THE REGISTRATION OF BAROQUE ORGAN MUSIC

THE REGISTRATION OF *Baroque*

Organ Music

BARBARA OWEN

INDIANA UNIVERSITY PRESS

Bloomington and Indianapolis

This book is a publication of

Indiana University Press
601 North Morton Street
Bloomington, IN 47404-3797 USA

http://www.indiana.edu/~iupress

Telephone orders 800-842-6796
Fax orders 812-855-7931
E-mail orders iuporder@indiana.edu

Library of Congress Cataloging-in-Publication Data

Owen, Barbara.
      The registration of baroque organ music / Barbara Owen.
         p.   cm.
      Includes bibliographical references and index.
      ISBN 0-253-33240-0 (cloth : alk. paper)
      1. Organ—Registration.   2. Organ music—17th
   century—History and criticism.   3. Organ music—18th
   century—History and criticism.   4. Performance practice
   (music)—17th century.   5. Performance practice (music)—
   18th century.   I. Title
      MT189.094   1997
      786.5'09'032—dc20   96-33081

ISBN 0-253-21085-2 (paper : alk. paper)

2   3   4   5   04   03   02   01   00   99

CONTENTS

Until the latter part of the fifteenth century, organs, whether large or small (and some were of considerable size), were essentially large mixtures of open Principal pipes, capable of a single tone color and intensity—the so-called *Blockwerk.* Toward the middle of that century a small step had been taken which heralded the beginning of the art of registration: Some builders began to make a single Principal rank separable from the rest of the plenum. The second logical step followed not long afterward, when the still formidable mixture was broken down into two smaller ones, of low and high pitches. While organists still had little choice of color, they now commanded three levels of intensity.

Small organs had coexisted with large ones in churches of all sizes for some time, and a fourth option became available after the midpoint of the century, when in some areas a small organ (positive) was attached to a large one in such a way that it could be played from a keyboard adjacent to that of the larger instrument. This ancient juxtaposition of large and small organs is perpetuated in our modern terminology—Great, Grand orgue, or Hauptwerk for the larger; Chaire (Choir), Positif du dos, or Rückpositiv for the smaller.

In two remarkable decades—those framing the year 1500—it may be said that the modern organ was born. The accepted birthplace is the lower Netherlands region, but the new developments spread quickly along the coast to France, Spain, and Italy to the south, and to England, the northern Netherlands, and Baltic Germany to the north, as well as inland, to Paris and central Germany. Keyboard size and compass became more standardized, mechanism more sophisticated, and—of greatest importance to us here—the realization that certain sets of pipes could be made playable to the exclusion of others brought about a rapid proliferation of new pipe constructions and sounds. Most of these, in both name and function, were frankly imitative of existing ensemble instruments of the time. The "orchestral organ" is by no means a twentieth-century concept.

Before the turn of the century flute stops, both stopped and open, are recorded. Evidence for reed stops before 1500 is scant, but as early as 1505 a large organ in Antwerp is recorded as having, besides flutes of 8' and 4' pitch, a Zink, Regal, Krummhorn, and Trumpet, representing the three classifications of reed stops found in modern organs (fractional-length, half-length, and full-length) [176, p. 32–3]. Four years later another Antwerp church contracted for an organ containing, along with a Trumpet, Shawm, and Zink, such flute varieties as the Quintadena, Waldhorn, and Schweigel flute [182, p. 71]. A treatise published by the Heidelberg organist and theoretician Arnolt Schlick in 1511 adds tapered flue stops (Gemshorns at 8' and 4') to the list of available colors. Not long after this, directions for the use of the stops in various kinds of music began to appear, first in treatises and organ contracts, and later in the music itself. From that time to the present, registration has been an important aspect of organ performance practice.

It is not the purpose of this book to chronicle in detail the history of the organ or its music, but rather to relate that history to the registration of the increasingly diverse regional styles of organ composition and tonal design as they evolved from the period following the Reformation through the Baroque to the beginning of the Classical era. The reader is therefore encouraged to use one or more of the standard modern histories of the organ and its music as background material.

While all organists are encouraged to familiarize themselves with historic organs in various countries, as well as a growing number of replicas or historically influenced instruments in the United States (see the Appendixes), it is recognized that the large majority will be playing modern instruments most of the time. For this reason a certain amount of standardization in nomenclature and pitch designation has been deemed advisable for the stoplists herein cited. While stop names will be given in the language of the country under discussion, they will be in modern, rather than archaic, spelling, with explanations where necessary. Similarly, while many organs of the Renaissance period were based on a low C of 6' or 5' pitch, it is felt that the use of the modern 8' pitch basis will help to avoid confusion in registering on modern organs. Thus, 12' or 10' = 16', 6' or 5' = 8', etc. Modern pitch designations will also apply to seventeenth- and eighteenth-century English organs and early nineteenth-century American instruments, even though the bass of the compass in these organs usually descended a half octave below the normal modern compass, to 10 2/3' G. For most cited stoplists dating from before the mid-eighteenth century, it may be assumed that pitch designations are editorial. The British system of note/pitch designation will be used throughout: CCCC = 32', CCC = 16', CC = 8', C_o = 4', c_1 = 2', c_2 = 1', c_3 = 1/2', c_4 = 1/4'.

A chronological approach to organization has been chosen over a regional one (although regional styles appear as subheadings) because it was felt that, particularly in the early part of the period under discussion, the similarities between the music and the tonal composition of organs in different regions are more important than the differences. Recognition of these similarities can often help in understanding the basic musical applications of registration in a given period, especially when they were not all equally well recorded in every region.

The recent emphasis on the study of the performance practices in fingering, tempi, and phrasing prevalent in various periods and regions has helped performers immeasurably in the understanding, appreciation, and sensitive interpretation of the literature. For the organist, registration is also a facet of performance practice, equally necessary for the proper interpretation and understanding of the music. It is the author's hope that this book will help to further the appreciation and informed performance of an important segment of the vast body of great music written for the most multifaceted of instruments.

ACKNOWLEDGMENTS

This study has evolved over a fairly long period of time, during which I have received much help and encouragement from a number of people. I would like to express especial gratitude to David Fuller and Peter Williams, who not only took time out of their busy schedules to read an early version of the manuscript but also contributed useful ideas and helpful criticisms, suggestions of additional source material, and, most important, encouraging words.

For their encouragement, too, I am grateful to several fine organ teachers, particularly David Craighead, Joan Lippincott, Marilyn Mason, and Max Miller. It is my earnest hope that they and their students will find this volume useful.

Many others have generously shared ideas and material, including Geoffrey Cox, Greg Crowell, Lynn Edwards, Christopher Kent, Charles Krigbaum, Orpha Ochse, Guy Oldham, Stephen Pinel, Umberto Pineschi, Susan Tattershall, Harald Vogel, and the late Susi Jeans. In addition, I am indebted to the resources of the American Organ Archive, the British Library, the Boston Public Library, the Mugar Library of Boston University, the Organ Library of the Boston Chapter, A.G.O., and the Westfield Center for Early Keyboard Studies for supplying much source material.

Finally, since any project of this nature entails many out-of-pocket expenses, I acknowledge with gratitude the very real help provided by grants from the American Guild of Organists chapters in Boston, San Francisco, and Washington.

PART I. PROLOGUE: RENAISSANCE & REFORMATION

1 | The Music, Composers, and Organs

The early and middle years of the sixteenth century encompassed many swift and sometimes startling changes in the political, religious, and cultural life affecting the organ and its music. Technological skills and the wealth of the Church made large organs possible, and the invention of stop controls opened the door to the introduction of new and colorful stops, many of them imitative of ensemble instruments. Accessory, or "toy," stops appeared early in the century. The most common were the Zimbelstern (possibly a relic of the medieval cymbalum or Zimbel, an instrument of small bells often used in churches), drone (for bagpipe effects), drum (either two or three de-tuned open wood pipes in the 4' range, or a real drum), and birdcall. The Tremulant too appeared sometime before the middle of the sixteenth century, and organs of more than two manuals began to be built in the northern regions.

During the early years of the sixteenth century organs and organ music exhibited marked similarities throughout Europe. This is not surprising in view of the unity in church and liturgical life, and the rather remarkable amount of traveling done by musicians and organ builders. To cite a single example, members of the Flemish Langhedul family of organ builders were active for over a century in Flanders, France, England, Italy, and Spain, and it was by no means uncommon for both musicians and instrument makers to settle and work in some country other than the one in which they were trained.

Without question the most influential religious event of the sixteenth century was the Reformation. Begun in the early decades of the century, this movement had by around 1575 wrought changes in the musical portion of the liturgy in Germany, the northern Netherlands, Switzerland, and England that ranged from inconsequential to radical. In the countries influenced by John Calvin, organ music was severely curtailed or banned outright; in those where Martin Luther's influence prevailed the organ retained its importance as a liturgical instrument, but the increasing emphasis on congregational singing soon set the stage for significant changes in both organ music and organ design.

The Music

Liturgical music makes up a large percentage of the surviving written organ literature of this period in all countries. Plainsong-based, it comprises *alternatim* organ masses, settings of office and feast-day hymns, antiphons, and offertories intended for church use. It must not be forgotten, however, that the organ has always had a secular side, and that not all organs were in churches. Thus settings of folk songs and dances appear side by side with liturgical music in early sixteenth-century German tablature books, and in 1517 the Italian publisher Andrea Antico issued a book of *frottole* (secular song) settings, "intabulated for playing on the organ." An early (1530) French publication by Pierre Attaingnant included liturgical music in a compilation intended for the organ, spinet, or clavichord. Since there is no evidence for the use of stringed keyboard instruments in church, the use of them in domestic devotions—which is well documented in later periods—must be assumed here.

Free musical forms are less commonly met with in the early period, but they appear most frequently in the Spanish, English, and Italian literature under generic titles such as tiento (Spain), verse or voluntary (England), or toccata (Italy). Also found are more general instrumental forms such as the ricercar or the canzona. The latter are often freely based on secular or religious folk songs.

Of the keyboard composers from this early period, the names of Redford, Tallis, Schlick, Gabrieli, Merulo, Cabezón, and Santa Maria are the most familiar. Their music is the most accessible in modern editions (not all of which are faithful to the original), and is representative of the genre as a whole.

The Organs

Until the final years of the fifteenth century, large organs consisted simply of an undivided Principal chorus—a massive mixture, or Blockwerk, containing all pitches, many of them multiple (especially in the treble). The first stop to be made separable was the 8' (or, in large organs, 16') Principal. Early names for this rank (Sourd, Doeff = soft or muted) attest to its function in providing a quieter foundational alternative to the brilliant full organ sound. Stopped wooden pipes also began to make their appearance, particularly in the upper Rhine region.

Recorded stoplists of early sixteenth-century organs are scarce, but those that have been found show a remarkable similarity regardless of their country of origin. Even in the earliest decades of the sixteenth century, however, Flemish organs and those of northern and central Germany began to acquire characteristics that set them apart: the more imitative stops (unison and quint flutes; reeds) were often placed on a separate chest, or Oberwerk, above the Principal chorus (a divided or undivided Blockwerk), and were played from either the main manual or a separate manual; it is not unusual in some of the earliest sources to find such stops described as "new." The northern organs were also the first to have independent Pedal stops. Thus from a very early stage, Netherlands-German organs could be found having as many as three manuals and an independent Pedal division, with a large number of colorful stops, although usually with a manual key compass of no more than 45 notes.

The organs of England, Italy, the Iberian peninsula, and, to some extent, France tended to have one, or at the most two, manual divisions. Their compass sometimes (especially in Spain and Italy) exceeded 45 notes, with either only a pulldown (coupled) pedalboard or none at all, and a somewhat smaller variety of color stops. These latter were, however, of the same sort as found in the northern organs—flutes at unison and quint pitches, and a few reeds, usually of short length. While the Principal chorus in the north usually remained at least partially undivided (the higher-pitched ranks being grouped into mixtures), many organs in the southern countries had completely divided Principal choruses, a characteristic that allowed the Principal mutations to be used with the same flexibility as the Flute mutations and that persisted in Italy into the eighteenth century.

Before the middle of the sixteenth century, single-manual organs with some or all stops divided between treble and bass appeared in Flanders; they quickly spread to Spain, England, and northern France. Such organs offered increased registrational flexibility by allowing contrasting or solo effects, and this characteristic was increasingly exploited in certain areas in the following centuries.

Toward the end of the period, two-manual organs consisting of a large (Great) and small (Positive) division began to occur with increasing frequency in France, and occasional independent pedal stops began to appear in Parisian organs. While low-pitched bass extensions (Trompes or Bordunen) were known in the fifteenth and very early sixteenth centuries, the independent pedal stops that developed in France and Germany as the sixteenth century progressed were at first solo stops—8' and 4' reeds, 8', 4' and 2' flues—intended for playing *canti firmi* in plainsong- and chorale-based pieces.

A word should also be said here about positives and regals. Most churches of any size had more than one organ during the sixteenth and seventeenth centuries. One or two of these, located on the wall of the nave or quire (chancel), upon the pulpitum (rood screen), or in a west end gallery, would have qualified as a "Great" organ (Hauptwerk, Grand Orgue), but the rest, usually found in chapels (and in England, particularly, the Lady Chapel) could be classified as "little" or "small" organs (Positivs). These were often of 4' or even 2' pitch, and while some were stationary, others were small enough to be moved from place to place in the building, or, as church records from the period attest, even loaned out to other churches or for use in mystery plays.

It is possible that the introduction of separable stops first occurred in these smaller organs, and this may also be true of the introduction of certain color stops, especially short-length reeds. Before the middle of the sixteenth century a distinct type of small organ known as the regal appeared. The smallest of these instruments consisted of but a single reed stop, but larger ones often contained one to three flue stops as well; both types are illustrated in Praetorius's *Syntagma Musicam* of 1619 [128, p. 73].

Apparently introduced from Flanders, regals enjoyed considerable vogue in England, Spain, and central Europe in the middle and later decades of the sixteenth century. Henry VIII of England owned no fewer than 27 "regalls" along with a few positives and claviorgana (instruments combining pipes and plucked strings) [57, p. 292], and several are also recorded as being used in Spanish court chapels. During the years following the death of Henry VIII, when English government fell into Calvinist hands, the use of the large organs in churches was discouraged, but many continued to use regals, perhaps to give the pitch and provide discreet guidance for psalm singing. Organs of all sizes continued in use in most continental regions, however. Just as the "little organ" is analogous to the Chaire, or Rückpositiv, so the flue-and-reed regal may be said to have been the forerunner of the Brustwerk in the northern countries.

Composers

England

Richard Allwood (fl. mid 16th century)
William Blitheman (153?–1591)
Avery Burton (c1470–1543)
Nicholas Carleton (fl. mid 16th century)
Robert Coxsun (fl. mid 16th century)
Richard Farrant (c1530–1580)
Thomas Preston (fl. early 16th century)
John Redford (c1486–1547)
Philip ap Rhys (d. c1559)
John Sheppard (Shepherd) (fl. 1542–1556)
Thomas Tallis (15??–1585)
John Taverner (c1495–1545)
Robert White (Whyte) (153?–1574)

France and Flanders

Pierre Attaingnant (fl. early 16th century)
Eustache du Caurroy (1549–1609)
Guillaume Costeley (c1531–1606)
Claude le Jeune (c1530–1600)

Italy

Vincenzo Bell'haver (1530?–1587)
Jachet Buus (1505–1564)
Girolamo Cavazzone (fl. early 16th century)
Marco Antonio Cavazzone (fl. 1490–1559)
Giacomo Fogliano (1468–1548)
Andrea Gabrieli (c1510–1586)
Fiorenzo Maschera (c1540–1584)

Claudio Merulo (1533–1604)
Antonio Mortaro (d. 1595)
Annibale Padovano (1527–1573)
Giovanni Pierluigi da Palestrina (1525–1594)
Giulio Segni (1498–1561)
Antonio Valente (c1520–c1600)

Spain and Portugal

Juan Bermudo (c1510–1565)
Antonio de Cabezón (1510–1566)
Antonio Carreira (c1525–c1590)
Cristobal de Morales (c1500–1553)
Alonso Mudarra (c1506–1580)
Heliodoro de Paiva (1502–1552)
Francisco Fernandez Palero (fl. 1550–70)
Francisco de Salinas (1513–1590)
Tomas de Santa Maria (c1510/20–1570)
Francisco de Soto (c1500–1563)
Pedro Alberto Vila (1517–1582)

Germanic Countries

Elias Nikolaus Ammerbach (c1530–1597)
Hans Buchner (1483–c1540)
Paul Hofhaimer (1459–1537)
Leonhard Kleber (c1490–1556)
Johannes (Hans) Kotter (c1485–1541)
Gregor Meyer (d. 1576)
Konrad Paumann (c1415–1473)
Arnolt Schlick (c1460–c1521)
Bernhard Schmid Sr. (1535–1592)
Fridolin Sicher (1490–1546)

Representative Organs

England

ALL HALLOWS, BARKING, LONDON
Anthony Duddyngton, 1519 [19]

Manual
Double Principals (in all probability a complete Flemish type of chorus from 8', based on either two 8' ranks or 8' and 4')
"Basses" (downward extension of 8' Principal)

"as few stops as may be convenient" (could possibly refer to color stops—unison and quint flutes; perhaps even reeds)

[N.B. The enigmatic contract for this organ is subject to various interpretations; see 19 and 320 in Bibliography.]

VICTORIA & ALBERT MUSEUM, LONDON
Claviorganum by Lodowicus Theewes, 1579 [155, p. 40]

Manual
Stopped Diapason (stopped wood) 8'
Flute (stopped wood) 4'
Fifteenth (wood and metal) 2'
Cimball Irk 1/4' (repeating)
Regal (wood) 8'

ESTATE OF KING HENRY VIII
Two regals built before 1547 [57, p. 294]

I.	II.
Stopt Diapason 4'(?) (tin)	Stopt Diapason 4' (wood)
Cimball (Irk repeating?)	Cimball (Irk repeating?)
Regall 8'(?) (tin)	Regall 8'(?) (varnished paper)

France

CHURCH OF ST. SEURIN, BORDEAUX
Arnaud de Guyssaurret, 1514 [39, p. 294]

Manual
Principal 16' (?) (Montre, "double")
Principal 8' ("second principal")
Grosse Flute 8'
Principal 4'
Petit Flute 4'
Douzaine 2 2/3'
XXII (22nd) 2'
(Octave) Douzaine 1 1/3'
XXIX (29th) 1'
(Octave) XXIX 1/2' or Petit flute 2'

CONVENT OF ST. JEAN, VALENCIENNES
Charles Waghers or Waquet, 1515 [177, p. 156]

Manual I
"Grand Ouvraige" (full principal chorus or *Blockwerk)*

Manual II: Cheyere (Rückpositiv)
Principal 8' ("double" of the Principal)
Principal 4' (Prestant)
Flute 4'

Octave 2' ("treble octave")
Cymbale

[N.B. While they were not exactly accessory stops, this organ also had a wind-driven "turning sun" and a grotesque tooth-clacking head in its case.]

CHURCH OF NOTRE DAME, ALENÇON
G. deCailly & S. leVasseur, 1537–1540 [39, pp. 46, 136]

Grand Orgue	**Positif**
Principal 16'	Trompette 8'
Principal 8'	Voix humaines (8'? reed?)
Bourdon 8'	Harpes (8'? regal?)
Principal 4'	
Flute 4'	
Double Flute 4'	
Flute 2'	
Flute 1 1/3'	
Flute 1'	
Fourniture VIII	
Cymbale	

Accessory Stops
Tremblant
Rossignol (bird)

ST. GENEVIEVE-DES-ARDENTS, PARIS
Positive by Antoine LeFèvre, 1549 [215, p. 69]

Manual
Flûte 8' (stopped?)
Montre 4'
Doublette 2'
Nazard 1 1/3'
Fourniture II–III
Cymbale

Accessory Stops
Tremulant
Tambourin, Rossignol (bird), Stars

CHURCH OF ST. ETIENNE, TROYES
Unknown builder, 1551 [28, p. 76]

Manual
Plein Jeu (complete Principal chorus, from 8')
Bourdon 8'
Voix humaine (four beating ranks of flues?) 8'
Flute d'Allemand 4'(?) (chimney flute)
Nazard 2 2/3'
Flûte a neuf trous 2'(?) (recorder)
Doubles Flûtes (?)

Fifres 1' (?)
Cymbales
Cornet, 4 ranks (?)
Doulcine (reed) 8'
Harpe (regal?) 8' (?)
"Falsetto" (regal?) 4' (?)

Accessory Stops
Tambourin
Tremulant?
Musette (drone?)

HOUSE ORGAN OF PIERRE DE LABATUT, BORDEAUX
Jehan Pistre, 1558 [39, p. 58]

Manual
Principal 4'
Octave 2'
Fifteenth 1'
Regal 4'

Accessory Stops
Tremulant

PARISH CHURCH, SARCELLES, FRANCE
Unknown builder, 1559 [39, p. 57]

Manual
Montre 8'
Principal 4'
Recorder 4'
Nazard 2 2/3'
Doublette 2'
Petit Nazard 1 1/3'
Cymbale (mixture) 1'
Petite cymbale
Saqueboutte 4' (reed)

Accessory Stops
Tremblant
Rossignol (bird)
2 Etoiles (cymbalstars)
2 trumpeting angels

SAINTE-CHAPELLE, DIJON
François des Oliviers, 1560 [40-I, p. 69]

Manual
Principal 8' (prestant)
Flutes d'Allemand 8' or 4'? (chimney flute)
Octave 4'

Flutes à neuf troux 4' or 2'? (recorder)
Nazard 2 2/3' (possibly 2 ranks)
Fifre 2' (or 1'?)
Cimballe
Douzaine (possibly two-rank 12th & 15th, or Dulzian reed)
Hautbois & Cornet 8' (?) (possibly a divided reed stop)
Trompette 8'

Accessory Stops
Tremulant

ABBEY, NEUFMOUSTIER (LIÈGE)
Art Waingon, 1567 [177, p. 131]

Manual
Bourdon 8'
Doff (Principal) 4'
Flute 4'
Flute 2'
Mixture
Simbale
Cornet
Trompet 8'

Accessory Stops
Tabure (drum)
Ouseaulx (bird)

Italy

BASILICA OF SAN PETRONIO, BOLOGNA
Lorenzo da Prato, 1471–75 [105, p. 36]

Manual
Principale 16' (doubled from C_o)
Principale 8' (doubled from C_o, tripled from c_1)
Ottava 4' (doubled from c_1)
Flauto in ottava 4'
Flauto in duodecima 2 2/3' (added 1563)
Duodecima 2 2/3'
Quintadecima 2
Decimanona 1 1/3' ⎫
Vigesimaseconda 1' ⎬ these four stops break back at 1/4' pitch
Vigesimasesta 2/3' ⎪
Vigesimanona 1/2' ⎭

Pedal
20 notes, coupled to manual

[N.B. This organ has a 54-note keyboard compass, which is longer than usual for this period.]

SANTA MARIA DELLA PACE, ROME
Giovanni Donadio, 1506 [108, p. 394]

Manual
Principale 8'
Ottava 4'
Quintadecima 2'
Flauto in Quintadecima 2'
Decimanona 1 1/3'
Vigesimaseconda 1'
Vigesimasesta 1/3'

CHURCH OF SANTA MARIA DE LA SCALA, SIENA
Antonio Piffaro, 1517–19
[stoplist from the organ]

Manual
Principale 8' (doubled from $C\sharp_o$)
Ottavo 4' (doubled from $C\sharp_o$, tripled from f_1)
Flauto in ottava 4' (open)
Flauto in Quintadecima 2'
Decimaquinta and Vigesimanona 2' and 1/2'
Vigesimaseconda and Vigesimaquinta 1' and 1/4'
Decimanona and Vigesimasesta 1 1/3' and 2/3'

Pedal
Coupled to Manual

OLD CATHEDRAL, BRESCIA
Gian Giacomo Antegnati, 1536 [108, p. 394]

Manual
Principale I 8'
Principale II 8' (with added bass octave for pedals)
Ottava 4'
Flauto in ottava 4'
Quintadecima 2'
Flauto in quintadecima 2'
Decimanona 1 1/3'
Vigesimaseconda 1'
Vigesimaseconda II 1' (large scale)
Vigesimasesta 2/3'
Vigesimanona 1/2'
Trigesimaterza 1/3'

Pedal
Coupled to Manual

CHURCH OF SAN MARTINO, BOLOGNA
Giovanni Cipri, 1556–57 [108, p. 394]

Manual
Principale 8'
Ottava 4'

Flauto grosso in ottava 4'
Flauto in duodecima 2 2/3'
Ripieno (divided upperwork)
Cornamuse 8' (reed)

Accessory Stops
Tremulant

CONSERVATORY OF MUSIC, PARMA
Positive, said to have belonged to Claudio Merulo, 16th century [60, p. 16]

Manual
Principale 8' (stopped in bass?)
Ottava 4'
Flauto 4' (or 2'?)
Vigesimaseconda 1'

Pedal
9 notes, permanently coupled to manual

Spain and Portugal

CHURCH OF ST. MATHIEU, PERPIGNAN
Gabriel Cap de Bos, 1516 [40-I, p. 83; 11, p. 7]

Manual II (Positiv added to an older 16' "blockwerk" of 1499)
Flautat 8'(?) (prestant)
Musetes (4' or 2', octaves?)
Forniment (large mixture)

In 1524 the Blockwerk (Manual I) was broken down into:

Flautat 16' (prestant)
Octavas 8'
Quinsenas 4' and 2'
Mixtura VIII (?)

Pedal
Recorded in 1524 as having ten "Contres" (basses) of 16' pitch.

[N.B. Although Perpignan was later annexed to the southeastern edge of France, it was part of Spain in the sixteenth century.]

CHURCH OF NUESTRA SEÑORA DEL PINO, BARCELONA
Pedro Flamench, 1540 [181, p. 237]

Manual
Flautado 8' (prestant)
Octavo 4'
Flautado de roure 4'(?) (chimney flute)
Forniment III 2 2/3' (mixture)
Forniment V 2'
Simbalet III

CATHEDRAL, LERIDA
Mateo Telles, 1543 [92, p. 232]

Organo Mayor
Flautat 8' (prestant)
Flautat II 8'
Flautat octavo 4'
Flautes naturals 4'(?) (recorder)
Pifanos 2'? (flute)
Plenum (mixture)
Cimbales (mixture)
Xaramellat (Shawm) 8'
Trompeta 8' ("German" = full length?)
Clarins 8' or 4'(?)

Accessory Stops
Multiple tremulants on both manuals
Tambors (drums)
Campanas (bells)
Ruisenyors (birds)

Cadireta (Positive)
Flautes tapates 8' (stopped)
Flautat octavo 4'
Flautat octavo II 4'
Flautes quinzenes 2'
Decimal II, treble (cornettino?)
Pusicio II, divided (mixture)
Clarins de mar 8' (regal?)

CATHEDRAL, SEVILLA (EPISTLE ORGAN)
Builder unidentified, 1579 [11, p. 9]

Manual I (divided?)
Flautado 16'
Bordon 16'
Octava 8'
Octava Bordon 8'
15a 4' (principal)
15a 4' (flute)
22a 2'
Lleno en 15a (4' mixture)
Trompetas 8'(?)
Xavegas 8'(?) ("Arabian flute"; a short-length reed?)

Manual II
Bordon 8'
Octava 4'
12a 2 2/3'
15a 2'
19a 1 1/3'
22a 2'
Trompetas Bastardas 8'(?)

OLD CATHEDRAL MUSEUM, SALAMANCA
Francisco de Salinas's positive, 16th century [253]

Manual
Flautado tapado 8' (stopped)
Flautado abierto 8' (open, possibly a treble stop)
Octava 4'
Docena 2 2/3'
Lleno (mixture)
Zimbala (mixture)
Orlos 8' (reed)

Netherlands, Germany, and Central Europe

PARISH CHURCH, ST. WOLFGANG, AUSTRIA
Michael Khall, 1497 [131, p. 26]

Hauptwerk
Principal 8'
Hölzern Octav 4' (wood)
Quint 2 2/3'
Octav 2'
Scharfe Mixtur
Zimbel

Rückpositiv
Gedackt 8'
Flöte 4'
Hölzern Principal 2' (wood)
Hintersatz (mixture)

Pedal
Principal 16'
Octave 8'
Zimbel

ST. MICHAEL'S CHURCH, ZWOLLE
Johann van Kovelen (?), 1505 [176, p. 33]

Hauptwerk
Blockwerk 16' (c. 32rks)

Oberwerk
Prinzipal 8'
Oktav 4'
Scharfe Stimme (2'?)
Mixtur (possibly divided)
Grosse Zimbel

Rückpositiv
Hohlpfeife 8'
Prinzipal 4'
Scharf (mixture)
reed stop (8'?)

Pedal
Coupled to Blockwerk, no independent stops

ST. ANDREAS'S CHURCH, WORMS
Unknown builder, c1510 [176, p. 37]

Manual
Grosse Hohlflöte 16'(?)
Prinzipal 8'
Kleine Hohlflöte 8'(?)
Oktave 4'
Quinte 2 2/3'
Mixtur
Zimbel
Trompete 8'
Reed stop (Regal 8?)

Pedal
Prinzipal 8'
Oktave 4'
Mixtur

Accessory Stops
Tremulant
Drum
Ventil

REPRESENTATIVE STOPLIST SUGGESTED BY ARNOLT SCHLICK (1511) [152, Ch.V]

Hauptwerk
Principal 16'
Principal and/or Flute 8' (II)
Octave 4'
Gemshorn 4'
Schwegel 2'
Hintersatz (large mixture)
Zimbel
Rauschpfeife/Zink 8' (regal)
"Hulze Glechter"★

Positiv
Principal 8' ("wood or tin"; stopped?)
Principal 4'
Gemshorn 2' (?)
Hintersätzlein (Scharff Mixture)
Zimbel

Pedal
Principal 16'
Octave 8'
Octave 4'
Hintersatz (Mixture)
Posaune 16'
Trompete 8'

★Various writers have speculated widely on the nature of this stop, which is also recorded in a 1513 organ in Innsbruck, where it is called Hölzern Glechter [131, p. 27]. Guesses include a high-pitched mixture, a wood flute, a regal, a tremolo, a hurdy-gurdy, and a percussion stop. Peter Williams argues for its being a wooden Quintadena (then a new stop). Schlick describes its sound as "like hitting a pot with a spoon," so a wooden percussion stop (xylophone?) is also not an impossibility.

CATHEDRAL, TRIER
Peter Briesger, 1537 [193, p. 13]

Hauptwerk
Prestant 16'
Octaaf 8'
Hohlpfeife 8' (bass)
Nachthorn 8' (treble)
Mixtur 4'
Zimbel
Bazuin 8' (bass)
Zink 8' (treble)

Positiv
Quintadena 8'
Prestant 4'
Hohlpfeife 4'
Flöte 2'
Oktaaf 1'
Querpfeife 1' (or 2')
Scharfzimbel
Schalmey 8' (or 4')

Pedal
Quintade 16' (from HW by transmission)
Prinzipal 8' (from HW by transmission)
Zimbel (from HW by transmission)
Flötenbass 2'
Trompete 8'

Accessory Stops
Trommel (drum)
"Zwergpfeife" (lit. "Dwarf-pipe"; possibly a drone)

OLD CHURCH, AMSTERDAM
Hendrik & Herman Niehoff, 1539–42 [181, p. 32]

Hauptwerk
Prinzipal 16'

Oberwerk
Prinzipal 8'

Oktave 8' & 4'
Mixtur
Scharf

Rückpositiv
Prinzipal 8'
Quintadena 8'
Oktave 4'
Holpijp 4'
Mixtur
Scharf
Baarpijp 8' (possibly flue)
Krummhorn 8'
Regal 8'
Schalmei 4'

Accessory Stops
Tremulant
OW/RP and HW/RP Couplers

Holpijp 8'
Quintadena 8' (or 4')
Offenflöte 4'
Gemshorn 2'
Sifflöte 1'
Terzzimbel
Trompete 8'
Zinck 8' (treble?)

Pedal
Nachthorn 2'
Trompete 8'

BENEDICTINE ABBEY, WEINGARTEN
M. Ruck, 1554–58 [181, p. 65]

Hauptwerk
Praestant 8'
Gross Hohlflöte 8'
Quintadena 8'
Oktave 4'
Klein Hohlflöte 4'
Superokave 2'
Schwegel (flute) 2'
Mixtur
Zimbel
Rauschwerk (reed stop) 8'?

Positiv
Hohlflöte 8'
Praestant 4'
Oktave 2'
Schwegel 1' or 2'
Hörnli (reed) 8'(?)

Pedal
Praestant 16' or 8'
Oktave 8' or 4'
Superoktave 4' or 2'
Mixture
Posaune 16'

Accessory Stops
Tremulant
Vogelsang (bird)

[N.B. The first four Pedal stops may have been borrowed from Hauptwerk.]

HOFKIRCHE, INNSBRUCK
Jörg Ebert, 1561 [148, p. 234]

Hauptwerk
Principal 8'
Gedeckt 8'
Octav 4'
Quint 2 2/3'
Quintez 2' (15th)
Hörndl II
Hintersatz V–X
Zimbel II

Rückpositif
Gedeckt Flöte 4'
Offenflöte 4'
Hörndl II
Mixture III–V
Zimbel II

Pedal
Coupled by means of a ventil to 19 lowest
notes of HW

Trummett 8'
Regal 8' (divided)

Accessory Stops
Zitter (internal Tremulant to entire organ)

KUNSTHISTORISCHES MUSEUM, VIENNA
Claviorganum, c1580 [256, p. 13]

Manual
Gedackt 4' (wood)
Flute 2' (wood)
Zimbel I (metal, repeating)
Regal 8' (metal)
Regal 4' (wood)

The organs in these three regions display considerable similarity in their tonal makeup, especially in the first half of the sixteenth century. The majority are one-manual instruments, although some of them (the "great" organs) are of fair size and are based on either the 8' or the 16' series. Although the very earliest organs consist entirely or nearly entirely of Principal tone, one soon finds a separate grouping of flutes at various pitches and, finally, reeds.

It is a mistake to think of these "great" organs as having dainty or overly refined tone. Surviving pipework has open toes and open windways which, along with medium-to-high mouth cut-ups, suggests wind pressures in excess of 3" in some instances, and a robust but unforced sound. The wonderfully pervasive effect of such pipework in a resonant masonry building can still be experienced in a few places, notably the Basilica of San Petronio in Bologna. The "little" organs, often based on the 4' pitch, are smaller versions of the larger scheme, frequently incorporating a fractional-length reed stop. As they were used in smaller spaces, they may be expected to have had a more refined sound. A few regals survive in museums, and their sound is throaty, articulate, and surprisingly strong.

Even when not specifically indicated, some of the larger organs probably had a rudimentary pull-down pedalboard of eight or ten notes, but no independent pedal stops, unless the occasional 16' extensions of manual stops (Bassys, Trompes, Bordunen, Contres) could be counted as such. Certainly pedal solos, even of a simple *cantus firmus*, would have been out of the question on such organs, and there is evidence, particularly in Italian music, that these early pedals were used only as a convenience, a "third hand," to double the bass notes in cadential passages or for long sustained "pedal points." There is, however, evidence for both divided stops and half-stops on the manuals in the latter part of this period (even some of Henry VIII's regals had divided stops), which presumably had some solo function.

Despite the technical simplicity of these organs, the player had considerable tonal material to work with, which can be broken down into the following broad categories for an 8' organ (in a 4' organ all pitches would be an octave higher):

1. Plenum or Full Organ (principal chorus with upperwork)
2. Principal 8'
3. Principal 8' colored by various components of the upperwork
4. Flute tone (usually 4', but sometimes 8', 2 2/3', 2', and higher)
5. Reed tone (usually 8'; only short-length reeds recorded in England and Italy in this period)
6. Combinations of 2., 4., and 5. with upperwork components

The first two represent the very earliest options open to a sixteenth-century organist and can safely be applied to much of the earliest liturgical literature. The remaining four came into use in the early decades of the sixteenth century, almost as soon as the stop mechanism that made them possible became widespread. It is significant that, in the earliest sources, the art of registration was often intentionally imitative of other instruments and even of natural sounds such as birdcalls.

Some of the earliest directions for registration come from southern France and Spain. No Italian registration instructions are known prior to the first decade of the seventeenth century, although these later formulae largely confirm and expand upon what is known of French and Iberian usages of the previous century, suggesting that similar usages were common in Italy as well. Only in England have no indications of registration practice been found earlier than the late seventeenth century, yet up to the middle of the sixteenth century English musical culture was so closely tied to that of Flemish-influenced Spain and France that it is probable that the same basic premises applied in England. Cabezón visited England after the middle of the sixteenth century, during the reign of Queen Mary, and there were many continental instrumentalists in the courts of Henry VIII and Edward VI.

The earliest French source, found in the records of the Church of St. Michel in Bordeaux, pertains to an organ of 1510 by Loys Gaudet. Unfortunately the stoplist of this nine-stop organ has not been found, but several attempts to reconstruct it have been made based on the registration list. It seems probable that this organ, like many other larger southern organs of the period (such as the ten-stop organ of 1514 in the church of St. Seurin, Bordeaux), contained no reed stops. Rather, imitative colors were synthesized by combinations of flue stops to obtain the effect of hautboys, horns, cornets, and sackbuts as well as the sounds of human voices and birds [39, p. 22–23]. Around the same period, Luis Zapata Chaves, a contemporary of Cabezón's, described the "admirable" tonal effects of a large organ near Madrid. In addition to the basic plenum and 8' Principal (also found in the French sources), he mentions the reed and accessory stops and the imitative sounds presumably produced by combinations: cornets and other wind instruments, human voices, and viols [252, p. 58].

In all, at least six French contracts from the period 1510–1548 include listings of possible color combinations (*jeux*); indeed, the builders appear to be bragging a bit about how many wonderful sounds one can synthesize on their nine- to twelve-stop single-manual organs: recorders, German (traverse) flutes, hautboys, cornets, flageolets, sackbuts, human voices, birds—even ducks! But they do not tell us how some of these combinations are made up or how they are to be used in the music. Scholars such as Douglass, Vente, Hardouin, Gravet, and May have taken their turn in trying to unravel the St. Michel *jeux* (see Bibliography), thus far without agreeing. All that one can be assured of is that these combinations achieved their effect by adding selected higher-pitched flute and principal unisons and quints to an 8' or 4' basis.

Certain of these early combinations persisted in later practice, however, and from some of these later sources, along with an occasional clue from the early period, one may make an educated guess here and there. Certainly there is little question concerning the *Plein jeu* (full organ), which appears at the beginning of most of the lists, and which would consist of principal-toned pipes only, with no reeds and only occasionally an 8' flute, usually in the north. This plenum sound was probably used, as it was later in Italy and Spain, for certain music on feast days, and for intonations and introits.

The *jeu de nazard* is frequently listed, and it plainly refers to a combination including a fifth-sounding mutation. In the 1537 contract for a church in Alençon one finds the notation "for the nasard" attached to the 8' Bourdon, 2' Flute, and 1 1/3' Flute, with a further notation that addition of the 1' Flute made the *petit jeu de nasard* [39, p. 46]. A 1535 contract for an organ in Chalon-sur-Saône mentions flute stops of 2 2/3' and 2' pitch that can "serve for a nasard," and later contracts of the period occasionally call for a two-rank Nazard stop [39, p. 51–52]. This usage is confirmed in French and Spanish sources from the seventeenth century. French sources from around the middle of the next century cite a variety of combinations called "nazard," all of them based on the 8' Bourdon, and one may assume that in the earlier period the nazard combinations also presumed an 8' or 4' foundation. These nazard combinations were ubiquitous by the middle of the sixteenth century. In the region north of Paris, a contract for an organ in St. Walburga's Church of Bruges, dated 1569, mentions that the "quint flute" (2 2/3') used with the 8' Hohlpijp constitutes the nazard, but when it is used with the 8' Principal it imitates the gemshorn [177, p. 41].

Although the third-sounding tierces that were part of the standard "cornet" combination in the seventeenth century had yet to make their appearance, a "cornet" registration occurs in many early sources. This would appear to have been created by adding the "little nasard" or Larigot 1 1/3' to the unison flutes, probably 8', 4', and 2'. A 1559 contract from Sarcelles notes that the "little nasard is for playing with the flutes to make a cornet registration" [239, p. 167]. Although reed stops became more common toward the end of the sixteenth century, reed instrument colors (such as the cornet) continued to be synthesized from flue combinations for some time.

The stoplists of the organs, and the knowledge that registration was a matter of combining mutations with foundations in colorful (and often imitative) ways, gives part of the answer to the question of how music in the early and middle sixteenth century was registered in France, England, Italy, and the Iberian peninsula. The music itself must provide the remaining clues. Strangely, little of this has come down to us from France, despite the fact that organ building flourished there and that colorful registration was obviously a matter of some importance. But from England, Italy, and Spain we have a substantial corpus of organ music, particularly in the works of Redford, Cabezón, and Cavazzone.

The works of just these three giants suggest that they may well have taken into account the different sizes and types of organs available to them. Cabezón's son, in his edition of his father's works, implies that the secular compositions (diferencias, canciòns, glosadas, etc.) are suitable for any keyboard instrument and may even be played on the harp or the viol. Clearly, then, registrations drawn from the resources of the positive or regal are the most suitable for such pieces. The use of 4' and even 2' as the basic pitch is appropriate, whereas the use of any pitch lower than 8' is not.

Some of Cavazzone's works follow a similar pattern, and it will be noted that his canzonas are generally of lighter texture than the ricercares and liturgical works. The fact that the left-hand texture in some of the canzonas is quite dense (thirds and fifths near the bottom of the staff, as in the obviously secular *Il e bel e bon*) would seem to suggest a 4' pitch line. Because canzonas in general are based on the vocal idiom, single unison and/or octave colors would seem more suitable than the complexities of mutations and higher pitches, although reeds of the regal family would also be suitable if they are mixed with unison or octave flue stops, as they doubtless were in the small reed-and-flue type of regal/positive.

The liturgical works are another matter, for churches possessed both large and small organs. Both Cavazzone and Redford, as organists respectively of St. Mark's in Venice and St. Paul's in London, would have had at least one large organ, probably with a compass down to 16' (10', 12'), at their disposal; Cabezón, as court organist, may also have had one fairly substantial organ of at least 8' pitch. All would also have had one or more smaller organs at their disposal. St. Paul's in London is known to have had a sizable Lady Chapel, where, prior to the Reformation, masses associated with the cult of the Virgin Mary were regularly said; such a chapel could well have had an 8' or a 4' organ.

Bearing in mind the different organs available to the composers, one realizes that the music itself often suggests the type of organ it was written for. Willi Apel notes that "even a superficial examination of Redford's organ works reveals several different types of composition, some of which are in strong contrast with each other" [7, p. 144]. He cites as examples of the extremes the plain and rather stiff *Miserere* [124, p. 23] and the fluid and subtle *Salvator withe a meane* [124, p. 57], with its far more interesting rhythmic texture. A third type is exemplified in the contrapuntally sophisticated *Glorificamus* [124, p. 17]. A cursory examination of Redford's complete works, as well as those of his Spanish and Italian contemporaries, will reveal many other examples of all three types.

Until past the middle of the sixteenth century, most of the larger organs were probably somewhat unwieldy, and many may have been older undivided or only partially divided *Blockwerks*. Liturgical works of a slow and spare texture, such as Redford's *Miserere* and the *Glorificamus te* from Cavazzone's *Missa de Beata Virgine* are probably intended for such organs, to be played either on the separable 8' Principal or on a fairly full chorus. The same would apply to the short *Te Deum* segments in Attaingnant's 1530 publication and other works of a similar foursquare nature.

Other pieces by some of these composers, often office hymns, combine the characteristic of a fairly dense left-hand line with a high tessitura. The left-hand part never descends below tenor C, and, as in the case of certain Redford pieces, the right-hand part sometimes ascends to a_3—exactly an octave above the highest note of most organs of the period. Cavazzone's *Exultet coelam* and *Pange lingua* exemplify this, and a Magnificat by Redford (*The VIII tune in c fa ut*, now thought to be a work by Avery Burton) actually carries the direction "Play bothe parts VIII nots lower" [124, p. 125]. Office hymns and those associated with the Virgin may well have been played at daily masses in chapels having smaller organs, and if pieces such as those mentioned are played at a 4' pitch line—whether written up an octave or not— they will be found to sound more convincing and interesting than if played at 8' pitch.

The matter of the use of solo lines in music of this period is not at all clear. If registrations such as the nazard or cornet combinations were used, it does seem logical to assume a solo role, although these light combinations also suit thin- textured (two- or three-part) music that seems to want to move at a brisk tempo. Because some music contains clearly differentiated sections, manual and stop changes are also a possibility. Cabezón's rather startling and varied *Tiento del Primer Tono No. 2* could possibly call for the concurrent use of two manuals on the last page, and Santa Maria's short *Fantasia del modo de tañer a corcheas* is the type of piece that, if written by a northern composer, could call for a bright right-hand combination (a Nazard combination?) against a more subdued registration in the left hand. Similarly, in the English repertoire one occasionally encounters pieces such as Blitheman's fourth setting of *Eterne rerum conditor*, where the plainsong cantus in long notes could be played either on a solo manual or on the upper half of a divided manual, against what, from its texture, would be a fairly light registration in the moving left-hand part. In general, however, such usages are probably the exception rather than the rule.

The pull-down pedals found on the larger organs could not, by their nature, have had any solo function in this period, although they may have been used to double a low-pitched *cantus firmus* at the octave in organs with bass extensions to the 8' Principal, and almost certainly would have been used cadentially or as sustained "pedal points," as in later Italian music. The presence of a third-staff independent or solo pedal line in a modern edition of English, Iberian, or French music from this period is inauthentic and should be taken as evidence of severe editorial meddling; such editions usually also contain misleading and improbable registration sugges- tions and are not to be trusted in this regard.

3 | Netherlands, Germany, and Central Europe

Despite their common connection to the Flemish tradition, the organs of the Rhineland and central Europe began to break away stylistically from those of the more southerly regions even before the opening of the sixteenth century, and these differences became more pronounced with the passing of time. While the northern organs held many characteristics in common with the longer-compass one- and two-manual instruments of France, Spain, and Italy, they are set apart by the occasional presence of a third manual and solo pedal stops (which may well have existed even before 1500), as well as a greater variety of color stops and reeds. The Quintadena, a narrow-scaled stopped pipe, is also unique to the northern area in this period. Many registrations for the southern instruments can apply equally to the Germanic organs (and indeed their counterparts occur in northern registration sources), but there are other possibilities to exploit as well.

Arnolt Schlick's invaluable *Spiegel* of 1511 is one of the earliest sources of registration practice found in any country. His discussion begins with this disarming statement: "With eight or nine good registers, which go well together and yet are interchanged with one another, one may give much pleasure to the hearer" [152]. This sounds very much like the statements made by the French builders of the same period and points to the same sort of "coloration" style of registering. Organs with inseparable *Blockwerks* were still much in evidence in 1511, at least in the north, but Schlick disapproved of them, recommending that at least the Principal 8' and Octave 4' be capable of being separated from the large mixture, or *Hintersatz*. In the area around present-day Austria, organs with separable stops were found as early as the 1490s; there the main chorus already had a very "modern" appearance, only the high-pitched ranks remaining undivided as often sizable mixture stops.

In describing the stops of his ideal organ, Schlick mentions in passing the following combinations:

1. Principal and Zimbel (but "the zimbel sounds well with all registers")
2. Rauschpfeife (Regal) and Trompete, with the Mixture

3. Rauschpfeife and small Mixture in the Positiv
4. Principal 8' and Octave 4' in the Pedal, or Octave alone; also Trompetes and Posaunes
5. "Wood pipes with the octave" (probably Gedeckt 8' and Principal 4')

Obviously these are obviously not all of the possible combinations but apparently the ones Schlick particularly liked; and the combination of reeds with mixtures, which is little exploited in modern usage, occurs in other sources as well. Something Schlick seems not to have cared for was fifth-sounding mutation stops, although they were found throughout Flanders and central Germany in this period, and were much in favor as color stops in France and Spain.

Schlick's comments on the use of the compound stops finds some confirmation in a contract for a six-stop organ built a few years later, in 1522, by the Flemish builder de Buus for the church of St. Denys in Veurne. Here the builder mentions that the Scharf mixture plays with the Principal (8') and Octave (4'), while the double Cimbel (i.e., repeating Cimbel of two ranks) can play with all the registers [177, p. 160]. It is clear from these and other references that the Cimbel is regarded as a color stop rather than a part of the chorus.

A contract of 1537 for an organ in Trier Cathedral, and a companion manuscript of 1538 dealing with the same organ, contain a few suggestions for use. The Trier registrations are broken down into four categories:

1. *Organo pleno* (full organ)
2. *Kuppel* (combinations including the 8' Principal)
   a. With Quintadena
   b. With Quintadena and Zimbel
   c. With Quintadena, Hohlpfeife, and Zimbel
3. *Quintadein* (combinations including the 16' Quintadena)
   a. Quintadena alone
   b. With Hohlpfeife
   c. With Zimbel
4. Reed and other solo combinations [194, p. 115]

A corresponding group of combinations is listed for the Positiv division: For No. 2, the Quintadena 8' and Principal 4'; these two with the 2' Flute added; these three with the Zimbel added. For No. 3, the Quintadena alone, or with the Zimbel, 2' Flute, or Querpfeife 2' (or 1'). This last is called *fleit fogel* (lit. bird-flute) and one wonders if it is the German equivalent of the mysterious French *jeu de papegay* (bird registration). Among the solo combinations listed are Quintadena with 4' Schalmey, and these two stops plus 2' Flute and Zimbel—note again the seemingly unorthodox commingling of reeds with flues and mixtures.

The reeds (Kornett treble) and some flue stops (Flute bass) were divided or half-stops after the Flemish fashion, and the writer points out that this enabled the organist to play trios from the same manual. For trios involving two manuals and pedal, ten combinations are given, using the previously described registrations. The fact that no off-unison mutations are cited perhaps supports Schlick's dislike of them, although such stops do appear in combinations from a slightly later period. The term "trio" here in all probability refers simply to any three-part composition (the form of many chorale-based works) in which the parts may be played on separate manuals (or half-manuals) plus the pedal.

The Pedal division of the Trier organ had two independent stops (8' Trompete and 2' Flute), plus the Principal and Quintadena borrowed from the Great. Combinations given are Quintadena alone, with Principal, and with Principal and Trompete. The 2' Flute was to be used in trios, or for a *cantus firmus*—one of the earliest specific references to the solo use of a Pedal stop [194, p. 115].

Three central German documents confirm the general premises of the Trier registrations. One, from Worms (dated 1556, but possibly relating to the 1510 organ in St. Andreas's Church), gives the following combinations; they are interesting in that some of them combine narrow (principal) and wide (flute) stops:

1. The Prestant 8', Holfluit 8', and Holfluit 4' may all be used alone, or with the 4' Octave. The Pedal Principal (16'?) should be used with these stops.
2. Combinations that sound well with the Tremulant are: Principals 8' and 4'; Principal 8' and Flute 8'; Principal 8' and Flute 4'; Flutes 8' and 4' with Quint 2 2/3' ("this is the best"). But the Tremulant should never be used with the reed stops.
3. Instrumental imitations: Holfluit 8', Regal 8', and Quint 2 2/3' make a "good loud Zink"; Regal 8' and Holfluit 8' make a "loud Krummhorn."
4. The large manual and pedal Mixtures should only be used with the full organ, but the Zimbel sounds best with the 8' and 4' flutes—again confirming its use as a color rather than a chorus stop.
5. Neither the manual Regal nor the pedal Posaune should be used alone.
6. The Drum is best used in pieces in the key of C [193 II, p. 9; 127, p. 269].

Twenty years later we find some registration instructions for a two-manual organ in the Cistercian Monastery of Schöntal laid out on similar lines:

Full organ: Principal 8', Octave 4', Quint 2 2/3', Mixture, Zimbel
Reeds: Should be drawn with the Principal or Gedeckt, along with the Octave and Quint.
Principal and/or Gedeckt:
   a. Either alone or together
   b. With Octave and Quint
   c. With Octave and Flute 4'
   d. With Flute 4' and Quint [193 III, p. 16]

Here again one notes the mixing of "narrow" and "wide" stops, as well as the use of the Quint, and the necessity of always combining reeds with flues (a practice which, as will be seen, continued into the nineteenth century).

The authors of these 1576 instructions also give an interesting rule of thumb for registering when the Hauptwerk and Positiv are used together: Always have one more stop on the Positiv than on the Hauptwerk, i.e., if there are two stops drawn on the Hauptwerk, there should be three on the Positiv. This may possibly refer to the playing of solos on the Positiv or to trio playing.

Concerning the Tremulant, this source confirms the suggestions of the Worms document: It should not be used if more than three stops are drawn, for "it is lovelier than it is when many stops are drawn"; nor should it be used with the Posaune (Trumpet) or Regal, "or they will be ruined." A few years earlier, in some instructions left by the builders of an organ in Amorbach in 1568, one finds an almost identical stricture: never use the Tremulant with more than three stops or with reeds. How much the wind systems of the day had to do with these cautions is not certain, but in all likelihood this was a factor.

The Schöntal source also confirms the use of wide and narrow stops together as well as with reeds, the all-flue plenum, the use of 8' Principals and Flutes alone, and the popularity of combinations containing the quint mutation. Of even more interest is the fact that it repeats almost verbatim the rule about drawing one more stop on the Positiv than is drawn on the Hauptwerk, noting that "this is more pleasant than drawing many stops" [181, p. 67].

From the Stiftskirche in the south-central city of Würzburg (not far from Worms) comes a set of directions dated 1568, which specifies such combinations as:

Principal 8', Gedackt 8', and Spitz Octave 4'
Gedackt 8' and Spitz Octave 4'
Quintadena 8'(?), Fifteenth 2', and Zimbel
Octave 4' and Rausswerck (reeds)
Octave 4', Klein Basaun (Posaune?) and Zinck
Gedackt 8', Spitz Octave 4', and Flöte (4'?)
Gedackt 8' and Klein Flöte (2'?)
Gedackt 8', Octave 4', and Klein Flöte (2'?)

The Tremulant is again mentioned; it "goes with the Gedackt and Spitz [octave]" [193 III, p. 14]. The Würzburg document differs from the others in making no mention of quints and in including registrations combining flues and reeds— although the latter may simply be another way of stating the Worms prohibition against using reeds alone.

With the exception of instructions for the use of pedals and multiple manuals, these Germanic directions do not differ significantly from those set down a little later in more southern regions. The Principal and Flute (or Quintadena) at either 8' or 4' could be used alone or together, and other stops could be added to color them. Whereas the earliest Plenum consisted solely of the Principal and its upperwork, a second category of Plenum which included reeds appeared around the middle of the sixteenth century—a distinction perpetuated in subsequent centuries in the French *Plein jeu* (principals through mixtures) and *Grand jeu* (reeds instead of mixtures). While the Zimbel is sometimes included in the Plenum toward the end of the century, it is more often used simply to color lighter combinations.

In registering the Catholic liturgical music of the late fifteenth and early sixteenth centuries, such as that in the *Buxheimer Orgelbuch*, the same general observations affecting the music of Redford or Cavazzone may safely be applied. The music is still on two staves, with no manual or pedal designations or registrations. What appears to be the intermittent transfer of the bass part to the Pedal in *Sanctus Angelicum* from the Buxheimer book has never been satisfactorily explained; in all probability it is put on a separate staff simply because it crosses the tenor line. In the music from the sixteenth-century tablature books of Kleber, Sicher, Buchner, etc., however, one finds clear examples of music where solos in manual or pedal are indicated. For example, Sicher's *In Dulci Jubilo* and one of the *Resonet in Laudibus* settings from the same collection have the *cantus* in the tenor voice of a three-voice setting. Because of wide intervals and crossed parts, these pieces are awkward and make little sense when played only on the manual. If, however, the tenor part is played with the left hand on a 4' or 2' flute or light 8' or 4' reed (preferably with a corresponding flute) against one of the 8' (or 8' and 4') manual combinations, and the bass is played on an 8' pedal stop, the elegant sophistication of these little trio-like works becomes apparent.

Even some of the plainsong-based pieces from this period, such as Buchner's *Recordare* and many of Kotter's settings, plainly call for solos, although usually in the soprano part and highly ornamented. Thus they may be played on a second manual, preferably the Positiv, with a colorful combination such as a "Nazard" or one including the Zimbel and/or a Regal.

Side-by-side with plainsong and chorale settings in the early sixteenth-century German tablature books one finds dances, settings of popular songs, and an occasional free composition, such as a preludium, praeambulum, fantasia, or fugue. Some particularly good examples of the latter are found in Kotter's 1513 collection [101, pp. 57–66]. In some of them, the spacing of the left-hand parts and general relegation of the faster ornamentation to the upper registers suggest performance on a large organ employing a fairly strong Principal plenum. In a few, however, rapid notes and close harmonies in the left hand suggest a smaller organ or a 4' pitch basis.

The song and dance pieces are equally at home on a plucked string keyboard instrument, a regal, or a positive, and light combinations based on 8' Flutes or 4' Principals or Flutes are appropriate here. Here too one may use the short-length reeds, the Zimbel, and, most certainly, the "toy" stops—birds, bells, and drums—wherever it seems appropriate.

In our modern organs we have the tonal materials of both the large and the small organs. For the purpose of registering early music, however, it is necessary to mentally separate this tonal material. This is relatively easy with a classically conceived organ having a Rückpositiv or a Brustwerk—the legacy of the "little organs"—but a bit more difficult with a mid-twentieth century "all-purpose" chambered instrument, and even more so with an earlier twentieth-century organ having little in the way of lightly voiced stops or upperwork. The irony of this situation is that the Renaissance organ was every bit as much an "orchestral" organ as the organ of the 1920s. The difference is simply in the vastly different instrumentarium of the two periods.

Within recent years several organs based on early models have been constructed, often for educational institutions. Assuming the average (and more common) "eclectic" modern instrument of two or three manuals, however, the best approach to early keyboard music is a process of elimination, and the player must have a clear mental catalog of what may be used and what is best avoided. A good clear Principal chorus, based on a reasonably foundational but not bottom-heavy 8', is a requisite; if a suitable 16' Quintadena is available, it may be used in the Plenum in some of the

Germanic literature, but foundational Romantic 16' Bourdons are out of character. Modern strings too have no place in this music—until the Baroque period, the string-color equivalent in the organ was either the 8' Principal or the Regal.

With regard to flutes, lightness, color, and contrast are the keys. The basic types of stopped flute in this period were the Germanic Gedeckt or Hohlpfeife, which could be of wood or metal, and the French Bourdon, which was usually of metal; all of them were fairly foundational in tone, although neither weak nor reticent. To these may be added the thin and quinty metal Quintadena, a stop usually used only for coloring. Whether the English had yet developed the characteristic quinty wooden Stopped Diapason of the succeeding period is uncertain, although stopped wood pipes of some sort were found in early English regals.

It will be noted that the Recorder or Blockflute appears in many stoplists, usually at 4' or 2' pitches. It was usually an open flute, frankly imitative of its namesake, which in the Renaissance had a wider bore and a sweeter, stronger sound than the narrow-bore Baroque recorder. Somewhat less common was the so-called German Flute, which imitated the lighter, more mellow traverse flute and was probably smaller in scale than the recorder.

On a modern organ a mild 8' Gedeckt or Chimney Flute with a trace of quint is a useful voice for early music, and in the 4' and 2' registers a fairly foundational open or tapered flute will likewise be useful. Flute-toned Quints or Nazards of 2 2/3' are always good for coloring, but as there is no evidence that third-sounding stops (Tierces, or compound stops containing them, such as the Sesquialtera or the Cornet) were in use this early, they should be avoided. "Cornet" effects in this period were achieved with high-pitched quint and unison mutations, especially the 1 1/3'. While "gapped" combinations (ones which omit one or more of the elements of the overtone series) are occasionally mentioned, they were usually associated with special effects and should be used very sparingly.

Three basic kinds of reeds were common in the sixteenth century, the oldest of which is the fractional-length Regal type. Half-length cylindrical reeds are represented by the Krummhorn, and the Schalmey is something of a hybrid between these two. Full-length conical reeds (Trumpets) appeared in France, Spain, and Germany by the middle of the sixteenth century, but there is no hard evidence that they were employed in England or Italy. A light Oboe is often a good substitute for the Schalmey, and if an organ has Trumpets on more than one division, the lighter of the two is probably preferable, especially for French and Spanish music and for Plenum use. Full-length reeds should probably be used very sparingly for solo purposes, if at all.

The Pedal in this period was usually not a 16' division, save in Germanic organs with a 16' manual division, and while pull-down pedals in all regions were almost certainly used to sustain pedal points and to double bass notes in cadences, the solo use of the pedals in the northern countries was of far greater musical importance. For this purpose 8' or 4' light reeds (preferably combined with a light stopped flute) or 4' or 2' flutes are required, and if they are not to be found in the Pedal division of a particular organ, they should be coupled down from one of the manuals.

Players are encouraged to use (or simulate) the "toy stops" in appropriate music (usually seasonal or secular, but not liturgical). A number of organs built after the

1950s have Zimbelsterns, but a page-turner with a string of little brass "Sarna bells" is an acceptable substitute. A few more recent organs have birds and drums, but the commonest form of drum stop is simply two or three de-tuned open wood pipes of around 4' pitch, and this effect can thus be simulated by treading rhythmically on the highest C and C♯ of the pedalboard with the 16' Open Diapason alone drawn (especially if it is a large-scaled wooden one).

Above all it must be remembered that the Renaissance organ was a colorful instrument, but that the colors were largely achieved by the mixing of foundations with mutations and, occasionally, flues with reeds. Registering early music on a well-designed organ of ten or twelve stops can be a rewarding exercise—as Schlick and others suggest—but it must also be conceded that there are some organs on which it will be an exercise in futility.

Europe did not burst from the Renaissance to the Baroque overnight, but many of the political events and cultural developments of this transitional period did sometimes crowd upon each other in rapid succession, especially at the beginning. They all made their mark on the history of the organ and its music.

In England, the administration of Elizabeth I was gradually loosening the hold of the Puritans on the Church of England, but the hiatus in the building (and playing) of organs that had occurred during the mid-century reign of the boy king Edward and the ecclesiastical confusion of Mary's tragic reign had cut the island nation off from continental developments. The organs built in England during the Elizabethan and Jacobean reigns that bracketed the beginning of the seventeenth century seem curiously spartan when compared to those found in parts of France and Germany during the same period.

Spain kept control of Flanders (Catholic Netherlands) for some decades after the defeat of her Armada by the English in 1588, and there were strong cultural and economic connections between Madrid and Antwerp for the remainder of the seventeenth century. Just to the north, in the United Provinces of the Protestant Netherlands, a creative truce had been declared between the Calvinists, who eschewed the use of instruments in their worship, and the civic authorities, who owned and maintained the organs in the large churches, using them regularly for recitals on weekdays and after the church services.

France, meanwhile, had begun winning some of her long-standing battles with the Habsburgs and was becoming more of a unified entity, culturally centered around Paris. The French classic organ, growing out of the Flemish tradition, came into its own during the final decades of the sixteenth century, and a school of composers began to rise around it. In 1643 the accession of Louis XIV, the "Sun King," ushered in a golden age for the arts and sciences that lasted until the eighteenth century. In the same period Italy continued to build on a well-established organ tradition and produced some of her greatest composers and theoreticians. The Iberian peninsula, bankrupted by the excesses of its rulers, was beginning a slow economic decline, but its musical golden age had not yet ended and was in fact establishing roots in the New World.

Germany at this time did not exist as a country, but was rather a fluid confederation of small duchies and free cities. The wealthy Hanseatic trading cities on the North Sea became a center for opulent music and extravagant organ building, attracting musicians and instrument makers from less affluent areas. But much of central and south Germany, Austria, and Hungary were devastated by the Thirty Years War of 1618–48, and cultural and economic recovery in this area was not complete until well past the middle of the seventeenth century.

The organs and music of all countries were becoming unique and more distinctive, yet certain threads continued to bind them together. Perhaps the greatest distinction, by the end of this period, was between the organ culture of the Protestant countries (north and central Germany, northern Netherlands, and England) and the Catholic countries (southern Germany, Austria-Hungary, Poland, Italy, Spain, Portugal, France, and Spanish Netherlands). Liturgical usage played no small part in this.

The Music

The organ mass and office hymn settings still formed an important part of the literature in the Catholic countries, but free forms such as the toccata, ricercar, verset, and canzona became more prominent, particularly in Italy. In France, the gradual expansion and elaboration of the organ mass would eventually lead to the virtuoso offertoires and registration-oriented shorter movements of the Baroque period. Some significant compositional activity was beginning to appear in south Germany, subtly influenced by Italy through individuals such as Frescobaldi's German pupil Froberger.

In Protestant northern Europe, a cultural explosion was taking place, particularly in the the large Dutch market towns and the Hanseatic cities. The use of the organ in the Lutheran service generated chorale preludes, chorale variations, and elaborate chorale fantasias, while the significant secular use of the instrument in Holland and northern Germany promoted the composition of flamboyant praeludia, toccatas, fantasias, and fugues, as well as variations on secular melodies. In England, major composers (many of them recusant Catholics) again turned their talents to the organ, largely in free forms such as preludes, fantasias, and voluntaries, but also, despite the repressive character of England's Protestantism, in stylized plainsong-based works.

Conspicuous among the composers of this period are the great teachers Frescobaldi and Sweelinck, who left their mark on this and the subsequent era; the English keyboard virtuosi Bull, Byrd, and Gibbons; Normandy's enigmatic Titelouze and the first of the Parisian Couperin dynasty; and such heralds of the mature German Baroque school as Scheidt, Scheidemann, Weckmann, and Tunder. Despite their relative familiarity to modern players, all have suffered in years past at the hands of cavalier editors and arrangers, although it is now increasingly possible to find good scholarly editions of their work.

The Organs

The organs built in the final years of the sixteenth century not only summed up the developments and international influences of the previous decades but also set the tone for the regional styles that prevailed during much of the seventeenth century. A significant case in point was the organ built in 1580 by Nicolas Barbier for the church of St. Gervais and St. Protais in Gisors, France. This instrument represented the synthesis of Flemish and Iberian elements that was to make the Parisian Baroque organ unique: full Principal choruses, Chimney Flutes, flute mutations, the five-rank treble-compass Cornet (containing a Tierce), three types of reed stop (conical Trompette, cylindrical Cromorne, short-length Voix Humaine), Trompettes at 8' and 4' on the Grand Orgue, and 8' reed and flue stops in the Pedal.

In 1583, the Fleming Sebastian Hay built a large two-manual organ for the Church of St. Apollinare in Rome. It contributed new elements, notably reeds and chimney flutes, to the standard ripieno-based Italian tonal scheme. However, Graziadio Antegnati's 1581 organ for the Church of St. Giuseppe in Brescia differed little from instruments built by his family a half century earlier. Iberian organs followed a similar pattern of development, gradually increasing in the number of stops (particularly reed stops) but, as in Italy, France, and England, never exceeding two manuals. With a few notable exceptions, such as the organ completed by the Flemish builder Brebos for El Escorial in 1584, they possessed only the most rudimentary Pedal divisions.

England, still sporadically plagued with religious troubles, seemed cut off from the developments across the channel. Between 1580 and and the renewed Puritan onslaught of the 1640s, her artisans picked up the almost-lost thread of what had once been a thriving organ culture, but the one- and two-manual organs they built were devoid of the reeds, tierces, and other color stops now standard on the Continent.

Because of the Calvinist troubles in Holland after 1566, many Netherlands organ builders, such as the de Mare and Maas families, moved northeast and began building large organs for the wealthy German cities on the North Sea. A not untypical example was the three-manual, 44-stop organ built between 1587 and 1591 for St. Peter's Church in Lübeck, which had a large Pedal division based on the 32' Principal. Some unusually large organs were also being built in central Germany, Austria, and Czechoslovakia in this period, including a truly mammoth (for that time) instrument of four manuals and 74 stops (21 of which were in the Pedal), said to have been completed in 1588 by the brothers Rudner for the Cathedral in Prague [133, p. 32]. Needless to say, such extravagant organs were always the exception, with modest instruments of one, two, or three manuals being much more the rule.

4 | England

Composers

John Bull (c1562–1628)
William Byrd (1542/3–1623)
Nicholas Carleton (d. c1630)
Benjamin Cosyn (fl. 1622–43)
Christopher Gibbons (1615–1676)
Orlando Gibbons (1585–1625)
John Lugge (fl. 1602–1645)
Peter Philips (c1560–c1638)
Richard Portman (c1610–1656)
Benjamin Rogers (1614–1698)
Thomas Tomkins (1573–1656)
Thomas Weelkes (d. 1623)

Representative Organs

ORGAN GIVEN BY ELIZABETH I TO THE TURKISH SULTAN
Thomas Dallam, 1597 [100, p. 79]

Manual
Open Principal 4'
Unison Recorder 4'(?)
Octavo Principal 2'
Flute 2'(?)

Accessory Stops
Shaking stop (tremulant)
Nightingale, Drum

[N.B. This was a self-playing organ.]

ETON COLLEGE, ETON
Thomas Dallam, 1613–14 [172, p. 2]

Manual
(Stopped) Diapason 8'
Principal 4'
Fflute 4'
Octavo to the Principal 2'
Fifteenth 1'(?)

Accessory Stops
Shaking stop

CATHEDRAL, WORCESTER
Thomas Dallam, 1613–14 [228, p. 65]

Great	**Chaire**
2 Open Diapasons 8'	(Stopped) Diapason 8' (wood)
2 Principals 4'	Principal 4'
Recorder 4'(?)	Flute 4'(wood)
Twelfth 2 2/3'	Small Principal or 15th 2'
2 Small Principals 2'	

Accessory Stops
2 Stars (cymbalsterns)

KNOLE HOUSE, SEVENOAKS, KENT
Anonymous "chest organ," c1623 [228, p. 37]

Manual
Stopped Diapason 8'
Principal 4'
Twelfth 2 2/3'
Fifteenth 2'

CASTLE CHAPEL, CHIRK
John Burward, 1631–32 [30, p. 39]

Upper Keys	**Lower Keys**
Stopt Diapason 8'	Diapason 8' (stopped?)
Open Diapason 8' (treble)	Principall 4'
Principall 4' (prestant)	Small Principall 2'
Small Principall 4' (or 2'?)	
Recorder 2' (or 4'?)	
Fifteenth 2'	
Two and Twentieth 1'	

CATHEDRAL, LITCHFIELD
Robert Dallam, 1639 [191, p. 6]

Great	**Chaire**
2 Open Diapasons 8'	Stopped Diapason 8' (wood)
2 Principalls 4'	Principall 4' (prestant)

Small Principall 2'
Two and Twentie 1'

Flute 4'? (wood)
Small Principall 2'
Two and Twentie 1'

Registration

It is possible that two-manual organs were not known in England before 1600, but in the first decade of the seventeenth century new organs of two manuals are recorded (King's College, Cambridge, 1605) as is the addition of a second division to older single organs (St. George's Chapel, Windsor, 1609). The second division was, as on the Continent, a smaller organ located on the gallery rail, and a "double organ" consisted of the Great (main organ) and Chaire (small organ). Neither additional divisions nor pedals occurred between 1580 and the 1640s, and the organs under discussion may thus be said to fall into the following categories:

1. Double organs (two divisions, based on 8' and 4' Principals)
2. Large single organs (8' pitch)
3. Small single organs (4' pitch)
4. Chamber organs or positives

It should be noted that modern pitch equivalents are given here. The English church organs of this period were so-called transposing instruments, with low C of the keyboard playing a pipe that was actually 10' or 5' in length, sounding a pitch between a third and a fourth lower than modern pitch.

Regals, so popular in the preceding period, had all but disappeared, and indeed there is no record of the use of either reed stops or mixtures in English organs of any size until after the Restoration of the Monarchy in 1660, although references continue to be found to accessory stops such as tremulants and "turning stars."

As for the previous period, no written suggestions for registration survive, and the character of the music and the organs must again serve as a guide. Just which keyboard music from this period was intended for the organ and which for virginals or harpsichords is still open to question, although it may probably be safely said that any piece carrying the original (not editorial) title of "Voluntary" is an organ piece; this distinctive term in fact originates in this period. Many of the Fantasias (or Fancys) are also suitable for the organ, unless their style plainly dictates otherwise. A work by Byrd is entitled "Fantasia" in the *Fitzwilliam Virginal Book* and "Voluntary" in *My Ladye Nevells Booke*, indicating a certain amount of inter-changeability between the two terms, both of which are analagous to the continental Praeludium, Toccata, or Tiento in indicating a freely composed piece. Some of these free Fantasias or Voluntaries were calm and dignified, somewhat reminiscent of the early Italian Toccatas, and more suited to the sustained organ style than that of the harpsichord or the virginal. Yet Bull, Gibbons, and others also occasionally wrote Fantasias in a light and brilliant "Netherlandish" style that are equally effective on the organ and the harpsichord.

Although liturgical music with a plainsong basis was no longer a required (or even desired) part of the reformed Church of England service, pieces of this type,

primarily *Misereres* and *In Nomines*, occur throughout this period in the works of
Bull, Byrd, Tomkins, and others. The source for many of these is the *Fitzwilliam
Virginal Book*, actually the musical "commonplace book" of the Paget family. The
title by which this important manuscript is now known is relatively modern, and
its contents are by no means all intended for the virginal. The knowledge that Bull,
Byrd, and the Pagets were all recusant (illegal or "underground") Catholics suggests
that the plainsong pieces could well have been intended for liturgical use in private
chapels.

The few "double organ" voluntaries of this period, chiefly by John Lugge,
Orlando Gibbons, and Richard Portman (although a few other works not specifically
so named may also belong to this genre), are certainly intended for a full-sounding
church organ having a stoplist similar to those of the Worcester or Litchfield organs
cited above. Lugge was organist of Exeter Cathedral, where there was an organ at
least as large as (and possibly larger than) the cited examples. Although its stoplist
has not been preserved, it was described in 1634 as "a delicate, rich and lofty organ
which has more additions [stops?] than any other" as well as possessing "faire pipes
of an extraordinary length and of the bigness of a man's thigh"—presumably a
"trompes" type of bass extension down to 10' pitch [97, p. 2].

The same writer (backed up by entries in the Cathedral records) notes that at this
time other instruments—viols, cornets, and sackbuts—were used in the services
along with the organ and choir. Such usages are referred to in records of other
cathedrals and may well be associated with the increasingly elaborate anthems that
began to be written in the early seventeenth century. What would appear to be the
fairly widespread use of supplementary instruments, at least on the cathedral level,
may also partially explain why reeds and other imitative stops were not regarded as
a necessary part of English organs in this period.

While intended for an organ of two manuals, the double organ Voluntaries are
closely related in compositional style to the *medio registro* pieces of Spain and the
Spanish Netherlands as well as the *basse et dessus* pieces of seventeenth-century
France. In Spain and France such pieces often made use of cornet mixtures and
reeds, stops not known in England until after 1660. The sturdy character of double
Voluntaries like Lugge's suggests that these pieces are meant to pit the full chorus
of the Great against that of the lighter Chaire, particularly since the part assigned
to the Great is, in this period, always in the bass, and, as is often characteristic of the
style in general, both hands go to the Great at the end.

Substantial Voluntaries or Fantasias, even though intended only for "single"
organ, should likewise have a fairly full principal-family registration, but not one
including mixtures. In view of their possible liturgical function in chapels with
smaller organs, a more restrained registration (such as 8' Stopped Diapason and 4'
Principal or Flute) is suggested for the plainsong-based pieces, and the short verses
and pointes will usually benefit from an even lighter registration, perhaps involving
some of the higher-pitched stops. Some verses and shorter fantasias (good examples
of which are found in the works of Bull and Tomkins) can sound extremely well
on a single 8' (or even 4') Principal or Diapason, provided that it is of a suitable
"singing" character—rich in texture but not too loud, "sizzly," or foundational, and
having a slight rise in intensity toward the treble.

Finally, there is the unresolved question of the secular use of the organ in England and the applicability of the various song- and dance-based keyboard pieces to the organ. Certainly the use of domestic chamber organs was widespread during the sixteenth and seventeenth centuries and beyond. And during the period of the Puritan repression (1642–1660), when the liturgical use of organs was prohibited, one may find references to the secular use of those few larger organs that remained in use—chiefly, it would appear, in college chapels. John Milton in 1644 recommended organ music to soothe the "travailed spirits" of students with fugues or the "artful" embellishment of chordal music played on a soft stop, and the use of the organ for accompanying "religious, martial, or civil Ditties" [153, p. 151]. Robert Hooke, the philosopher, learned to play twenty pieces on the organ at Christ Church, Oxford, "in those days when the church musique was putt down"; and in 1654 the diarist Evelyn heard Christopher Gibbons give some visitors "a taste of his skill and talents" on the organ at Magdalen College, Oxford [153, p. 242].

It is generally accepted that, along with their Fantasias and other free pieces, Sweelinck and his contemporaries played secular music, including variations on popular songs and dances, on the municipally owned organs in the large Dutch churches on secular occasions, even though these organs were silent during the Calvinist church services. While the widespread destruction of church and cathedral organs during the Commonwealth period precluded this practice in most English churches, references such as those quoted above indicate that similar usages may well have obtained in those college chapels that retained their organs.

The secular song variations, dance pieces, and "battles" are, for the most part, "generic" keyboard pieces, whether Dutch or English, and unless they are of a distinctly "lutenistic" style, more appropriate to the virginal or harpsichord (broken chords, thick left-hand chords), they may be played on the organ. Examples of both styles can be found in the *Fitzwilliam Virginal Book, My Ladye Nevells Booke*, the *Dublin Manuscript*, and similar volumes, as well as in the collected works of the various composers in the invaluable *Musica Brittanica* series; sorting them out can be a rewarding stylistic exercise for the student.

Since the secular pieces would have been most commonly played on chamber organs, light stops and combinations appropriate to a small "single organ" would be the most suitable registrations. In variations, registrations can be changed with each section, and the player should not be afraid to use some imagination. The use of 4' and even 2' stops as the basic pitch line has precedent on the Continent and in the existence of "ottavino" instruments in the sixteenth and seventeenth centuries. It is encouraged wherever the tessitura and texture of the music suggests it. It is thus possible on a very small Positive consisting of only 8' Flute, 4' Principal, 4' Flute and 2' Principal to obtain different registrations for as many as a dozen variations.

In registering this music on a modern organ, care must be taken to preserve its transparent nature. The typical wooden English Stopped Diapason, with its characteristic quinty flavor (not to be confused with the more foundational Gedackt, Hohlflute, and Bourdon) evolved during the seventeenth century and was common to both large and small organs. It is an ideal blending stop, useful on its own, giving a unique color to the Open Diapason, and combining well with other stops. Unfortunately it is not available on many modern organs, where one must settle for the lightest or brightest stopped or chimneyed flute. Despite its somewhat quinty quality, it should not be confused with the metal Quintadena, which lacks much of the fundamental inherent in the English stop.

Often the most suitable principal chorus will be found on a secondary division in large modern organs, although some very characteristic English sounds (including good Stopped Diapasons) are often found in early nineteenth-century American organs. Heavy and opaque 8' Principals should be avoided at all costs, and it is probable that the use of the 8' Stopped and Open Diapasons together, which was well established in the following period, was also observed in the early seventeenth century.

Despite the arrangements and editorial registrations in some badly butchered editions, the player should avoid 16' manual stops, reeds, and, above all, the use of the pedal to preserve the clear texture of seventeenth-century English music, although the addition of a not-too-overpowering mixture will not harm some of the more robust Fantasias. On paper, the organ that Byrd, Bull, Gibbons, Lugge, and Tomkins wrote for may seem uninteresting, but it is very doubtful that it sounded so under the fingers of one with the "skill and talents" of a Gibbons or a Bull, and it is the modern organist's challenge to bring this music to life without distorting it in the process.

| **Grand Orgue** | **Positif** |

France and Catholic Netherlands

Composers

Jean-Henri d'Anglebert (1628–1691)
William Browne (Brouno) (fl. early 17th century)
John Bull (c1562–1628) (in later years)
Pieter Cornet (1570/80–1633)
Louis Couperin (c1626–1661)
Richard Deering (d.1630)
Henry Du Mont (1610–1684)
Jean-Nicolas Geoffroy (fl. 1633–94)
Charles Guillet (d. 1654)
Abraham van den Kerckhoven (1627–1702)
Karel Luython (1557/8–1620)
Samuel Mareschall (1554–1641)
Peter Philips (c1560–1628) (in later years)
Charles Racquet (1597–1664)
Etienne Richard (c1621–1669)
François Roberday (1624–1680)
Jehan Titelouze (1563/4–1633)

Representative Organs

CHURCH OF ST. GERVAIS AND ST. PROTAIS, GISORS
Nicolas Barbier, 1580 [40, p. 122; 39, p. 59]

Grand Orgue	**Positif**
Montre 16'	Bourdon 8'
(Principal) 8'	(Principal) 4'
Bourdon 8'	(Principal?) 2'
Prestant 4'	Petite Quinte 1 1/3'

Flûte 4'
Nazard II (2 2/3' and 2'?)
Quinte flûte 2 2/3'(?) (chimney)
Doublette 2'
Sifflet 1'
Cornet V (from middle C)
Fourniture IV–VI
Cimballe III
Trompette 8'
Voix humaine 8' (?) (regal)
Clairon 4'

Accessory Stops
Tremblant

Cimballe II
Cromhorne 8'

Pedal
"Pedal stop" 8' (wood, large-scale)
Sacqueboutte 8'(?) (Sackbut; reed)

ST. BAVO'S CHURCH, GHENT
Aert de Smet, 1592 [176, p. 118]

Manual
Bourdon 16'
Prestant 8'
Holpijp 8'
Octaaf 4'
Gedackt Fluit 4'
Nasard 2 2/3'
Gemshoorn 2'
Siffluit 1'
Cornet (from middle C♯)
Mixtuur
Scherp
Trompet 8' (divided?)
Schalmei 4' (divided?)

Pedal
Coupled to Manual

Accessory Stops
Tremulant
Nachtegaal (bird)
Trommel, Harp

CHURCH OF ST. MARTIN-DES-CHAMPS, PARIS
Valeran de Héman, 1618 [240, p. 8]

Grand Orgue
Montre 16'
Bourdon 16'
Montre 8'
Bourdon 8'
Prestant 4'
Flûte 4'
Nasard 2 2/3'
Quinte 2 2/3'
Doublette 2'
Quarte (de nasard) 2'

Positif
Montre 8'(?)
Bourdon 8'
Montre 4'
Flûte bouchée 4'
Doublette 2'
Larigot 1 1/3'
Fourniture III
Cymbale II
Cromorne 8'
Régale 4'

Flageolet 1'?
CornetV (treble)
Trompette 8'
Voix humaine 8'
Clairon 4'

Pedale
Coupled to Grand Orgue

CATHEDRAL OF OUR LADY, ANTWERP
Mathieu Langhedul, 1626 [177, p. 18]

Manual
Holpype 8'
Prestant 4'
Fluyte 4'
Quintefluyte or Nazard 2 2/3'
Superoctave 2'
Tierce 1 3/5'
Nagthoorne (a Cornet stop, treble only)
Trompet 8'
Schalmey 4'

Accessory Stops
Nagtegael (bird)
Trommel (drum)

ST. VICTOR ABBEY, MARSEILLE
D. & G. Eustache, 1630 [181, p. 185]

Grand Orgue
Montre 8'
Bourdon 8'
Prestant 4'
Flûte 4'
Nasard 2 2/3'
Doublette 2'
Fourniture II–III
Cymbale II
CornetV
Trompette 8'
Voix humaine 8'

Accessory Stops
Tremblant
Rossignol (bird)

Positif
Bourdon 8'
Montre 4'
Larigot 1 1/3'
Fourniture III

Pedale
Flûte 8'(?) (open)

CHURCH OF ST. GODARD, ROUEN
Guillaume Lesselier, 1632 [40, p. 110]

Grand Orgue
Montre 8'★
Bourdon 8'★
Prestant 4'★
Flûte 4' (stopped)

Positif
Montre 8' (stopped bass)
Prestant 4'
Nazard 2 2/3'? or 1 1/3'?
Doublette 2'

Nazard 2 2/3'
Doublette 2'★
Petit flûte 2'
Petit nazard 1 1/3'
Sifflet 1'
Cornet V (treble)
Fourniture IV★
Cimballes III★
Trompette 8'
Voix humaine 8' (regal)
Clairon 4'

Fourniture III
Cromorne 8'

Pedal
Bourdon 8' (wood and metal)
Trompette 8' (large-scale)
Flûte 4' (open, large-scale)

Accessory Stops
Tremblant
Rossignol (bird)
Tambour (drum)

★ "All these stops serve as the Plein Jeu."

JACOBIN MONASTERY, LYON
Sylvio Reynon, 1650 [12, p. 20]

Manual
Montre 8'
Bourdon 8'
Octave 4'
Gros nazard 2 2/3'
(Principal) 2'
Tierce 1 3/5'
Petit nazard 1 1/3'
Vingt-deuxième (22nd) 1'
Cornet
Fourniture II
Trompette 8'
Voix humaine 8'

Pedal (8 notes)
(unnamed wood stop) 8'

PARISH CHURCH, LANVELLEC, BRITTANY
Robert Dallam, ★1653 [202, p. 76]

Manual
Bourdon 8'
Prestant 4'
Quinte (Nasard) 2 2/3'
Doublette 2'
Tierce 1 3/5'
Larigot 1 1/3'
Flageolet 1'
Cornet V (treble)
Fourniture III
Cymbale II
Cromorne 8' (divided)
Voix humaine 8' (divided)

Accessory Stops
Tremblant?

*The English Dallam, being a Catholic, fled England in 1642 to escape the persecution of the Roundheads. Once in France he adopted the French style completely.

Registration

Reed stops of all types (full-length, half-length, and fractional-length) had been in use in central and northern Europe since the middle of the sixteenth century, as had "German" (chimneyed) flutes and wide-scaled mutations (Nasards, etc.). These elements all came together in a unique way in the late sixteenth-century organ of Gisors, and the organs of central and northern France adhered very closely to this general model for the better part of the succeeding century. Like the Italian organ, the French organ was rapidly becoming sufficiently standardized for basic registration conventions (*jeux*) to be established, and, in France, more than in any other country, these conventions helped to shape the organ compositions of several generations of organists.

Until the later years of the seventeenth century, French organs had no more than two manuals. If Titelouze is correct (in the preface to his 1623 *Hymns de l'eglise*) about the recent "perfecting" of the organ with "two separate manuals for hands" and pedalboards of up to 30 notes [259, p. 4], the second (*Positif de dos*) division must have been introduced only a few decades before it appeared in England. Indeed, the Gisors instrument may have been one of the first two-manual organs on French soil. Thus, with the exception of the significantly greater variety of stops, French and southern Flemish organs of the early seventeenth century may be said to fall into the same general categories as those in England: two-manual (8' and 4' or 16' and 8') organs, large (8') and small (4') single-manual organs, and positives or chamber organs. The single-manual organs were very likely to have divided reed stops, which, with the treble-compass Cornet—a relatively new stop containing the tierce—allowed solo possibilities.

While abstract descriptions of *jeux* occur early in the sixteenth century, their musical use, with a few exceptions, is not entirely clear, even in the light of later usages. The earliest instances of registration directions connected with specific pieces of music come not from Paris but Liège and possibly Antwerp. Two manuscripts of vast importance, the *Liber Fratrum Cruciferorum Leodiensium* (1617) and Christ Church Ms. 89 (c1620)—both sizable collections of liturgical organ pieces from Flanders—foreshadow the direction that French liturgical music would take later in the century. Most of the pieces in these manuscripts are anonymous, but among the identifiable composers are Cornet, Merulo, Gabrieli, Sweelinck, Scronx, and at least two English Catholic expatriates, Peter Philips and William Browne (Brouno), as well as Richard Deering, who may be the author of some anonymous pieces. An interesting international melange!

Two pieces in the Liège manuscript have registrational titles, an *Echo pour Trompette* and a *Fantasie por le Cornetto*. In addition, there is a Fantasia by Browne that could well be a double organ Voluntary, and several echo pieces, which also suggest access to a two-manual organ. Indeed, in four of the pieces, repeated (echo) passages are written in red ink in the manuscript, apparently to alert the player to a manual change [336, p. 23]. All the Christ Church manuscript pieces appear to be for a single-manual organ, but one with some divided stops, presumably reeds. Certain pieces, such as the third verset of Cornet's *Regina Caeli*, are unmistakably in the Flemish-influenced *Medio Registro* style coming into use in Spain. They drop below middle C♯ before and between solo sections, and their florid style suggests that they are probably for the Cornet (or some similar bright combination of stops), even though this is not specified. Similar pieces appear in the Liège manuscript. Three other pieces are specifically labeled "for the Cornet"; each contains active right-hand lines against a slow-moving left-hand accompaniment, which is presumably to be played on the standard *jeu doux* registration of 8' and 4' principals or flutes specified for similar pieces by later French writers, such as Nivers and Lebègue. Pieces such as these usually require two manuals on modern organs, especially since the division between bass and treble sometimes occurs one or two whole tones higher than the middle c or c♯ that later became standard in divided-manual organs.

One other lower Netherlands source deserves mention here. In 1613 John Bull left England abruptly (possibly for religious or political reasons) and entered the court at Brussels; he became organist of the cathedral in Antwerp in 1617 and remained there until his death in 1628. The cathedral had at least three organs, one of the smaller ones having been installed just two years before Bull's death. The largest organ was a two-manual instrument built in 1565–67 by the Flemish master Gilles Brebos. It contained a full principal chorus, a rich variety of flutes and flute mutations, four reeds, and a treble Cornet stop (from d above middle c). A somewhat smaller two-manual instrument of 1572 had similar resources [176, p. 123].

These organs were very different from the instruments Bull had known in England, and one may safely assume that a virtuoso player such as he would have reveled in their colorful possibilities. Late in his life Bull wrote an organ piece in three sections based on the Flemish folk song *Laet ons met herten reijne*, in which he included a registration that was prophetic in terms of later usage in both France and England. The final section begins with a melody in long notes played by the right hand on the Cornet, located in the Hauptwerk. As its pickup note overlaps the ending of the previous section, that section would have had to have been played on the Brustwerk (if the larger organ was intended) or Rückpositiv (if for the smaller organ). Although a short rest allows for a minor left-hand registration change, it might not have been necessary for the running figuration accompanying the Cornet solo, for the secondary division in both of the Antwerp organs was fairly small, consisting mostly of light flutes and high-pitched mutations.

Thus far the piece partakes of the same character as the Liège and Christ Church pieces. But in the sixth measure the texture changes: The running figures transfer to the right hand, which is again marked "Cornet," as if for emphasis; and at the pickup to the chordal left-hand part is the word "Cromhoren"—the Cromorne/Krummhorn of the secondary division. Finally, at the start of the five-measure coda (which echoes in embellished form the theme at the opening of the piece) is the indication *Voll Register* (full organ). This type of closing section recalls the double voluntaries of Bull's English contemporaries, but the juxtaposition of Cornet against reed in this piece was the first recorded usage of a registration that was to reappear toward the end of the century in both France and England. It is unlikely that Bull was the originator of such registrations; the organs that made them possible had, after all, stood in the Antwerp Cathedral for almost four decades before he arrived.

South of Flanders, in central and northern France, were organs not very different from those in Bruges and Antwerp. Jehan Titelouze, in the preface to his *Hymns de l'eglise* of 1623, mentions that having two manuals and a Pedal with 8' stops (as he certainly must have had in Rouen) allowed one to play four lines separately (one on the Pedal, one with the left hand, two with the right hand), but in his music he gives no clue as to where and how this might be applied. The first versets of all the hymns have the plainsong melody in whole notes in the bass; as he suggests, they can easily be played with an 8' reed in the Pedal, the tenor part on one manual (Great?) and the alto and soprano parts on the other (Positive?), the registrations for these manuals being of a dynamic level that will not obscure the Pedal solo. Other versets place the plainsong in the tenor part, where it could also have been played on the Pedal (described by Titelouze as having "28 or 30" keys).

In a few versets the plainsong appears in the alto or soprano, and this is a bit more problematic. The stoplist of Titelouze's organ in Rouen Cathedral is not known, but if, like the organ Titelouze designed for St. Godard's Church, it had a 4' Flute in the Pedal, the solo could have been played on such a stop an octave lower than written. Some of these same considerations might be applied to those of the Magnificat verses having the plainsong in long notes, but many of the movements will work well on a single-manual combination. Perhaps the most problematic piece is the third verset of the *Pange lingua*, where the *cantus* migrates from the soprano, to the alto, and finally to the tenor. Vicki Riley, applying Titelouze's prefatory suggestions, offers the following plausible solution to this piece:

> By using the pedal eight-foot flute for the bass line, registering the positif with a similar eight-foot flute, and drawing a light solo stop or combination on the grand orgue, one can effectively play the verset up to the fermata sign, bringing out the chant quite satisfactorily. When the chant is carried in the soprano, the alto and soprano on the solo stop sound like an accompanied duet; when the chant is carried by the alto this duet sounds like a cantus with descant, and the chant melody is still quite clear; when the chant is carried by the tenor, the manuals can be exchanged so that the tenor is on the solo combination and the soprano and alto on the accompanying manual. After the fermata, the character of the piece changes; the cantus is in the soprano only and there is brilliant figuration, requiring both hands and all four parts on one manual with a brighter and bigger sound. [142, p. 70]

One might add that the type of concluding section described here has a somewhat familiar ring; it may well have been played on full organ, as in some of the previously described English and Flemish works involving solo lines in preceding sections.

In neither the hymns nor the magnificats does there seem to be any opportunity for florid Cornet solos such as are found in the Flemish manuscripts, but a tenor line played on a reed is a possibility in movements like the *Deposuit potentes* of the Magnificat in the First Tone. Some movements, like the fourth verset of *Ave Maris Stella*, are in a fugal style much akin to the *fugues graves* of later writers, such as the Couperins, which were usually intended to be played on the reed stops. Whether this practice was already in use in Titelouze's day is not known, but it may well have been. A *reglement* of 1630 from Troyes Cathedral instructs the organist to begin and end the Kyrie with the *Plein Jeu* and to use "the particular registrations," including reeds, for the second, third, and fourth versets [245, p. 57]. This usage again relates to what is known of Flemish practices. Indeed, these northern practices have more in common with the organs and liturgical music of this and later periods in France than do the quirky and hard-to-decipher imitative *jeux* recorded in the previous period, which, perhaps because of their generally southern origins, seem more linked to Iberian practices.

Just thirteen years after the publication of Titelouze's liturgical pieces, the theoretician Marin Mersenne, in his *Harmonie Universelle*, attempted a list of registrations, drawing his information from some local organ builders and Charles Racquet, organist of Notre Dame, Paris. While Racquet's much-rebuilt instrument (still retaining its ancient 16' Blockwerk) cannot be regarded as typical, it is noteworthy that the Positif, added in 1610, was thoroughly up-to-date in its appointments, which included three reeds and a treble-compass Cornet [63, p. 13].

There are a number of inconsistencies in Mersenne, largely having to do with proper pitches of stops, but one finds the beginnings of standardization of formulae for such combinations as the *cornet decomposé* and nasard. Mersenne regarded the plein jeu (full organ) as the "most important" registration. As indicated by Lesselier in his 1632 Rouen contract, it consisted only of the Montre and Bourdon 8', the Principals 4' and 2', and the two Mixtures. With the exception of the 8' flute, this constitutes the Plenum of the previous period. Mersenne, writing a few years later, adds the 16' Bourdon and the Tierce—stops just beginning to migrate to France from the north—but these two descriptions probably define the limits of the plein jeu in this period.

Reeds seem still to have been routinely combined with flues, usually 8' and 4' foundations. In Mersenne too is one of the earliest references to the existence of two kinds of Tremulant—the internal (*tremblant doux*) and external (*tremblant fort*), which were to remain standard in French organs into the beginning of the nineteenth century. Mersenne indicates that they were used with a rather wide variety of combinations, including flutes 8' and 4', flutes with mutations (Nasard, Flajolet, etc.), 8' Flute and 4' Principal, but only in one instance with a combination containing a reed ("with or without")[39, p. 168]. Unfortunately Mersenne, like other theoreticians, may have been more interested in numerical possibilities than in musical usages, and he does not give examples of the types of music in which his registrations were to be used.

We do however have one mid-century indication that within the relatively short period following the publications of Titelouze and Mersenne some of the conventions that would govern French registration for the next century and a half were rapidly falling into place, at least in Paris. The source is a privately owned manuscript book (the Oldham Ms., believed to be a holograph), of organ pieces by Louis Couperin, the dated compositions falling within the decade 1650–60. Along with retrospective fugues and fantasias related to the style of Titelouze and his predecessors, this manuscript also contains duos, trios, and several pieces with registrational titles such as *Fugue sur le Cromhorne, Fugue sur la Tierce* (with and without Tremulant) and *Basse de Trompette*. The registration for the *Fugue sur la Tierce* must almost certainly be the combination of unison flutes, upperwork, and Tierce later known as the *Jeu de Tierce* [276, p. 31].

Fenner Douglass dates the beginning of the so-called French Classical period from the publication of Nivers's *Premier Livre d'orgue* in 1665, and the period under discussion above may be seen as a prologue to it. In view of the great number of luminaries who crowded the scene in France's Classical period, it is surprising to find so few just immediately preceding it. The works of Louis Couperin, Titelouze, Roberday (probably as much influenced by Froberger as by the Flemings), and d'Anglebert are virtually all that is accessible from south of the Low Countries. And d'Anglebert is really a transitional figure, with one foot in the Baroque period, as evidenced by his publication in 1689 of an early four-part piece (for three manuals and pedal) obviously intended to show off the player's skills on a large three-manual organ.

While French Classical registration practices began to be codified in this period, they would appear to have been—Mersenne notwithstanding—less extensive and elaborate than they were soon to become. Independent Tierces were still fairly rare in early seventeenth-century organs, but the treble-compass Cornet very quickly became a fixture. The higher-pitched (1 1/3', 1') mutations and Cymbals remained and were still doubtless used for coloration, but they gradually disappeared during the ensuing period, save in large instruments. Reeds had definitely established a role of continuing importance, for both solo and ensemble purposes.

On modern organs, even those with a French Classical bias (which are most often based on the "Dom Bédos" organ of the late eighteenth century), excesses should be avoided in the music of the pre-Classical period. One should probably even avoid the Classical *Grand Jeu*, since nothing prior to Nivers suggests use of this full-organ combination of flues and reeds. The 16' stops also should be employed sparingly, since only the largest organs of this period had stops of this pitch, and then only on the manuals.

The only solo voices specifically mentioned in music or writings of this period are the basic Trompette or Cromorne and the Cornet, along with a few of the older combinations such as the *jeu de nasard*. The Classical French Trompette is a bright and quick-speaking stop, and heavy or overly loud stops of the trumpet family should be avoided. The Cromorne is a cylindrical reed of some strength and foundation, more like an English Clarinet than the thinner-sounding German Krummhorn. On organs without a Cornet stop, a combination of 8' and 4' flutes with mutations of 2 2/3', 2', and 1 3/5' pitches will give the same effect, and where no third-sounding mutation is present, the older "cornet" combination substituting the 1 1/3' mutation for the Tierce will also be effective.

The use of the Pedal should be confined to the 8' and 4' reeds and flues: the reeds and 4' Flutes for solos, and the 8' flues to play bass lines of an accompanimental nature. It would indeed be some time before 16' Pedal stops were to play a significant part in French music.

6 | *Italy*

Composers

Costanzo Antegnati (1549–1624)
Adriano Banchieri (1567–1634)
Serafino Cantone (d. 1627)
Antonio Cifra (1584–1629)
Fra Antonio Croci (fl. 1641)
Girolamo Diruta (1557–1612)
Giovanni Battista Fasolo (fl. 1645–59)
Girolamo Frescobaldi (1583–1643)
Giovanni Gabrieli (1557–1612)
Giuseppe Guami (c1540–1611)
Luzzasco Luzzaschi (1545–1607)
Giovanni di Macque (c1550–1614)
Ascanio Mayone (c1570–1627)
Tarquinio Merula (c1595–1665)
Ercole Pasquini (c1560–c1620)
Giovanni Picchi (fl. 1615–1625)
Luigi Rossi (1597–1653)
Michelangelo Rossi (c1600–c1674)
Bernardo Storace (fl. 1640–65)
Gregorio Strozzi (fl. 1634–87)
Giovanni Maria Trabaci (c1575–1647)

Representative Organs

CHURCH OF ST. GIUSEPPE, BRESCIA
Graziadio Antegnati, 1581 [295]

Manuale

Principale 16' (divided at tenor F)
Fiffaro 16' (undulating de-tuned Principal, probably from middle C)
Ottava 8'
Flauto in ottava 8'
Flauto in duodecima 5 1/3'
Quintadecima 4'
Flauto in quintadecima 4'
Decimanona 2 2/3'
Vigesimaseconda 2'
Vigesimasesta 1 1/3'
Vigesimanona 1'
Trigesimaterza and Trigesimasesta 2/3' and 1/2'

CHURCH OF ST. APOLLINARE, ROME
Sebastian Hay, 1583 [205, p. 96]

Organo Grosso

Principale 16'
Ottava 8'
Flauto in ottava 8' (chimney flute)
Flauto in duodecima 5 1/3'
Quintadecima 4'
Flauto in quintadecima 4'
Decimanona 2 2/3'
Vigesimaseconda 2'
Vigesimasesta 1 1/3'
Vigesimanona 1'
Cimbalino doppio II (repeating)
Tromboni 8' (full-length?)

Positivo Tergale (*Rückpositiv*)

Principale a cannelli 8'(chimney flute)
Ottava 4'
Flauto in vigesimaseconda 2'
Vigesimanona 1'(?)
Tromboncino 8' (regal?)

Accessory Stops

Tremolantibus
Rosignoli (bird)
Timpanis (drum)

METROPOLITAN CHURCH, MILAN
Costanzo Antegnati, c1608 [60, p. 18]

Manuale

Principale 8' (divided)
Principale Grosso 16' or 8'(?) (treble)
Fiffaro 8' (undulating)
Ottava 4' (divided)
Flauto in Ottava 4' (divided)
Flauto in duodecima 2 2/3'
Quintadecima 2'

Pedale

Contrabassi 16' (downward extension of Principale)

CONVENT OF ST. DOMENICO, PISTOIA
Cosimo Ravani, 1617 [147, p. 160]

Manual
Principale 8' (doubled in treble)
Voce Umana 8' (treble, undulating)
Ottava 4' (doubled in treble)
Flauto in Ottava 4'
Decima Quinta 2'
Decima Nona 1 1/3'
Vigesima Seconda 1'
Vigesima Sesta e Nona 2/3' and 1/2'
Cornetto Soprano IV (treble)
Trombe 8' (divided; possibly replacing a 2 2/3' Flute)

Pedal
(Permanently coupled to manual)
Contrabassi 16'

Accessory Stops
Tirapieno (draws Principal chorus)

CHURCH OF S. MARIA DELLE GRAZIE, MONTEPULCIANO
Anonymous, early seventeenth century [stoplist from organ]

Manuale
Principale 8'
Ottava 4'
Flauto in Ottava 4'
Flauto in duodecima 2 2/3'
Flauto in decimaquinta 2'
Quintadecima and Decimanona 2' and 1 1/3'
Vigesimaseconda and Vigesimanona 1' and 1/2'

Pedal
Permanently coupled to Manual

Accessory Stops
Tremulant
Grillo (cricket)

[N.B. All pipes in this organ are of cypress wood.]

SANTO SPIRITO PRIORY CHURCH, PISTOIA
Willem Hermans, 1664 [147, p. 172]

Manuale
Principale 8'
Flauto 8' (stopped)
Ottava 4'
Flauto in duodecima 2 2/3' (treble)
Quintadecima 2'
Decimanona 1 1/3'
Vigesimaseconda 1'
Flautino basso 1' (bass)
Vigesimasesta/Vigesimanona/Trigesimaterza 2/3', 1/2', 1/3'
Cornetto IV (treble)
Musetto 8' (reed, treble)

Pedale
Contrabassi 16'

Voce Umana 4' (reed, bass)
Trombe 8' (reed, divided)

Accessory Stops
Tremolo
Usignoli I and II (birds)
Timpano

Registration

By the final decades of the sixteenth century the Italian organ had assumed the essential form that would, with minor variations, define it for the next two centuries and even beyond. Building on this well-established tradition, the first half of the seventeenth century became the golden age of Italian organ composition, with centers in Venice, Rome, Florence, and Naples.

The principal chorus of completely separated ranks, with one or two flutes at 4' pitch or higher, remained the basis of the Italian organ. Because the numerical designations of the Ripieno or chorus components (also used in reference to flute pitches) can cause some linguistic problems, the following table may be helpful:

Principale (Principal, Diapason) 8'
Ottava (Octave) 4'
Duodecima (12th) 2 2/3'
Quintadecima (15th) 2'
Decimanona (19th) 1 1/3'
Vigesimaseconda (22nd) 1'
Vigesimasesta (26th) 2/3'
Vigesimanona (29th) 1/2'
Trigesimaterza (33rd) 1/3'
Trigesimasesta (36th) 1/4'

The series is always based on the pitch of the Principale, so that if this stop is of 16' pitch, then the Ottava is 8', the Quintadecima 4', etc.; conversely, in small organs based on the 4' Principale, the Ottava would be of 2' pitch. Pitches here are given in modern equivalents; as in England many early Italian organs were "transposing," with low C playing a pipe of greater than 16' or 8' length.

During the last few decades of the sixteenth century a uniquely Italian stop made its appearance in the north: the Voce Umana, or Piffaro/Fiffaro, a second set of Principal pipes at unison pitch (usually a treble stop, beginning around middle C), slightly de-tuned to produce a warm, undulating effect—a "principal celeste," in modern terms. It was used only in slow, solemn chordal music.

The *effeti speziali* (accessory stops)—tremulants, drums, birdcalls, drones, and bells—appeared during the second half of the sixteenth century. One of the earliest recorded uses was in the 1555 organ in the Church of San Martino, Bologna. The Italian Tremulant was of the internal type, and the bird effects were produced by two or three small pipes with their tops dipped in a container of water to produce a warbling sound. A later variant, found in the Florence area, is the *Grillo* (cricket), a "dry" bird effect made by two or three small de-tuned pipes producing a shrill chirp. The *Zampogna*, a bagpipe-like drone, first appeared around the turn of the century in Rome and usually consists of a single wooden reed pipe. The Drum effect is produced by two or three large-scaled open wood pipes of about 4' pitch, but de-tuned to beat, producing a surprisingly drumlike sound. Bells—small chimes or "saucer" bells struck by hammers connected to the keys—appeared late in the sixteenth century to complete the Italian "toy counter."

These accessory stops are substantially the same as those which apparently originated in Flanders and appeared from the middle of the sixteenth century onward in the Netherlands, Germany, England, France, and Spain; the exception is the Zimbelstern, which never seems to have migrated south. They are described in detail here because some of the oldest extant examples are to be found in Italy, and their construction and use there continued well into the nineteenth century. Although such stops are found throughout Europe during the Renaissance and Baroque periods, it is in Italy that we find the clearest picture of their musical uses.

With the exception of a few organs built by Flemish builders from the north (Hay, Hermans), Italian organs of this period, regardless of size, typically had only a single manual and often had no reed stops. The normal pedalboard for over two centuries rarely had more than eight keys (short octave) located to the player's left; the drum, birdcall, or other special effects being played by pedals to the right. A peculiarly northern Italian phenomenon of the early seventeenth century were the *organi di legno*—organs, sometimes of substantial size, all of whose pipes were of wood.

By 1600 Italian organs had become fairly standardized in their design. The first decade of the seventeenth century saw the appearance of several important treatises, intended for the instruction of church organists: Banchieri's *L'organo suonarino* (1605), Part II of Diruta's *Il transilvano* (1609), and *L'arte organica* (1608) by the Brescian organist, organ builder, and composer Costanzo Antegnati. The treatises contained suggestions for registration, usually related to the style of the music and its place in the mass, although Diruta's seem somewhat quaint and backward-looking, relating as they do to Zarlino's concepts of the "mood" or "affect" of the various modes [297, p. 17].

Perhaps because Antegnati was an organist and composer as well as an organ-builder, his instructions are the clearest. They are cast in the rather engaging context of a dialogue between a father (the teacher) and his son (the pupil). The following is a summary of these instructions (all translations in quotes are by L. F. Tagliavini, from notes used in his seminars):

Ripieno (Full Organ)

All the principal-toned stops together, from Principale 16' through the highest pitches. The flutes are omitted because without them "the ripieno comes out livelier and more humorous, and a gentler harmony is heard." (But note below where in the milder "half ripieno" the 4' Octave is doubled by the 4' Flute.) The Ripieno is normally used for intonations and introits, "also in finishing at the Deo

Gratias with toccatas, and with pedal." It should be noted here that all the higher-pitched stops in Italian organs break back at around 1/8' c; the Ripieno in the treble has thus some of the effect of a modern Principal chorus with breaking mixtures.

Half Ripieno

Principale, Ottava, Flauto in ottava, Vigesimanona, Trigesimaterza (on the large Cathedral organ), or:

Principale, Ottava, Flauto in ottava, Vigesimaseconda, Vigesimasesta (on a smaller organ)

[Note that Antegnati relaxes his rule against the use of flutes in these smaller ripieno combinations.]

Other Combinations

Principale, Ottava, Flauto in ottava

Principale, Flauto in ottava ("for doing all kinds of things, and accompanying motets in concertato style")

Ottava, Flauto in ottava, Decimanona, Vigesimaseconda ("for the concerto style ... these four stops together resemble a consort of cornets.")

Ottava, Flauto in ottava ("excellent for playing with diminutions and for *Canzoni alla francese*"; if diminutions [florid passages] are not played, the tremulant may be used with this combination.)

Principale and Flauto in duodecima

Principale, Ottava, and Flauto in duodecima (good for *Canzoni alla francese* "and florid things")

Principale and Flauto in quintadecima (good for diminutions)

Principale, Ottava, Flauto in quintadecima

Fiffaro, or Voce Umana

"Must be played with the Principale alone, nor must anything else be used with it, for everything would be out of tune; and it must be played adagio [i.e., "at ease"] with slow movements and as legato as possible."

Stops that may be used alone

Principale (" ... very delicate; I usually play this at the Elevation of the Mass"; it can also be used with Tremulant, "but slowly and without diminutions.")

Flauto in ottava (may be used with Tremulant)

Ottava (in large organs; that is, where it is an 8' stop)

While half-stops occur fairly frequently, organs with full divided stops were not common in Italy although, as in other areas, they did exist. Antegnati cites an organ in the Church of San Marco, Milan, as having the Principale, Ottava, and Flauto in ottava divided, explaining that the organist wanted this done "in order to play dialogues." He also refers to a different sort of divided stop at the Brescia Cathedral: the second Principal, which was played from the manual from tenor D upward, the lowest twenty pipes being played by the Pedal. By using this stop with the Flauto the effect of a solo with accompaniment was obtained, since the Flauto sounded alone in the bass, but this would appear to be a virtually isolated case.

Diruta, in *Il Transilvano*, confirms many of Antegnati's directives by generalizing:

The flute stops, and other extraordinary instruments, must not be used with the ripieno [principal-scaled ranks] of the organ, seeing that they do not blend well. The principals may [in non-ripieno combinations] be combined with various stops, including flutes, according to the tonal effect required by the different modes.

He then goes on to prescribe registrations for the various modes:

First Mode (serious): Principale, Ottava, Flauto, "or even the Quintagesima"
Second Mode (melancholy): Principale with Tremolo
Third Mode (lamentation): Principale, Flauto in ottava, or "other stops which give the same effect"
Fourth Mode (sad): Principale with Tremolo, "or some flute stop played at its natural pitch [8'?] with appropriate modulations"
Fifth Mode (happy): Ottava, Decimaquinta, Flauto in ottava
Sixth Mode (devout): Principale, Ottava, Flauto in ottava
Seventh Mode (gay): Ottava, Decimaquinta, Vigesimaseconda
Eighth Mode (charming): Flauto in ottava, alone or with Ottava or Decimaquinta
Ninth Mode (gay, sweet): Principale, Quintadecima, Vigesimaseconda
Tenth Mode (melancholy): Principale and Ottava
Eleventh Mode (lively): Flauto in ottava, alone or with Quintadecima or Quinta-decima and Vigesimaseconda
Twelfth Mode (sweet, lively): Flauto in ottava with Quintadecima or alone

Diruta admits that "no set rules may be laid down for these combinations of stops, seeing that organs are not all alike," but cautions that "it is useless to play a sad piece on joyful stops, or a joyful thing on mournful ones." Joyful stops, in Diruta's canon, are generally those of octave pitch or higher, whereas the Principale with Tremolo, or the Flauto played an octave down, are more sombre and are particularly recommended for "the elevation of the Holy Body and Blood of our Lord Jesus Christ." It is noteworthy that Diruta bases almost as many registrations on the octave pitch as on the unison and that, unlike Antignati, he avoids the use of the quint ranks. Soehnlein suggests that this may be because Diruta was more concerned with vocal accompaniment than with solo playing [297, p. 25].

Registration directions in Italian music are rare in any period, but a few that occur in music appended to the later editions (1622, 1638) of Banchieri's *Organo Suonarino* confirm some of Diruta's indications. A *Sonata Grave* for the Elevation is marked *col Principale*; a *Bizaria* in the First Tone for the Graduale is *col Flauto all' Ottava* (and the tempo, which increases in speed twice during this short piece, does indeed seem a bit bizarre); and a more sedate *Bizaria,* also in the First Tone, calls for Flauto in duodecima. Certain other pieces by Banchieri specify the Ripieno, and in his *La battaglia* he calls for *Ottava e Flauto* in an Allegro passage and for the Principale in an Adagio. In one short *Diologo*, Banchieri specifies three stop changes: He begins on the Principale 8' and Ottava 4', calls for the Ottava to be taken off at the fifth measure, and then directs that the *Pieno* (full organ) be drawn in the penultimate measure.

In another publication, *Concluzioni nel suono dell'organo* (1609), Banchieri is more concerned with service playing and the general philosophy of it all. But he does touch briefly on registration when he suggests the use of the "serious, full sound" of the Principale alone (with the case-doors closed!) for funerals of "prelates or principal dignitaries." He also cites further liturgical use of the Ripieno, to be played upon from the time the celebrant left the sacristy to the beginning of the *Deus in adjutorum* [14, p. 13, 16].

The imitative side of the organ is alluded to in Banchieri's description of the organ in St. Peter's Church, Gubbio, which had, in addition to its twelve registers of principals and flutes, "many others which imitate . . . Swiss pipes, a regal, trombones, a loud trumpet, voices, cornettos, a viol, drums, tremolo, and nightin-gales" [14, p. 11]. The last three were *effeti speziale*; the others were probably reed stops. The "Swiss pipes" and "cornettos" may have been combinations of stops: in his dialogue Antegnati points out that the combination of Ottava, Flauto in ottava, Vigesimaseconda, and Decimanona "gives the effect of cornets"; indeed this very combination was called "cornet" in southern France during the previous period. As third-sounding stops (Tierces) were not introduced to Italy until late in the seventeenth century [272, p. 4], the older form of cornet registration would appear to have persisted there longer than in other areas.

Little is said in the treatises about the use of the pedals, although when composers specify them, as Frescobaldi does in some of his toccatas, the purpose is clear enough—to sustain long pedal points under moving passages. Occasionally their use will also be suggested musically in cadential passages, but they were never intended to play moving passages or a *cantus firmus*, and, indeed, it is virtually impossible to do so on the standard old Italian eight-key pedalboard.

Some of the earliest references to stop changes are found in these sources. Both Diruta and Antegnati recommend changing stops during a piece, a practice that is particularly appropriate in some of the sectional ricercares and toccatas of Frescobaldi, Gabrieli, Merula, and others, where the mood and texture can sometimes change noticeably. Banchieri actually gives us an example (the *Diologo*, previously mentioned, as well as a *Batalla*); and Antegnati states, "I praise changing stops from time to time," adding that this way "one never becomes bored." Stops were also changed in accompaniments, as attested to by the registrations in Monteverdi's *Vespri* of 1610 [303, p. 369]. Although they consist largely of the 8' Principale (piano) with 4' Ottava (mezzo-forte), or these two plus the 2' (forte), they are often changed between movements and occasionally within a movement.

Stop-levers on Italian organs were usually in a vertical row to one side (usually the right) of the keyboard and moved right and left (rather than in and out). Thus, changing stops without the aid of assistants was easier than on some of the northern European organs, although it was largely confined to the taking off or putting on of single Ripieno components. Modern organists should understand that subtle variation, rather than novelty, is the key here. There are no dramatic contrasts or solo possibilities suggested by the Italian organ or its music in this period; rather, registration consists largely of coloring the unison Principale with the higher-pitched stops, and the judicious use of the accessory stops.

In terms of contemporary organs, the key to the successful interpretation of early Italian music is the availability of a good, warm-sounding Principal stop—not too heavy, thin, edgy, or loud. In a large modern organ, a warm Principal on a secondary division may be best, although the 8' Great Open Diapason on some nineteenth-century organs often works well. Care must also be taken in selecting the upperwork, since few modern organs have the breaking-back mutations of the Italian organ, and, while mixtures are an acceptable substitute in the Ripieno, some may be too low-pitched. In the smaller combinations it is best to work with individual upperwork ranks of 2', 1 1/3', or 1' pitch when available, although Tierces should be avoided. If pitches above 2' are unavailable, an octave coupler can sometimes be useful in obtaining the desired effect.

The player should avoid heavy foundational flutes, especially at 8' pitch, as well as thin voices such as strings and Quintadenas. As Italian flutes were usually open metal stops, a light open or large-scaled tapered flute will serve best for the 4' and 2' flute voices. Reeds are not really addressed by the treatise writers. They should be used very sparingly, perhaps only in lighter sections of Capriccios or Variations. Remember that the few reeds found in Italian organs of the period were nearly always short, and even the occasional full-length ones would have had a fairly light sound. A light Oboe or Regal may be occasionally useful, but there is no place for loud full-length reeds.

The hauntingly warm and vocal sound of the Voce Umana may well be the most elusive sound to synthesize, although on an organ with mechanical stop action it is sometimes possible to couple the Principal to a similar stop—another Principal, or perhaps a Gemshorn—with the knob not quite fully drawn, to de-tune it. The deceptive simplicity of the early Italian organ and its music makes a reasonably authentic Italian sound perhaps the most difficult thing to achieve on many modern organs.

7 | *Spain and Portugal*

Composers

Sebastian Aguilera de Heredia (1561?–1627)
Diego de Alvorado (d. 1643)
Pablo Bruna (1617–1679)
Bernardo Clavijo del Castillo (d. 1626)
Manuel Rodriguez Coelho (c1555–1635)
Francisco Correa de Arauxo (c1581–c1663)
Agostinho da Cruz (c1590–1633)
Joseph Jiminez (José Ximinez) (d. 1672)
Gabriel Menalt (d. 1687)
Jeronimo Peraza Sotomayor (c1560–1617)
Francisco Perazo (1564–1598)
Lucas Puxol (fl. late seventeenth century)
Diego de Torrijos (1640–1691)

Representative Organs

CHURCH IN MATARÓ, BARCELONA
Joseph Bordons, 1595 [11, p. 29]

Clavier Principal
Flautat 8' (prestant, tin)
Flautat 8' (wood?)
Octava 4' (tin)
Dotzena 2 2/3'
Quinzena 2' (lead?)
Quinzena 2'(?) (tin)
Plé IV (Mixture)
Cimbalet III

Cadireta
Flautat 8' (wood? stopped?)
Flautat 4' (prestant)
Quinzena 2'
Dotzena 1 1/3'(?)
Quinzena 1'(?) (tin)
Cimbalet III

Pedalier
Contrabaxes 16(?)

CHURCH OF SAN JUAN DE LAS ABADESAS, BARCELONA
Lorenzo Saurcot, 1613 [181, p. 244]

Manual
Flautado 8' (prestant)
Unisonus 8' (wood flute)
Octava 4'
Docena nazarda 2 2/3'
Quincena llarga 2'
Decinoctava doble II (22nd and 26th, breaking back?)
Vintidocena 1' (breaks back)
Simbalet III

Accessory Stops
Tremblant

CATHEDRAL, LÉRIDA
Antoni Llorens, 1624–25 [39, p. 163]

Organo Mayor
Flautat tapado 16' (stopped)
Flautat 8' (prestant)
Flautat 8' (wood)
Octava 4'
(2nd) Octava 4'
Flautat tapado 4'
Docena 2 2/3'
Quincena 2'
Quincena nasarda 2' (flute)
Alemanna VI (mixture)
Simbala III
Tolosana III (cornet)

Cadireta (*Rückpositiv*)
Flautat tapado 8'
Flautat 4' (prestant)
Flautat tapado 4'
Octava 2'
Desenovenas (19th and 22nd?)
Docena nasarda 1 1/3' (flute)
Quincena nasarda 1' (flute)
Tolosana III (cornet)
Simbala III

Accessory Stops
Tremulant
Drums

CATHEDRAL, BADAJÓZ (Epistle Organ)
Anonymous, mid-seventeenth century [313, p. 156]

Bass
Flautado 8'
Octava 4'
Tapadillo 4' (stopped flute)
Quincena 2'
Docena 1 1/3'
Vientidocena 1'
Clarin 8' or 4'?

Treble
Flautado 8'
Octava 4'
Tapadillo 4'
Quincena 2'
Docena 2 2/3'
Octavin 4'
Clarin 8'

CHURCH OF SAN JERÓNIMO, MEXICO CITY
Anonymous Spanish positive, c1670 [214, p. 35]

Bass (left jamb)
Violón 4'

Treble (right jamb)
Violón 4'

Flautado 2'   Flautado 2'
Docena 1 1/3'   Docena 1 1/3'
Quincena 1'   Quincena 2'
Diez septina 4/5'   Diez septina 1 3/5'
Diez novena 1/2'   Diez novena 1 1/3'
Vientidocena 1/2'   Vientidocena 1'

Registration

The opening of the seventeenth century saw an increase in both the size and the complexity of Iberian organs and an emergence of two regional styles. Catalonian (northern) organs often had no reeds. The 1625 Lérida organ was of this type, although the contract does specify "two ranks of regalies," the location of which is unclear. But two Regals in an organ of this size are a far cry from the variety of reed stops found in this instrument's 1543 predecessor. Reed stops appeared with greater frequency in central or southern (Castilian) organs in this period.

As in Italy, single-manual organs were the norm, although occasional two-manual organs are found throughout the period. Divided stops and half-stops, probably introduced from Flanders, had been known since the sixteenth century, particularly in smaller organs, but toward the middle of the seventeenth century, large single-manual organs began to be built in which most if not all of the stops were divided, the so-called *medio registro*. This arrangement is increasingly reflected in music assigning solos to the right or left hand, written by composers such as Perazo, Bruna and Correa de Arauxo, and was to become an important element in Iberian organ design and musical composition.

On the Iberian peninsula, registration lists are most commonly found in directions included by the builder with organ contracts. One of the earliest applies to the organ built in 1613 for the church of San Juan de las Abadesas in Barcelona [192; 60, p. 149]. The registrations cited may be grouped into the following categories:

Lleno (full organ)

Pleno: All stops, including the wide-scaled ones
Pleno "for less important feast days": Principals only, 8' through Simbalet, without the 8' flute (Unisonus) and wide-scaled Docena nazarda
Pleno "for common feast days and for playing variations": Principals 8' and 4', Decinoctava doble (2'), Simbalet
Cadireta [i.e., Positiv] effect, "for Sunday masses": Principals 4' through Simbalet, with Docena nazarda

Flautado combinations

Flautado [Principal 8'] alone, with or without Tremulant
Flautado and Unisonus [8' flute], "more solemn"
Flautado, Unisonus, Octava
Flautado and Octava
Unisonus and Quincena 2'

Nasardo [flute] combinations

Docena nazarda with either Flautado, Unisonus, or Octava

Docena nazarda with Quincena llarga and Tremulant is called "an attractive registration"

The player is cautioned against using the high-pitched mutations and mixtures by themselves (i.e., without foundations), but the Flautado alone is recommended for accompanying voices or instruments. One special effect cited is the combination of Unisonus, Simbalet, and Tremulant, "to imitate bells."

A registration list in the 1624 Lérida contract follows a similar pattern, although, being for a two-manual organ, it also includes solo combinations [39, p. 164–65]. In the Organo Mayor, four Pleno combinations mirror those of the Barcelona directions—and, coincidentally, some of the Italian directions—in being of varying strengths. All but one use the 8' Flautat (principal) as their basis, some include the 8' wood flute, and all but one exclude the wide-scaled mutations. The one exception incorporates not only the 16' flute but the Tolosana (Cornet) as well—almost like a French *Grand jeu*. The eight Pedal bass pipes may be used with any of these combinations.

Flautat combinations consist of principals and flutes at 8' and 4', alone or combined with each other, with or without the Tremulant. The *Nasardo* combinations are sometimes gapped (lacking some intermediate pitches) and may also be used with or without Tremulant. Some Organo Mayor nasardos are flutes at 8', 4', and 2 2/3'; 8' and 4' principals and flutes with 2 2/3'; the same with the 2' added, etc. Cadira nasardos include principals at 4' and 2'; flutes at 8', 4', and 2 2/3'; flute 8', principal 2', and 19th 1 1/3', etc.

Mistura combinations are also given. Some are similar to the Pleno combinations, but with the inclusion of wide-scaled mutations. Others include the Tolosana (tierce mixture), combined with Principal 4' or 4' and 2'. Still other Misturas include the Simbala, either with the 8' Principal alone, or in various colorful combinations, such as one calling for Flutes at 16' and 2 2/3' plus Simbala. These fit in with Correa's definition of Misturas as a catchall category for a wide variety of flue combinations (including unorthodox and gapped combinations), usually of no more than two to five stops, intended for special effects or distinctive colors [25, p. 9].

The Pleno, Nasardos, and Misturas combinations of the Cadireta are similar to those of the Organo Mayor, and additional combinations are given for using both manuals:

Unisonus

Organo Mayor	**Cadira**
Principal 8'	Principal 4'
Flutes 8' and 2 2/3'	Flutes 4' and 2'
Flute 4'	Flute 4'
Flutes 8' and 4'	Flutes 8' and 4'

While the Tremulant may or may not be used, it is recommended. The right hand should be on the Organo Mayor, the left on the Cadira.

Flaviolas (flageolets or flutes)

Organo Mayor	Cadira
Principal 8'	Flutes 4' and 2'
Principal & Flute 8'	Flutes 8', 2 2/3', 2'
Principal 8'	Flutes 4' & 2 2/3'
Principal 8' and Flute 4'	Flutes 4', 2 2/3', 2'
Principal 8'	Flutes 4' & 2 2/3', Principal 2'

Should be played without the Tremulant or bass (pedal) pipes, the left hand on the Organo Mayor, the right on the Cadira.

Gaytillas (bagpipes or musettes)

Organo Mayor	Cadira
Principals 8' and 4'	Flutes 4' and 2 2/3', Cymbale
Principals 8' and 4', Flute 8'	Principal 4', Flute 2 2/3', Cymbale
Principals 8' and 4'	Principal and Flute 4', Tolosana
Principal 8', Flute 4'	Flute 4', Principal 2', Tolosana
Principal 8'	Flute 4', Tolosana

The usual manner is to play with the left hand on the Organo Mayor and the right on the Cadira, but this can be reversed if the player chooses.

Cornetillas

Organo Mayor	Cadira
Flute 8', Tremulant	· Octave 2', with pedals
Principal 8'	Nasard 2 2/3', Principal 2'

The right hand plays the Organo Mayor, the left the Cadira, but the 2' pitch basis of the latter would actually make it sound above the Organo Mayor. The mention of Pedals is interesting, but apparently this refers only to pull-downs, since the player is specifically instructed not to use the "large bass pedals."

The *Regalies* (short-length reeds) are referred to in such a way as to suggest that they have their own manual and chest, perhaps in a quasi-*Brustwerk* position. Registrations are cited which use the Regalies against foundations and flutes on either the Organo Mayor or the Cadira. The various combinations of resources possible are summed up as "solo Organo Mayor, solo Cadira, Organo Mayor and Cadira together, Regalies with Organo Mayor, and Regalies with Cadira."

The one Iberian organ treatise of the period, Correa de Arauxo's *Facultad Organica*, published in 1626, was apparently written with the organists of smaller churches in mind. While the Barcelona and Lérida directions are more applicable to the Catalan type of organ, then containing few if any divided stops or reeds, Correa's treatise is applicable to the Castilian type of organ, which had not only reed stops but also the divided manual, or *medio registro*. Although divided stops had been known since the middle of the sixteenth century, Correa suggests that the completely divided organ was a more recent development. He regards it as a "celebrated invention" and credits Francisco Perazo, who died in 1598, with being the first to write music expressly for this type of organ [246, p. 16].

While the *Facultad* does not provide a table of registrations in the manner of the

Italian treatises, its 69 pieces include a number specifically designated for *medio registro* usage, with both left-hand (*mano izquierda de baxon*) or right-hand (*mano derecha de tiple*) solos. Several of the tientos also include registration indications—one of the earliest instances of their use in published music in Spain, although they also appear in contemporary works by Bruna and Menalt.

The registration indications in the *Facultad* are infrequent and not too specific, but they can probably be interpreted in the light of the Catalan directions. In Tiento XLVII the accompaniment is to be played on "the three voices of Flautado," which would suggest one of the combinations of 8' and 4' principals and/or flutes mentioned in the Catalan lists as an accompanimental registration. For Tiento XXXV, Correa suggests that in large organs of 8' or more the player should "take off the lowest Principal or Flute and leave the Octave or the [4'?] Flutes in order that the piece can sound clearer." Tiento LIV suggests that Mistura and Trompeta combinations were often used as solos. Sometimes, as in Tiento LXIX, Correa leaves the solo to the player's discretion, although in this instance he specifies the Flautado 8' for the accompaniment, which is in the bass. Mistura is the general term for colorful flue combinations, usually involving mutations and/or compound stops, and occasionally gapped. Trompetas were often combined with flue stops, usually foundations but sometimes mixtures as well.

Distinct from the *medio registro* idiom is the *tiento lleno*. It is used as a title by Jiminez, Bruna, and others, although it is generally thought to apply to similar pieces with no specific designation. While *lleno* can mean Plenum or full organ, in this instance it appears simply to indicate pieces where the registration is the same in both hands and no solos occur. In these pieces the style and texture of the music, along with regard for clear voice leading, must serve as a guide in one's choice of stops. Some of these tientos may sound well with a fairly full combination, but others will work best with a light foundational registration.

As in other music of this period, care must be taken in adapting registrations to modern organs. Iberian fluework is, like that of Italy and France, full but somewhat relaxed and understated, the mutations and mixtures bright but not (as in some modern organs) shrill or overbearing; indeed, Iberian organs usually have a balanced and well-blended Plenum. The Iberian reed stops have a characteristic sound—bright, a bit nasal; assertive without being overpowering. While they work well as solo stops, they characteristically blend into the full chorus in a way that colors the sound without dominating it. Some experimentation may be needed to find such well-balanced combinations of reeds and flues on many organs.

Many registration directions call for the 8' Principal to be used to accompany a fairly light solo combination. Heavy, loud, or raspy principals will not do here, and a light 8' principal on a secondary manual, perhaps combined with a light 8' flute, may often be the best choice. Heavy and overpowering reeds are also not appropriate for this music; nor are modern horizontal Trumpets, especially if they are located in a remote part of the building, for while horizontal reeds did in fact originate in Spain, they were unknown in the period under discussion.

The *medio registro* pieces were written for one-manual organs of all sizes, from positives to quite large instruments with a wealth of colorful reeds and mutations.

On most modern organs they will require two or more manuals with undivided stops. Each hand will of necessity be on a different manual, and the player must take pains to observe (and, for safety's sake, mark) the division of parts at either middle B/C or middle C/C♯—since this indication is often lacking in the score. These pieces can also, of course, be played on one of the many small divided-manual positives that are coming into increasing use in churches, chapels, schools, and homes, although the variety of possible combinations and dynamics will be more limited.

James Wyly suggests that a good rule of thumb for *medio registro* pieces is to use flues (with or without reeds) in wide pitch spreads (including combinations beginning on a 16' and ranging to the higher mutations), to emphasize right-hand solos, and reed color in narrow pitch spreads (based on 8' or 4'), to emphasize left-hand solos [325, p. 9]. Some pieces may require a left-hand solo combination of 4' or even 2' basic pitch, against a right-hand accompaniment of 8'.

Modern organs of the eclectic type, or even those with a French Classical bias, are generally suitable for Iberian music, especially if they are large enough to contain some variety of reed and mutation colors. But early twentieth-century organs or any with a preponderance of heavy sounds and a dearth of the essential upperwork cannot be expected to do justice to this sunny and occasionally whimsical literature.

Composers

Anthoni van Noordt (c1613–1675)
Gerard Scronx (fl. early seventeenth century)
Henderick Speuy (c1570–1625)
Gisbert van Steenwick (d. 1679)
Jan Pieterszoon Sweelinck (1562–1621)

Representative Organs

ST. PANKRATIUS CHURCH, LEIDEN
Peter Jans de Swart, 1565 [176, p. 130]

Hauptwerk
Prestant 8' IIrks
Hohlpfeife 8'
Oktave 4'
Flöte 4'
Nasat 2 2/3'
Gemshorn 2'
Sifflöte 1'
Mixtur
Scharf
Trompete 8'
Zink 8' (treble)

Brustwerk
Quintadena 8'
Flöte 2'
Krummhorn 8'
Schalmei 4'

Pedal
Trompete 8'
Touzyn 8' (short-length reed)

ST. LEONHARD'S CHURCH, ZOUTLEEUW
Rebuilt by Jan van Weert, 1620 [176, p. 162]

Hoofdwerk
Blockwerk, 16' or 8'

Rugpositief
Principal 8'
Hohlpfeife 8'
Oktave 4'
Flöte 4'
Quintflöte 2 2/3' or 1 1/3'
Superoktave 2'
Sifflöte 1'
Kornett
Mixtur
Krummhorn 8'

Accessory Stops
Tremulant
Nachtigall (bird)
Trommel (drum)

ST. STEVEN'S CHURCH, HASSELT
Jan Jacobs, 1625 [161, p. 42]

Hoofdwerk
Prestant 8'
Octaaf 4'
Mixtuur
Scherp

Rugwerk
Roerfluit 8'
Octaaf 4'
Octaaf 2'
Mixtuur
Scherp
Kromhoorn 8'

Bovenwerk
Roerfluit 8'
Quintadeen 8'
Octaaf 4'
Openfluit 4'
Gemshoorn 4'
Nasard 2 2/3'
Sifflet 1'
Cimbel
Kromhoorn 8'
Trompet 8'

REFORMED CHURCH, TERBAND
Tobias Baders, 1640 [73, p. 12]

Manual
Holpyp 8'
Prestant 4'
Baarpyp 4' (flute)
Octaaf 2'
Quint 1 1/3'
Sifflet 1'
Sexquialter (bass)
Mixtur I–V (treble)

Accessory Stops
Tremulant
Nagtegaal (bird)

[All stops divided.]

ST. MICHAEL'S CHURCH, ZWOLLE
Jan Morlet, 1644 [161, p. 12]

Hoofdwerk (*Blockwerk*)
Prestant 16'
Octaaf 8'
Superoctaaf 4'
Mixtuur 2 2/3'

Rugwerk
Prestant 8'
Quintadeen 8'
Dwarsfluit 8' (treble)
Octaaf 4'
Holpijp 4'
Superoctaaf 2'
Sexquialter 2 2/3'
Mixtuur 1'
Scherp
Schalmei 4'

Accessory Stops
Tremulant
Nachtegael (bird)
Trombel (drum)

Bovenwerk
Prestant 8'
Roerfluit 8'
Octaaf 4'
Openfluit 4'
Speelfluit 2'
Quintfluit 1 1/3'
Sifflet 1'
Sexquialter (treble)
Tertscimbel
Trompet 8'
Vox Humana 8'

Pedal
Trompet 8'

ST. LAURENTIUS'S CHURCH, ALKMAAR
Galtus & Germer Hagerbeer, 1645 [176, p. 150]

Hoofdwerk
Prinzipal 16'
Prinzipal 8'
Oktave 4'
Mixtur
Grosser Scharf
Kleiner Scharf
Tertian
Trompete 8'

Bovenwerk
Bordun 16'
Prinzipal 8'
Hohlpfeife 8'
Quintadena 8' (treble)
Oktave 4'
Offenflöte 4'
Echo Hohlflöte 4'
Superoktave 2'

Rugpositief
Prinzipal 8'
Quintadena 8'
Oktave 4'
Flöte 4'
Superoktave 2'
Terz 1 3/5'
Nasat 1 1/3'
Quintanus 1 1/3'
Sifflöte 1'
Mixtur III–IV
Scharf IV
Sesquialter (treble)
Trompete 8'

Pedal
Prinzipal 8'
Oktave 4'
Trompete 8'

Terz 1 3/5'
Nasat 1 1/3'
Gemshorn 1 1/3'
Sifflöte 1'
Sesquialter II
Trompete 8'
Vox Humana 4'

Registration

The northern Netherlands organ of this period was a curious amalgam of
contiguous styles. While large organs often had three manuals, the main division
(*Hoofdwerk*) was often just a partly divided *Blockwerk* consisting only of principal-
toned stops. On the other divisions one finds most of the flutes, mutations,
compound stops, and reeds current in France and Germany. The Pedal remained a
small *cantus firmus* division even in the largest organs, and in small organs it was
often just a "pull-down" Pedal coupled to one of the manuals, with no independent
stops of its own. Even the three-manual organ played by Sweelinck in Amsterdam's
Old Church, built by Jan van Kovelen in 1539–42 and rebuilt in 1567 to a stoplist
closely resembling that of Morlet's 1644 Zwolle organ, had in its Pedal division
only a Trumpet 8' and a Nachthorn, the latter probably of 2' pitch, although
presumably the pedal keys could be coupled to one of the manuals [16, p. 21]. Such
Pedal divisions remained typical in Protestant Holland until well into the eighteenth century, and obbligato pedal parts (other than a simple *cantus firmus*) do not
occur in the music of the sixteenth and seventeenth centuries.

The music of the northern Netherlands is a small corpus—of exceedingly high
quality, but small nonetheless. In some ways it is closer stylistically to the English
and Flemish repertoire than to that of its continental neighbors. While the great
fantasias, toccatas, and praeludia of Sweelinck, like those of Bull or Byrd, may be
played on the organ, they are just as much at home on the harpsichord, and the same
may be said for the Fantasias of van Noordt. Even the echo fantasias, with their
carefully indicated dynamic changes (marked *piano* and *forte*), may be played on the
modern harpsichord. Two-manual harpsichords capable of playing echos did not
however exist in Holland during Sweelinck's lifetime, and the echo genre was thus
clearly associated with the organ, where alternating between the lower *Rugwerk*
and the more remote *Hoofdwerk* or *Bovenwerk* would have produced a quite
dramatic "stereo" effect.

The range of styles for organ music in Calvinist Holland is small. In addition to
the free forms mentioned above, we have only psalm settings, chiefly by Sweelinck,
Speuy, and van Noordt, along with a few anonymous examples like those found in
the Susanne van Soldt manuscript (1599). Sweelinck's and van Noordt's are often
in variation form; perhaps at the instigation of his German pupils, Sweelinck also
wrote some variations on Lutheran chorale melodies. His largest output in the
variation genre consists of secular song settings, and while they, like their English

counterparts, may have been played on large organs, their structure often points more to the harpsichord or the chamber organ.

That there is no real liturgical music is due, of course, to the unique situation at this time vis-à-vis the organ in church. The German Protestants used their organs in the liturgy, the English ultimately destroyed theirs, but the Dutch did neither. The organs, usually the property of the town, remained in the churches, but they were never played during the service. They were nonetheless cared for and used for recitals, sometimes before and after the service, a practice that annoyed some of the stricter Calvinists. About two decades after Sweelinck's death the organ began to be used in the services for the support of psalm singing, and thus while van Noordt's 1659 psalm settings may have been used in the same manner as German chorale-preludes, Sweelinck's earlier ones most certainly were not, at least during his lifetime [199, p. 205].

One looks in vain for any hint of registration indications in the music of the seventeenth-century Dutch composers; and there do not seem to be any treatises. Around 1580 Jan Roose, a Netherlands organ builder, wrote some registration directions for a *Blockwerk*-and-*Positiv* organ built in Münster. They applied, of course, to the *Positiv* only: The Plenum is based on the Principal and Flute 8', with the Octave, Superoctave, and Mixture; a smaller version with both 8's and the 4' Principal is also given. The remainder of the directions consists largely of various ways of coloring the 8' and 4' flutes with upperwork and mutations in two- and three-stop combinations, much in the same manner as in France, Spain, and Italy. The Trumpet may be combined with a variety of principals, flutes, and even mutations, as well as with the Plenum. The Tremulant is not to be used with the Trumpet or accessory stops (bird, drum) but is recommended for use with the 8' Holpyp (stopped flute) [39, p. 151].

An even shorter list of combinations accompanied the organ in St. Leonhard's Church, Zoutleeuw. It was again for the *Positiv* and was probably written around 1620. They are classified as:

1. One-stop registrations: Principal 8', Holpyp 8', with or without the Tremulant
2. Two-stop registrations: Principal 8' with either Holpyp 8', Octave 4', Flute 4', Superoctave 2', or Mixtur (with or without Tremulant); Holpyp 8' with either Principal 8', Quintflöte 2 2/3', Superoctave 2', or Mixtur
3. Three-stop registrations: Holpyp 8' with either Principals 4' and 2', Octave 4' and Cornett, Octave 4' and Mixtur, or Quintflöte 2 2/3' and Superoctave

The player is also cautioned against using the Tremulant with the Blockwerk [176, p. 161]! This seems an odd admonition, since presumably the Tremulant was meant to affect only the *Positiv*, but perhaps in this particular organ it disturbed the wind system sufficiently to affect the *Hoofdwerk* as well.

There is nothing surprising about these combinations (although the Zoutleeuw registrations omit some seemingly important stops, such as the Kromhoorn and the Sifflet). They accord with the universal principle of coloring the foundation stops prevalent in the previous century and still observed in the countries to the south.

As to their use in the music, the music itself must be the guide. Certainly the various two- and three-stop combinations can be put to good use in the variations, but the fantasias and toccatas are more likely to call for either a Plenum or simple 8' and 4' combinations. It is rather doubtful that the *Blockwerk* or full *Hoofdwerk* were used in the Echo Fantasias, save in the smaller two–manual organs. Despite the *forte* and *piano* dynamics indicated in the score, the nature and texture of the music suggest that lighter combinations from the *Bovenwerk* and *Rugwerk* (or a *Hoofdwerk* with separable stops) would be more suitable.

Solos are plainly called for in some of the psalm and chorale settings of Sweelinck and van Noordt. When the melody is embellished it is usually in the soprano, and variations may, depending on their character, be played on one manual or two, without pedal. If florid soprano melodies are to be played on a separate manual, the *Positiv* is the best choice, having the lighter and more colorful stops, and perhaps the rule about having one more stop on the *Positiv* than on the main manual, cited elsewhere, is applicable here.

A long-note *cantus firmus* can occur in any part, but it is most often found in the soprano and tenor. It is quite possible to play any of these on the pedals, using the 8' Trumpet for the tenor and bass melodies, and the 2' Flute for those occurring in the alto or soprano. Sweelinck's works are now available in reliable editions, but unfortunately the only readily available modern edition of van Noordt is misleading in this respect, as some variations are put on three staves, with a moving bass line in the Pedal and the long-note *cantus* in the right or left hand. Alas, it would have been impossible, given the resources of the Pedal divisions, to play the music in this manner on a seventeenth-century Dutch organ, and the performer should be discouraged from attempting to do so on a modern organ. If the performer does choose to play it this way, however, no 16' Pedal stop should be used, the pedal being simply coupled to the accompanying manual.

Sweelinck was unquestionably the greatest of the northern Netherlands composers, and his works have long been in the modern repertoire. The Protestant North has been treated separately from the Catholic southern Netherlands because of certain differences in the organ-building style and musical repertoire, but there were also many similarities. Sweelinck knew and interacted with his Flemish and English colleagues as well as with his numerous northern German students. With regard to the registration of his organ works, one should take into consideration not only the few northern Netherlands sources but also the generally similar practices of Flanders, and probably also the suggestions of Sweelinck's student, Scheidt. In view of the size and resources of many of the northern organs, there is little question that, within the boundaries of accepted practice, Sweelinck would have made good use of their colorful possibilities in his own highly acclaimed playing, especially in the variations.

Many modern organs, including eclectic instruments and certain recent instruments based on late Renaissance or early Baroque models, possess resources necessary for the performance of the music of Sweelinck and his contemporaries, provided that the player stays within the limits of the Netherlandish organs that

Sweelinck knew, avoiding 16' Pedal stops and using mutations and light reeds for color and variety.

The music often also works well on organs of the neo-Baroque type, especially if they possess an 8' Principal. Some of the lighter two- and three-stop combinations can even be approximated on organs that seem otherwise inappropriate, provided that strings, fat Principals, loud reeds, and overly foundational flutes are avoided. And if no appropriately light and colorful sounds can be found on the organ available, much of this music also sounds very well on the harpsichord.

9 | North and Central Germany

Composers

David Abel (d. 1639)
Johann Rudolf Ahle (1625–1673)
Johann Heinrich Bach (1615–1692)
Samuel Friedrich Bockshorn (Capricornus) (c1629–1665)
Johann Decker (1596–1668)
Andreas Düben (c1590–1662)
Christian Flor (1626–1697)
Nicolaus Hasse (1617–1672)
Peter Hasse the Elder (c1585–1640)
Ewald Hintz (1614–1668)
Wilhelm Karges (1613–1699)
Jacob Kortkamp (c1615–1664/65)
Marcus Olter (fl. early seventeenth century)
Jacob Praetorius (1586–1651)
Michael Praetorius (1571–1621)
Heinrich Scheidemann (c1596–1663)
Gottfried Scheidt (1593–1661)
Samuel Scheidt (1587–1654)
Melchior Schildt (1592–1667)
Paul Siefert (1586–1666)
Johann Steffens (1559/60–1616)
Delphin Strungk (1601–1694)
Franz Tunder (1614–1667)
Matthias Weckmann (1621–1674)

Representative Organs

ST. MARY'S CHURCH, STRALSUND
Nicholas Maass, 1592–94 [181, p. 134]

Hauptwerk
Prinzipal 16'
Quintadena 16'
Oktave 8'
Spillflöte 8'
Gedackt 8'
Tolkaan 8' (Dolcan)
Octave 4'
Quinte 2 2/3'
Mixtur XII
Zimbel III

Rückpositiv
Prinzipal 8'
Gedackt 8'
Quintadena 8'
Oktave 4'
Hohlflöte 4'
Spillflöte 2' (?)
Mixtur
Zimbel
Trompete 8'
Fagott 8' (? or 16'?)
Schnarrwerk 8' (? or 4'?) (Regal)

Brustwerk
Prinzipal 4'
Gedackt 4'
Sifflöte 2'
Nasat 1 1/3'
Schweizerflöte 1'
Mixtur
Zimbel
Krummhorn 8'
Regal 8'
Geigendregal 4'
Querpfeife (8' flute? treble?)

Pedal
Untersatz 16'
Prinzipal 8'
Gedackt 8'
Oktave 4'
Quintadena 4'
Nachthorn 2'
Bauernflöte 1'
Zimbel II
Posaune 16'
Trompete 8'
Cornett 4' (reed)

ST. MARTIN'S CHURCH, KASSEL
Hans Scherer the Younger, 1610 [3, p. 232]

Hauptwerk
Principal 16'
Quintadehn 16'
Octave 8'
Holpfeife 8'
Flöiten 4' (Flute, open?)
Rauschpfiefe II (2 2/3' & 2')
Mixtur
Scharff

Oberwerk
Principal 8'
Holpfiefe 8'
Gemshorn 4'
Waldflöte 2'
Nasatt 1 1/3'

Rückpositiv
Principal 8'
Gedackt 8'
Quintadehn 8'
Octava 4'
Querpfeife 4'
Mixtur
Scharff
Krummhorn 8'
Messingregal 8' (brass resonators)

Pedal
Principal 32'
Octave 16'
Untersatz 16' (stopped)
Gedackt 8'

Zimbel
Trommette 8'
Zincken 8' (short length)

Rauschpfeife II (4' & 2 2/3')
Trommette 8'
Cornet 2' (reed)

ST. LEVIN'S CHURCH, HARBKE
Gottfried Fritzsche, 1622 [83, p. 49]

Manual
Gedackt Untersatz 16'
Principal 8'
Rohrflöte 8'
Octave 4'
Quintaden 4'
Blockflöte 4'
Quinta 2 2/3'
Sifflöte 2'
Schweigel 1'
Mixtur IV
Cimbel II
Krummhorn 8'

Pedal
Untersatz 16'
Schweitzerbass 1' (flute)
Cimbelbass 2' (mixture)
Posaunenbass 16'
Fagott 8'
Singend Cornett 2' (reed)

Accessory Stops
Tremulant
Vogelsang (bird)
Trommel (drum)

ST. MORITZ'S CHURCH, HALLE
Heinrich Compenius, 1624 [181, p. 135]

Hauptwerk
Quintadena 16'
Principal 8'
Gedackt 8'
Octave 4'
Gedacktflöte 4'
Nasat 2 2/3'
Octave 2'
Mixtur III
Trompete 8'

Pedal
Offenflöte 16'
Quintadena 16' (from HW)
Octave 8'
Octave 4'
Spitzflöte 1'
Posaune 16'
Dulzian 8' *
Cornett 2' *

Accessory Stops
Tremulant
Vogelsang

Rückpositiv
Gedackt 8'
Quintadena 8'
Principal 4'
Gedacktflöte 4'
Octave 2'
Gemshorn 2'
Sifflöte 1 1/3'
Spitzflöte 1'
Mixtur III
Krummhorn 8'
Schalmei 4'

Zimbelstern
Trommel

*These two reed stops on a "Brustpedal" chest.

ST. JAKOBI CHURCH, LÜBECK
Friedrich Stellwagen, 1636 [188, p. 155]

Hauptwerk
Prinzipal 16'
Oktave 8'
Spielpfeife 8' (tapered)
Oktave 4'
Nasat 2 2/3'
Rauschquinte II (2 2/3' and 2')
Mixtur IV
Trompete 8'

Rückpositiv
Gedackt 8'
Quintatön 8'
Prinzipal 4'
Hohlflöte 4'
Sesquialter II
Scharff III–IV
Trechterregal 8'
Krummhorn 8'

Brustwerk
Gedackt 8'
Quintatön 4'
Waldflöte 2'
Zimbel II
Regal 8'
Schalmei 4'

Pedal
Subbass 16'
Spielpfeife 8' (from HW)
Bordun (?) 4'
Posaune 16'
Trompete 8' (from HW)
Regal 2'

Accessory Stops
Brustwerk/Hauptwerk Coupler

PARISH CHURCH, WESTERHUSEN
Jost Sieborg, 1642 [76, p. 247]

Manual
Gedackt 8'
Quintatön 8'
Prinzipal 4' (Prestant)
Oktave 2'
Quinte 1 1/3'
Mixtur III
Trompete 8'

Pedal
Coupled to Manual

Accessory Stops
2 Zimbelsterns

Registration

There was much cross-fertilization in the continental Protestant organ world during this period. Attracted by the wealth of the Hanseatic churches, master organ builders from both the Netherlands (Maas) and central Germany (Fritzsche) converged on the North Sea and Baltic region, and there was also considerable mobility among the musicians of the region. Scheidemann and Jacob Praetorius from Hamburg in the north studied with Sweelinck in Amsterdam, as did Scheidt, a native of the central German city of Halle, and Schildt from Hannover. Düben, a Swede, studied in Leipzig as well as in Amsterdam; and Weckmann was led by his professional life from his native Mühlhausen to Dresden, Copenhagen, and Hamburg.

The influence from Calvinist northern Holland to the northern German cities was essentially one-way, as the Dutch masters passed the flame of their art eastward. But the traffic between northern and central Germany was very much a two-way street, remaining so until about the time that a central German teenager named J. S. Bach took an unauthorized vacation from his first church position, in Arnstadt, to see what he could learn up in Lübeck and Hamburg. Neither he nor another young central German visitor, G. F. Handel, seems to have been greatly tempted to stay in the North, however; by the early eighteenth century it had begun to lose some of its lustre.

Organs of more than two manuals, containing a colorful variety of flute, reed, and mutation stops in addition to the basic principal chorus, were common to both the Netherlands and north/central Germany. What primarily distinguished the German organs was their Pedal divisions. Save in the smallest village church organs, they were laid out virtually as an additional manual, with chorus stops, a variety of reeds, and flue stops from 32' or 16' pitch up to 1' pitch. The function of such a Pedal division in trio and solo playing (as well as in the increasingly flamboyant praeludia) is self-evident, and it contributed to significant differences in the compositional style of north and central Germany during this period.

Sources of registration information are varied. In the first decade of the seventeenth century, a manuscript document on organ inspection by composer Michael Praetorius and organ builder Esaias Compenius makes a few random references to the use of stops. Unlike some other sources from this and the earlier period, it prohibits the drawing of two stops of the same pitch (considered "dull") along with the use of the 8' flute in full organ. Full organ itself should "not be muddied with extensive passage-work," which is in agreement with those sources which recommend the plenum for more solemn or dignified music. But nothing is said about solo stops or smaller colorful combinations.

Perhaps most interesting is the confirmation that the Germans, as well as the French, had two types of Tremulant in this period. The milder, internal type is recommended for use with flue stops, while the stronger, external type (*Bock-tremulant*) is "best and most lovely" when used with reeds [339, pp. 25–31]. The same two authors, in their *Orgeln Verdingnis,* published in 1619, suggest playing a motet on manuals and pedals to test the Tremulant, but it is uncertain whether this indicates a common use or not [341, p. 23].

Some of the registration practices of Protestant Germany in the early seventeenth century are succinctly summarized by Samuel Scheidt in the preface to his *Tabulatura Nova* of 1624:

> All organists who possess an organ of two manuals and pedals can perform [the Magnificat, Hymns and Psalms], whether [the melody] is in the top or tenor parts, on the Rückpositiv with keen, sharp-toned stops, in order to render the chorale melody clear and distinct. If, in a bicinium, the melody is in the upper part, it may be played by the right hand on the Great

... and the second part with the left hand on the Rückpositiv. If the chorale melody is the highest of four parts, it will then be played on the Rückpositiv with the right hand, the two middle parts being played on the upper manual, the other parts [interludes?] played on the upper manual, and the bass on the pedals.

Scheidt goes on to cite some alternate ways to play four-part compositions, such as playing the soprano on the Great, the alto on the Rückpositiv, and the tenor and bass on the Pedal—provided that the tenor goes no higher than middle C ("as the D is rarely found on the pedals") and the tenor and bass are not too far apart. But, Scheidt concludes, "the easiest and most beautiful way of all is to play the contralto on the pedals"—but only "if one knows how to use the 4' and 8' stops well," since the Positiv must be at 8' and the Pedal at 4'. As the compass of the pedals rarely went higher than middle C, the transposition of the alto part down an octave is implied. There is more than a hint of Titelouze's prefatory remarks here.

It can readily be seen from these comments that Scheidt regarded the Pedal as a "third hand." He not only has no compunction about playing two parts on the Pedal but also thinks it a nice idea to let it play the alto part, while the right hand solos the melody on the Positiv and the left hand plays the tenor and bass on the Great. Students looking for a good sightreading exercise can try playing hymns this way!

Scheidt concludes with a few sample registrations. For solos on the Positiv he suggests Quintatön or Gedackt 8', Gedackt or Principal 4', with Mixture, Zimbel, or Superoctave 2'. For accompaniment on the Great, Gedackts 8' and 4', or Principal 8' alone. For Pedal solos he recommends a variety of colors: Subbass and Posaune 16' or 8', Dulzian 16' or 8', Schalmei, Trommette, Baurflöte or Cornet— "and anything else you might find in small or large organs." None of these combinations are sweet or foundational; indeed, they are rather robust and bright— revealing how Scheidt and his contemporaries viewed the performance of chorale-based pieces.

In his music, Scheidt gives further clues by indicating in which line the chorale melody occurs ("choralis in alto," "choralis in basso," etc.), but the only actual registration he cites is *Organo pleno*. This occurs in verse 8 of *Warum betrubst du* and in verses 1 and 3 of *Wir glauben all*. There is also the six-part (double pedal) *Modus ludendi pleno Organo pedaliter* ("manner in which to play full organ with pedal"), all in long notes with many suspensions—possibly a didactic piece or a model for improvisation.

Registration indications in German music of this period are scarce, but a hint is found in Weckmann's chorale variations on *Es ist das Heil uns kommen her*. The third variation, with the chorale in the bass, calls for Trumpet and Gedackt 8' or Trumpet 8' and 4' in the Pedal, with Principal 8' on the *Positiv* and Trumpet 16' on the Great. In Verse 6, the solo is on the *Positiv*, for which all the stops are required, while the Great is registered with soft stops (probably the Flutes 8' and 4' or Principal 8' suggested by Scheidt) and the Pedal with the Cornet (a 2' reed rather than a compound stop in German organs of this period). Verse 7 calls for full organ with the chorale in the tenor. In *O lux beata*, which begins, like *Es ist der Heil,* with a full organ verse, one finds a verse in which the melody is on the Pedal 8' Trumpet, while the right hand plays on a soft 8' combination and the left hand plays on an 8' Trumpet with a 16' flue stop [334, p. 52].

These combinations of reeds and flues, and wide- and narrow-scaled stops, continue the practices of the previous period and point to a long tradition of spicy and (to modern ears at least) occasionally bizarre sounds. A rare firsthand account by Johann Kortkamp records the actual registrations used by Weckmann in auditioning for the organist's post at St. Jakobi in Hamburg in 1655. Improvising on the chorale *An Wasserflüssen Babylon*, he used what Kortkamp described as a favorite registration of Jacob Praetorius: Trommete and Zincke 8', Hohlfleute 4', Nassat 2 2/3' and Gemshorn 2' on the Oberwerk; with principals 8' and 4' on the Positiv for "the soft middle part"; and on the Pedal, Prinzipal-Bass 24', Posaune 16', Trommete 8' and 4', and Cornet 2'. Weckmann concluded the improvisation with a "lively fugue" on the full organ [164, p. 227]. One wishes one knew something about the structure of the piece!

The practice of playing *cantus firmus* solos on the *Positiv* (accompanied on the Great), especially when of the florid or ornamented type, seems to have been of long standing. It continued well into the succeeding period, at least in the north, although bass and tenor solos were often played on the Pedal, and slow long-note solos could be played on the stronger, more fundamental stops of the Great. A Polish source, the Pelplin Tablature of circa 1630, contains many chorale preludes and fantasias by north German composers Tunder, Hasse, Abel, and Scheidemann, some of which include registrations. A fantasia on *Komm Heiliger Geist* by Abel calls for the Posaune (16') for its pedal *cantus* in whole and half notes, but a somewhat livelier *Allein Gott in der Höh* by Hasse has the pedal *cantus* in half and quarter notes marked for the Cornet (reed at 4' or 2') [307III, p. 266].

A slightly later source is Matthaeus Hertel's *Orgel Schlüssel* of 1666, which gives a list of combinations "for making the Choral [melody] clearly audible." They range from mild to "sharp" and include a stop just coming into use, the Salicional:

1. Grobgedackt 8', Kleingedackt 4'
2. Quintadena 16' and 8'
3. Quintadena alone
4. Quintedena and Zimbel
5. Quintadena and Salicet or Salicional
6. Salicional alone (because it is slow-speaking, it should only be used for slow playing)
7. Salicional and Kleingedackt
8. Principal alone
9. Principal and Sedecima (1 3/5')
10. Principal and Salicional
11. Salicional and Mixture IV
12. Grobgedackt alone
13. Krummhorn 8', Superoctave 4', Quint 1 1/3' ("very lovely")
14. All reeds, 16', 8', and 4', "work well in chorales"
15. Principal 4', Superoctave 2', Sedecima 1 3/5' ("sharp")
16. Open or Stopped Flute, Superoctave, Quint 1 1/3' ("sharp")

Hertel also has some suggestions for the use of accessory stops. The Tremulant (earlier described by Scheidt as "a dignified and important stop") "should not be employed in every piece"; it should be avoided especially in happy music or music in triple time, but it may be used for slow, sad, or penitential music. Drum stops may be used with Trumpets, and, interestingly, they are suggested for Christmas music. For playing continuo, Hertel recommends either the Principal or the Gedackt 8' on the Great, the Quintadena 8' or Kleingedackt 4' ("also strong enough in the pedal") on the Positiv, and 16' Gedackt or 8' Principal on the Pedal [307IV, p. 73–75].

It is clear that there was wide latitude in solo combinations during this period, and the player must let the nature of the particular piece be the guiding element. The livelier solos would call for the more "sharp" or spicy combinations. Some of the slower or more florid solos will benefit from registrations that are milder or smoother but still bright, with or without tremulant, depending on the character of the piece. Solos in long notes suggest either a strong pleno registration or a full-sounding reed stop. Many modern organs have satisfactory ingredients for some of these combinations, unorthodox as they may seem by present-day standards, and a bit of experimentation off the beaten track should prove rewarding. An ordinary Clarinet or Oboe combined with a 4' flute and mutations at 2 2/3' and 2', or with principals at 2' and 1 1/3', can, for example, make a quite convincing "sharp" solo.

Nearly all the sources from this period deal largely with the playing of chorale preludes and fantasias. It is likely that many of the same combinations were used in trio playing. But the only hint we have concerning the registration of fugues is in the description of the improvisation by Weckmann at his 1655 audition, when he is said to have played a lively fugue on full organ. He may well have employed the all-principal full organ described by Michael Praetorius in his 1619 *Syntagma Musicum II*: Principals 8', 4', 2', 1 1/3' Mixture and Zimbel; with the Sub Bass 16', the latter presumably added to the Pedal plenum. Note that this is the rather standard all-principal plenum in use throughout Europe in the sixteenth and early seventeenth centuries. But other types of plenum were also coming into use, and for a slower or more solemn fugue, a less brilliant combination, or one including reeds, would not be out of the question.

Two things are noteworthy in Protestant Germany and the Netherlands in this period: The importance of organ music based on the congregational hymns, and the colorful (and even adventurous) manner in which this music was both composed and registered. A dull-sounding organ with little in the way of reeds or mutations will leave the player with very few options, but an instrument having good coloring stops and good foundations can be exploited to the fullest.

Composers

Johann Benn (c1590–c1660)
Wolfgang Ebner (1612–1665)
Christian Erbach (c1570–1635)
Johann Jakob Froberger (1616–1667)
Hans Leo Hassler (1564–1612)
Jacob Hassler (1569–1622)
Carl von der Hofen (c1589–c1647)
Johann Kaspar Kerll (1627–1693)
Johann Erasmus Kindermann (1616–1655)
Alessandro Poglietti? (d.1683)
Adam Steigleder (1561–1633)
Johann Ulrich Steigleder (1593–1635)

Representative Organs

CATHEDRAL, ULM
Kaspar Sturm, 1576–78; rebuilt and enlarged by Konrad Schott, 1595–99 [54, p. 302]

Hauptwerk	**Rückwerk**
Gross Principal 16'	Principal 4'
Principal 8'	Gedeckt 4' (8' pitch?)
Octav 4'	Octav 2'
Hohlflöte 4'	Gedeckt 2' (4' pitch?)
Gedeckt 4'	Quint 1 1/3'
Duodez 2 2/3' (Twelfth)	Hörnlin (compound stop)
Doppelte Octav 4' & 2'	Mixtur
Mixtur IX	Regal 4'
Cymbal V	

Brustwerk
Principal 4'
Octav 2'
Gedeckt 2'
Quint 1 1/3'
Hörnlin (Sesquialter)
Mixtur
Cymbal

Pedal
Principal 16'
Hülziner Bass 16' (wood bass)
Principal 8'
Mixtur VI
Fagot 16'
Fagot 8'
Posaun 8'

Accessory Stops
Tremulant
Heerpauken (drums)
Vogel (bird)

[A transposing mechanism on the Rückwerk made it possible to switch from German to Italian choir pitch.]

AUGUSTINIAN ABBEY CHURCH, KLOSTERNEUBURG
Scherer organ of c1550, rebuilt and enlarged by J. G. Freundt, 1636–42 [181, p. 68]

Hauptwerk
Prinzipal 8'
Prinzipalflöte 8'
Coppel 8'
Quintadena 8'
Oktave 4'
Offenflöte 4'
Dulcian 4' (flue stop)
Oktavkoppel 4'
Quinte 2 2/3'
Superoktave 2'
Mixtur XII–XIV (4')
Zimbel II (1/2')
Grossposaune 16'
Posaune 8'

Brustwerk
Coppel 4'
Prinzipal 2'
Spitzflöte 2'
Regal 8'

Rückpositiv
Nachthorngedackt 8'
Prinzipal 4'
Spitzflöte 4'
Kleincoppel 4'
Oktave 2'
Superoktave 1'
Zimbel II
Krummhorn 8'

Pedal
Portunprinzipal 16' (prestant)
Subbass 16'
Oktave 8'
Choralflöte 8' (open)
Superoktave 4'
Mixture VI–VIII (4')
Rauschwerk III (2')
Grossposaune 16'
Posaune 8'

Accessory Stops
Hauptwerk-Rückpositiv Coupler

[The *Hauptwerk* and Pedal pipes occupy the same windchest, and the 16' and 8' reeds are probably borrowed by the Pedal from the *Hauptwerk*.]

ST. PETER'S CHURCH, SALZBURG
Daniel Heyl, 1618 [131, p. 38]

Hauptwerk
Prinzipal 8'

Rückpositiv
Copula 8'

Copula 8'
Octav 4'
Flauto 4'
Quint 2 2/3'
Superoktav 2'
Cornet V (4')
Mixtur VIII (2')
Zimbel IV (1')

Prinzipal 4'
Flauto 4'
Superoktav 2'
Quinta minor 1 1/3'
Zimbel II (1 1/3')

Pedal
Grossbass 16'
Subbass 16'
Prinzipal 8'
Oktav 4'
Superoktav 2'
Mixture IV (4')
Posaune 8'

FORMER STIFTSKIRCHE, ARDAGGER
Johann George Freundt, 1630 [131, p. 38]

Hauptwerk
Principal 8'
Gedackt 8'
Spitzflöte 4'
Gedackt 4'
Quint 2 2/3'
Octav 2'
Mixtur

Rückpositiv
Gedackt 8'
Flöte 4'
Principal 2'
Octav 1'
Mixtur

Pedal
Bordun 16'
Octav 8'
Flötenbass 4'

MARIENKAPELLE, WURZBURG
Johann Leonhard Schannad, 1642 [269, p. 172]

Manual I
Prinzipal 8'
Quintaton 8'
Oktav 4'
Spitzflöte 4'
Kleine Gedackt 4'
Superoktav 2'
Mixtur V

Manual II
Gros Gedackt 8'
Quintaton 8'
Prinzipal 4'
Kleine Gedackt 4'
Oktav 2'

Pedal
Subbass 16'
Posaun 8'

FRANCISCAN CHURCH, VIENNA
Johann Wöckherl, 1641–42 [131, p. 39]

Hauptwerk
Principal 8'
Quintade 8'
Gedeckt 8'
Octav 4'
Gedeckt 4'

Positiv
Copula 8'
Principal 4'
Spitzflöte 4'
Octav 2'
Superoctav 1'

Superoctav 2'
MixturVI (1 1/3')

Mixtur III (2/3')

Pedal
Offenbass 16'
Octav 8'
Principal 4'
Quint 2 2/3'
Mixtur IV (2')
Trompete 8'

PARISH CHURCH, BREGENZ
Michael Schnitzer, 1650 [54, p. 40]

Manual
Principal 8'
Coppel 8'
Octav 4'
Flöte 4'
Superoctav 2'
Mixtur IV (2')
Zimbel II(?) (1/2')

Pedal
Subbass 16' and 8'

Registration

While organists to the north circulated between the central German cities, the Baltic cities, and the Netherlands, those in the south tended to circulate between the urban centers of southern Germany and those of Austria, with occasional excursions to Italy; and some of the Italians occasionally migrated across the Alps to Germany and Austria. Kerll, the mentor of Murschhauser and Pachelbel, studied with Carissimi and held important positions in Munich and Vienna. Froberger, a native of Stuttgart, studied under Frescobaldi in Italy but spent most of his life as a court organist in Vienna. Their contemporary Alessandro Poglietti, a Tuscan, was connected with the Viennese court for most of his life. The Nürnbergers Hans and Jacob Hassler both studied with the Gabrielis and were court musicians in Augsburg, although Hans later went to Dresden and Jacob to Prague. Also from Nürnberg was Kindermann, who likewise studied in Italy.

The organs of the region also show southern influences. One- and two-manual schemes are the norm, with three-manual instruments being rare. With the exception of instruments like the Klosterneuburg organ, which was rebuilt by Freundt of Passau from an older organ by the northern builder Scherer, the Pedal divisions tend to be smaller, with fewer high-pitched stops.

Perhaps most noticeable as the seventeenth century progresses is the sparsity and even absence of reeds on the manuals; one is occasionally found in the Pedal, usually at 8' pitch. This lack is usually attributed to Italian influences (although larger Italian organs often had at least one manual reed stop), but it is also likely that it was influenced by the Catholic East, Poland and Czechslovakia. For example, a two-manual, 23-stop organ built by Hans Hummel in 1623 for the parish church in

Olkusz, Poland, contained no reeds at all. Also significant is that the only off-unison stop in this organ was a 2 2/3' Quint on the main manual [79, p. 183]. In the Germanic and Slavic South and East, the decline in colorful reeds was paralleled by a decline in mutations, something that was by no means true in Italy.

These tendencies became even more pronounced in the succeeding period. The instruments of the southeast were intended largely for the playing of Catholic liturgical music, rather than the colorful chorale variations, flashy praeludia, and secular works of the North. Surviving instruments, despite dispositions that owe more to Germanic tradition than to Italian, tend to be gentler and more understated than their northern counterparts. The latter not only had to play a different literature but were also called upon to support congregational singing after the middle of the seventeenth century.

While a few composers made occasional forays into chorale-based works—Steigleder wrote a set of 40 variations on *Vater Unser*; Kindermann is credited with a prelude on *Was mein Gott will*—the vast majority of the southern Catholic organ works were cast in the classic Renaissance forms of the ricercare, canzone, capriccio, intonation, toccata, praeambulum, and fugue. Many of these pieces were based on the church tones, obviously intended for use in the mass, although pieces with specific liturgical titles are surprisingly few. Erbach wrote a number of works based on the traditional hymns of the Church, and some of the others wrote magnificats, but the free forms predominated, as they did in Italy.

Few registration sources dating from the seventeenth century have been found from the southern Catholic regions. However, sources from the early eighteenth century show that (allowing for the introduction of newer stops) there is surprisingly little difference in the type of combinations cited from those described in the previous section from Catholic sources in Worms, Würzburg, and Schöntal: largely combinations of 8' and 4' principals and flutes, with the occasional addition of the Quint and, less commonly, the Zimbel or a reed. The full organ, of course, continued to include the mixtures.

A 1676 manuscript by Poglietti, perhaps intended for publication as a didactic work for players of keyboard instruments, is held in the Abbey of Kremsmünster in Austria. It contains a list of registrations for an organ of two manuals and eighteen stops which provides a tangible link between the sixteenth- and eighteenth-century sources [242].

On the main manual, ten combinations are based on the 8' Principal, most of them three-stop groups linking the Principal with (1) 8' Flute and 2 2/3' Quint, (2) 8' and 4' Flutes, (3) 4' Principal and Flute, (4) 4' and 2' Principals, (5) 4' Flute and 2 2/3' Quint, (6) 4' and 2' Flutes, (7) 4' Flute and 2' Principal. The largest combination is of Principal 8', Principal and Flute 4', Principal 2' and Quint 2 2/3'; the second largest omits the Quint. In addition, the Spitzflute (possibly a 4' stop) alone is cited, as is the "Principal alone with Tremulant."

On the Positiv manual, the 4' Principal is combined with the Flute 8'; these two stops plus Flute 4'; and these three plus Quint. It is also used with the Schwebelflaut, apparently an undulating or de-tuned stop, and probably of open or tapered pipes. The Schwebelflaut is also used with the Copula (the stopped 8' Flute), perhaps a Viennese version of the Italian Voce Umana.

As with some early French directions, there is no hint of how the combinations cited in the sixteenth- and seventeenth-century sources are to be used in the music, although liturgical use within the Mass is implied. But because of the strong Italian influences on the music, it seems reasonable to assume that registrations colored by some of the Italian usages, adapted to the resources of the south German organs, would be appropriate. In his discussion of Froberger's Toccatas, James Kosnik suggests

> that manual changes should be restricted to the clear structural divisions within the toccatas, for the coherence of the musical form is destroyed by frequent and abrupt manual alternations. The use of two plenums on different manuals for the free and strict writing is most successful: the larger division corresponds to the non-imitative sections, for they often contain the most dramatic music, rapid passagework, and dissonant harmonic material. Occasionally the use of a transparent solo registration such as a four-foot flute stop is conducive to certain types of imitative writing. The registration of these pieces, however, should not include excessively brilliant reed stops, a feature more characteristic of North German organs. [82, p. 104]

Froberger's Dorian Toccata in D minor, consisting of an introduction and four short sections, illustrates how some of these possibilities might be employed. Use of the plenum on the main manual is suggested by the nature of the introduction, with the sustained bass notes played on the Pedal in the Italian manner. The secondary manual plenum could suit the Allegro, with perhaps a 4' combination for the Presto, one of the principal combinations for the Andante, and one of the brighter registrations including the Zimbel or a light reed for the concluding Allegro. While the Italianate use of the Pedal is only hinted at by Froberger and Scherer, composers did write works with more clearly defined pedal lines, particularly Kerll, as in his Passacaglia and in the Toccata *per li Pedali*. In such instances the Pedal is used only for the bass line, as Pedal *cantus firmus* solos never occur in this southern literature.

Texture is also a clue to the registration of Scherer's Intonations. The initial piece in each set is somewhat in the character of a French *Plein Jeu* piece, while the others in the set are usually of a lighter construction, suggesting smaller and brighter combinations. For the ricercares and canzonas of Erbach and Hassler, combinations of 8' and 4' principals and flutes are often suitable, unless the nature of the piece clearly dictates otherwise.

Although the south German literature is somewhat out of the mainstream of modern repertoire, it contains many works of real merit. Because it does not demand as broad a palette of either reed or mutation colors as some of the north German or French literature, much of it works quite well on smaller modern organs, as well as on many organs built in the early or middle nineteenth century. As in other music of this period, excesses of bottom- or top-heaviness should be avoided, and light, balanced combinations should be sought.

This music is suitable for experimenting with the changes that may be rung on simple combinations of stops found in a wide variety of organs—8' and 4' principals and flutes, with the occasional addition of 2 2/3' and 2' pitches or lightly voiced reed stops.

From the middle of the seventeenth century, the period we know as the Baroque was, politically, a relatively peaceful time. Many small political entities had coalesced under a strong monarchy, particularly in France. Even in Germany, with no central head of state, weaker rulers tended to unite under stronger ones. Something approaching a balance of power had been achieved, although it was a fragile one.

During the Renaissance, two factors had caused constant turmoil—national boundaries and religion. Both were in a more settled state during the Baroque period, particularly after the end of the devastating Thirty Years' War in Germany. Spain and Portugal were in decline; but those erstwhile enemies, France and England, were in the ascendant, while Italy and the Netherlands held their own. More and more the areas to the east—Austria, Hungary, Czechoslovakia, and Poland—were making significant contributions to the cultural life of Europe.

On the spiritual level, the sixteenth century had seen not only that great schism in the Christian Church, the Reformation, but also the beginnings of a more humanistic outlook. In its best manifestation, it brought a healthy spirit of inquiry to bear on both Catholic and Protestant thought; mysticism remained an important element but was no longer everything. Perhaps this shift of emphasis also helped to bring about the cautious truce and growing tolerance that would culminate, by the end of the Baroque period, in greater freedom of religion than had existed before.

All of these conditions nurtured the arts. Peaceful rulers could afford to spend more on such things, and one finds even minor princelings vying with each other in their expenditures for opulent residences and lavish musical organizations. To be a court composer or even just a court fiddler represented job security for a growing number of musicians. And the beginnings of a democratic society, in which a man of humble birth might attain affluence and position through trade and hard work, were generating a new class of patrons of the arts, particularly in England and northern Europe.

The churches too were more at peace—Protestants had now existed for several generations, and the various factions had coalesced geographically, each with its distinctive liturgical and musical traditions. The Church of Rome had, through its Counter-Reformation, cured some of its besetting ills, and was again turning its attention to the embellishment of its services and churches. As a result, church musicians of both persuasions were also able to have a better standard of living, and the craft of organ building was flourishing almost everywhere.

Perhaps one of the most striking characteristics of Baroque art (which includes music and organs) is its nationalism. The gradual separation of styles and practices observed throughout the previous period becomes an accomplished fact in the High Baroque: here at last one can say without dispute that this music sounds German, this French, this Spanish. And the organs too spoke their own particular language; Luigi Tagliavini has observed that the Italian organ, like Italian speech, emphasizes the smooth vowel sounds, while the German organ speaks more with the crisp consonants of the Teutonic tongue.

The Music

All the keyboard forms prevalent in the earlier period continued in widespread use, but with continued development and elaboration and, in some instances, even metamorphoses. The fugue developed into a major and complex form in the northern countries, the praeludium into a multipartite fantasia, and the gentle Renaissance toccata began its evolution into a virtuosic showpiece. The chorale-prelude likewise was undergoing continuous development in the parts of Germany where Lutheranism flourished. Showy chorale fantasias appeared, and simple variations grew into complex partitas. Chorale-based pieces became less like introductions to congregational singing and more like major compositions, although the shorter and more utilitarian chorale-preludes continued to be written in quantity.

In France, the same kind of transformation affected the liturgical music of the organ mass. The music of the liturgy and the office hymns became more and more a vehicle for displaying the characteristic sounds of the organ. Dialogues between the main and secondary manuals appeared, and the offertoire became an impressive fantasia, often sectional in structure. Most significantly, titles implying registration appeared with increasing frequency from the middle of the seventeenth century onward.

In Italy and the Iberian peninsula, and indeed in Austria and southern Germany, evolution moved more slowly; but in Spain certain forms such as the *batalla* took on greater prominence and elaborateness, and the south German school expanded into larger compositional forms. In England, the depradations of the Puritans caused a general hiatus in church music in the middle of the seventeenth century, but upon the Restoration of the Monarchy in 1660 a rich infusion of outside influences, particularly from Italy and France, spurred the development of the voluntary into a varied, sectional, and often elaborate form. Indeed, by the early years of the eighteenth century, each of the northern countries had its own version of an extended, sectional, often virtuosic organ composition—in Germany the praeludium, in France the offertoire, and in England the voluntary. In the south, the simpler toccatas, tientos, and fantasias continued to be written.

While music for other instruments has always had some effect on keyboard music, this influence became more prominent during the Baroque period. The trio sonata—heretofore an ensemble idiom—found a natural keyboard counterpart when it was adapted to the two manuals and pedal of an organ, and outright transcriptions from the concerted repertoire began to appear. At the same time, the line of idiomatic demarcation between the style of writing for the organ and for stringed keyboard instruments became sharper, particularly in France.

The Organs

Many of the trends that shaped the organs of France, England, and Germany for most of the eighteenth century can be traced to the late seventeenth century. In France, the organ became so stylistically locked in that basic stoplists and registration conventions changed surprisingly little from the late seventeenth century to the French Revolution. In England, a whole new instrument was born during the Restoration period, as tonal concepts from France and the Netherlands were grafted onto the earlier English rootstock, but by the opening of the eighteenth century it too had stabilized into a form that was recognizable into the early decades of the nineteenth century.

In northern Germany and particularly in the Netherlands, the tonal evolution of the organ slowed. The growing edge had shifted to the central German region and Bohemia, where string stops and other innovations began appearing early on, and where the *Rückpositiv* gradually fell into disfavor as the eighteenth century progressed.

Something that did not change significantly in this period was the status of the pedal organ. The central and northern German organs continued to have substantial independent Pedal divisions, while those in the Netherlands were more sparse. French pedals were still largely limited to a *cantus firmus* function, and in England pedals hardly appeared at all until late in the eighteenth century. Both German and French organs could be found with three and even four manuals (St. Gervais in Paris had five, although not all were of full compass), and the Echo made its appearance as the third manual division in England, to be gradually transformed into the Swell as the century wore on.

Further south, in Italy, Spain, and Portugal, the organ remained not too far removed from its seventeenth-century mode well into the nineteenth century. The addition of horizontal reeds was the chief Spanish innovation, but in none of these countries did the Pedal develop beyond a short-compass keyboard that simply pulled down the bass manual keys or played one or two bass stops. Similarly, in this region the number of manuals rarely exceeds two, and, as in the Renaissance, some fairly substantial instruments were built with but a single keyboard. In Spain and Portugal it was usually divided, and the Iberian organs were in fact almost as flexible registrationally as those with multiple manuals.

11 England

Composers

Thomas Augustine Arne (1710–1778)
Charles Avison (1710–1770)
John Barratt (c1674–c1735)
George Berg (fl. 1746–71)
John Blow (1649–1708)
William Boyce (1710–1779)
William Croft (1678–1727)
William Felton (1715–1769)
Christopher Gibbons (1615–1676)
Maurice Greene (1675–1755)
George Frederick Handel (1685–1759)
Philip Hart (c1676–1749)
William Hayes (1706–1777)
William Hine (1687–1730)
John Humphries (1707–c1730)
John James (d. c1745)
John Keeble (c1711–1786)
Matthew Locke (1630–1677)
James Nares (1715–1783)
John Christopher Pepusch (1667–1752)
Peter Prelleur (1705?–1741)
Henry Purcell (1659–1695)
John Reading (1677–1764)
John Robinson (1682–1762)
Thomas Roseingrave (1690–1766)
Charles John Stanley (1713–1786)
Simon Stubley (d. 1754)
John Travers (1703?–1758)
William Walond (1725–1770)

Representative Organs

CATHEDRAL, EXETER
John Loosemore, 1665–66 [97, p. 6]

Great
Double Diapason 16' (14 bass pipes)
Open Diapason I 8'
Open Diapason II 8'
Stopped Diapason 8'
Principal 4'
Twelfth 2 2/3'
Fifteenth 2'
Sesquialtera III
Cornet III (V?) (treble)
Trumpet(?) 8'

Chaire
Stopped Diapason 8'
Principal 4'
Flute 4'
Fifteenth 2'
Bassoon(?) 8'

CHURCH OF ST. MARY-AT-HILL, LONDON
Bernard Smith, 1692–93 [270, p. 62]

Manual
Open Diapason 8'
Stop Diapason 8' (wood)
Principal 4'
Recorder 4' (wood)
★Great Twelfth 2 2/3'
★Fifteenth 2'
★Tierce 1 3/5'
Cornet V (treble)
★Mixture III
★Trumpet 8'
★Vox Humane 8'

Accessory Stops
Trimeloe (Tremulant)

[The stops marked with an asterisk were divided (treble & bass) "for the Benefit of increasing
the Variety of the Organ." The description of the organ also mentions an "Echo to the
Whole," which might be interpreted as some manner of primitive swell enclosure.]

ST. PAUL'S CATHEDRAL, LONDON
Bernard Smith, 1695–97 [55, p. 34]

Great
Open Diapason I 8'
Open Diapason II 8'
Stop Diapason 8'
Principall 4'
Hol Fleut 4'
Great Twelfth 2 2/3'
Fifteenth 2'
Small Twelfth 1 1/3'

Chaire
Quinta Dena Diapason 8'
Stop Diapason 8'
Principall 4'
Hol Fleut 4'
Great Twelfth 2 2/3'
Fifteenth 2'
Cimball (II?)
Voice Humane 8'

Sesquialtera (III? bass?)
Cornet (V? treble?)
Mixture (IV?)
Trumpet 8'

Crum Horne 8'

Echo (from tenor C)
Diapason 8' (stopped)
Principal 4'
Nason 4' (flute)
Fifteenth 2'
Cornet (III?)
Trumpet 8'

[Each manual on this organ had a different compass: Great, 60 notes (CCC, DDD–c³); Chaire, 54 notes (FFF, GGG, AAA–c³); Echo, 37 notes (c⁰–c³).]

ST. JOHN'S CHURCH, PORTSMOUTH, NEW HAMPSHIRE
A chamber organ of the Smith school, ca. 1700 [stoplist from extant organ]

Manual
Stopped Diapason 8' (wood)
Principal 4' (open wood)
Fifteenth 2'
Sesquialtera II (bass)
Cornet III (treble)

CATHEDRAL, SALISBURY
Renatus Harris, 1710 [98, p. 9]

Great
Open Diapason I 8'
Open Diapason II 8'
Stopped Diapason 8'
Principal 4'
Flute 4'
Twelfth 2 2/3'
Fifteenth 2'
Tierce 1 3/5
Larigot 1 1/3'
Sesquialtera IV
Cornet V (from Middle C)
Trumpet 8'
Clarion 4'
Cromhorn 8'
Vox Humana 8'

Chaire
Open Diapason 8' ("to Gamut G")
Stopped Diapason 8'
Principal 4'
Flute 4'
Twelfth 2 2/3'
Fifteenth 2'
Bassoon 8'

Echo (from Middle C)
Open Diapason 8'
Stopped Diapason 8'
Principal 4'
Flute 4'
Twelfth 2 2/3'
Fifteenth 2'
Tierce 1 3/5'
Larigot 1 1/3'
Trumpet 8'
Cromhorn 8'
Vox Humana 8'

Accessory Stops
Drum Pedal tuned to CC

[With the exception of one of the 8' Open Diapasons and the Cornet, all stops of the Great were playable on a fourth manual, the "Borrowed Great," by a rare early system of "duplexing."]

CHURCH OF ST. MARY REDCLIFFE, BRISTOL
Bridge & Byfield, 1726 [30, p. 70]

Great
Open Diapason I 8'
Open Diapason II 8'
Stopped Diapason 8'
Principal 4'
Twelfth 2 2/3'
Fifteenth 2'
Tierce 1 3/5
Sesquialtera III
Cornet V (from Middle C)
Trumpet 8'
Clarion 4'

Pedal
(13 notes, from CC)
Coupled to Great

Swell (from Tenor G)
Open Diapason 8'
Stopped Diapason 8'
Principal 4'
Flute 4'
Cornet III
Trumpet 8'
Hautboy 8'
Vox Humana 8'
Cromorn 8'

Chair
Stopped Diapason 8'
Principal 4'
Flute Almain 4' (chimney flute?)
Flute 2' (or 4'?)
Bassoon 8'

TRINITY CHURCH, NEWPORT, RHODE ISLAND
Richard Bridge, 1733 [282, p. 115]

Great
Open Diapason 8' (treble)
Stop Diapason 8'
Principal 4'
Flute 4'
Fifteenth 2'
Sesquialtera III (bass)
Cornet III (treble)
Trumpet 8' (treble)
Vox Humane 8'

Echo (short compass; middle C?)
Open Diapason 8'
(Stopped) Diapason 8'
Trumpet 8'

ST. MARY'S CHURCH, FINCHLEY
John Snetzler, 1749 [225, p. 34]

Great
Open Diapason 8'
Stopped Diapason 8'
Principal 4'
Flute 4'
Twelfth 2 2/3'
Fifteenth 2'
Sesquialtera IV

Swell (from Tenor G)
Open Diapason 8'
Dulciana 8'
Principal 4'
Cornet II

SMITHSONIAN INSTITUTION, WASHINGTON, D. C.
John Snetzler, 1761 (a chamber organ) [49, p. 6]

Manual
Open Diapason 8' (from Middle C)

Stopped Diapason 8'
Flute 4' (stopped wood)
Fifteenth 2'
Sesquialtera II (bass)
Cornet II (treble)

Accessory Stops
Shifting Movement (pedal, silences 2', and mixtures)

Registration

There is a startling difference between these stoplists and those cited for the previous period. The reed stops, mixtures, and mutations (including the Tierce) that appeared shortly after 1660—as well as the third manual—were due largely to the influence of two builders, their families, and their pupils. Renatus Harris, born in Brittany, was the son of an expatriate builder, and his mother was a Dallam. When he and his relatives returned to England at the Restoration of the Monarchy, they brought with them many current French tonal concepts.

Harris's chief competitor, Bernard Smith, emigrated to England during the 1660s from the Netherlands. Long thought to have been another expatriate, he is now believed to have been of Dutch or north German origin; he has been identified as the Barendt Smit who built several organs in Holland. His north European contributions are indeed quite similar to the French innovations of Harris—reeds, mixtures, the Cornet stop—and by the second generation these two influences had blended to produce a very idiomatic English instrument. Curiously, although Harris was familiar with the solo Pedal divisions of France and Smith with the more substantial Pedals of northern Europe, neither attempted seriously to introduce independent Pedal divisions to English organs, and both adopted the peculiarly English "long compass" for the manuals, descending to GGG below modern CC. Both also adopted and continued the long-established English use of wooden Stopped Diapasons, which is also unique to England.

The basic design of English organs was already quite standardized by 1700, and it remained so, with but minor permutations, for most of the subsequent century. By mid-century, however, the Cremona and the Hautboy had largely supplanted the Vox Humana as the light solo reed, and around the same time the Swiss immigrant Snetzler had added a third 8' flue stop, the Dulciana, to the basic Open and Stopped Diapasons [318, pp. 11–13]. Snetzler is also credited with the introduction of 16' manual stops (as in the Great of his 1754 instrument at St. Margaret's Church, Kings Lynn—Dr. Charles Burney's church) but in general he conformed to the prevailing English style [225, p. 34].

The short-compass Echo, imported from the Continent and enclosed in a wooden box to mute its sound, made an early appearance as a manual division. In 1712 Abraham Jordan improved upon it by adding a primitive mechanism to allow the organist to open and close the Echo box and thus be able to control the gradation, or "swelling," of the sound. The Echo/Swell quickly became popular (in 1720 Shrider added a swell mechanism of some sort to the Echo of Smith's organ in St. Paul's Cathedral), although it remained a short-compass division until the end of the century.

Also during the first half of the eighteenth century, the Chaire began to migrate from its older "Ruckpositive" position, outside the main organ case, to a location within the main case; and it began to be referred to as the Choir division, although exterior Choir divisions were still occasionally built. Pedals, however, remained almost nonexistent until the end of the eighteenth century, notable exceptions being those added by Shrider to the organ in St. Paul's Cathedral and the thirteen-note pulldown pedals on John Byfield's 1726 organ for St. Mary Redcliffe in Bristol.

Chamber organs continued to be popular in England throughout the eighteenth century, and, like their larger counterparts, they became quite standardized in design. The presence of half (treble) stops and divided stops, as well as a "shifting movement," which drew or retired the upperwork, made these instruments surprisingly flexible, allowing the playing of solos and (with the shifting move-ment) echo pieces—thus mimicking the effect of a two-manual organ. A number of eighteenth-century composers wrote voluntaries tailored to divided-keyboard organs, in which the solo never descends below the dividing point and the accompaniment never ascends above it.

Like certain instrument makers, some musicians found it prudent to be out of the country while Cromwell was in power; and they too absorbed foreign ideas, particularly in France. In addition, the Stuart kings imported French and Italian musicians for their courtly musical establishments, and the accession of the Hanoverian Georges in the early eighteenth century added an influx of German musicians (notably Handel) to London's already cosmopolitan musical community.

The French and Italian influence can readily be seen in the organ music of the late seventeenth and early eighteenth centuries. The organ works in Locke's *Melothesia* (1673) display strong French tendencies, particularly in their ornamen-tation, and his Voluntary for a Double Organ (a classic Cornet voluntary, although no registration is given) owes more stylistically to the florid Franco-Flemish idiom than to the pre-Commonwealth double voluntaries of Locke's compatriots. Continental influences, probably absorbed from the musicians with whom Purcell associated in the court of Charles, also mark that composer's keyboard writing, although Blow is more conservatively English in orientation.

As noted in the previous section, some rudimentary solo registration indications first appeared across the English Channel in Flanders fairly early in the seventeenth century. But the first known occurrence of registrations in French music is in the mid-century Louis Couperin manuscript, and hardly more than a decade later registrations appear in the music of John Blow and Christopher Gibbons.

For his Double Voluntary in A, Gibbons specifies a registration of Sesquialtera and Trumpet (possibly divided stops) for a left-hand solo on the Great, and the Great Cornet (a treble stop which included the 8' and 4' pitches in its five ranks) for the right-hand solo. Similar registrations can be found in France and Germany. Although Purcell specifies no registration for his better-known Double Organ Voluntary in D minor, the use of Gibbons's registrations is quite electrifying in this work. Gibbons prescribes a similar combination for his longer Double Organ

Voluntary in D minor and assumes some stop changes and/or additions—for the Cornet, Sesquialtera, and Trumpet are specified separately as solos in various sections.

In one of Blow's double organ voluntaries (No. 28 in the Watkins Shaw edition), variously called "Vers for the Cornett and Single Organ" (Gostling Ms.) and "A Voluntary for the Cornett Stop" (Davis Ms.), the entries for the Cornet solo in the treble are clearly marked [204, p. 4]. Another early example is an anonymous double organ voluntary from a manuscript in the Hereford Cathedral library in which "C" stands for Cornet and "D" for Diapasons, indicating that the fragmented Cornet solos are accompanied (and echoed) by the Open and Stopped Diapasons on a secondary manual [84, pref.]. A Voluntary in C attributed to either Purcell or Barratt has a "Diapason and Flute [4']" section, followed by solos for the Cornet (in the treble) and Sesquialtera (in the bass, and with appropriate foundations). These are all very reminiscent of the earlier Franco-Flemish registrations in which the Cornet or Trumpet are accompanied by the *jeu doux*.

Before the beginning of the eighteenth century, registration indications are found only in double organ voluntaries (i.e., those requiring two manuals). For registering pieces requiring only one manual, the player must still rely on the nature of the piece and knowledge of period instruments. One small hint is found in Blow's voluntaries and verses. Some, including the more ambitious and heavily textured, are marked "for the Organ"; since Blow had access to a two-manual organ, this would appear to indicate the Great, in the same way that *das Werk* refers to the main manual in German sources from the same period.

Other pieces, mostly shorter and lighter in texture, are "for the Single Organ"— i.e, the Chaire—and thus call for a lighter registration based on the 8' Stopped Diapason. A few of Blow's works are given registration indications only in later manuscripts. Thus the thin-textured and fugal No. 16 (Shaw) is called "Voluntary for the two Diapasons [Open and Stopped] and flute" in the c1721–45 Davis manuscript. This piece indeed sounds well when played on a light 8' Diapason, an English-style Stopped Diapason, and a mild 4' open Flute.

With regard to tonal resources, the organ of the Restoration set the standard for organ design in the British Isles for more than a century afterward. The same is true of the registration conventions that it inspired. The voluntaries and verses composed in the late seventeenth and early eighteenth centuries still followed the forms of the early seventeenth century—single voluntaries in fugal or ricercare style, double voluntaries in Franco-Flemish solo style. Either form usually appeared as a single-movement piece, a notable exception being Purcell's Voluntary in G, which has an Italian flavor and prefigures the many two-part "prelude and fugue" type of voluntaries composed throughout the eighteenth century. Although Purcell gave no registrations for this piece, it should probably be registered as later examples were: the "prelude" (reminiscent of an Italian *durezze e ligature* piece) on the Great Open and Stopped Diapasons; the "fugue" on a brighter combination, possibly on a secondary manual, or, as in some later examples, on full organ.

On the basis of some of the musical evidence described above, suitable registrations for music of the Restoration period (late seventeenth century) may be summed up as follows:

For Single Voluntaries:
  Diapasons (Open and Stopt 8' together)
  Stopt Diapason alone
  Diapasons 8' with Principal or Flute 4'
  Stopt Diapason 8' with Principal or Flute 4'
  Full chorus through Twelfth and Fifteenth
  Full chorus through Mixture (Sesquialtera)
For Double Voluntaries:
  Treble solo: Cornet V (or equivalent); Trumpet 8'
  Bass solo: Sesquialtera (with foundations); Trumpet 8'
  Accompaniment: Diapasons 8' with Principal or Flute 4'
The Trumpet should always have the Open or Stopped Diapason drawn with it.

The recent discovery in a psalm book formerly used in St. James's Church, Piccadilly, London, of a set of handwritten "Rules for the Organ" dating from around 1700, provides one of the earliest indications of the way organs were used and registered for church services at the opening of the eighteenth century [262, p. 29]. The St. James's organ, installed second-hand by Bernard Smith in 1691, had sash windows on the front of the case (as did the Smith organ in St. Paul's Cathedral originally); they appear to have been used as a primitive "open or closed" expression device to control volume. Normally they were kept open when the organ was in use, the exceptions being "Ashwednesday, Good Friday, and all Other solemn fasting days," when no voluntaries were played, and only soft stops were used to introduce the psalm tunes.

References to registration suggest that the organ was not to be played loudly during the course of the service. The Voluntary before the Lesson was to be played "only on soft stops; as the Diapason [i.e., 8' stops] of the Little [Chaire] and Great organ, or Both," but on State Festivals the organist could "take a greater liberty in his voluntaries." The introduction to the congregational singing of the psalm was also "ordinarily play'd only on the soft stops." The organist might however play the "exit" [postlude] after morning or evening prayers "as he pleases," which probably meant loudly or brightly, for on days when Communion followed the service, he was admonished to play "only on the soft stop, and as gravely as may be" until the minister was ready.

During the first half of the eighteenth century the single-movement Restoration voluntary gave way increasingly to voluntaries of multiple movements. At first they were simply fugues or Cornet pieces (bass-clef solos disappeared almost entirely) preceded by a slower movement for Diapasons or full organ, and this type of simple two-section voluntary continued to be written throughout the century. But by the 1740s longer voluntaries of multiple movements were also being written.

Although, as we have seen, solo-voice voluntaries were written before the beginning of the eighteenth century, their use may at first have been restricted to special occasions or to the end of the service, as is suggested in the Piccadilly "Rules." Eventually these showier voluntaries began to replace the quiet ones prescribed for the interval between the Psalm and the Lesson. The historian

Hawkins, writing after the death of Handel, puts the blame on the London organists Greene and Robinson for popularizing the playing of lively reed and Cornet pieces in this part of the service, stating scornfully that Greene "affected in his voluntaries that kind of practice on single stops, the cornet and the vox humana for instance, which puts [the organ] almost on a level with the harpsichord" [69, p. 884]. Hawkins may well have been prejudiced, however, for elsewhere he states his preference for fugues and "solemn music" on the organ, and he regards the Tremulant (which he incorrectly believes to be a modern invention) as "offensive to the ear" [69, p. 614].

With increasing variety in compositional style came more variety in registration. In 1737 John Reading completed a manuscript collection of voluntaries which he later presented to the Chapel Royal. In it one finds, in addition to the expected Cornet, Trumpet, Diapasons, and Full Organ movements, some of the earliest indications of the use of the 4' Flute stop as a solo voice: there are three voluntaries "for Cornett and Flute" and a Siciliano "for the Flute stop"—the latter title an indication of the Italian influence beginning to be felt in English organ composition.

In the Reading manuscript there are also some transcriptions from instrumental works, including an "Aire for French Horns and Trumpet," actually a movement from Handel's *Water Music*. Toward the middle of the century a Horn (or French Horn) stop began to appear on some larger organs, and "horn call" effects began to appear in voluntaries as well as transcriptions. The earliest of these Horn stops (like that in St. Dionis Backchurch, London, 1724) were only half-stops, from middle C, although Horn stops of longer compass occasionally appeared later in the eighteenth century [332, p. 11].

From a slightly later period (c1750) comes another manuscript, now in possession of the Royal College of Organists in London. It is curious in that many of the pieces are of composite authorship, the majority being of the two-section type—an introductory slow movement (usually marked "Diapasons") followed by either an Allegro for Cornet or Trumpet, or a fugue for full organ. But one looks in vain for any registrational innovation here [251, p. 237].

The pieces in John Stanley's three sets of voluntaries, published between 1748 and 1752, represent in almost encyclopedic form the broad stylistic range that characterized the English voluntary by the middle of the eighteenth century. The Cornet or Trumpet pieces preceded by a slow movement are still present, as are voluntaries of the prelude-and-fugue type. But Voluntary I of Book II begins with a Siciliano played on the Swell, followed by a movement in which the Vox Humana is the solo stop—one of the last such instances, for by this time the weak and often unstable Vox Humana was being supplanted by the more popular Hautboy or Cremona. In the same book, Voluntary V consists of three sections, and Voluntary VI of four, each with a different registration.

An insight into the registration of "horn-call" movements is found in Voluntary VI of Volume III, where the second section calls for "Corno or Diapasons," implying that if no Horn stop is present, the Diapasons could be substituted. About the only solo stop not called for by Stanley is the Cremona, a cylindrical reed whose name is a corruption of the French *Cromorne*. But this stop does appear in voluntaries by some of Stanley's contemporaries, as in the slow movement of Peter

Prelleur's three-section (Diapasons, Cornet, Cremona) Voluntary in D minor. While the Dulciana was making its appearance at mid-century, it does not begin to occur in registration directions until later.

Although the Great Trumpet (unlike the Cremona or the Swell reeds) was almost always a full-compass stop in eighteenth-century English organs, Trumpet bass solos seem to have gone entirely out of fashion by mid-century. The Trumpet is usually called for in a treble solo line against a softer accompaniment, but occasionally, as in portions of Voluntary V of Stanley's Volume II, it is written for chordally, and in such places it is appropriate to play both hands on the Trumpet. William Ludham, a contemporary of Stanley's writing in 1772, makes the following observation concerning this particular voluntary:

> The Trumpet is an imitation of that instrument and is used as such with the diapasons. The bass, in trumpet voluntaries, is played soft on the stopped diapason, though sometimes the trumpet breaks out suddenly in the bass.
>
> A remarkable instance of this is in Stanley's voluntaries, opera sesta, Volun. V, line 6th of the trumpet part; where the trumpet and echo answer to each other. In that place, the trumpet bass on the great organ should undoubtedly be used, though not particularly directed; and when you come to the holding note on A [line 6, measure 4] the left hand should come down to the lower row of keys belonging to the lesser organ [Choir], having the stopped diapason only drawn [266, p. 562].

It should also be noted that at the place in question, the right-hand Trumpet line, having been in two- and three-note chords for several measures, briefly reverts to single notes. Ludham concludes that "there are many instances in these voluntaries, where the good taste of the player must supply the want of more particular directions for the management of stops." One wishes that he had given us more of his own insights!

Percy Young has recently unearthed another contemporary source of commentary on registration during the Stanley period: letters from Sir Samuel Hellier (1736–1784) to the organist of the Womborne parish church, where a one-manual organ of seven stops (including a divided Trumpet and a divided Sesquialtera/Cornet) had been installed in 1767. Hellier's remarks suggest how music written for a larger organ was adapted to a smaller one:

> Am glad you can play the Trumpet Voluntary Mr. Bond gave you . . . [but] you must learn several: some for the Flute stop, some for French Horn. It is by playing in the Horn manner upon the two Diapasons only & has a sweet effect.
>
> Walond's Voluntaries you will find exceedingly pretty but as you have no Swell [division] upon the organ in the church the Swell part must be played on the soft organ, raking the loud stops off with your foot [i.e., using the shifting movement] and the parts which are wrote for the Flute stop as you have no stop of that kind must be played with the Stop't Diapason [327, p. 53].

Hellier supports several other sources when he notes that the Cornet "is the stop constantly used when a psalm is given out" for singing in the church service. This usage appears to be a Dutch practice that crossed the Channel after the Restoration. The most illustrious contemporary of Stanley and Walond was, of course,

George Frederick Handel, who left barely a dozen works for organ solo, only the *Six Fugues or Voluntaries for the Organ* (1735) having been published during his lifetime. These had no registration indications, although some other Handel voluntaries, published around 1780 by Longman and Broderip, do. Whether they are Handel's or an editor's is not of great importance, since with one interesting exception they are quite standard: Diapason or Full Organ introductions, Cornet or Trumpet solos. The exception is the second (Allegro) movement of the Voluntary I in C, where the Principal alone is called for as a solo stop. This stop is found only at 4' pitch in English organs, and it may be that because of the character of the piece it was thought more suitable than the more usual Flute 4'.

Organ concertos became a popular genre during Handel's lifetime and remained so through the end of the century, being written by a number of composers in addition to Handel. They were not usually performed in churches but on the small-to medium-sized chamber organs in theatres (such as London's Covent Garden); thus registrational options were limited. In only two instances did Handel record a registration in a concerto holograph. One occurs in the solo second movement of the Concerto in F, Op. 4, No. 4. The tessitura of this movement is relatively high, and that may be why Handel calls for the rather dark combination of Open Diapason 8', Stopped Diapason 8', and Flute 4'. In the second movement of the Concerto in A (No. 14) there are some less clear directions: "or flauto" (Flute 4'), "or diapa[sons]," and, in one place, simply "more," which presumably calls for added stops [237, p. 71].

Despite a plenitude of corrupt editions and some older recordings made with large organs and orchestras, one must not lose sight of the fact that these concertos are chamber works, and that the organs on which Handel played them were all small, without pedals, and usually of one manual. Much misinformation is still current on this matter: A supposedly scholarly book on Handel, published in 1995, makes the remarkable statement that at the first performance of a concerto [Op. 7, No. 1] in 1740 the organ must have been located in the center of the hall so that the audience could admire Handel's pedal technique in the opening flourish! In 1937 French organist Marcel Dupré published a three-stave arrangement of the Handel Concertos for solo organ in which this passage is indeed assigned to the Pedal—but by Dupré, and not by Handel. We are probably fortunate that the author in question did not also quote Dupré's French registrations.

Small organs were also used for continuo or obbligato parts in oratorios. Donald Burrows recently found a written-out organ part to Handel's *Alexander's Feast*, dated 1736. It is contemporary with Handel but not in his handwriting. It contains the following registrations:

Overture: Open and Stopped Diapasons 8', Principal and Flute 4'
Recitatives: Stopped Diapason 8', Flute 4'
A Solo (Air): Open Diapason 8', Stopped Diapason 8'

Unusual are two places where playing an octave lower is indicated, one being the Largo section in the solo, "Revenge, Timotheus cries," where the registration given is 8' Diapasons. This may perhaps have been a conscious effort to enhance the gloomy and foreboding nature of the text.

Two sources from the end of the period under discussion give further insights into the registration of small organs, although they do not relate to specific compositions. One is a set of directions, possibly contemporary with the instrument, pasted on the stopjambs of the 1765 Byfield organ now in the Finchcocks collection, Goudhurst, Kent. The stoplist of the organ is typical: Stop Diapason 8' (divided), Open Diapason 8' (treble only), Principal 4', Flute 4', Twelfth 2 2/3' (divided), and Fifteenth 2'. The suggested combinations are:

1. Open Diapason and Flute
2. Open and Stop Diapasons
3. Diapasons and Fifteenth
4. Diapasons and Principal
5. Stop Diapason and Flute
6. Diapasons, Flute, and Fifteenth
7. Diapasons and Twelfth
8. Diapasons, Principal, and Flute [286, p. 113]

Combinations 3 and 7 are "gapped," lacking the 4' pitch; possibly they are intended for a lighter sort of literature than was usually played on church organs. It is also possible that No. 7 may have intended the treble half of the Twelfth only, allowing for a quasi-Cornet solo to be played against the Stop Diapason bass. Leaving off the Twelfth bass in No. 7 does in fact create a very effective treble solo color on this organ, while putting it on results in a rather muddled-sounding bass which distracts from the solo line.

The second source comes from a very similar instrument built in 1762 by Daniel Gray for Charlton Hill House in Shrewsbury. Its stoplist was quite standard: 8', 8', 4', 2 2/3', 2', Sesquialtera/Cornet and Trumpet 8', the Trumpet being a treble stop, and the Open Diapason going down only to tenor E. The only unusual feature was that the 4' was a Flute instead of a Principal, but it was presumably an open stop and was perhaps designed as a kind of hybrid.

The registration instructions Gray left with the organ are nothing out of the ordinary, but they are interesting in that they relate the registrations to dynamic levels, a practice which became commoner after the turn of the century. Thus we have the following:

pp = Stopt Diapason
p = Open and Stopt Diapasons
mf = 8', 8', 4'
f = 8', 8', 4', 2 2/3', 2'
ff = Full with Trumpet

Gray also suggests that for "a brilliant or quick passage," the Stopt Diapason 8', Flute 4', and Fifteenth 2' be used, "perhaps without the 4'" [255, p. 27]. This combination corresponds to the third Finchcocks registration, again indicating that gapped combinations were permissible in fast, light-textured music.

The Finchcocks instrument, like many of the smaller church and chamber organs built throughout the eighteenth century, has divided stops and half-stops.

Many voluntaries for such small organs (usually Cornet pieces) were written after 1660, beginning with Purcell and Blow, and they are later found among the works of Hine, Prelleur, James, Reading, Walond, Heron (a Trumpet voluntary), and others. One of the James works alternates the Cornet entrances with "Eccho" sections in the right hand, conveniently bracketing them with eighth rests, which would allow the use of the shifting-movement pedal to put the Cornet on or off.

By the middle decades of the eighteenth century, virtually all published and manuscript sources of organ music contained registrations, a notable exception being the twenty pieces published by Roseingrave in 1728 and 1750. However, they are largely single-movement pieces, many of them fugues, and the registrations can be fairly accurately gauged from the composer's dynamic markings: 8' Diapasons and/or Flute for *piano*, the addition of the 4' Principal for *mezzo*, and full organ through Fifteenth or Mixture for *forte*. The second half of the eighteenth century added a new soft stop (Dulciana) to the organist's palette and expanded the solo stop possibilities somewhat, but there were no substantial changes.

The overall sound of English church organs in this period was still sturdy, bright, and well-balanced—neither retiring nor overpowering, and well suited to rooms with a live acoustic, whether large or small. The Open Diapason is rich and warm, but it is balanced by the rest of the chorus; and the Stopped Diapason has a pleasant "quinty" quality which allows it to blend well. The Dulciana is more a soft Diapason than a string, and all flutes are light in quality. The reeds are quick-speaking and have considerable harmonic development, the Trumpet in particular being of a quality that makes it useful as either a solo or a chorus stop.

Much of the music of this period sounds good on organs of moderate size having a full principal chorus and a few flutes and reeds. In adapting the music to a larger modern organ, it is often wise to choose the principals and reeds of a secondary division if those of the Great are too opaque, gritty, or (in the case of Trumpets) overbearing. If a light 8' flute is not available, it is better to use the 8' Diapason or Principal alone rather than attempt to blend it with an overly loud or foundational Gedeckt. A modern Clarinet (not a loud French Cromorne) or Oboe is usually a good stand-in for the Cremona or Hautboy, but a French Voix Humaine or some of the better German short-length reeds may be closer to the old English Vox Humana than a twentieth-century Vox of the closed-sounding "orchestral" style—it is not always safe to simply go by the name.

A Tierce 1 3/5' or tierce-containing mixture stop is useful in synthesizing a Cornet where no such stop exists, especially on a smaller organ, but stops of 2 2/3' and 2' pitch combined with 8' and 4' flutes are an acceptable substitute for Cornet solos where no Tierce is available. Small organs having no 8' Open Diapason present some problems, although a Gemshorn may be combined with a Rohrflute for a "Diapasons" movement. Many American organs built in the middle of the nineteenth century or earlier (especially from the New York or New England region) are often ideal for eighteenth-century English music, since their design and voicing are an outgrowth of the English style.

Many players still tend to avoid the 8' Diapason tone and to make excessive use of gapped combinations when playing English music (particularly the Handel

Concertos!), even though such combinations were only rarely encountered in the eighteenth century. Similarly, the term "Diapasons" should not be understood as meaning full organ, or the intent of the gentle Adagio movements will be distorted. The player should always attempt to obtain up-to-date editions of the music (fortunately now readily available) which include original registrations, and shun those older editions in which pedal parts and inappropriate registrations have been editorially added.

Composers

Jean-François Babou (1709–17??)
Jacques Boyvin (c1653–1706)
Antoine Calviére (1695–1755)
Marc-Antoine Charpentier (1634–1704)
Lambert Chaumont (fl. 1690s)
Louis-Nicolas Clérambault (1676–1749)
Gaspard Corrette (c1680–c1712)
François Couperin (1668–1733)
François Dagincour (1684–1758)
Jean-François Dandrieu (1682–1738)
Pierre Dandrieu (c1660–1733)
Jean-Henri d'Anglebert (1628–1691)
Louis-Claude Daquin (1694–1772)
Nicolas deGrigny (1672–1703)
Antoine Dornel (c1685–1765)
Pierre DuMage (c1676–1751)
Joseph Hector Fiocco (1703–1741)
Nicolas Gigault (c1627–1707)
Jean-Adam-Guillaume Guilain (fl. c1700)
Gilles Jullien (c1653–1703)
Mathieu Lanes (1660–1725)
Nicolas Lebègue (1630–1702)
Louis Marchand (1669–1732)
Christophe Moyreau (fl. 1743–53)
Guillaume Nivers (1632–1714)
Dieudonné Raick (1702–1764)
André Raison (d. 1719)
Nicolas Siret (d. 1754)

Representative Organs

CATHEDRAL, CHARTRES
Etienne Enocq, 1667 [217, p. 22]

Grand Orgue
Montre 24'
Bourdon 16'
Montre 8'
Bourdon 8'
Prestant 4'
Flûte 4'
Grosse Tierce 3 1/5'
Nasard 2 2/3'
Doublette 2'
Quarte de Nasard 2'
Tierce 1 3/5'
Cornet
Fourniture IV
Cymbale III
Trompette 8'
Voix humaine 8'
Clairon 4'

Pédale
Flûte 8'
Flûte 4'
Trompette 8'

Accessory Stops
2 Tremulants (strong and weak)

Positif
Montre 8'
Bourdon 8'
Prestant 4'
Flûte 4'
Nasard 2 2/3'
Doublette 2'
Quarte de Nasard 2'
Tierce 1 3/5'
Larigot 1 1/3'
Cornet
Fourniture IV
Cymbale III
Cromorne 8'

Echo (34 notes, Tenor F)
Cornet
Cymbale
Cromorne 8'

Récit (treble)
Cornet

CHURCH OF ST. GERVAIS, PARIS
Alexandre Thierry, 1685 [64, p. 6]

Grand Orgue
Montre 16'
Bourdon 16'
Montre 8'
Bourdon 8'
Prestant 4'
Flûte 4'
Grosse Tierce 3 1/5'
Nasard 2 2/3'
Tierce 1 3/5'
Fourniture III
Cymbale III
Cornet (from Middle C)
Trompette 8'
Clairon 4'
Voix humaine 8'

Positif
Bourdon 8'
Montre 4'
Flûte 4'
Nasard 2 2/3'
Doublette 2'
Tierce 1 3/5'
Larigot 1 1/3'
Fourniture III
Cymbale III

Echo (from Tenor C)
Cornet III
Cymbale
Cromorne 8'

Cornet (from Tenor C)
Cornet séparé

Pédale
Flûte 8'
Flûte 4'
Trompette 8'

Accessory Stops
Tremulants
Coupler: Positif to Grand Orgue

CHURCH OF ST. DENIS, ROUEN
Clément & Germain Lefebvre, 1688–98 [39, p. 92]

Grand Orgue	**Positif**
Bourdon 16' (wood bass)	Bourdon 16' (wood bass)
Montre 8' (tin)	Prestant 4' (tin)
Bourdon 8' (wood bass)	Flûte 4' (stopped, metal)
Prestant 4' (tin)	Nasard 2 2/3'
Flûte 4' (stopped, metal)	Doublette 2' (tin)
Nasard 2 2/3'	Quart de nasard 2'
Doublette 2' (tin)	Tierce 1 3/5'
Tierce 1 3/5'	Larigot 1 1/3'
Cornet V	Fourniture III
Fourniture IV	Cymbale II
Cymbale III	Cromorne 8'
Trompette 8'	
Cleron 4'	**Cornet d'Echo** (Tenor F)
Voix humaine 8'	Bourdon 8'
	Prestant 4'
Cornet de Récit (Middle C)	Nasard 2 2/3'
Cornet V	Doublette 2'
Trompette 8'	Tierce 1 3/5'
	Cromorne 8'
Pedalle	Voix humaine 8'
Bourdon 8' (wood)	
Flûte 4' (open)	

Accessory Stops
Tremblant doux (mild)
Tremblant à vent perdu (strong)

ABBEY CHURCH, EBERSMUNSTER, ALSACE
Andreas Silbermann, 1730–32 [3, p. 196]

Grand Orgue	**Positif**
Bourdon 16'	Bourdon 8'
Montre 8'	Prestant 4'
Bourdon 8'	Nasard 2 2/3'
Prestant 4'	Doublette 2'
Nasard 2 2/3'	Tierce 1 3/5'
Doublette 2'	Fourniture III
Tierce 1 3/5'	Cromorne 8'

Fourniture III
Cymbale III
Trompette 8' (divided)
Voix humaine 8'
Clairon 4'

Récit (from Middle C)
Bourdon 8'
Prestant 4'
Cornet III
Trompette 8'

Pédale
Subbass 16' (open wood)
Octave 8' (open wood)
Bombarde 16'
Trompette 8'
Clairon 4'

Accessory Stops
2 Tremblants
Coupler: Positif to Grande Orgue

[N.B. Although the manual divisions are virtually indistinguishable from those of Parisian organs, the 16' Pedal division marks this instrument as Alsatian.]

CHURCH OF ST. JACQUES, HOUDAN
Louis-Alexandre Cliquot, 1734 [25, p. 38]

Grand Orgue
Montre 8'
Bourdon 8'
Prestant 4'
Nasard 2 2/3'
Doublette 2'
Quarte [de nasard] 2'
Tierce 1 3/5'
Cornet V (treble)
Fourniture IV (1 1/3')
Trompette 8'
Clairon 4'
Voix humaine 8'

Positif (interior)
Bourdon 8'
Flûte 4'
Nasard 2 2/3'
Doublette 2'
Tierce 1 3/5'
Plein Jeu V (1')
Cromorne 8'

Récit (from Middle C)
Cornet V
Trompette 8'

Pédale
2 octaves, coupled to Grand Orgue

Accessory Stops
Tremblant doux, Tremblant fort
Tiroir (Shove coupler, Positif to Grand Orgue)

PARISH CHURCH, ST. QUIRIN, MOSELLE
J. A. Silbermann, 1746 [86, p. 70]

Grand Orgue
Bourdon 8'
Prestant 4'
Flûte 4'
Nasard 2 2/3'
Doublette 2'
Tierce 1 3/5'

Écho (from Middle C)
Bourdon 8'
Prestant 4'
Cornet III

Pédale
Bourdon 8'
Trompette 8'

Cornet V (treble)
Fourniture III
Cymbale II
Cromorne 8' (divided)

Accessory Stops
Tremblant doux

CHURCH OF NOTRE-DAME DE GUIBRAY, FALAISE
Henri Parisot, 1752 [86, p. 32]

Grand Orgue
Bourdon 16'
Montre 8'
Bourdon 8'
Flûte 8'
Prestant 4'
Nasard 2 2/3'
Doublette 2'
Tierce 1 3/5'
Larigot 1 1/3'
Cornet V (treble)
Plein Jeu IV
Cymbale III
Trompette 8'
Voix humaine 8'
Clairon 4'

Pédale
Soubasse 16'
Flûte 8'
Flûte 4'
Trompette 8'
Clairon 4'

Positif
Bourdon 8'
Dessus de flûte (treble)
Prestant 4'
Flûte 4'
Nasard 2 2/3'
Doublette 2'
Quarte [de nasard] 2'
Tierce 1 3/5'
Plein Jeu III
Cymbale II
Cromorne 8'

Récit
(from Middle C)
Cornet V
Trompette 8'

Écho
(from Tenor G)
Cornet V
Hautbois 8'

Accessory Stops
[Not given, but presumably they included tremulants and a Positif–Grande Orgue coupler.]

Registration

The French organ of the Baroque period was a gradual and natural outgrowth of the Renaissance organ, but around the middle of the seventeenth century some important additions were being grafted onto the basic matrix. The Grosse Tierce 3 1/5' is first recorded in an organ built by Enocq in 1660 for the church of the Jacobins in Paris (which also had a 16' Bourdon), and around the turn of the century the Hautbois made its first appearance. In 1647 we have the earliest recorded instance of a third manual (the Écho) at Chartres Cathedral and the Church of St. Merry in Paris. To this latter organ Thierry added a fourth manual, called Récit, in 1664, and organs of four manuals became common in large churches and cathedrals from this time onward.

Another development of the 1660s was the use of double channels in the windchests of some organs to allow the borrowing of the 8' Trompette from the Grand Orgue to the Pedal in organs not large enough to have an independent Pedal Trompette, such as the compact but versatile Cliquot organ in Houdan [240, pp. 22–27].

It is important to note, however, that the third and fourth manuals which appeared in the mid-seventeenth century were not, as in Germanic countries, of full compass, nor did they commonly contain more than two or three stops. They never extended below tenor G or F, and in many instances began no lower than middle C. The basic instrument was still essentially a two-manual organ, with the Récit and Écho little more than registrational aids, making available the most common solo stops (usually Cornet and Trompette) without the necessity of changing stops on the two main manuals. As the Écho was located in a box (not, in this period, expressive), it provided, as its name implies, a quieter echo of the solo stops located in the other divisions.

The Pedal too was largely used as a solo division, save where a unison (8') flue bass was needed. Sixteen-foot Pedal stops were rare save in some Alsatian instruments, even up to the end of the eighteenth century, and then usually only in larger organs. The eighteenth century brought some additions but no real changes in the overall scheme. The Hautbois (Oboe) and open Flûte 8' (as distinct from the stopped metal Bourdon) began to appear around mid-century. As early as 1733 the large organ in Notre-Dame of Paris acquired a fifth manual, the Bombarde, which controlled a single strong 16' reed on its own windchest. However, even an instrument of this size still had no 16' Pedal stop beyond the Bombarde, which was not independent but was borrowed from the fifth manual. [63]

The year 1662 may well be regarded as a turning point in French liturgical music. Before then, only Titelouze had published a volume of music expressly for the church service, although some works of this type by Louis Couperin and some lower Netherlands composers exist in manuscript. What little else we have consists largely of secular works and fantasias that could be played by instrumental ensembles as well as on the organ. In 1661 the *Caeremoniale Parisiense* was published, and although some earlier ceremonials (handbooks of church ritual) had mentioned the use of the organ in the mass, the 1662 Paris ceremonial determined the role of the great west-gallery organ in the liturgy until the end of the eighteenth century.

This development, in turn, led to the publication of a remarkable succession of *livres d'orgue* containing music for the mass and the office hymns according to the Paris ceremonial. Many of them contained directions for the registration of organs that were, especially in Paris and Normandy, already very standardized in tonal design. These directions, or tables, spell out in detail the combinations of stops that make up the shorthand registration formulae in the titles of the pieces. A chronological listing of these organ books by composer includes the following (*indicates prefatory registration tables):

Nivers: *1665, 1667, 1675
Lebègue: *1676, *1678, 1685, 1688
Gigault: *1685

Raison: ★1688
Boyvin: ★1689
F. Couperin: 1690
Jullien: ★1690
Chaumont: ★1695
deGrigny: 1699
Corrette: ★1703, ★1737
Guilain: 1706
DuMage: 1708
Clérambault: 1710
Marchand: c1732
Dandrieu: c1738

The music in these collections was composed expressly for liturgical use, although the format varies. Boyvin's organ book is organized into "suites" according to the eight church tones. Couperin's two masses ("for parish churches" and "for convents") each contain short pieces intended for alternatim use in the various parts of the mass (Kyrie, Gloria, Sanctus, Agnus Dei, and Deo Gratias) plus a longer and more virtuosic offertoire, which exploits more fully the power and variety of the organ. DeGrigny gives us both a mass and alternatim settings of five office hymns. Later composers such as DuMage and Clérambault revert to the organization of pieces in suites on various church tones, but Guilain's suites are based on the Magnificat.

With the exception of offertoires and dialogues, most of the pieces in these collections are fairly short. What distinguishes them is the actual or implied references to registration in their titles—*Basse de Cromorne, Récit de Nasard, Tierce en taille, Basse et dessus de Trompette, Dialogue sur les grands jeux,* etc. Most of the later organ books did not contain registration tables. While many of the registrational titles in these books are explicit, it would appear that the composers assumed that by this time all organists knew the formulas, as indeed they undoubtedly did. For present-day organists, however, brought up in different traditions and not playing standardized organs, those composers who provided registration tables have performed a valuable service.

The earliest organ books with registration directions are those of Nivers and Lebègue. Nivers gives us the compositions of some of the most basic registrations, but Lebègue goes into greater detail and also gives suggestions concerning musical applications. Juxtaposed, they provide a fairly consistent picture of the practices of the late seventeenth century, which, as later registration lists confirm, continued well into the eighteenth century. In the following summary, [N] = Nivers; [L] = Lebègue:

Plein jeu: Bourdon 8', Prestant 4', Doublette 2', Fourniture, Cymbale; with Montre 16' and Bourdon 16' when available. Used for playing preludes and *Plein jeu* pieces [N]. May also include the Bourdon 16' [L]. Note that reeds, quints, and tierces are not used in this combination in these early sources. Prelude and *Plein jeu* pieces are to be played slowly and, if on the Positif, lightly [L]. Raison concurs, stating that the *Grand plein jeu* should be played slowly and legato, and Boyvin recommends that the two main manuals be coupled.

Jeu de tierce: Bourdon 8', Prestant 4', Quinte 2 2/3' and Tierce 1 3/5'; may also include the Doublette 2' and Montres 16' and 8' [N]. With the Doublette, but without the Montres, this combination is used in duos and trios [L]. With the Montre and the Tremulant it is suitable for *Fugues graves*, and Nivers calls this the *Gros jeu de tierce*. Chaumont makes the distinction between the *Fugue grave* and the less frequently encountered *Fugue gaye*, preferring a reed combination for the former and the *Petit jeu de tierce* (i.e., without Montre) for the latter. It will be seen from this that there is more than one *Jeu de tierce,* and the type employed depends on the musical application.

Grand jeu: The *Jeu de tierce*, with Montres, to which is added the Trompette 8', Clairon 4', Cromorne 8', and Cornet — and also the *Tremblant fort* [N]. Lebègue adds *Grand jeu* combinations for the Positif (Bourdon 8', Montre 4', Nasard 2 2/3', Doublette 2', Tierce 1 3/5') and Écho (Bourdon 8', Prestant 4', Nasard 2 2/3', Doublette 2', Tierce 1 3/5', Voix humaine or Cromorne), all with the strong tremulant [L]. Gigault and Raison also require the strong tremulant for the Grand jeu. Note that there are no chorus mixtures in these combinations; this may explain why the tremulant, which was prohibited in earlier times with any kind of full organ registration, is permissible here.

Jeu doux: There are several possibilities: Bourdon 8' and Flûte 4'; Bourdon 8' and Montre 8'; Bourdon 8' and Prestant 4' ("a little stronger"); the same with Doublette 2', Montre 8', or even a 16' flue stop ("still stronger") [N]. These may be used alone, but they are usually accompaniment registrations, to be used against reeds or the Cornet, and the particular *Jeu doux* chosen should balance well with the stops to be accompanied.

Duos: *Petit [jeu de] tierce* (treble) and *Grosse tierce* (bass); or Cornet (treble) and Trompette (bass) [N]. Positif *Jeu de tierce* against Grand Orgue *Grosse tierce* with Bourdon 16' (in large organs). Duos should be played "boldly and quickly" [L]. Raison concurs with these combinations, but also adds Cornet against Bourdon 8' with Flûte or Prestant 4' as another possibilty.

Trios: These are not mentioned by Nivers, but Lebègue cites two kinds: the *Trio à deux dessus* (trio with two trebles) and the *Trio à trois claviers* (trio on three keyboards). In the former, the bass is played on the Grand Orgue *Jeu de tierce* and mild tremulant, or on the Trompette alone. The two treble parts are played on the Positif, with either the Cromorne alone (Flute or Principal 8' or Flute 4' may be added if it is not strong enough), or on the Positif *Jeu de tierce*. In the latter type of trio, the third keyboard is the Pedal, using the 8' Flûte (in French organs, actually a mild Principal). The top part may be played on a Cornet or *Jeu de tierce* on either manual, the middle part on another manual with a Cromorne or Voix humaine plus Bourdon 8', Prestant 4', and Tremulant. Another version gives the top part to the Trompette 8' and the middle part on the Positif *Jeu de tierce*, but in all instances the bass part is played on the Pedal Flûte 8'. Raison cites similar Trio registrations, as do Boyvin, Chaumont, and Corrette. Gigault alone cites an optional scheme for playing a *Trio à deux dessus,* although a Grand Orgue with some divided stops is required: Top part on Grand Orgue (no registration given—Cornet?); middle part on the Positif Cromorne, played with the right thumb; and bottom part on the

Grand Orgue with a *Jeu de tierce*. This may well be the earliest reference to the practice of "thumbing" (later to be used in Quatuors), although it was clearly the exception and not the rule.

Fugues graves: To be played on the *Gros jeu de tierce* with tremulant, or Trompette without tremulant [N]. Here Lebègue differs somewhat, recommending Bourdon 8', Prestant 4', Trompette 8', and Clairon 4', or, on smaller organs, Bourdon 8' and Cromorne 8' [L]. Boyvin echoes Lebègue, but without the Clairon, and adds the 4' flue color to the "small organ" registration. Chaumont adds the Nasard to the Trompette combination, and Corrette suggests that the two main manuals be coupled.

Dialogues: Nivers does not mention Dialogues, but virtually every other writer does. Lebègue gives three *Grand jeux* (Grand Orgue: Bourdon 8', Prestant 4', Trompette 8', and Cornet, the same with the Clairon 4' substituted for the Cornet, or the full *Grand jeu* described above, including the strong tremulant), and two *Petit jeux* (Positif: Bourdon 8', Montre 4', and Cromorne 8', or the same with Nasard 2 2/3' and Tierce 1 3/5' added). Raison and Boyvin both state that dialogues should use all four manuals when available, or at least three, although they can also be played on a two-manual organ. It is in the more elaborate dialogues (as well as in the offertoires of Marchand, Couperin, and others) that one can most easily understand the usefulness of the two short-compass solo divisions, since they eliminate the necessity of changing stops anywhere in the piece. Some version of the Grand Jeu appropriate to each division is always indicated, however, and a little later, in 1703, Corrette requires that the two main manuals (Grand Orgue, Positif) be coupled (the others were incapable of being coupled in organs of this period).

Quatuors: A few isolated pieces with this title appear around the end of the seventeenth century and in the early eighteenth. They are clearly designed to show off an organist's skill (several writers warn that they are not easy to play!) as well as to display all the colors of the French four-manual organ. The precursor of these pieces was a single Quatuor published by d'Anglebert around 1660, based on a Kyrie. With its suspensions and overlapping themes it is more like a composition for strings than for keyboard, and indeed all the organ Quatuors have a certain "non-organ" character to them. D'Anglebert, while not citing registrations, specifies that the four parts should be played on three manuals plus pedal, "with stops of equal weight but different timbre" [151, p. 123]. Other quatuors occur in the works of Guilain (1706) and Marchand (c1732)—all, like d'Anglebert's, fugal, and scored on four staves for three manuals and pedal. Jullien mentions quatuors in his preface, but he is referring only to his four-part fugues, which he suggests can be played with soprano and alto on the Grand Orgue (Cornet séparé) and tenor and bass on the Positif (Bourdon 8', Prestant 4', Cromorne 8') or some variation of this, and with the mild tremulant. Boyvin also refers to four-part fugues as quatuors and suggests as an alternative to Jullien's method, the playing of the top and bottom parts on the Grand Orgue *Jeu de tierce*, especially if there is a manual to pedal coupler (not all organs had this!), and the two middle parts on the Positif Cromorne with the 8' flues. But he also suggests the method d'Anglebert hints at, which may be indicated in all quatuors written on four staves: playing on three manuals and pedal, with

Bourdon 8', Prestant 4', and Nasard 2 2/3' on the Grand Orgue; *Jeu de tierce* on the Positif; and Trompette 8' on the Récit. This registration implies some thumbing, but as we have seen, this practice had already been suggested by Gigault for trios a few years earlier.

Récits, Tailles, Basses, and Basse et Dessus pieces: Nivers lumps these works together with diminutions, echos, and cornets, stating that while the registrations are given in the music, "they can all be changed and played on other combinations at one's discretion, and according to the specification of the organ" [39, p. 179]. He does, however, note that the Voix humaine should be combined with the Bourdon 8', with optional Flûte 4' and mild tremulant. The Nasard may also be added [N]. If the Voix humaine is in the bass, then the treble should be played on a suitable *Jeu doux*, but if it is in the treble, the bass should be a Cornet (presumably the Cornet séparé) or a Bourdon 8', Montre or Flûte 4', and Nasard 2 2/3'. Voix humaine pieces are to be played slowly, in a singing style [L]. Raison and Boyvin concur with these suggestions, although in place of the Cornet, Boyvin suggests a *Jeu de tierce.*

Lebègue, whose treatment of solo registrations is more detailed than Nivers's, characterizes the *Basse de trompette* as "hearty" (Raison calls it "bold"; Corrette "daring"). To the Trompette stop may be added the Bourdon 8' and Montre 4', with the Bourdon 8' and Prestant 4' of the secondary manual for accompaniment. But pieces of this type may also be played on the Positif Cromorne 8' with the Montre 8', Nasard 2 2/3', and Tierce 1 3/5' added, accompanied by 8' and 4' stops on the Grand Orgue. For a *Dessus de trompette,* however, only the Bourdon 8' should be added to the Trompette stop, and it should be accompanied on the Bourdon 8' and Montre 4' of the Positif [L]. Raison cites a similar *Basse de trompette,* but also suggests a somewhat unusual alternative: Clairon 4' and Bourdon 16'. Boyvin would augment the Trompette stop with the Prestant 4' and Nasard 2 2/3', regarding the 8' Bourdon as too sluggish in speech, and adds the option of the strong tremulant— the only composer to do so.

The Cromorne is a versatile stop, used for solos in the bass, the treble, and the tenor (*en taille*). For treble solos it is combined with a Bourdon 8' and accompanied on a *Jeu doux* of 8', or 8' and 4'. For a tenor solo it is combined with the Bourdon 8', Montre 4', and Nasard 2 2/3' (Corrette omits the Nasard); with an 8' and 4' *Jeu doux* in the treble and 8' Flûte in the Pedal. In the treble, the Cromorne solo is "sweet and agreeable" (Raison says "tender"), but in the tenor it is "serious" [L]. Raison is of the opinion that when it is played in the treble the Cromorne may be used alone, but Chaumont states that when it is used for a bass solo it should be combined with the Montre 4', Nasard 2 2/3', and Tierce 1 3/5', and played more boldly. Corrette makes a revealing statement concerning the Cromorne in the bass: "The *Basse de Cromhorne* imitates the bowings, nuances, and passage-work of the *Basse de Violle*" [39, p. 196]. The orchestral connection seems never to have been very far from the minds of the French organists.

The *Tierce en taille* is one of the unique solo registrations; it is the indicated registration for some of the most expressive compositions in the French literature of the seventeenth and eighteenth centuries. Indeed, Lebègue refers to *Tierce en taille* versets as "the most beautiful and distinctive of all organ pieces," and Corrette says that they should be played with nuance and movement [39, p. 181, 196]. The solo registration consists of Bourdon 8', Montre 4', Flûte 4', Nasard 2 2/3', Doublette 2', Tierce 1 3/5', and Larigot 1 1/3' on the Positif, accompanied in the right hand (Grand Orgue) by Bourdon 8', Prestant 4', and possibly the 16' Bourdon or Montre, and with the Flûte 8' on the Pedal. Chaumont cites an almost identical registration, as does Corrette, although both regard a 16' stop on the accompaniment manual as obligatory.

Around the turn of the century more solo registrations appear. Boyvin in 1689 and Corrette in 1703 mention the *Récit de nasard* (Bourdon 8', Prestant 4', and Nasard 2 2/3' on the Positif, against an 8' and 4' *Jeu doux*), and *Dessus de petit tierce* (the same, with Tierce 1 3/5' added). The former was popular with some of the eighteenth-century composers, notably Clérambault.

An anonymous c1710–20 manuscript from Tours adds the 2' stops to the Nasard combination and cites some imitative combinations not called for in any known music. They are reminiscent of certain combinations from the previous period, which may have lingered on in some areas south of Paris: *Flageollet* (Bourdon 8', Flageolet 2'), *Violon* (Prestant 4', Flûte 4', Clairon 4'), *Bombarde* (Montre 8', Bourdon 8', Flûte 4', Clairon 4') and *Musette* (Montre 8', Doublette 2', Nasard 2 2/3', Tierce 1 3/5', and Larigot 1 1/3') [236, p. 215]. They include almost the only examples of gapped combinations (i.e., those skipping pitches in the harmonic series) found in French sources and were perhaps intended for use in transcriptions, improvisations, or secular pieces.

Corrette's instructions of 1703 and 1737 are the earliest sources for certain other combinations, largely non-solo, which are called for in his and others' music after 1700. They include the *Fond d'orgue* or *Jeu de fond* (flutes and principals 16', 8', and 4', main two manuals coupled), *Les flûtes* (Flûte Almande 8', Montre 8', Bourdon 4' with tremulant; Flûtes and Bourdons in the Pedal), and *Musette* (Cromorne alone played by both hands, with 8' Flûte in the Pedal). The last, rather than the Tours combination, is the *Musette* called for in works of Dandrieu and others.

The Flûte Almand (later called Flûte à biberon = "bottle flute") was a chimneyed flute; it also appears in a trio combination (*Jeu de flûte*), where the *Flûtes* combination previously cited is drawn on both Grand Orgue and Positif, with Flûte 8' and Bourdon 8' on the Pedal, and mild tremulant. There is only one earlier reference to an all-flute combination, Boyvin's *Concert de fluste,* for which the 8' and 4' flutes on both main manuals are drawn, with the mild tremulant, and the manuals are coupled. Corrette was the last of the composers to include detailed registration tables in an organ book.

A very different type of source comes to us from Alsace, dated 1746. This manuscript relates to the Andreas Silbermann organ in Marmoutier and may even have originated with the builder himself. Although it is generally in line with Parisian usages, it is the one source to mention the 16' Pedal stops, which came into general use earlier in Alsace than in the western area. The only real surprise is the use of the Cromorne as the basis for the *Tierce en taille,* and the 4'-based accompaniments for the *Basse de Trompette.* The following combinations are described:

Grand jeu. Grand Orgue: [Montre 8'], Prestant 4', Nazard 2 2/3', Tierce 1 3/5', Gros Cornet, Trompette 8', Clairon 4'. Positif: Similar to Grand Orgue but with Cromorne 8', coupled to Grand Orgue. Pedal: Bombarde 16', Trompette 8', Clairon 4' (Grand Orgue coupled).

Plein Jeu. Grand Orgue: Montre 8', Bourdons 16', 8', and 4', Prestant 4', Doublette 2', Fourniture, Cimballe. Positif: similar to Grand Orgue. Pedal: Bombarde 16', Trompette 8', Clairon 4'.

Duos. 1. Grand Orgue: Cornet (treble); Positif: Cromorne with Prestant 4' and Bourdon 4' (bass). 2. Grand Orgue: Montre 8', Prestant 4', Bourdon 4', Nazard 2 2/3', Tierce 1 3/5' (treble); Positif: Montre 8', Bourdon 4', Nazard 2 2/3', Tierce 1 3/5' (bass).

Récit de Cornet. Grand Orgue: Cornet (treble). Positif: Montre 8' and Bourdon 4' (bass).

Récit de Tierce. Positif: Montre 8', Prestant 4', Bourdon 4', Nazard 2 2/3', Tierce 1 3/5' (treble). Grand Orgue: Montre 8', Bourdon 4' (bass).

Tierce en taille. Grand Orgue: Montre 8' and Bourdon 4'. Positif: Prestant 4', Doublette 2', Nazard 2 2/3', Tierce 2 3/5', Cromorne 8'. Pedal: Bourdon 8'.

Basse de Trompette. 1. Grand Orgue: Both Trompettes 8' and Clairons 4', with Prestant 4'; Positif: Prestant 4', Doublette 2', Larigot 1 3/5'. 2. Grand Orgue: Trompette 8', Clairon 4', Prestant 4'; Positif: Bourdon 4' and Larigot 1 1/3'.

Jeu de flûte, Trio. Grand Orgue: Montre 8', Flute Almande 4', Bourdon 4'. Positif: "the same." Pedal: Bourdon 16', Flûte 8'. Mild tremulant with this combination.

Prelude. "All the Bourdons, Montre, Fourniture, Simballe, Prestant, 16 foot [stops]" [40, p. 683]. This is virtually the same as the *Plein jeu,* but perhaps it refers to a specific usage.

In France, as in England, it was the late seventeenth century that set the pattern for virtually all of the eighteenth century, both in organ design and in registration conventions. The key was color—in the design and voicing of the organs, and in the distinctive liturgical compositions which exploited that color. The organs of this period possess warm Principals and Flutes, assertive Cornets, and intense reeds that, in addition to their solo functions, are intended to add a very characteristic blaze to the chorus. Even the cylindrical reed, the Cromorne, is stronger than similar reeds in other countries; it is meant to do for the Positif chorus what the Trumpet does for the chorus of the Grand Orgue. Most French churches are fairly large buildings, often with masonry ceilings, and perhaps no style of organ demands a reverberant room more than does the French organ.

The distinctive sounds of the French classic organ are not always easy to approximate on modern organs. However, since the 1960s, various North American builders have been producing instruments which to some degree take the needs of this literature into account. A variety of mutations is essential, as is the Tierce color (alone or in a Cornet or Sesqualtera), but even without these features many of the *Jeu doux, Flûtes,* and reed-solo pieces can be played if a few lightly voiced and bright stops in these categories are available. This usage is particularly important in the choice of Trumpet stops; unfortunately one is sometimes subjected in recitals to a parody of a *Basse et dessus de Trompette* hammered out on a modern ear-splitting high-pressure horizontal Trumpet, totally out of balance with the rest of the organ.

It is also important to know that the mutations and Cornets of a French classic organ are of a wider (fluty) scale rather than the narrower principal scale. Thus narrow-scaled mutations found in many modern "neo-baroque" organs, which may be the only mutations available, can give an unnatural edginess to certain combinations, especially if the prohibitions against gapped combinations are ignored—it is not unusual to hear a piece calling for a *Jeu de Nasard* played on a Flute 8' and Quint 2 2/3', without the mandatory 4'.

French 8' principals are not overpowering, and they tend toward a warm timbre; an authentic 8' Montre is refreshingly devoid of edginess and "sizzle." With the 8' Bourdon it provides a solid if unobtrusive foundation for the various full organ combinations. In organs with too little foundation, multiple 8' stops may be needed to achieve this effect; in organs with overly heavy foundations, more lightly voiced 8' stops should be used to achieve the desired top-to-bottom balance.

Perhaps one of the most problematic areas is the use of the tremulant. Few modern organs give one the choice of a mild and a strong tremulant, although some do have adjustable tremulants. While most tremulants (if not too fast or "chattery") will be satisfactory in the softer flute or solo registrations, they may not be appropriate for the louder registrations with which they were sometimes used, and it will be better to leave them off. The player's taste and discretion are important here.

On organs not really designed to allow for French music one will of necessity have to experiment and make adjustments, but, as Joseph Sauveur wrote in 1704,

> One does not draw stops indifferently . . . but one is guided first according to the nature of the pieces that are played which require differing registrations, and second according to the taste and caprice of the organist, who, in the manner of cooks, prefer their stews to be more or less piquant. [263, p. 16]

But piquant in some degree, and always containing certain essential ingredients.

13   *Italy*

Composers

Tommasi Giovanni Albinoni (1671–1750)
Giulio Cesare Aresti (1617–1692/4)
Floriano Arresti (d. 1719)
Giovanni Battista Bassani (c1657–1716)
Giovanni Maria Casini (c1670–1715)
Giovanni Paolo Colonna (1637–1695)
A. B. Della Ciaia (1671–1755)
Francesco Durante (1684–1755)
Francesco Feroci (1673–1750)
Fabrizio Fontana (d. 1695)
Antonio Lotti (c1667–1740)
Benedetto Marcello (1686–1739)
Domenico Palafuti (fl. mid-eighteenth century)
Bernardo Pasquini (1637–1710)
Jacopo Antonio Perti (1661–1756)
Giovanni Battista Pescetti (1704–1766)
Carlo Francesco Pollaroli (c1653–1722)
Nicolo Antonio Porpora (1686–1768)
Domenico Scarlatti (1685–1757)
Antonio Vivaldi (1678–1741)
Pietro Andrea Ziani (c1630–1711)
Domenico Zipoli (1688–1726)

Representative Organs

CHURCH OF SANTA MARIA LATERINA, AREZZO
Unknown builder, c1700 [37, p. 65]

Manuale
Principale 4'
Ottava 2'
Duodecima 1 1/3'
Decimaquinta 1'

[N.B. This is a typical Italian 4' positive.]

CHURCH OF S. TOMMASO CANTUARIENSE, VERONA
Giuseppe Bonatti, 1716 [108, p. 248]

Grand' Organo
Principale 8' (divided)
Voce umana 8' (treble?)
Fluta reale 8'
Ottava 4'
Flauto in ottava 4'
Decimaseconda 2 2/3'
Flauto in duodecima 2 2/3'
Decimaquinta 2'
Decimanona 1 1/3'
Vigesimaseconda 1'
Vigesimasesta 2/3'
Vigesimanona 1/2'
Trigesimaterza e sesta 1/3' & 1/4'
Cornetto II/III (2' - 1 3/5')
Pastorale 8' (regal)

Positivo Tergale
Principale in eco 4' (st. flute)
Frazolé 2' (flute)
Ottava 1'
Duodecima doppia 2/3' & 1/2'

Accessory Stops
Grillo I and II (cricket)
Rosignuolo (bird)
Tiratutti (pleno combination, presumed to be a later addition)

[N.B. A three-stop Pedale was added to this organ in 1786.]

MONASTERY OF S. CATERINA, SAN MARCELLO PISTOIESE
D. F. Cacioli, 1730 [147, p. 248]

Manuale
Principale Fisso 8'
Voce Umana 8' (treble)
Ottava 4'
Decimaquinta 2'
Decimanona 1 1/3'
Vigesimaseconda and sesta 1' and 2/3'

CHURCH OF S. GIUSTINA, PADUA
Pietro Nacchini, 1737 [60, p. 21]

Organo Grande
Principale primo 8'
Principale secondo 8'
Voce umana 8' (treble?)
Ottava prima 4'
Ottava seconda 4'
Flauto in ottava 4'
Decimaseconda 2 2/3'
Flauto in dodecima 2 2/3'
Decimaquinta 2'
Flauto in quintadecima 2'
Decimasettima 1 3/5'
Decimanona 1 1/3'
Vigesimaseconda 1'
Vigesimasesta 2/3'
Vigesimanona 1/2'
Trigesimasesta 1/4'
Cornetta (divided)
Tromboncini 8' (divided)
Fagotti 8'? (treble?)

Accessory Stops
Bells
Drum
Birds
Tiratutti (draws plenum)
Fistara (? possibly drone?)

Organo di Riposta (Positive)
Principale 8'
Voce umana 8' (treble?)
Ottava 4'
Flauto in ottava 4'
Decimaquinta 2'
Flauto in quintadecima 2'
Decimanona 1 1/3'
Vigesimaseconda 1'
Vigesimasesta 2/3'
Cornetta (treble?)
Tromboncini bassi (8' or 4'?)

Pedale
Contrabassi 16'
Contrabassi in duodecima 4'

OSPEDALETTO, VENICE
Pietro Nacchini, 1751 [208, p. 4]

Manuale
Principale 8' (divided)
Voce umana 8'
Ottava 4'
Flauto in ottava 4'
Flauto in duodecima 2 2/3'
Quintadecima 2'
Ottavina soprani 2' (treble flute; originally a Cornetta)
Decimanona 1 1/3'
Vigesimaseconda 1'
Vigesimasesta 2/3'
Vigesimanona 1/2'
Trigesimaterza 1/3'
Trigesimasesta 1/4'
Tromboncino 8' (divided)

Pedale
Contrabassi 16'
Ottava 8'

Accessory Stops
Tremolo
Timballi (drum)
Tiratutti

CHURCH OF S. MARIA DELLE GRAZIE, PISTOIA
Antonio and Filippo Tronci, 1755 [147, p. 180]

Manuale	**Pedale**
Principale 8' (doubled in treble)	Contrabassi 16'
Voce Umana 8' (treble)	
Ottava 4'	
Flauto 4'	
Decimaquinta 2'	
Decimanona 1 1/3'	
Vigesimaseconda & Vigesimasesta 1' and 2/3'	
Cornetto 2 2/3' and 2' (treble)	
Trombe 8' (divided)	

Accessory Stops
Tremolo
Timpano (drum)
Tirapieno (pleno combination)

Registration

Both organ building and organ composition seem to have lost momentum in Italy after the deaths of such masters as Frescobaldi, Merula, and Trabaci. The only composers of real stature and significant output in the subsequent period were Bernardo Pasquini and his pupil Domenico Zipoli, both of whom wrote in a style that combined the old with tantalizing hints of the new. The best-known composer, Domenico Scarlatti, regrettably left very little in the way of organ music, although at least three (and possibly as many as eight) of his 555 keyboard sonatas can with some certainty be identified as organ pieces (although perhaps they were intended only for chamber organ) [249, p. 91].

It is not unusual in the music of this period to find traditional canzonas, toccatas, versets, ricercares, and elevations interspersed with newer and lighter forms—such as the pastorale, the lively postcommunio, and the virtuosic offertorio—or with pieces such as Pasquini's *Toccata con lo Scherzo del cuccu*, with its ingenuous bird imitations.

The organs built in this period were still firmly rooted in the early seventeenth-century style. Foreign influences continued to make their presence felt, however. Willem Hermans, a Fleming, settled in Genoa in 1648, and his northern European influence was subtly felt for a long period of time in Tuscany and the surrounding area. Eugenio Casparini, an Austrian or central German who circulated from central Germany to northern Italy after the 1670s, also left his mark. Particularly influential in the North was Pietro Nacchini (Petar Nakich), a Dalmatian active in Venice from around 1729, where he ultimately built over 200 organs. All these builders worked mainly within the older Italian tradition, although in northern Italy these central European expatriates were undoubtedly responsible for the larger number of organs built with more than one manual, and the more frequent occurrence of reed stops.

The typical Italian organ continued to be a one-manual instrument (occasionally quite sizable) with many *Ripieno* mutations, sometimes with the addition of a small Positivo and/or a short-compass Pedale of one or two stops. A large four-manual and pedal organ with an unsually large complement of reeds was built in 1733 by Azzolino della Ciaia for the Church of St. Stephen in Pisa, but it was decidedly an exception [60, p. 20]. However, by the early eighteenth century one begins to find the 2 2/3' principal mutation in 8' organs occurring more frequently, and a greater variety of flutes, although usually all still 4' and above in pitch, save in the work of Hermans.

Hermans and Casparini were probably responsible for the introduction of the third-sounding mutation (Tierce) in the second half of the seventeenth century, although it was more likely to appear as part of a compound stop (Cornet or Sesquialtera). In the early eighteenth century compound stops containing the Tierce appeared regularly in the work of Nacchini as well as in organs by the Italian-born builders Bonatti and Traeri, but only rarely did the Tierce (Decimasettima) appear as an independent chorus mutation [272, pp. 3–5] .

The short-length Tromboncino remained the most widespread reed stop, although full-length reeds do appear in organs built or influenced by the non-Italian builders, largely north of Rome. Save in the very largest organs, the pedal remained rudimentary—of short compass and containing only one or two bass stops. Less is known about the organs of southern Italy than those of northern Italy in this period, but in general the southern organs appear to have been more conservative in style, with fewer "concertino" stops or other transalpine influences.

The Renaissance-style "toy" stops—birds, bells, drum, and drone—remained in use. But a useful new registrational aid began to appear during the first half of the eighteenth century. Called *Tiratutti* or *Tirapieno*, it was a knob that drew or retired the upperwork of the full Ripieno, making quick dynamic changes and echo effects possible.

No registration treatises have been found from this period, but there is every reason to believe that, despite some minor changes in the nature of the tonal resources, the basic directions of Antegnati, Diruta, and Banchieri are still applicable. The few directions left by organists and organ builders in the late seventeenth century tend to confirm this assumption. Directions pertaining to an organ of c1691 in the Basilica of S. Antonio in Padua repeat the prohibition on the use of flutes in the Ripieno, as does another, dated 1697, from the Church of the Carmine in Padua. The latter also confirms the continuing use of the Voce Umana ("so noble a register") for slower music [90, pp. 87–88].

References to the use of the Cornetto appear in a booklet published in connection with a two-manual organ built by Casparini in 1687 for a church in Trent. It explains that while the manuals might be coupled, they should normally be used separately to play dialogues, or in echo manner [181, p. 222]. Among the echo registrations are: 1. Manuele I: Principale I or II, Tromba, Tromboni; Manuele II: Principale, Ottava, Voce Umana. 2. Manuele I: Both Principali, Ottava, Cornetto;

Manuele II: Principale, Ottava, Cornetto. When manuals are coupled, the writer (Casparini?) suggests that similar tone colors be drawn on both manuals—either just the Principals, or the two Ripienos, or (and this seems a bit odd!) the reeds and Voce Umana. A possible explanation for the last might be that in this northern-influenced organ, the Voce Umana was a reed stop and not the normal Italian undulating principal.

Some additional combinations for the main manual are given in the Casparini source. Most appear to be solo (flutes 8', 4', and 2 2/3' or flutes 8', 4', 2', and Sesquialtera) or novelty registrations. There are some rare references to the use of the accessory stops: Flute 4' with either the 2 2/3' or the Drum and Nightingale; Flute 2 2/3' and Drum. For improvising bagpipe-like pieces, the player may play [hold] a note or two on the Voce Umana with the left hand and above play the Flute, Trumpet, or Cornetto ... adding the Drum and Nightingale if desired [181, p. 223]. It is probable that such novelty registrations increased in use in the North during the eighteenth century, although for liturgical use the older conventions still largely applied.

Some newer musical styles were coming into vogue, however. Zipoli's 1716 *Sonate d'Intavolatura per Organo e Cimbalo*—essentially liturgical organ music, despite the "Cimbalo" designation—contains a quite traditional Toccata in the Frescobaldi style and five sets of four Versos plus a Canzona in different keys, presumably (because of the brevity of the Versos) to be used in the Mass. It also contains two typical slow Elevations and three pieces in the newer style: an *Offertorio*, a *Post Communio*, and a *Pastorale*. Such pieces would soon become a staple of the repertoire, particularly in Zipoli's home province of Tuscany, but perhaps because they were at the time less familiar, Zipoli included some registration directions for them.

The *Post Communio* and the middle Allegro section of the *Pastorale* are marked *co'flauti* (with flutes). Zipoli's Hermans organ at the Jesuit Church in Rome may have had an 8' flute, but most other Italian organs had either only a 4' flute or flutes at 4' and 2', and the context would seem to support a 4' pitch line. The other registration direction, *Piva*, is in the final Largo section of the *Pastorale*. Tagliavini points out that it could refer either to the character of the piece (bagpipe-like)or to a short-length reed such as the Musetto in Hermans's Pistoia organ cited above [304, pref.]. It could also, of course, apply to a much more common stop, the short-length and rather nasal-sounding Tromboncino, and because of the dronelike structure of the left-hand part, both parts may be played on the reed stop (preferably reinforced with an 8' flue stop) to good effect. And perhaps also, in accordance with Casparini's suggestions, the Drum and Nightingale may also be employed, if available.

Interestingly, two sonatas by Scarlatti contain registrational hints. Although dating from his Spanish period, they seem more applicable to the type of Italian two-manual organ he would have known in Rome. Sonata K. 287 in the Parma Ms. is inscribed for a two-manual chamber organ and marked *Flautato e Trombone*. "Flautado" is the Spanish term for Principal, and the Trombone (since no analogous term was used in Spain) could well mean the Italian Tromboncino; hence, a piece for 8' Principal and 8' short-length reed. In K. 328 alternating sections are marked "Org°" and "Fl°." The likeliest interpretation, which is upheld by the musical context, is an alternation ("echo") between Ripieno (*Organo*) and 8' Principal (*Flautado*), which would imply either an organ of two manuals or a one-manual organ with a Tiratutti.

Beginning around the middle of the eighteenth century, northern Italian organ builders often left suggestions for registration with their organs, a practice which may have come from such transalpine builders as Casparini, and which continued well into the nineteenth century. A set inscribed on the music rack of an organ built by Nacchini in 1750 for the Church of Maria Maddalena in Udine (since relocated to Turgnano) cites three different Ripienos: The Simple Ripieno (Principale 8' plus Ottava 4', Quintadecima 2', Decimanona 1 1/3', Vigesimaseconda 1', Vigesimasesta 2/3', and Vigesimanona 1/2'), the Mixed Ripieno (the same plus the Voce Umana, Flauto, Cornetta, and Contrabassi), and the "Orchestra" Ripieno (all stops plus Drum). The inclusion of the Voce Umana in the Mixed Ripieno is curious, since most other sources from both before and after the period under discussion prohibit the use of this stop in any kind of Ripieno combination because of its intentional out-of-tuneness.

The registration for the *Elevazione* is the traditional Principale and Voce Umana. Finally, there are four registrations suggested for different types of music: *Spiritosa* (Principale 8' and Flauto 4'), *Cantabile* (Principale and Flauto with Voce Umana), *Andante* (Principale, Flauto, and Cornetto), and *Arpeggio* (a 4'-based combination— Ottava and mutations through Vigesimasesta, plus Flute 4' and Cornetta) [79, p. 49]. There are no real surprises in any of these combinations, although one will notice a slight increase in the mixing of wide- and narrow-scaled stops.

As far as the more traditional compositions of Zipoli, Pasquini, and their contemporaries are concerned (toccatas, versets, canzonas, elevations), there is no indication of any departure from the older registration conventions. Thus many of the same suggestions and cautions concerning performance on modern organs cited in the previous section also apply to pieces of this type.

When using a 4' flute alone, a light open or tapered flute will give the best effect, although a 4' Harmonic Flute may also produce the desired effect if it is not too loud. Full-length reeds should still be generally avoided, but a modern Clarinet, Regal, or mild Oboe is often an acceptable substitute for the Tromboncino or Musette in pieces of the pastorale type. And the suggestions found in the previous section regarding the Ripieno and Voce Umana are applicable in this period.

Composers

Juan Baseya (late seventeenth century)
Juan Bautista José Cabanilles (1644–1712)
Sebastián Durón (1660–1716)
José Elias (1675–1749)
Francisco Llusá (Llissa) (fl. c1700)
Miquel Lopez (1669–1732)
Antonio Martin y Coll (c1660–c1740)
Juan Moreno y Polo (d. 1776)
Pablo Nassarre (1664–1724)
José Antonio Carlos Seixas (1704–1742)
José de Torres y Vergara (1661–1727)
Diego Xarava (late seventeenth century)

Representative Organs

CHURCH OF SANTA MARIA, TOLOSA
Joseph Echevarria, Jr. and Sr., 1688 [323, p. 44]

Manual
Flautado 16'
Flautado 8'
Flautado Menor/Octava Abierta 4' (open)
Flautado Menor Tapado 4'(?) (stopped flute)
Docena Abierta 2 2/3'
Nasarte Mayor 2 2/3' (flute)
Quincena 2'
Diecinovena 1 1/3'
Gran Corneta VII (mounted Cornet)

Corneta in Eco (treble, enclosed)
Chirumbela (tierce mixture)
Claron (tierce mixture — high pitched?)
Lleno IV (mixture)
Zimbala III
Sobrezimbala III
Trompetas Reales 8' (interior)
Dulzainas 8' (Regal, probably exterior)
Trompeta Magna 16' (treble; exterior?)
Clarines 8' (treble, exterior Trumpet)
Ecos de Clarines 8' (treble, interior, enclosed)
Bajoncillos 4' (bass; exterior?)

Accessory Stops
None listed, but this organ almost certainly had the array of bells, birds, drones, and drums found in other organs by the same maker.

[N.B. Many if not all stops were probably divided.]

CHURCH OF PURÍSMA CONCEPCIÓN, MEXICO CITY
Félix de Izaguirre, 1699 [150, p. 177]

Manual
Flautado 8' (principal)
Flautado de Bourdon 8' (stopped, bass octave wood)
Rochela 8'(?) (an open flue register)
Octava 4'
Docena 2 2/3'
Quincena 2'
Diez y novena 1 1/3'
Lleno en viente docena III (1' pitch)
Trompetas reales 8'

Accessory Stops ("People's stops")
Cascabeles III ("throughout the keyboard"; apparently small pipes of indeterminate pitch on a common channel, which played whenever any key was depressed)
Tambor de guerra (military drum, "essential for battle pieces")
Pájaros (birds)

NEW CATHEDRAL, SALAMANCA (Epistle Organ)
Unknown builder, 1702 [stoplist recorded by Hiroshi Tsuji, restorer]

Bajones (Bass)	Tiples (treble)
Flautado I 8'	Flautado I 8'
Flautado II 8'	Flautado II 8'
Octava Real 4'	Octava Real 4'
Octava Tapada 4' (stopped flute)	Octava Tapada 4'
Docena 2 2/3'	Docena 2 2/3' & 2'
Quincena 2'	Quincena 2' & 1 1/3'
Lleno III	Lleno III
Zimbala y Sobrezimbala IV	Zimbala y Sobrezimbala IV
Clarin de Bajos 8'	Corneta en Eco 8' (8', mounted)
Bajoncillo 4'	Trompeta Magna 16'

Trompeta Real 8'
Clarin 8'

Accessory Stops
Tambores II, Timbales II (drums)
Pájaros II (bird; 2 tin pipes)
Campanilla del Entenador (blower's signal)
2 pedals to control the 2 Cornets

[N.B. Exterior (horizontal) reeds were added in 1732–38.]

CHURCH, VILLASANDINO (BURGOS)
Pedro Merino de la Rosa, 1734 [11, p. 41]

Bass	**Treble**
Flautado 8'	Flautado 8'
Tapadillo 4' (stopped flute)	Violon 8'
Octava 4'	Octava 4'
Docena 2 2/3'	Docena 2 2/3'
Quincena 2'	Quincena 2'
Decinovena 1 1/3'	Decinovena 1 1/3'
Lleno III	Lleno III
Cimbala III	Cimbala III
Sobrecimbala III	Corneta VI
Trompeta Real 8'	Trompeta Real 8'
Bajoncillo 4' (exterior)	Clarin de Eco 8'
Violeta 2' (exterior)	Clarin de Battalla 8' (exterior)
	Clarin 8' (exterior)
Pedal	Trompeta Magna 16' (exterior)
8 Notes, pulldown	

Accessory Stops
Rossignol (bird)

NEW CATHEDRAL, SALAMANCA
Gospel organ, Echevarria, 1744–45 [92, p. 240]

Organo Mayor	**Cadereta Interio**
Flautado 16'	Flautado 8'
Flautado 8' (front)	Flautadillo 4'
Flautado 8' (back)	Nasarte en 12a 2 2/3'
Violon 8'	Nasarte en 17a/19a 1 3/5' & 1 1/3' (treble)
Octava 4'	Nasarte en 17a (bass)
Flautadillo 4'	Nasarte en 19a (bass)
Docena 2 2/3'	Corneta real (treble)
Nasarte en 12a 2 2/3'	Lleno III
Nasarte en 15a 2'	Zimbala III
Nasarte en 19a 1 1/3'	Trompeta real 8'
Corneta real (treble)	Bajoncillo 4' (bass)
Lleno IV	Clarin 8' (treble)
Zimbala III (bass)	Obue 8' (treble)
Trompeta magna 16'	
Trompeta real 8' (interior)	**Pedal** (8 notes)
	Contras 16' or 8'

Trompeta de batalla 8'
Trompeta magna 16' (exterior, treble)
Clarin 8' (exterior)
Chirimía 4' (exterior, bass)
Clarin 8' (exterior, treble)
Dulzayna 8' (exterior, short-length)

Accessory Stops
Tremulant
Expression box (possibly for Cadireta Cornet and reed trebles)

CHURCH, SANTA MARIA TONANZINTLA, PUEBLA, MEXICO
Unknown Mexican builder, 1750 [178, p. 127]

Manual (all stops divided)
Bordón 8'
Flautado Mayor 4'
Octava clara 2'
Docena clara 1 1/3'
Quincena clara 1'
Trompeta 4'(?) (horizontal)

Accessory Stops
None recorded (organ is in ruins), but probably included the usual drum and birdcall.

Registration

As in the previous period, the names of some distinguished composers stand out, notably Cabanilles, Seixas, and Durón. Their compositions tend to be in a somewhat antique (if expanded) style. Cabanilles, by far the most prolific, wrote tientos and toccatas on the church tones, some of them specifically for *medio registro* (divided keyboard), as well as pasacalles, gallardas, diferencias (variations), and the increasingly popular batallas (battle pieces).

Durón, Cabanilles's slightly younger contemporary, wrote in a similar vein and left some very spirited and idiomatic *medio registro* works. The younger Seixas wrote for both organ and harpsichord, and it is in his music that the spirit of the Baroque is most evident. Organists can be particularly indebted to Martin y Coll, a monastic organist in the Basque region and Madrid, for preserving the works of many Spanish composers of the turn of the century period in a five-volume collection published in 1706–9.

As in Italy, at the beginning of the Baroque period, the organ in Spain was still firmly rooted in the Renaissance. Typically it was a one-manual instrument, although often of substantial size, with many (and occasionally all) stops divided. Increasingly (particularly across the sea in Mexico) one finds quite different stoplists for the bass and treble. The most significant trend in this period was the increase in number and variety of reed stops, particularly after the beginning of the eighteenth century. Notable too is the increasingly elaborate casework of Iberian organs.

Tonally, the most significant development of the second half of the seventeenth century was the introduction of horizontal reed stops, which projected from the façade of the organ case. James Wyly has traced the earliest use of such reed stops to the Basque region, where in 1659 Joseph Echevarria introduced a treble half-stop of Clarines (full-length Trumpets) in his organ for the Convent of San Diego de Alcalá de Henares. They were "placed in the main cornice like cannons," and Echevarria boasted that such a stop had never before been made [323, p. 42]. He and his son later placed similar stops, including short-length reeds, in documented organs built in 1677 and 1688, and the novelty seems to have caught on quickly. Wyly observes that "by 1700 façade reeds seem to have been installed nearly everywhere except in Cataluña."

Some organs had both interior and exterior reeds. The interior Trompeta Real was voiced in a more refined manner, but the voicing of the exterior trumpet-type stops, called Clarins, was brash and open. The 8' Clarin was sometimes called Trompeta de Batalla—a reference to its use in the increasingly popular "battle" pieces—and it was often reinforced by two half-stops, a 4' Bajoncillo in the bass and a 16' Trompeta Magna in the treble, which helped to even out the dynamic range and had solo uses as well.

After the beginning of the eighteenth century, bass reed stops of 2' and 1' pitch called Chirimía or Violetas began to appear in some large organs, as well as 4' reed stops in the treble. Such stops are found in the turn-of-the-century organs in the Cathedral of Mexico City, among others. Whatever their names, all these reed stops are full-voiced trumpet-type reeds and of similar scaling. The short-length Dulzayna, or Orlos, also began to appear among the façade reeds around the end of the seventeenth century. Usually a rather loud and raucous stop, its function seems to have been to add harmonics to the Clarins rather than to be used alone.

The exterior Trompetas did not replace the interior ones, but complemented them, giving the organist a greater choice of reed colors. Depending on context, the player had the choice of the evenly regulated interior Trompeta (which could be used in pieces not calling for divided stops), or the exterior Clarins at 8' or 4' in the left hand and 16' or 8' in the right hand, or a combination of the trebles and basses of interior and exterior reeds. James Wyly, a writer with extensive experience of Iberian organs, comments on one of the frequently used registrations:

> Contrary to what might be expected, a listener is not upset by the disparities between written and actual pitches when the 4' [bass]/16' [treble] ranks are employed. I cannot account satisfactorily for this, yet from experience I know it to be true. Perhaps it has to do with the extreme brilliance of the harmonics plus the extremely sharp attack of the pipes; one is dazzled by a mass of sound which seems differentiated more by percussive attacks of notes and harmonies than by discernible changes in pitch or register. Even so, I doubt that the effect would succed in any but a very large, very reverberant space. [326, p. 17]

The Cornets and tierce mixtures (Tolosanas) that had begun to appear in Iberian organs during the seventeenth century came into greater prominence during the eighteenth. By mid-century it was possible to find a large instrument, such as that built in 1747 for the Cathedral of Granada. It was unusual in that it had three manual divisions (Organo Mayor plus Cadereta Exterio and Cadereta Interio)— with three Cornetas, a Tolosana, a Claron mixture (apparently the bass to the Organo Mayor Corneta), and a wide variety of reeds both interior and exterior, divided and undivided. This organ also contained such intimations of things to come as a Flauto Traversiere, a Violon, and a two-rank (possibly undulating?) *Imitacion de Violines* [92, p. 242].

It is harder to pinpoint the introduction of the Echo box. Treble stops such as Cornets and, later, reeds, were placed in such boxes before 1700, as in France. But by the 1740s one finds the term *Caja de exprésion* ("expression box") in use; and indeed by this time it was increasingly common to find Echo boxes with some sort of hinged lid or sliding shutter controllable by the organist. An interesting registration aid also appeared in the early eighteenth century in the form of a pedal device that allowed the player to shift quickly between the unenclosed Cornet to the enclosed (Eco) Cornet.

In a description of an organ built c1680, Echevarria notes in passing that the 8' Flautado Suave (light principal) should be used with the 8' Voz humanas (a reed), but registration hints from organ builders are rare in this period. The first specific registration instructions to be found in Spanish music occur in Martin y Coll's five-volume *Flores de Musica* of 1706. Most of them pertain to the use of the Clarins: *Entrada de clarines*: Clarins in the right hand (in a Medio Registro piece); and a Canción "for Clarin, with Echo [probably the enclosed Cornet], at the player's discretion." Indications found in similar sources include "Pieces for Clarins" and a Canción "for the Cornet with an Echo"—a specific allusion to the enclosed Cornet [203, p. 44].

Although the eighteenth-century Iberian organ still had close ties with that of the early seventeenth century, the later additions to the tonal palette and an increasingly complex and ornamented musical style led inevitably to virtuosity on the part of the players and registrational diversity in musical practice. In 1723, in his *Escuela Música*, Pablo Nassarre observed (with some disapproval) that, despite the options available in a larger organ of two divided manuals, "the organists, not content with this, have secured the invention of so many registers and have such a love for them, that it is an ear-flattering marvel . . . that draws the attention to this instrument more than any other kind of music" [203, p. 44]. Among other things, Nassarre was referring to the new practice of *medio registros doblados*, where, by drawing different combinations on each half of the keyboards of a two-manual organ, four-part pieces could be played with a different color on each part. Like quatuor playing in France, this largely improvisational technique was probably practiced only by the more virtuosic players; no known written music actually calls for it, although it may have been employed in some way in the performance of contrapuntal music.

Nassarre also comments on some Lleno registrations, for, as in France and Italy, there were several possibilities for "full organ" combinations. None of Nassarre's combinations involve the reed stops, however. On 16' organs, the Lleno may include mixtures and/or mutations up to the 26th and even the high-pitched Zimbala and Sobrezimbala, in order to maintain clarity and keep a balance with the

16' pitch. On 8' organs the Lleno may contain everything from 8' through the 19th, with possibly the Zimbala, but the extremely high pitches are not recommended. The idea was to balance the low and high pitches so that neither predominated, although a full Lleno on a large 16' organ must have been an impressively complex sound.

A word should be said here concerning "battle" pieces (*batallas*). Works of this type appeared as early as the late sixteenth century not only on the Iberian peninsula but also in Italy, England, and the Germanic countries. Not all were written for the organ (the English examples are virginal pieces), but during the seventeenth and eighteenth centuries such pieces did become a staple of organ composition (and improvisation) in Spain, Portugal, and Latin America. It should be borne in mind, however, that early examples (before 1660) obviously do not call for the use of horizontal Clarins, and some can—and even should—be played with no reeds at all. But later Spanish batallas do require the exterior as well as interior reeds, particularly in sections imitating trumpet calls and fanfares, and, as M. S. Kastner points out,

> the structure of *batallas* specifically intended for horizontal trumpets is distinctly different from those in which the trumpet stop is not intended. In those *batallas* where there is an intervention of trumpets *en chamade* it is necessary to distinguish the polyphonic parts in which the trumpets do not participate, from the more homophonic sections in which the motifs of trumpets and clarions predominate. These *batallas* require a minimum of two different registrations. [74, p. 76]

As suggested in the contract specification of the Mexico City organ cited above, the use of the drums was common in the playing of *batallas*, and indeed, in the eighteenth-century *batalla* there is ample opportunity for the player to make imaginative use of all the "toy" stops. No drum stop available? A rhythmic tramping on 4' C and C♯ of any substantial 16' open wood Pedal stop is a quite effective substitute.

In playing Iberian music on modern organs, the player should still avoid flue tone that is too foundational or too top-heavy, and strive for a good balance between the available extremes of pitch with no gaps between the lowest and highest pitches. In the Lleno (full organ) pieces, there is much to be said for following Nassarre's advice—to balance a 16' pleno with higher-pitched stops, but to curtail the use of higher-pitched mutations and mixtures when employing an 8' pleno. Thus, on a modern organ, a high-pitched Cymbel, Sharp, or Terzzimbel mixture would be appropriate to a 16' full organ but not to an 8' full organ, where such stops might lead to top-heaviness. Indeed, this advice could well apply to much music other than the Iberian.

Many of the conventions of the previous period would still be in effect, and some of the lighter pleno combinations suggested in the Lérida instructions in the previous chapter may be used when the texture of the music calls for it, as it often does in some of Cabanilles's tientos. As in the Italian toccatas, there are places in some tientos where registrations may be changed, usually by the addition of stops.

Specific Echo pieces are rare, but one can find examples of "repetition echos" in several pieces, where it would seem appropriate to play the repetition on a quieter combination (or simply close a swellbox to imitate the transition from unenclosed to enclosed echo Cornet or reeds). Cabanilles's Tiento XVI (*Coreado o de ecos*) is a large-scale, complex piece, not far removed in style from the Echo Fantasias of Sweelinck. It would appear to be a work for two-manual organ, and although the echo sections are not specifically marked, they are musically discernible. The texture suggests a fairly strong plenum for both manuals, possibly with stop changes between sections.

Many modern organs have horizontal reeds of some sort—sometimes they are located at the opposite end of the room from the rest of the organ! Some of these modern reeds are indeed voiced in a classical, fast-speaking, relatively low-pressure way that would make them suitable for Iberian music. But many are too heavy, slow-speaking, or blatant to be appropriate to this lively, fast-paced music. The Iberian reeds have a snappy attack and are loud and brilliant (especially the horizontal Clarins), but not unbearably so. Since all of them are in buildings of magnificent acoustical properties, their effect is one of pleasant excitement. Many American horizontal reeds are in buildings with poor-to-marginal acoustics, and their loudness sometimes approaches the threshhold of pain. They do no justice to the Iberian literature of any period, and in such cases it is prudent to use a lighter reed stop, even if it is an interior one.

Reeds for the playing of this music should thus be chosen judiciously. French-style reeds often work well, while heavier Romantic or German (including German Baroque) types are considerably less successful. The 16', 8', and 4' pitches may be combined where available, especially for solos, balanced with a suitably bright (but not overwhelming) flue pleno combination. For playing with both hands (normally done on an interior Trumpet), a more restrained 8' Trumpet is suitable, perhaps on a secondary division. When combining reeds with flues, the reeds chosen should add color to the ensemble without overpowering it. But above all, the player should not lose sight of the often fresh and exuberant character of the music written in this period, and play it accordingly.

Northern Germany, Holland, and Scandinavia

Composers

Georg Böhm (1661–1733)
Nicolaus Bruhns (1665–1697)
Dieterich Buxtehude (1637–1707)
Daniel Erich (1689?–1712)
Christian Flor (1626–1697)
Carl Gottfried Geilfus (d. 1740)
Christian Geist (1640?–1711)
Daniel Magnus Gronau (d. 1747)
Johann Nicolaus Hanff (1665–1711/12)
Peter Hasse the Younger (1659–1708)
Konrad Friedrich Hurlebusch (c1695–1765)
Andreas Kneller (1649–1724)
Georg Dietrich Leyding (1664–1710)
Vincent Lübeck (1654–1740)
Martin Radeck (1640?–1684)
Johann Adam Reincken (1623–1722)
Johann Christian Schiefferdecker (1679–1732)
Georg Philipp Telemann (1681–1767)
Quirinus Van Blankenburg (1654–1739)

Representative Organs

CHURCH OF ST. COSMAE, STADE
Berendt Huss, 1669–73 [185, p. 40]

Hauptwerk	**Rückpositiv**
Principal 16'	Principal 8'
Quintadena 16'	Rohrflöte 8'

Octav 8'
Gedackt 8'
Octave 4'
Rohrflöte 4'
Nassat 2 2/3'
Octav 2'
Mixtur VI
Cimbel III
Trommet 16'
Trommet 8'

Pedal
Principal 16'
Sub-Bass 16'
Octav 8'
Octav 4'
Nachthorn 1'
Mixtur V–VI
Posaune 16'
Dulzian 16'
Trommet 8'

Accessory Stops
2 Manual Couplers
Tremulant
Glockenspiel

Quintadena 8'
Octav 4'
Waldflöte 2'
Sifflöte 1 1/3'
Sesquialter II
Scharff V
Dulzian 16'
Trechter Regal 8'

Brustwerk
Querflöte 8' (wood, open)
Gedackt 8' (wood, stopped)
Flöte 4' (wood, open)
Octav 2'
Tertia 1 3/5'
Nassat Quint 1 1/3'
Sedetz 1' (Sedecima)
Scharff III
Krummhorn 8'
Schalmey 4'

PARISH CHURCH, LÜDINGWORTH, NIEDERSACHSEN
Arp Schnitger, 1682 [21, p. 8]

Oberwerk (Hauptwerk)
Quintadene 16' (to FF)
Principal 8'
Rohrflöte 8'
Octave 4'
Hohlflöte 4'
Nassat 2 2/3'
Octave 2'
Rauschpfeife (II?)
Mixtur
Zimbel III
Trommette 8'

Brustwerk
Gedackt 4'
Quintflöte 2 2/3'(?) (treble)
Octave 2'
Scharff III
Regal 8'

Accessory Stops
2 Zimbelsterns

Rückpositiv
Gedackt 8'
Principal 4' (tin)
Spitzflöte 4'
Octava 2'
Waldflöte 2'
Sifflöte 1 1/3'
Terzian II
Scharff IV–VI
Dulzian 16' (reed)

Pedal
Untersatz 16'
Principal 8'
Octava 4'
Nachthorn 2'
Rauschpfeife
Mixtur IV–VI
Posaune 16'
Trommett 8'
Cornet 2' (reed)

Vogelgesang, 3 pipes (bird)
Tremulant
Manual "shove" coupler

[N. B. Most of the stops in the HW, BW, and Pedal were re-used from the former 1598 organ by Antonius Wilde.]

CHURCH OF ST. LAURENTIUS, DEDESDORF
Arp Schnitger, 1698 [138, p. 103]

Unterwerk
Quintaden 8'
Gedackt 4'
Quinta 2 2/3'
Octav 2'
Sifflet 1 1/3'
Sesquialt II (2')
Mixtur IV (divided)
Trommet 8' (divided)

Oberwerk
Gedackt 8'
Principal 4' (tin)
Flöte 2'
Quinta 1 1/3'

Pedal
Coupled to Unterwerk

PARISH CHURCH, NIEUW-SCHEEMDA, HOLLAND
Arp Schnitger, 1698 [stoplist taken from extant organ]

Manual
Holpijp 8'
Quintadena 8' (treble)
Praestant 4'
Fluit 4'
Quint 2 2/3'
Octaaf 2'
Mixtuur III (1/2')
Trompet 8'

Pedal
Coupled to Manual

Accessory Stops
Tremulant

PARISH CHURCH, MARIENHAFE, OSTFRIESLAND
Gerhard von Holy, 1712/14 [stoplist taken from extant organ]

Hauptwerk
Bordun 16'
Prinzipal 8'
Gedackt 8'
Oktave 4'
Spitzfleute 4'
Quinte 2 2/3'
Oktave 2'
Spitzfleute 2'
Sesquialtera II
Mixtur III
Cymbel II
Trompete 8'

Rückpositiv
Rohrfleute 8'
Prinzipal 4'
Blockfleute 4'
Oktave 2'
Quinte 1 1/3'
Siffleute 1'
Scharff II
Krummhorn 8'

Pedal
Coupled to Hauptwerk

Accessory Stops
Cymbel-Stern
Tremulant

ST. MICHAEL'S CHURCH, HAMBURG
Arp Schnitger, 1712–15 [43, p. 65]

Hauptwerk
Principal 16'
Quintadena 16'
Octav Principal 8'
Rohrflöte 8'
Octava 4'
Spitzflöte 4'
Nasat 2 2/3'
Super Octava 2'
Rauschpfeiffe II
Mixtura IV–VI
Cymbel III
Trompeta 16'
Trompeta 8'
Vox Humana 8'

Pedal
Principal 16'
Subbass 16'
Rohr-Quinta 10 2/3'
Octava 8'
Octava 4'
Nachthorn 2'
Rauschpfeiffe III
Mixtura VI
Gross-Posaune 32'
Posaune 16'
Trompeta 8'
Trompeta 4'
Cornet 2'

Rückpositiv
Principal 8'
Gedackt 8'
Quintadena 8'
Octava 4'
Flute douce 4'
Gedackte Quinta 2 2/3'
Octava 2'
Spitzflöte 2'
Quinta 1 1/3'
Sesquialtera II
Scharff IV–VI
Dulcian 16'
Hautbois 8'

Brustwerk
Flute douce 8'
Octava 4'
Rohrflöte 4'
Quinta 2 2/3'
Octava 2'
Waldflöte 2'
Sifflet 1 1/3'
Tertian II
Scharff IV
Trichter Regal 8'
Schallmey 4'

Accessory Stops
Tremulants to Hauptwerk, Rückpositiv, Pedal
Cymbelsterns in Hauptwerk and Rückpositiv
Tympani
Vogelsang (bird)
3 Couplers
4 Sperrventils

JACOBIN CHURCH, LEEUWARDEN, HOLLAND
Christian Müller, 1724 [134, p. 11]

Hoofdwerk
Prestant 16'
Octaaf 8'

Bovenwerk
Baarpijp 8' (flue)
Quintadena 8'

Roefluit 8'
Octaaf 4'
Quint 2 2/3'
Super Octaaf 2'
Mixture IV–VIII (2')
Scherp IV–VI (1')
Trompet 16'
Trompet 8'

Rugpositief
Prestant 8'
Holpijp 8'
Octaaf 4'
Octaaf 2'
Mixtuur IV–VIII (1 1/3')
Cornet VI
Sexquialter (2 2/3')
Trompet 8'

Accessory Stops
Bovenwerk Tremulant
Rugpositief Tremulant

Viola di Gamba 8'
Octaaf 4'
Gemshoorn 4'
Nasard 2 2/3'
Nachthoorn 2'
Sexquialter II–IV
Cimbel III
Dulciaan 8'
Voxhumana 8'

Pedaal
Prestant 16'
Bourdon 16' (metal)
Octaaf 8'
Octaaf 4'
Quint 2 2/3'
Mixtuur IV (2 2/3')
Bazuin 16'
Trompet 8'
Trompet 4'

PARISH CHURCH, LÖFSTA BRUK, SWEDEN
Johan Niclas Cahman, 1728 [3, p. 238]

Huvudwerk
Quintadena 16'
Principal 8'
Rohrflöte 8'
Quintadena 8'
Octava 4'
Spitzflöte 4'
Quinta 2 2/3'
Octava 2'
Mixtur V
Trompet 8'

Ryggpositiv
Gedackt 8'
Quintadena 8'
Principal 4'
Flöte 4'
Quinta 2 2/3'
Octava 2'
Mixtur IV
Vox humana 8'

Pedal
Subbass 16'
Principal 8'
Gedackt 8'
Quint 5 1/3'
Octava 4'
Rauschquint II
Mixtur IV
Bassun 16'
Trompet 8'
Trompet 4'

PARISH CHURCH, OCHTERSUM, OSTFRIESLAND
Chr. Klausing, 1734 [76, p. 192]

Manual
Prinzipal 8'
Gedackt 8'
Octav 4'
Rohrflöte 4'
Quinta 2 2/3'
Octava 2'
Sesquialtera II
Mixtur VI (divided)
Trompete 8' (divided)

Accessory Stops
Tremulant

Pedal
Coupled to Manual

WALLOON CHURCH, LEEUWARDEN, FRIESLAND
J. M. Swartsburg, 1740 [73, n. p.]

Hoofdmanuaal
Prestant 8'
Holpyp 8'
Octaav 4'
Quint 2 2/3'
Octaav 2'
Cornet IV
Mixtuur IV–VI
Trompet 8'

Accessory Stops
Tremulant
Ventil

Bovenmanuaal
Prestant 8'
Quintadeen 8'
Sollycionaal 4' (Salicional)
Nachthoorn 2'
Dulciaan 8' (reed)

Pedal
Coupled to Hoofdmanuaal

PARISH CHURCH, TIMMEL, OSTFRIESLAND
Joh. Friedrich Constabel, 1740 [76, p. 223]

Hauptwerk
Prinzipal 8'
Gedackt 8'
Oktave 4'
Rohrflöte 4'
Quinte 2 2/3'
Oktave 2'
Sesquialtera II
Mixtur IV
Trompete 8'

Accessory Stops
Tremulant
Zimbelstern
Manual coupler

Brustwerk
Quintatön 8'
Flöte 4'
Oktave 2'
Repetier 1' (repeating Cymbel)

Pedal
Coupled to HW only

Registration

By the late seventeenth century, much of the activity in both organ building and organ playing in northern Europe centered around Hamburg and the free cities of Lüneburg and Lübeck, with some significant activity also in northeastern Holland, particularly in the Groningen area. Religious and political problems in the Netherlands had been gradually driving organists and organ builders east, from the late sixteenth century onward. Just as the heirs of Sweelinck's art were his north German pupils, so did north German organ builders take up the thread of Netherlandish organ building evolution in the latter part of the seventeenth century. In the Renaissance the flow of builders and instruments had been east, from the Netherlands to Germany; in the Baroque period the flow was reversed, and German organs, builders, and musicians began to appear in the northern Netherlands and in the Scandinavian countries.

By 1700 the hub of northern organ building was the Hamburg area, and central to the "Hamburg school" was the master builder Arp Schnitger. The elements that influenced Schnitger were diverse. The Fleming Hendrik Niehoff in the sixteenth century and the Saxon Gottfried Fritzsche in the early seventeenth were among those who contributed substantial foundation blocks to Schnitger's Baroque style. Descended from a long line of woodworkers, Schnitger apprenticed with and ultimately succeeded his cousin Berendt Huss. Backed by a well-staffed workshop, Schnitger was prodigiously active from the 1670s to his death in 1719. His organs are concentrated in the Hamburg, Bremen and Groningen areas. He was succeeded by his son Franz Caspar, but he also left numerous former apprentices and journeymen, such as Cahman, "the Swedish Schnitger," to carry on the distinctive tonal and visual tradition crystallized in his work. But while significant changes in style were becoming evident in other parts of Germany at the time of Schnitger's death in 1719, the essence of the "Hamburg organ" continued to exert a strong influence in the North for nearly a half-century afterward.

The tonal orientation of these organs, as seen in the stoplists given above, is a direct outgrowth of the late Renaissance style. By the middle of the eighteenth century, it was already something of an anachronism, although it persisted in northern Holland even into the early nineteenth century. Visually, too, these organs clung to an older style, now dubbed the *Werk-Prinzip* (a modern term, quite unknown to Schnitger's contemporaries), in which each division occupied a discrete place in the case façade. A number of the larger organs also contained pipework and other material retained from earlier organs, which also influenced their orientation toward an earlier style.

Although temperaments based on the meantone system persisted well into the nineteenth century in England and parts of Italy, by the early eighteenth century they were fast being supplanted by other, "well-tempered" systems in all parts of Germany save the North Sea area (and adjacent northern Holland). The retention of the older meantone-based systems in the North is thought to have had some influence on compositional style there. It probably also had something to do with the persistence of earlier organ design and registration practices in this area: pure-tuned tierces and short-length reeds with considerable harmonic development sound better in a tuning that contains some pure thirds, at least when played in the commoner keys.

The typical three-manual northern organ consisted of Hauptwerk, Brustwerk, Rückpositiv, and Pedal; two-manual organs were either Hauptwerk-Brustwerk or Hauptwerk-Rückpositiv, and small or medium-sized instruments often had no independent Pedal stops. Although the Brustwerk was going out of favor in other areas (or mutating into an Echo, Récit, or Unterwerk), it remained a standard feature in the North until a fairly late date. Schnitger, in a 1707 proposal for an organ in Delmenhorst, specified a Brustwerk of 8', 4', 2', 2', IV (mixture), and 8' (reed), stating that this division was necessary to provide "penetrating sharpness" [77, p. 169].

Although smaller organs in village churches frequently lacked an independent Pedal, in larger organs the Pedal division was still of significant size, and evidence suggests that the large Pedal was a peculiarly Lutheran phenomenon. For example, in 1709 a member of the Klausing family built an eighteen-stop organ for the Lutheran church in Höxter with a fairly substantial Pedal division that included a 2' reed and a 1' flute. But another eighteen-stop Klausing organ built in 1720 for the Catholic church in nearby Zwillbrock had only a pulldown pedal [319, p. 158].

In Holland, the only organs with large Pedal divisions were those that belonged to the large cities. Although housed in the (now Calvinist) churches, these organs have always had an important secular function. Indeed, it was not until the middle of the seventeenth century that they began to be used to support congregational singing, and in Amsterdam, this did not occur until 1680. This "new" use of Dutch organs prompted some minor changes in tonal design, most notably the addition of the Cornet stop (to "give out" the psalm melody) and the increased importance of 16' Pedal reeds. But as late as 1700 the Dutch builder Jan Duyschot built a large three-manual organ for the New Church in the Hague having only a coupler from the main manual to the Pedal [195, p. 2].

A particularly notable feature of the northern organ is the variety of its reed stops. The use of the colorful Renaissance "consort stops" in all divisions (including the Pedal), inherited from the Flemish tradition, persisted in northern Europe well into the middle of the eighteenth century. The reed resources of most of the organs in the rest of Europe north of Italy and Iberia had long since coalesced into the standard mostly 8' Trumpet/Cromorne/Hautboy/Vox Humana pattern (with an ocasional 4' Clarion), with conical Pedal reeds at 8' in France and at 16' and 8' in southern and central Germany. One of the major differences between the organs of northern Germany and those of the central and southern region in the early eighteenth century is the plethora of manual reeds on the former and the scarcity of them on the latter.

Possibly because of the longevity of some of the most noteworthy north German organist-composers of the period (Buxtehude reached 70, Böhm 72, Kneller 78, Lübeck and Telemann 86; and Reincken died at the astonishing age of 99), an older style of organ composition persisted into the early years of the eighteenth century as well, and with it many of the older registration conventions of the previous period. Most of the organ compositions fall into the categories of multi-partite *stylus phantasticus* Praeludia or chorale-based compositions. Among the latter the elaborate chorale fantasias of Buxtehude, Reincken, and Lübeck stand among the most significant examples of this genre, along with the earlier works of Buxtehude's father-in-law, Tunder. The works of Telemann are the exception. Although Telemann spent more than half his life in Hamburg (largely working in the secular sphere), in his youth he was a church musician in central Germany. Thus his organ works, which are small in scale and represent but a small part of his total output, belong more in the stylistic camp of Pachelbel, Walther, and the Bachs.

In Holland, despite the presence of substantial instruments, no important composers emerged in this period, and what little organ literature comes from that quarter consists mainly of simple psalm-tune settings. Those of Van Blankenburg are typical; they are largely homophonic, and a few have little fugal preludial sections. Nor (unless we count Buxtehude's sojourn there) does any music of great significance come from Scandinavia. Thus, despite the presence of large organs in these areas, it is in the north German cities that we find the bulk of the literature.

Harald Vogel states that "a fundamental guideline for North German registrational practice is the principle that the more complicated and consistently polyphonic the work, the fewer the stops that should be used." He then makes some pertinent observations on the registration of praeludia:

> Within the toccata-like sections of the North German *stylus phantasticus* repertoire, it is very important to alternate between the contrasting *plena* of the Rückpositiv and Hauptwerk (sometimes of the Brustwerk, as well). In this way large blocks of sound are clearly set apart and gain increased spatial depth. Alternating the pedal with contrasting manual *plena* adds still another dimension in works such as the Praeludium in D, BuxWV 139 of Buxtehude (mm. 13–16) or the Praeludium in d of Lübeck (mm. 35–40). The fugal sections can be registered with a wide variety of consort sounds (reed stops, especially, can be exploited here). Because of the great blending quality of the North German reeds, they can be registered not only singly but also in combination with principals or flutes or in the *plenum*. This arrangement applies equally to the reeds with full-length resonators (Trompet, Posaune, Schalmei, Cornet) and to those with half-length (Regal, Krummhorn, Dulcian, Vox Humana). In a reed *plenum* (based on a low-pitched reed stop such as the Trompet 16' or 8' or the Dulcian 16', with the principal chorus including the mixture), each individual voice in the polyphony retains its identity much more than in a pure principal *plenum*. The reed *plenum* is thus especially useful for many of the final fugues of the North German Praeludia, which, with their simpler rhythms, exhibit strong homophonic tendencies. In all fugues, the bass voice should be at the same pitch level as the rest of the voices, regardless of whether it is played in the manual or on the pedal. [316, p. 35]

The sectional nature of the praeludia is worth emphasizing, for it clearly calls for registration and/or manual changes between the sections, or, as Vogel suggests, the addition of reeds at the conclusion. On smaller organs stop changes can often be managed by the player without great difficulty, but on the larger organs of the period (where some stops were actually out of the reach of the organist), contemporary evidence points to the use of stop-pullers (registrants); on most modern organs the use of some sort of combination action achieves the same end. Stops are never changed during a section, however. As in the sectional toccatas of Frescobaldi, stop-changes only occur between clearly defined cadenced sections, where the necessary brief pause occurs.

Echo and alternation effects were still part of the canon of northern composers, and such places are usually well marked. Bruhns, in his Prelude and Fugue in E minor, marks his echo passages for "Org." (Hauptwerk) and "Echo" (Brustwerk); Buxtehude, in his chorale-prelude on *Nun lob, mein Seel, den Herren*, indicates alternation between Oberwerk (Hauptwerk) and Rückpositiv, as does Lübeck in his chorale-prelude on *Ich ruf' zu dir* and partita on *Nun lasst uns Gott dem Herren*. Many other examples can be found in the works of these and other composers. A true echo (repetition of a motif or short segment) is usually assigned to the lighter, more-reticent division (the Brustwerk), while alternations between more-extended sections are more likely to be between the more-assertive divisions (the Hauptwerk and Rückpositiv). Bright Rückpositiv solos in the earlier manner are also still very much part of this music, as in Böhm's transcendent *Vater Unser*, in which the florid right-hand solo on the Rückpositiv is accompanied on "OW piano" (soft stops on the Hauptwerk) by the left hand.

No real registration treatises are found from this period, nor did any of the northern composers of the late seventeenth or early eighteenth centuries include any registrations with their compositions. The theoretician Andreas Werckmeister of Quedlinburg made some references to registration in his *Erweiterte und Verbesserte Orgel-Probe* (handbook for "proving" or evaluating organs), published in 1698. He was somewhat critical of short-length reeds, and in a bit of doggerel verse describes poor ones as "fools' work," while admitting that if they are "good and pure" they can "refresh the heart and mind." A few of his observations, paraphrased here, give insight into his ideas on registration:

1. The Tierce is not very useful without the Quint, but Tierce and Quint combinations (Sesquialteras) can sound well in fast ("colored") passagework. [N.B. The use of an 8' and 4' foundation for this combination is of course assumed here; see No. 4.]

2. The Pedal Subbass 16' is a splendid stop for use in accompanying congregational singing.

3. Do not draw two stops of the same pitch but differing scales (e.g., a principal and a flute).

4. Avoid really peculiar combinations, such as basing a registration on a quint, or playing slow chords on just a Gedackt 8' and Quint 2 2/3—"nobody could have such a strange sense of hearing" as to do things like that! [179, p. 59]

One wishes Werckmeister had been a bit more specific on the topic of registration, but he states the truism that "a good ear is the best criterion" and advises neophyte organists to hear and understand all the stops on their instrument and use good musical judgement—sound advice in any context.

Another theoretician, Johann Mattheson of Hamburg, while perhaps on the periphery of the organ world, makes passing comments on organ registration in two of his works, *Das Neu-Eröffnete Orchestre* (1713) [NEO] and *Der Vollkommene Kapellmeister* (1739) [VK]. To these might be added his appendix to F. E. Niedt's *Musikalische Handleitung*, Part III (1721) [MH]. Even at these late dates, Mattheson clings to the old concept of using stops in families and contrasting (but not combining) the "thin" (principal) and "fat" (flute) families; reeds may be combined with flutes in some circumstances, however. Hans Klotz notes that Mattheson makes a distinction between the "mixture-plenum" and the "reed-plenum," much in the same manner that the French distinguished between the *Plein Jeu* and the *Grand Jeu* during the same period. He concludes that it is usually the the mixture-plenum that is meant by the direction *Volles Werk* [80]. Although reeds are excluded, very little else is; in *Der Vollkommene Kapellmeister* Mattheson gives this formula for the full organ:

> To the plenum belong the Principals, Sorduns, Salicionals (Weiden-pfeiffen), Rauschpfeifes, Octaves, Quints, Mixtures, Scharfs, Quintadenas, Zimbels, Nasats, Terzians, Sesqualteras, Superoctaves, and the Posaunes in the Pedal—not in the manual, for Posaunes are reed pipes, excluded from the manual plenum.

Some other registrational dicta culled from Mattheson may be summed up as follows:

1. Do not draw reeds with the manual fluework unless there is a reed on the pedal [NEO].

2. Reeds should be kept out of the *Vollem Werk* (mixture-plenum), but a 16' reed may be used in the Pedal [VK].

3. The Sesquialtera (principal-scaled tierce mixture) should not be combined with a 4' flute in solo combinations [NEO; presumably this means that the 8' foundation should not be omitted].

4. "Thin" and "fat" stops should not be mixed in the plenum, but the two families may be contrasted in solo or alternating registrations [NEO]. However, in VK Mattheson describes the plenum quoted above, which does indeed include both narrow- and wide-scaled stops; he seems to have changed his mind about full organ registrations during the quarter century that separated VK from NEO, perhaps because of improvements in wind stability.

5. Do not use two 8' stops together, but 8' and 4' combinations are good [VK]. Werckmeister also mentions this prohibition in his *Orgelprobe* (1698), citing a concern for tuning and wind stability.

6. Draw only one stop of each pitch length in any given combination [VK].

7. The 8' Gedackt is sufficient to accompany instruments such as the oboe or violin [VK].

8. Do not draw a reed and a flue of the same pitch together, as they are rarely in tune with each other [MH]. [Note that this contradicts the usage of almost every other region since the Renaissance!] That Mattheson's recommendation was not always adhered to in the North is attested to by the Dutch builder Christian Vater, who in 1755 recommended that the Gedackt 8' should be drawn with the Vox Humana "for a fuller sound" [307, p. 100].

9. Choose stops for echo effects with care [MH].

10. Let the sense of the words guide you in choosing registrations for chorale-preludes [VK].

11. The overuse of drums, cymbelsterns, and other "children's toys" is discouraged—at least by Mattheson [WK]. But such prohibitions are usually fair proof that there was active engagement in the disapproved activity.

In addition, Mattheson, in *Der vollkommene Kapellmeister*, cites some registrations used for chorale-preludes on the large organ in St. Catherine's Church, Hamburg:

For use on a single manual:
 Rohrflöte 8', Spitzflöte 4', Waldflöte 2', and Sifflöte 1
 Pedal: Principal 16' alone or with the Gemshorn 8'
For chorale-preludes written for two manuals and Pedal:
 Hauptwerk: Trommete 16', Spitzflöte 8', Octave 4'; or Oberwerk: Trommete 8', Zincke 8', Flöte 4', Nasat 2 2/3'
 Rückpositiv: Gedackt 8'
 Pedal: Subbass 16', Principal 16', Posaune 16', Dulcian 16', Trommete 8', Cornet 2'
[The rather overpowering Pedal combination is a bit puzzling, unless one assumes that the Hauptwerk, Oberwerk, and Pedal registrations are simply suggested solo registrations and not all meant to be used in the same piece.]
For playing on all four manuals (presumably in sectional works, since "quartet" playing seems not to have been practiced in this region as it was in France and Spain):
 Hauptwerk: Principal 16', Octave 8', Octave 4', Octave 2', Rauschpfeife II, Mixtur
 Rückpositiv: Principal 8', Quintadena 8', Octave 4', Sesquialtera II (Quintflöte 1 1/3' optional)
 Brustwerk: Principal 8', Octave 4', Scharff
 Oberwerk: Principal 8' and Scharff ("this is sufficient for the fourth")
 Pedal: Principal 32', Principal 16', Octave 8', Octave 4', Mixtur, Rauschpfeife, Gross Posaun 32', Posaun 16', Trommet 8', Schalmey 4' ("to be drawn with all [combinations]")
[It should be understood that all of these combinations, including those for the Pedal, were to be used independently; coupling of manuals (and even of manuals to Pedal in organs of this size) was still rarely employed in the North.]

Large instruments such as the organ in Hamburg's St. Catherine's Church (where Reincken presided for most of his long life and where young J. S. Bach was impressed with all the reed stops) are what we most often associate with the large praeludia and chorale fantasias. With the exception of mixing "thin" and "fat" colors and using too many stops of the same pitch (which may have been rough on the wind supply), along with cautions against gapped combinations still largely in force from the previous period, the sky was probably the registrational limit with these large organs, especially when a player improvised. But such organs were greatly outnumbered by the smaller "congregational-singing" organs in country churches. Yet they too were capable of color and variety, and it is obvious that a large portion of the simpler and shorter chorale-prelude literature was intended for these instruments.

Only one set of registrational directions has come down to us with regard to a small organ. It is included in the contract for Arp Schnitger's 1697 organ in Dedesdorf, a very minimal two-manual organ lacking even an 8' Principal—although the beefy Gedackt and foundational Trompete provide a very solid basis for the chorus, as well as for the lusty singing of the congregation. The Trompete and Mixtur are both divided, a procedure more common in Dutch than in German organs of this period. In his contract Schnitger states that "the Trompete may be used in the Pedal and the Scharf [upper half] may be separated from the Mixtur [lower half]" [138, p. 106].

This organ originally had no Pedal stop, but the Pedal was permanently coupled to the lower manual, containing the Trompete and Mixtur. Schnitger seems to be suggesting that the bass half of the Trompete and the treble half of the Mixtur be drawn on this manual (with appropriate foundation stops, probably at 8' and 4', or 8', 4', and 2'). Thus the Trompete could be used for a Pedal solo, or possibly as an element in a trio, with the Mixtur coloring the right-hand part and the left hand on the upper manual, probably with all four stops drawn. Schnitger followed his Dedesdorf organ with an almost identical instrument for the Church of St. Johannes in Strückhausen, which also had divided Trompete and Mixtur. One major difference was that in this organ both manuals could be coupled to the Pedal, affording a little additional flexibility. Indeed, the tonal design of these small twelve-stop organs with their two divided stops affords much more in the way of registrational variety and color than immediately meets the eye.

Another northern source of registration information originates some distance from Hamburg. During the second quarter of the eighteenth century, Daniel Magnus Gronau of Danzig, East Prussia (now Gdansk, Poland), on the easternmost fringe of the area, composed some chorale variations in which each movement is given a detailed registration. Gronau affects an Italianate terminology not only for his titles and musical directions but also for his organ stops. This is somewhat confusing, since the organ Gronau played in St. Mary's Church was, despite some eighteenth-century additions, a large Flemish/German instrument of the late sixteenth century.

Gotthold Frotscher has distilled some of Gronau's registrations into various categories; for the sake of coherence the stop names are here translated into modern equivalents:

1. "Forte" (full organ) registrations:
   Dark forte, often used in variations without Pedal: Principal 16', Quintadena 16', Principal 8', Quintadena 8', Flute 8', Octave 4', Superoctave 2'
   Reed forte, with manuals coupled: Principal 16', Principal 8', Flute 8', Octave 4', Flute 4', Twentysecond 1', Fagotto 16', Regal 8' or Trumpet 8'
   Bright forte: Principal 8', Flute 8', Gedackt 8', Octave 4', Superoctave 2' ("requiring also wider 8' and 4' voices and Mixtures, but without 16' stops")
   Silvery forte: Principal 8', Flute 8', Octave 4', Flute 4', Salicet 4', Flageolet 2'
2. Accompanimental registrations:
   Manual: Flute 8', Octave 4', Salicet 4'; or Flute 8' and Quintadena 8'; or Octave 8', Flute 8', Flute 4'; or Flute 8', Flute 4'
   Pedal: Subbass 16', Violone 16', Flute 8'; or Principal 16', Violine 16', Lieblich Gedackt 16', Octave 8', Flute 8
3. *Cantus firmus* registrations (representative):
   Principal 8', Quintadena 8', Flute 8', Superoctave 2'
   Principal 8', Gedackt 8', Octave 4', Flute 4', Salicet 4', Octave 2'

Flute 8', Principal 4', Flute 4',Twentysecond 1', Regal 8'
Principal 8', Gamba 8', Octave 4',Vox Humana 8'
Principal 8', Flute 8', Octave 4', Flute 4', Salicet 4', Oboe 8',Trumpet 8'

These are for a treble *cantus*; for a tenor *cantus* Gronau suggests Gamba and reed 8', and for a Pedal *cantus* all the reeds from 32' to 4' [54, pp. 1028–32].

What is curious about the Gronau registrations is their avoidance of off-unison mutations and reliance on some of the newer string colors along with the older reed colors. Gronau also mixes narrow and wide stops, and includes reeds in one of his full organ schemes. Despite the fact that Gronau is believed to have spent all his life in the Baltic city of Danzig, his music looks forward toward the "galant" style developing in central Germany rather than backward toward the old Sweelinck-pupil school, and he seems to have been more influenced by developments to the southeast than by what was going on to the west of him in Hamburg (a goodly distance away in his day). His registrations cannot therefore be regarded as typical for the North; they tend toward developments in the southern and central regions in the middle of the eighteenth century [229, p. 70].

Much of the music of the north European Baroque is familiar to organists, but it is often played and registered in a static and lackluster manner. This music is exuberant; the big pieces were meant to be exciting and even startling, and the small pieces offer endless opportunities for color. Perhaps part of our problem lies in the familiar brittle-sounding "neo-Baroque" instruments of the 1950s and 1960s that we tend to associate with this music, with their thin, top-heavy sound and unyielding wind supply. While it is true that the organs of northern Europe ostensibly provided the inspiration for this style, it is more of the letter than the spirit. They look all right on paper, but lack the substance to deliver musically.

The instruments for which Buxtehude, Bruhns, and Böhm wrote are red-blooded, warm, and colorful, with seeming faults—such as unequal temperament and wind systems of uncertain equilibrium—that turn to virtues when the right music is played on them. Since the 1970s several American builders have been taking the lessons of these instruments to heart and have built a number of organs based on their principles, some even intended as direct copies. For players who have access to these organs, the registrational practices of the seventeenth and early eighteenth centuries will have meaning, and the music will come alive. For those who do not, it will be more difficult, and some of the rules will have to be broken to approximate the right effect.

On organs with too much foundation and not enough in the way of mutations, supercouplers and reeds may have to be used in imaginative ways to achieve brightness and balance. On those with too little foundation and too much upperwork, the rule against multiplying 8' stops will have to be broken, and the upperwork perhaps used more sparingly in order to simulate a more authentic-sounding balance. As in all organs of the Renaissance and Baroque periods, a warm and singing 8' Principal is an indispensable stop, and modern organs lacking such a color are handicapped. Thus on those unfortunate instruments possessing no 8' Principal at all, every 8' flue stop available, regardless of color, may have to be marshalled to support and balance the plenum.

Despite the fondness of some present-day organists for gapped combinations, the regrettable fact is that in addition to being generally disapproved of in the Baroque period, they tend to sound worse on organs already foundationless and thin in tone color. Those in the habit of using an 8' Quintadena and a 1 1/3' Larigot for a solo in a chorale-prelude should experiment instead with a more colorful salad based on a stronger 8' flute, built up with 4' and 2' pitches and garnished with not only that Larigot but also with a Sesquialtera, a Cymbal, or a buzzy reed. The result will not only be more authentic but also more interesting.

16 Central Germany

Composers

Johann Friedrich Alberti (1642–1710)
Andreas Armsdorff (1679–1699)
Johann Bernhard Bach (1675–1749)
Johann Christoph Bach (1642–1703)
Johann Michael Bach (1648–1694)
Johann Sebastian Bach (1685–1750)
Arnold Melchior Brunckhorst (c1670–1720)
Johann Buttstedt (1666–1727)
Georg Friedrich Kauffmann (1679–1735)
Johann Tobias Krebs (1690–1762)
Johann Krieger (1651–1735)
Johann Philipp Krieger (1649–1725)
Johann Kuhnau (1660–1722)
Johann Pachelbel (1653–1706)
Christian Ritter (1645/50–c1725)
Nicolaus Adam Strungk (1640–1700)
Nicolaus Vetter (1666–1734)
Johann Caspar Vogler (1696–1763)
Tobias Volckmar (1678–1754)
Johann Gottfried Walther (1684–1748)
Friedrich Zachau (1663–1712)

Representative Organs

MARKET CHURCH, HALLE (Small organ)
Georg Reichel, 1664 [234, p. 132]

Manual
Grob–Gedackt 8' (wood)
Principal 4' (prestant)
Spillflöte 4'
Octava 2'
Super–Octav 1'
Sesquialtera II (1 3/5'–1 1/3')

[N.B. This church also had a large organ of three manuals and 55 stops built in 1712 by Christoph Contius of Halberstadt.]

CHURCH OF SS. PETER AND PAUL, WEIMAR
Christoph Junge, 1685 [18, p. 80]

Oberwerk
Quintadena 16'
Principal 8'
Grobgedackt 8'
Gemshorn 8'
Viol di Gamba 8'
Octava 4'
Quinta 2 2/3'
Super Octava 2'
Mixtur IV
Cymbel III
Trompeta 8'

Rückpositiv
Grobgedackt 8'
Quintadena 8'
Principal 4'
Klein Gedackt 4'
Spillflöte 4'
Viol di Gamba 4'
Octava 2'
Sifflöte 1'
Sesquialtera II
Cymbel Mixtur

Pedal
Subbass 16'
Posaunen 16'
Trompet Bass 8'
Cornet Bass 2'

Accessory Stops
Oberwerk Tremulant
Rückpositiv Tremulant
Cymbel Stern (Rückpositiv)
Couplers: Oberwerk-Pedal, Rückpositiv-Pedal, Rückpositiv-Oberwerk

CHURCH OF ST. GEORGE, EISENACH
Georg Christoph Stertzing, 1696–1707 [1, p.214]

Hauptwerk
Bordun 16'
Principal 8'
Viol di gamba 8'
Rohrflöte 8'
Quinte 5 1/3'
Oktave 4'
Flöte 4'
Nasat 2 2/3'
Sesquialtera III 4'

Oberseitenwerk
Quintatön 16'
Grossoktave 8'
Gemshorn 8'
Gedackt 8'
Principal 4'
Flöte douce 4'
Hohlflöte 4'
Hohlquinte 2 2/3'
Superoktave 2'

Mixtur VI 2'
Cymbel III
Trompete 8'

Brustwerk
Grobgedackt 8'
Kleingedackt 4'
Principal 2'
Supergemshörnlein 2'
Sifflöte 1'
Sesquialtera II

Pedal
Untersatz 32'
Principal 16'
Subbass 16'
Violon 16'
Oktave 8'
Gedackt 8'
Superoktave 4'
Flöte 4'
Bauerflöte 1'
Mixtur V
Posaune 32'
Posaune 16'
Trompete 8'
Cornet 2'

Blockflöte 2'
Sesquialtera III 2'
Scharf IV
Vox humana 8'

Unterseitenwerk
Barem 16'
Stillgedackt 8'
Quintatön 8'
Principal 4'
Nachthorn 4'
Spitzflöte 4'
Spitzquinte 2 2/3' Grosser
Oktave 2'
Rauschquinte 1 1/2'
Superoktave 1'
Cymbel III
Regal 8'

Accessory Stops
3 Tremulants
Cymbelstern
Glockenspiel 2' (Hauptwerk)
Hauptwerk-Unterseitenwerk coupler; Hauptwerk-Pedal coupler
2 Sperrventils

CHURCH OF ST. BONIFACE, ARNSTADT
Johann Friedrich Wender, 1699–1703 [207, p. 5]

Oberwerk
Prinzipal 8'
Viol da Gamba 8'
Quintadena 8'
Grobgedackt 8'
Gemshorn 8'
Quinta 5 1/3'
Octava 4'
Octava 2'
Mixtur IV
Cymbel III
Trompete 8'

Brustwerk
Stillgedackt 8'
Prinzipal 4'
Nachthorn 4' (capped)
Quinta 2 2/3'
Spitzflöte 2' (?)
Sesquialtera
Mixtur IV

Pedal
Subbass 16' (wood)
Prinzipalbass 8'
Hohlflöte 8'
Posaunbass 16'
(Cornetbass 2')

Accessory Stops
Tremulant
Glockenaccord (saucer bells, on Oberwerk)
Manual and Pedal couplers

[N.B. This stoplist is from the contract, but it also includes the Hauptwerk Octava 2' and Glockenaccord, which were added later, when the Oberwerk Cymbel and Brustwerk Mixtur were also enlarged by one rank. The Pedal Cornetbass is found in an estimate of 1701 but not in the contract, and it is not known whether it was actually included.]

CATHEDRAL, FREIBERG
Gottfried Silbermann, 1710–14 [52, p. 95–100]

Hauptwerk
Bourdon 16'
Principal 8'
Viola da Gamba 8'
Rohrflöte 8'
Octava 4'
Quinta 2 2/3'
Super-Octava 2'
Tertia 1 3/5'
Cornet V
Mixtur IV
Cimbeln III
Trompete 8'
Clarin 4'

Oberwerk
Quintaden 16'
Principal 8'
Quintaden 8'
Gedackt 8'
Octava 4'
Spitzflöte 4'
Super-Octava 2'
Flaschflöte 1'
Echo Cornet V
Mixtur III
Cimbeln II
Krummhorn 8'
Vox Humana 8'

Brust (Unterwerk)
Gedackt 8'
Principal 4'
Rohrflöte 4'
Nasat 2 2/3'
Octava 2'
Tertia 1 3/5'
Quinta 1 1/3'
Sifflöte 1'
Mixtur III

Pedal
Untersatz 32'
Octavbass 16'
Principalbass 16'
Subbass 16'
Octavbass 8'
Octavbass 4'
Pedalmixtur VI
Posaunenbass 16'
Trompetenbass 8'
Clarinbass 4'

Accessory Stops
2 Tremulants (one for Oberwerk, one for entire organ)
Sperrventils: Hauptwerk and Burst, Oberwerk
Manual couplers (shove couplers)

PARISH CHURCH, STÖRMTHAL
Zacharias Hildebrandt, 1723 [stoplist taken from extant organ]

Manual
Principal 8'
Quintadena 8'
Gedackt 8'

Pedal
Subbass 16'
Principalbass 8'
Lieblich Posaune 16'

Praestant 4'
Rohrflöte 4'
Nasat 2 2/3'
Octava 2'
Tertia 1 3/5'
Quinta 1 1/3'
Sifflet 1'
Cornet III
Mixtur III

Accessory Stops
Tremulant
Manual–Pedal coupler (Windkoppel)

PARISH CHURCH, REINHARDTSGRIMMA
Gottfried Silbermann, 1730 [stoplist taken from extant organ]

Hauptwerk
Principal 8'
Quintadena 8'
Rohrflöte 8'
Octava 4'
Spitzflöte 4'
Quinta 2 2/3'
Octava 2'
Cornet III (treble)
Mixtur IV 1 1/3'

Hinterwerk
Gedackt 8'
Rohrflöte 4'
Nassat 2 2/3'
Octava 2'
Tertia 1 3/5'
Quinta 1 1/3'
Sifflöte 1'
Zymbeln II 2/3'

Pedal
Subbass 16'
Octavenbass 8'
Posaunenbass 16'

Accessory Stops
Tremulant
Manual coupler (shove)
Pedal coupler (Windkoppel)

CASTLE CHURCH, ALTENBURG
Heinrich Gottfried Trost, 1739 [stoplist from extant organ and 56]

Hauptwerk
Gross-Quintadena 16'★
Flaute traverse 16'★
Principal 8'
Bordun 8'★
Spitzflöte 8'
Viol di Gamba 8'
Rohrflöte
Octave 4'★
Kleingedackt 4'
Quinte 2 2/3'
Superoctava 2'
Blockflöte 2'

Oberwerk
Geigenprincipal 8'
Lieblich Gedackt 8'
Vugara 8'
Quintadena 8'
Hohlflöte 8'
Gemshorn 4'
Flaute douce 4' (2 rks)
Nasat 2 2/3'
Octave 2'
Waldflöte 2'
Superoctava 1'
Cornet V

Sesquialtera II
Mixtur VI–IX★
Trompete 8'

Mixtur IV–V
Vox humana 8'

Pedal
Principalbass 16'
Violonbass 16'
Subbass 16'
Octavenbass 8'
Posaune 32'
Posaune 16'
Trompete 8'

Accessory Stops
Hauptwerk Tremulant
Oberwerk Tremulant
Glockenspiel (Hauptwerk; saucer bells)
Windkoppel (Hauptwerk-Pedal coupler)
Oberwerk-Hauptwerk (shove coupler)

★Stop also available on the Pedal by transmission.

PARISH CHURCH, GROSSHARTMANNSDORF
Gottfried Silbermann, 1741 [stoplist taken from extant organ]

Hauptwerk
Principal 8'
Quintaden 8'
Rohrflöte 8'
Octave 4'
Spitzflöte 4'
Quinta 2 2/3'
Octave 2'
Cornet III
Mixtur IV

Oberwerk
Gedackt 8'
Rohrflöte 4'
Nassat 2 2/3'
Octave 2'
Gemshorn 2'
Tertia 1 3/5'
Quinta 1 1/3'
Sifflöte 1'
Cymbel II

Pedal
Subbass 16'
Octavbass 8'
Posaunenbass 16'

Accessory Stops
Tremulant
Bassventil

PARISH CHURCH, BAD BERKA
Heinrich Nicolaus Trebs, 1742–73 [18, p. 170]

Hauptwerk
Quintadena 16'
Principal 8'
Gedackt 8'
Flöte 8'
Gemshorn 8'
Octave 4'

Brustwerk (Unterwerk)
Gedackt 8'
Quintadena 8'
Principal 4'
Nachthorn 4'
Quinte 2 2/3'
Octave 2'

Gedackt 4'
Quinte 2 2/3'
Nassat 2 2/3'
Octave 2'
Sesquialtera II
Mixtur V
Trompete 8'

Waldflöte 2'
Tritonus 1 3/5' (Tierce)
Cimbel III

Pedal
Subbass 16'
Principal 8'
Hohlflöte 4'
Posaunbass 16'
Trompete 8'
Cornett 4'

Accessory Stops
Manual coupler
Pedal coupler

PARISH CHURCH, ZSCHORTAU
Johann Scheibe, 1744–76 [18, p. 176]

Manual
Quintatön 16' (wood)
Principal 8'
Grobgedackt 8' (wood)
Viola di Gamba 8' (divided c/c♯)
Octav 4'
Fleute-Travers 4' (wood)
Hohe Fleute 2 2/3' (divided c/c♯)
Super Octava 2'
Super Octava or Sifflöte 1'

Pedal
Subbass 16' (wood)
Violon 8' (wood)
Posaunenbass 16' (wood)

Accessory Stops
Tremulant
Manual-Pedal coupler

CHURCH OF ST. WENCESLAUS, NAUMBURG
Zacharias Hildebrandt, 1746 [34, p. 189]

Hauptwerk
Principal 16'
Quintadehn 16'
Octav 8'
Spitzflöte 8'
Gedackt 8'
Octav 4'
Spitzflöte 4'
Octav 2'
Weitpfeiffe 2'
Sesquialtera II
Cornet IV
Mixtur VIII
Bombart 16'
Trompet 8'

Oberwerk
Bordun 16'
Principal 8'
Hohlflöte 8'
Unda maris 8' (treble)
Prestant 4'
Gemshorn 4'
Quinta 2 2/3'
Octav 2'
Waldflöte 2'
Tertia 1 3/5'
Quinta 1 1/3'
Sifflöte 1'
Scharff V
Vox humana 8'

Rückpositiv
Principal 8'
Quintadehn 8'
Rohrflöte 8'
Viol di Gamba 8'
Praestant 4'
Fugara 4'
Rohrflöte 4'
Nassat 2 2/3'
Octav 2'
Rauschpfeiffe II
Cimbel V
Fagott 16'

Pedal
Principal 16'
Violon 16'
Subbass 16'
Octav 8'
Violon 8'
Octav 4'
Nachthorn 2'
Mixtur VII
Posaune 32'
Posaune 16'
Trompett 8'
Clarin 4'

Accessory Stops
Tremulant (Rückpositiv)
Cimbelstern
Coupler (Windkoppel)
4 Ventils

Registration

Central Germany may be defined as an area largely within the former East Germany, extending from the Erzgebirge mountain range in the south (which effectively divides this mostly Protestant region from the Catholic South) to Celle and Berlin in the north. It extends west-east from Eisenach near the old East/West German border to Upper Lusatia on the Czech border, but the area of greatest organ building and playing activity was in the lower central part, Thuringia and Saxony. This region was the birthplace of J. S. Bach (and numerous other Bachs), Handel, Walther, the majority of the composers whose names appear at the beginning of this chapter, and some who made their mark elsewhere, such as Scheidt and Weckmann.

With the exception of a small group of Catholic musicians in Dresden, virtually all the composers in this area were Lutheran; and, as might be expected, there is a wealth of chorale-based music. Relatively short chorale-preludes predominate, suitable for preceding the sung chorales in the church service, but one also encounters more extended chorale partitas and fantasias. The shorter chorale-preludes provide a wealth of high-quality service music for present-day organists of all persuasions, for virtually all can be played on a two-manual organ, many are suitable for an organ of only one manual, and some do not even require the Pedal.

In addition we find fantasias, fugues, and paired preludes (or toccatas) and fugues, which were brought to their culmination by J. S. Bach. The toccatas of this time and place are no longer the gentle meditative pieces of the Frescobaldi school, but are rather virtuosic works more closely related to the *stylus phantasticus* idiom of the North. It is in the central German Baroque too that one begins to find instrumental forms, such as the trio sonata, adapted to the organ, along with outright transcriptions from instrumental works, often by popular Italian masters such as Vivaldi and Albinoni. Such practices may have been fostered by the active musical life of the courts in this area.

Possibly the greatest obstacle (as well as the greatest challenge) in dealing with this time and place is the matter of the "Bach organ." But J. S. Bach's professional life spanned a half-century during which much was happening in the evolution of the German organ, and Bach, depite his transcendent greatness, was but one of a number of organist-composers at work in central Germany in the late seventeenth century and the first half of the eighteenth. Neither the man nor his music can be wholly isolated from this milieu. The "Bach organ" of any given segment of this period was also the organ of Walther, Kauffmann, Buttstedt, Zachau, and, for a portion of their careers, even Pachelbel and Telemann.

During most of the seventeenth century the north German organ culture was of such innovative brilliance that the events of other areas fell into the shadows, and central German organs followed, in a general way, the northern pattern. But as that northern brilliance waned in the early years of the eighteenth century, it was central Germany that became the leading edge. A comparison of the stoplists at the beginning of this chapter and those in the previous one will show a widening gulf as the North continued to be locked into the pattern established by Schnitger (who died in 1719) while evolution and innovation were occurring just to the south.

Toward the end of the seventeenth century one finds significant changes in central German organ design that became fairly standardized well before the death of Bach. The Rückpositiv gradually fell out of favor. Eventually it was found largely in organs where older casework was re-used, such as Hildebrandt's splendid instrument of 1743–46 in the Church of St. Wenceslaus in Naumburg. The miniature Renaissance Brustwerk of the North evolved into the larger Unterwerk (although sometimes retaining its old name, as in Silbermann's Freiberg organ), and an essentially new division, the Oberwerk, began to appear in the space above the Hauptwerk. One also begins to find small enclosed elements ("echo" Cornets or reeds) during this period.

Sometimes the term "Oberwerk" came to designate the main division, and in some two-manual organs "Oberwerk" is synonymous with "Hauptwerk." This confusion of terminology is not limited to central Germany; it occurs in the northern region as well. Generally if the term "Oberwerk" occurs in a context that mentions other divisions (Unterwerk, Brustwerk, Positiv) but not anything specifically named Hauptwerk, it may be taken to designate the main division. If an organ has both a Hauptwerk and an Oberwerk, however, the Oberwerk is a subsidiary division located above the Hauptwerk.

Pedal divisions became proportionately smaller, reduced to the most essential stops, and lost their place in the façade. The whole so-called *Werk-prinzip* quietly disintegrated. Although the names of the divisions still generally denoted their position in the organ, none was individually encased or walled off, and the case itself was barely more than a loose (if still elegant) garment to screen the interior. The Pedal was still sometimes located at the sides of the manual divisions, but more often it was relegated to the back of the organ, causing an increase in the depth of the casework; and Seitenwerk divisions occasionally appeared at floor level when space would not permit a vertical piling-up of divisions.

Tonally, the most noticeable thing about these central German stoplists, aside from the general scarcity of manual reeds, is the gradual proliferation of 8' stops, especially string-toned and hybrid colors such as the Gamba, Salicional, Fugara, Gemshorn, and, in the Pedal, the all-important Violones at 16' and 8', which were usually made of wood. Toward the middle of the century other imitative stops, such as the Traverse Flute, made their appearance. Organists and their auditors wanted such stops, and the builders took pains to provide them. In his first proposal for the Altenburg Castle organ, dated 1733, Trost makes these revealing comments in his descriptions of the individual stops:

Viol de Gambe: "Specially voiced to sound like the genuine instrument."
Hautbois: "Very similar to the natural oboe, and can be used in its place in music."
Vox humana: "Closest of all to the human voice" [265, p. 173].

Bach's pupil Agricola attests to the success of Trost's imitative stops, noting that when the 16' Querflöte and 8' Gamba on the Altenburg organ are played in rapid runs and arpeggios, "the pleasant keenness that is found in both these stops comes as close to the attack of a bowstroke on a [stringed] bass as is possible to achieve with pipes." Agricola similarly praises the Vox Humana in this organ, while noting that many others are more like the voice of an "ill-trained choirboy" [221, p. 5]. Happily, the Altenburg organ still exists and has recently been restored, and its imitative stops are indeed impressive.

Another builder, Wagner, wrote comments similar to Trost's concerning his 1727 organ in Berlin's Garnisonkirche, stating that his Flute Traversiere was "like a real flute in the middle of its compass," and that his Vox Humana, enclosed in an expression box with its own tremulant, was "subtle, like a human voice" [181, p. 163].

As has been seen in previous chapters, imitative stops and registrations have always been associated with the organ. But in the eighteenth century a new generation of imitative stops (including string-toned stops) was appearing in central as well as southern Germany and countries to the east. The reasons for the popularity of such stops in this region can only be conjectured. In the free cities of the North, most organists, despite their fame as recitalists, were primarily church musicians and to some extent bound by the natural conservatism of things ecclesiastical. Ensemble instruments were indeed used in the larger churches, which could afford them, but which also could afford large, impressive organs.

In central and southern Germany, many organists (including Bach and Pachelbel) spent at least a part of their careers as court musicians for the numerous petty dukes, margraves, and electors who throve in this area well into the Classical period. They perforce came into greater contact with ensemble music: they wrote it, conducted it, and usually could play (and teach) instruments other than keyboard instruments. But both the organs and the instrumental establishments tended to be small in most court chapels, and versatility was important (note Trost's comment about his Hautbois stop being good enough to use in place of a real oboe). Some composers, notably Bach and Walther, were beginning to write keyboard transcriptions of instrumental works, which presuppose a certain amount of imitative organ color.

The occurrence of registration directions in central Germany was no greater or more organized than in other parts of Germany during this period. Two of the best-known sources are Kauffmann's *Harmonische Seelenlust*, of 1733, and directions left by Gottfried Silbermann with his two-manual organs in Fraureuth (c1739–42) and Grosshartmannsdorf (1741). It is possible that too much has been made of the latter and not enough of the former. Kauffman's work is a collection of 63 chorale-preludes, many of which have detailed registration directions. The preludes themselves are cast in a number of common forms used by other composers of the period (including Bach). Thus they offer some clue as to the kinds of registrations used with various types of chorale-preludes (which the Silbermann registrations do not).

What is perhaps mildly surprising is the number of pieces having registrations based on a 16' stop—Principal, Quintadena, Bordun, or Fagott. Some of these are light-textured manual pieces such as No. 3, *Ach Gott, mich armen Sünder*, which has a left-hand solo on the Rückpositiv Fagott 16', Quintadena 8', and Spitzflöte 2' against a triplet figure played on the Oberwerk Vox Humana 8', Gemshorn 8', and Spillpfeife 4'; the same 16', 8', 2' combination accompanies a Pedal solo of Violon 16', Trompete 8', Gemshorn 4', and Cornettin 2' in No. 14B, *Ein feste Burg*—an interesting instance of the same combination being used as both a solo and an accompaniment.

A three-part manual piece in sixteenth notes, No. 7, *Auf meinem lieben Gott*, is registered for Quintadena 16', Spillflöte 8', and Flaut-doux 4'; a stronger version is found in No. 9, *Christ lag in Todesbanden*, a work of four-part texture played on Quintadena 16', Principal 8', and Octava 4'. Another 4-part piece, No. 18B, *Freu dich sehr*, is registered for Principal 16', Gedackt 8', and Spillflöte 4'. Some fairly lively manual pieces make regular use of the 16' reed, such as No. 46B, *O Herre Gott* (Presto, 16th notes), with the Fagott 16', Quintadena 8' and Spitzflöte 2' in the right hand against Quintadena 16', Principal 8', and Gemshorn 8'; and No. 48, *Puer natus* (Vivace, eighth notes), with Fagott 16', Quintadena 8', and Principal 4'.

This frequent use by Kauffmann of the 16' pitch basis (and particularly the Fagott)—perhaps influenced by *basso continuo* practice in cantata settings—helps to put in better perspective Walther's shorthand account of Bach's registration of his *Ein feste Burg* at Muhlhausen in 1709. It is only good sense to assume that Bach did not play the opening left-hand Oberwerk part on the Fagott 16' alone, but rather on the Fagott with some suitable 8' and 4' (perhaps even 2') flue stops, just as he would hardly have played the right-hand Brustwerk part on the Sesquialtera mutations without giving them their usual 8' and 4' flute foundation.

It is a worthwhile exercise to experiment with this piece on a good three-manual organ (especially one with a sound historical basis) using some of Kauffman's combinations, not just for the opening section but for the Rückpositiv "bridge" sections (perhaps employing one of the lighter combinations based on an 8' flute) and also for the Pedal. It is likely that a Pedal registration change (or coupling of a strong manual) occurs at measure 25, where the chorale melody suddenly breaks in in augmentation, and reverts to a lighter sound for the second "bridge" at measure 35.

Some of Kauffman's quieter pieces employ one or more 8' stops or softer 8' and 4' combinations. No. 46A, *O Herre Gott*, marked *Con affetto,* is registered for Principal 8' and Gemshorn 8'; a livelier three-part No. 38B, *Nun freut euch*, is for Gedackt 8' and Spillpfiefe 4'. Some interesting solo combinations are found throughout. No. 4, *Allein Gott in der Höh'*, accompanies a Pedal solo of Posaune 16' and Violon 8' with Principal 8', Octave 4', and Sesquialtera on the manual; the Pedal solo in No. 34A, *Komm, heiliger Geist*, is for Violon 16', Trompete 8', Nachthorn 4', and Cornet 2' against the Vox humana 8', Salicional 8', and Spillpfeife 4' on the Oberwerk. In No. 19B, *Gelobet seist du*, a robust solo of Fagott 16', Quintadena 16', Gemshorn 8', and Kleingedackt 4' is accompanied in sixteenth notes on the Vox humana 8' and Salicional 8'. Occasional instances of gapped combinations are found, as in No. 37B, *Nun danket alle Gott*, where running sixteenth notes on the Hauptwerk Gedeckt 8', Nasat 2 2/3', and Spitzflöte 2' contrast with a chordal accompaniment on the Rückpositiv Principal 8', Gedackt 8', and Kleingedackt 4'. No. 54, *Warum betrübst du*, solos the Hauptwerk Cornet or Sesquialtera (presumably with 8' foundation) in the right hand against the Rückpositiv Gedackt 8' and Principal 4'.

One curious practice of Kauffman's deserves brief mention. In several of the chorale-preludes (notably those with an obbligato part for an oboist), the left-hand part is registered for a 4' stop, but the player is directed to play it an octave lower. Often this occurs where the right hand is playing on an 8' Principal, and the left hand is on a 4' Principal; this seems to be a device to give independence to the left-hand part and avoid awkward crossings. It could well be employed in other pieces by other composers, even if not so marked, and one writer suggests that some of the bicinia in Bach's *Clavierübung* (BWV 802–5) could possibly be played this way [274, p. 177].

The *Harmonische Seelenlust* is fortunately available in a recent modern edition (Pierre Pidoux, ed.; Bärenreiter, 1980), and is worthy of study. The pieces make useful service music, and stylistically one can find many parallels in other sources, including works of Walther, Pachelbel, and the recently published "Neumeister" chorale-preludes of J. S. Bach and his circle. There is sufficient consistency in the registrations to make them applicable to similar pieces by most of the central German composers. However, the player should also heed the admonition in Kauffmann's preface, that his registrations are only suggestions and that organists should always use their own judgment.

Other composers were far less generous than Kauffmann in their registration hints. In his chorale-preludes, J. G. Walther tells us little. In his *Plauener Orgelbuch* (1708–10) there is a prelude on *Hilf Gott, dass mir's gelinge*, in which the melody occurs in the soprano line and, in augmentation, in the Pedal. For this somewhat unusual setting Walther assigns a registration of 4' Principal plus Sesquialtera to the right hand, a Gamba 8' to the accompanimental left hand, and a 2' Kornett (reed) to the Pedal [170, p. 31]. His reason for being so specific in this instance is presumably that it is necessary to maintain the pitch levels indicated (4' right hand, 8' left hand, 2' pedal), since otherwise the two solo lines would not relate to each other as he intended. The registrations themselves are nothing out of the ordinary for the period.

Walther also frequently designates on which manuals he wants his solos and accompaniments played, thus offering a clue as to what is possible. No. 32, *Nun lasst uns Gott den Herren*, a piece in long notes to be played on the Oberwerk (Hauptwerk), is probably intended for Organo Pleno. Other chorale-preludes give more florid solos to the Rückpositiv, accompanied on the Oberwerk; these call for bright solo registrations against a quieter (and usually foundational) accompaniment. Manual directions of this kind can also be found in the works of other composers, including such earlier writers as J. M. Bach *(Allein Gott in der Höh sei Ehr*, which alternates chordal passages on the Oberwerk with lighter contrapuntal passages on the Rückpositiv).

From the same period as Kauffman and Walther come some more conservative chorale-prelude registrations that were used at a dedication in Lahm in 1732. The first solos Quintadena 16', Principal and Gedackt 8', and Octave 4' on Manual I against Gemshorn 8' and Flute 4' on Manual II, with a rather strong Pedal (16', 16', 12', 8', 6'). The second solos 8', 4', 2' plus Sesquialter on Manual II against Principals 8' and 4' on Manual I, again with a rather strong Pedal—16', 8', 4', and Posaune 16'. In the third, Principal and Trumpet 8' on Manual I are used against Gemshorn and Quintadena 8', with a strong Pedal similar to that of the first registration [330, p. 123]. Such examples confirm that 16'-based solos or strong Pedal registrations are by no means unique to Kauffman.

In his *Orgelbüchlein*, J. S. Bach gives only one registration: In No. 2, *Gott durch deine Güte*, he calls for a Principal 8' in the right hand and a Trompete 8' in the Pedal, thus placing the two parts of the canon an octave apart. As in the Walther example, concern for pitch levels is probably what prompted Bach to set down this registration. No registration is given for the left-hand part, but its *continuo* character would suggest something with a 16' basis—perhaps the Quintadena or Principal. In the same collection, No. 35B, *Liebster Jesu, wir sind hier,* has the right-hand (melody) part marked "forte" and the left-hand part marked "piano"; and although no registration is given for No. 33, *Komm, Gott Schöpfer*, its expanded version in the *Eighteen Chorales* is marked "Organo Pleno," which would be equally appropriate to the shorter version.

Of the other "Eighteen," the first, *Komm, heiliger Geist*, is also intended for full organ, as is the third setting of *Nun komm, der Heiden Heiland*, but Bach gives few other hints in this collection. Some of the solo chorale-preludes have a definite instrumental flavor akin to some of the Schübler settings. The walking bass in the first setting of *Nun komm, der Heiden Heiland* cries out for a distinct-sounding Violone, while the sectional nature of *O Lamm Gottes* offers a legitimate opportunity for stop or manual changes between sections.

Pitch and dynamic indications are given in Schübler's printed edition for some of Bach's *Sechs Chorale* (more familiarly known as the "Schübler chorales"). Since they are all transcriptions (for organs of two manuals and pedal) of chorale settings from his own cantatas, the instrumentation for the original versions of most of them is known and can offer a further clue to appropriate registrations. The pitches given have to do with the basis of the registration, and other pitches can be built upon this basis, as in Kauffmann's examples.

No. 1, *Wachet auf, ruft uns die Stimme*: Right hand and left hand (solo), 8'; Pedal 16'. The original instrumentation (in Cantata 140) is entirely for strings, with a tenor solo. This might suggest Gambas and/or Principals at 8' and 4' with Violone 16' as the Pedal basis, and a suitable light reed, qualified by some flues, for the solo. In this context, the common practice of playing the solo on a loud reed (yea, even a blatant Tuba), with a correspondingly loud accompaniment, is somewhat suspect.

No. 2, *Wo soll ich fliehen hin*: Manual I 8', Manual II 16', Pedal 4'. No original instrumentation is known, but the pitch bases and the "busy" nature of the music strongly suggest some of Kauffmann's registrations in which the 16' Fagott is called for on the manual, with a fairly strong 4' Pedal solo combination.

No. 3, *Wer nur den lieben Gott lasst walten*: Here only the basic pitch (4') of the Pedal line is given, and there is no indication as to whether the upper parts are to be played on one or two manuals. The original instrumentation (in Cantata 93) assigns the melody to strings, the two upper parts to singers, and the left-hand part to the *continuo*; thus a Pedal solo on a 4' Principal with a light reed might be appropriate, with the two upper parts played on 8'-based flutes and the left-hand part on a light 16'-based combination.

No. 4, *Meine Seele erhebt den Herren*: The only indication Bach gives is that the right-hand solo should be played "forte." The original instrumentation (in Cantata 10) gives the melody to two oboes and trumpet, the two inner parts to voices, and the bass to the *continuo*. The bass line (Pedal) could thus be played on a string at 16' and/or 8', with the melody on light, smooth reeds (with flues), and the inner parts on flutes and/or principals.

No. 5, *Ach bleib bei uns*: No directions given beyond "a 2 Clav. e Pedale." The instrumentation (in Cantata 6) gives the melody to the soprano voice, the accompaniment (left hand) to the Violoncello-piccolo, the bass to the *continuo*. A Principal (or possibly one of Kauffmann's Vox Humana combinations) would thus suit the melody, and a good Gamba (perhaps helped by a suitable 4' stop) the accompaniment, with a Pedal based on a 16' string.

No. 6, *Kommst du nun, Jesu, vom Himmel herunter*. In his revised version Bach called for a 4'-based Pedal solo here, although he originally put the solo in the left-hand part. The original instrumentation (in Cantata 137) assigns this solo to a singer, with *basso continuo* and a violin solo for accompaniment. This suggests a somewhat light registration, with perhaps a 4' Principal solo, a 16'-based left-hand *continuo*, and an 8' Gamba in the right-hand part.

Although they are transcriptions, Bach's *Schübler Chorales* have been discussed in some detail here because they are not incompatible with some of Kauffmann's registrational ideas. They also offer clues to chorale-preludes written in an "instrumental" style, such as Bach's *Herr Gott, nun schluss den Himmel auf* (No. 19 in *Orgelbüchlein*) and *An Wasserflüssen Babylon* (No. 3 in *Eighteen Chorales*). Indeed, such pieces foreshadow much of the chorale-prelude writing of the next generation, including works by Bach's sons and pupils such as Krebs.

Bach, Walther, Pachelbel, and others wrote a number of sets of variations on chorales, and presumably improvised them as well. The chorale-prelude registrations discussed are also applicable to variations, but it is interesting that a contemporary source makes special mention of them. In a booklet published at the time of the completion of Wagner's large organ for the Garnisonkirche in Berlin in 1725, we find the suggestion that the Hauptwerk Bourdon 16' is "useful in sets of variations; good with Quintatön 8' or Spitzflöte 4'." Also useful in variations are the

Gamba 8' (a mild, tapered stop) and Nasat 2 2/3' (when added to other stops). Strings 8' and 4' are, interestingly, suggested for "running basses and arpeggios" as well as for combining with heavier 16' and 8' stops for slower passages, but we must remember that these eighteenth-century strings were of a fuller and more robust character than modern ones, and a string-toned stop was expected to function somewhat like the stringed instrument in *continuo* work. In accordance with long and widespread custom, the five-rank Cornet and Prinzipal 8' are deemed useful for bringing out chorale melodies [181, p. 163].

The chorale-prelude was not the only genre to be affected by the "transcription" style. Bach and Walther made unabashed keyboard transcriptions of instrumental concertos by favorite Italian composers (Vivaldi and Albinoni), by Telemann, and by friends (such as Bach's patron, Duke Ernst). Although the only indications given are for manual changes (and an occasional *Organo pleno* or dynamic direction), these pieces are, after all, string and woodwind works, and registrations should at least make a nod in this direction. In particular, the brilliant and top-heavy neo-Baroque registrations one occasionally hears are surely less in character than more-restrained combinations drawing a bit more on foundational and unison sounds while still maintaining the clarity of real strings and woodwinds. The slow movements in particular take on a special elegance when registered "instrumentally."

Trio sonatas for two manuals and pedal are usually not transcriptions, but they are a definite borrow from instrumental style. They do not appear in German keyboard literature much before J. S. Bach's lifetime (simple trios, often for manuals only, had, of course, been a part of keyboard literature for much longer). The slow middle movements of at least two of Bach's Trio Sonatas are in fact transcriptions, however. That from the third Trio Sonata (BWV 527) was originally written for flute, strings, and clavier; and that in the fourth (BWV 528) is from a movement for oboe d'amore, gamba, and *continuo*. Using stops of similar color and dynamic on the organ, while nowhere mandated, nonetheless confers a feeling of authenticity.

The above discussion relates primarily to music written in the second quarter of the eighteenth century. Before this period registration directions in music are even scarcer, as in the North; and in music from the late seventeenth century and the opening years of the eighteenth, older registration conventions, as discussed in the previous section, are more pertinent. They would apply to the works of turn-of-the-century composers Armsdorff, Buttstedt, Strungk, and J. M. Bach as well as to some of the earliest chorale-preludes and partitas of J. S. Bach. However, today one would not go to the extremes of the editor of the 1928 Bärenreiter edition of Pachelbel's organ works, who suggested Praetorius's 1619 *Syntagma Musicum* stoplist as the ideal for this music! Pachelbel had much more up-to-date tonal resources to work with in his churches in Erfurt, Nürnberg, and elsewhere, and one must assume that he utilized them to the fullest.

Understanding the changes that were occurring after 1700 also helps to put into context Bach's much-discussed directions for improving the Muhlhausen organ in 1707 [36, p. 58]. Over the years various writers have tried to make a case for his wishing to make the organ more like northern instruments (which Bach had recently visited) or even to prove that he was trying to make it more like a French organ—a type of instrument which, despite his known interest in and knowledge of French music, Bach was never to see or play. It is true that the influence of French organs did begin to be felt in Germany around the mid-point of the century, partly because of the Alsatian influence of Silbermann and, later, of such Francophiles as Marpurg. But in 1707 Silbermann was still an apprentice, and Marpurg was yet to be born.

The truth appears to be that Bach was simply trying to bring an old organ up to the latest central German standards. He wanted a 32' Subbass to give the organ more "gravity"—a desirable quality increasingly alluded to by writers like Adlung as the century wore on, and mentioned by builders such as Silbermann and Trost in their proposals. The rebuilding of the 16' Posaune with larger resonators was also in the interest of greater gravity.

Bach wanted a Fagotto 16' on the Oberwerk for the same reason that Kauffmann included it so frequently in his registrations—it helped the *continuo* line. Wagner also recommended this prompt-speaking half-length reed for running basses and *continuo* work. The replacement of the Hauptwerk Gemshorn with a Viol di Gamba may well have been simply "keeping up with the Joneses"; 8' Gambas were appearing in central German organs everywhere, and Bach thought it would go well with the 4' Salicional already in the Rückpositiv. But possibly this too was requested with *continuo* playing in mind, for a few years earlier, in 1703, Christian Ludwig Boxburg, commenting on a new Casparini organ in Görlitz, recommended the Gamba 8' alone or with Salicet 4', Prinzipal 16', and perhaps the Flute 4', as being "particularly suitable for continuo" [223, p. 44].

The change from a principal-scaled 2 2/3' stop to a flute-scaled one in the Rückpositiv was again quite in line with what central German builders of the period were doing even before Alsatian-trained Gottfried Silbermann came along to reinforce them. Boxburg had especial praise for Casparini's 2 2/3' Spitzflöte in Görlitz, which he thought sounded particularly well with the Prinzipal 8' and Fleut Doux 4'. Combinations such as this were hardly new, as we have seen, for they are found as early as the sixteenth century. But they obviously remained useful in the eighteenth century.

Bach's proposed new Brustpositiv was not based on the old north German model, nor did it have any correlation with the small short-compass French Récit. It was a small *Unterwerk* with a mild Stillgedackt 8' and Fleute douce 4' for *continuo* playing, a Schallmey that probably was meant to sound like an Oboe, and a Quint 2 2/3', Octave 2', and Tertia 1 3/5' which combined with the 8' and 4' flutes to make a Cornet-like Sesquialtera. This combination was useful not only in chorale-preludes and in giving out chorale melodies but also in accompaniments. Bach is later recorded as using a Sesquialtera combination to reinforce the treble unison line, sung by boys, in the *O Lamm Gottes* and *O Mensch bewein* movements of the St. Matthew Passion (although it is possible that it might also have been a substitute for the voices) [126, p. 81]. The indication *Sesquialtera ad Organo* likewise appears in the *continuo* part of an alto aria in Bach's Cantata No. 161 [141, p. 14].

Bach's recommendations for Muhlhausen fall very much in line with the dicta of Jacob Adlung as set forth in his *Musica mechanica organoedi*; this life-work was begun in 1726 but was not published until 1768, after Adlung's death. This work includes an "ideal stoplist," which incorporates most of Bach's Muhlhausen ideas as well as the concepts embodied in many of the organs built in Thuringia and Saxony in the first half of the eighteenth century, including the large Hildebrand organ of 1746 in Naumburg [220, p. 2].

Like many of the central German builders of his time, Adlung disliked Rückpositivs and cared very little for reed stops—or at any rate less so than Bach, according to Adlung's editor, Bach's pupil Agricola. Adlung was also fond of the sound of tin flue pipes, then coming into fashion partly through Silbermann and his followers, and he favored wide-scaled mutations as well as mixtures containing tierces. All these features are found in central German organs of the Baroque period, and must be taken into account in registering music from the region.

Adlung himself makes only general comments on registration, since he seems to favor the experimental approach—"one must register according to one's fancy." But he comes on rather strongly concerning two topics—using more than one stop of the same pitch, and objecting to gapped combinations. Regarding the former, he is aware of the objections of Niedt and Werckmeister, but reasons that if the wind is steady and the bellows large enough there should be no objection to drawing more than one stop of a given pitch. Certainly one finds many examples of stops of the same pitch being combined in Kauffmann's registrations. It is probable that the newer organs in central Germany had better "lungs" than the older instruments to the north, and they also had more 8' and 4' stops. In the same context, Bach's pupil Agricola made this interesting observation in 1758:

> Our ancestors believed that two voices of different scale at the same pitch level would of necessity sound bad if they were drawn together. But if such stops are well constructed and purely voiced, then one can refute our ancestors any day by merely drawing such stops and using them together. I have heard a Lieblich Gedackt, Vugara, Quintadene and Hohlflöte played together on a certain organ, all at 8' and without any other stop, which produced a beautiful and strange effect. [221, p. 7]

Agricola, however, is old-fashioned enough to disapprove of the use of a Quint or Terz without their qualifying 8', 4', and 2' stops. In the same vein, Adlung finds it disagreeable to have unison and fifth-sounding stops too far away from each other in pitch. He is particularly bothered by the use of the Sesquialtera with the 8' pitch alone, without the intermediate 4' pitch to help blend it into a single voice, although such a combination is in fact called for by Silbermann in one of his Grosshartmannsdorf registrations. It would seem that gapped combinations were coming into use in solo and trio applications, however, and Agricola himself suggested that a 16' Quintadena and a 4' Flute could have a "good effect" in a trio, while cautioning against 8' and 2' combinations in chordal playing ("too hollow") [221, p. 7].

Adlung even gives a hint on the use of one of the newer stops beginning to make its appearance, the Unda Maris. This warm, undulating stop is sometimes made with metal pipes and sometimes in the form of double-sided stopped wood pipes. According to Adlung, it must be drawn with a Principal of the same pitch and nothing else—a usage reminiscent of the Voce Umana, which was still very much in vogue in northern Italy.

Another stop found in a number of central German organs and mentioned by Adlung is the Glockenspiel (or Glockenakkord), a limited-compass stop of tuned "saucer" bells with a light, tinkling sound, which Bach also recommended for Muhlhausen. It was probably used mostly in improvisations, for Adlung suggests using it in broken chords, and other sources add arpeggios, trills, and "light music" generally. It was still popular a century later, and Liszt is said to have used it in playing Bach's "Dorian" Toccata—something that may (or may not!) have surprised the composer [337, pp. 16–17].

Regarding the composition of the plenum, Adlung demolishes the carefully constructed full organ formulas of the previous generation in favor of an "everything-but-the-kitchen-sink" approach (and the kitchen sink seems to be the Unda Maris):

> Anyone who would like to know what to draw on the manual for the plenum need only to remember this: One must have registers which brighten. To this end the principal serves together with all the octaves, quints, and terzes, and best of all the compound voices such as the terzian, sesquialtera, mixtures, scharfs, cymbels, etc. If one does not desire such a strong combination, something may be left out—whatever one wishes. If one desires an even brighter plenum, then one can draw the appropriate stops on another manual and couple it to the main one. One must however also have stops which add gravity. For this purpose, gedackts work as well as the quintadena 16'; even better is the gedackt or rohrflöte 16' or a Bourdon of the same pitch (whatever is available), the gedackt 8', quintadena 8', rohrflöte 8', gemshorn 8', etc. [1, p. 168]

Adlung goes on to say that the Pedal plenum must match in both gravity and brightness, from the 32' stops on up through the mixtures, and if that is not sufficient, the manuals may be coupled to make it heard above the manual plenum. And in rapidly moving pedal passages, it is best to omit the 32' pitch for the sake of clarity [1, p. 171].

Although in his plenum, Adlung, like Mattheson, excludes the manual reeds, he nonetheless recommends adding reeds at 32', 16', and 8' to the Pedal plenum (but with the above-mentioned caveat regarding the 32' in rapid passages). The only limitation, in Adlung's eyes (and possibly Bach's as well), is the capacity of the wind supply. Agricola, however, tends to be a bit more conservative, recommending the full principal chorus only, and not eschewing the 8' and 4' Trumpets, "if they are in good tune." He also allows the possibility of coupling the plenum of the secondary manual, and utilizing a 16' flute color in the plenum if there is no 16' Principal, as well as using it to augment the "gravity" of the 16' Principal [221, p. 6].

While occasional chorale-preludes or variation movements by various composers are marked *Organo pleno* or *Volles Werk*, it is the longer free compositions—largely preludes and fugues—in which the full organ is most likely to be required, at least for the prelude. No fewer than twelve of Bach's are so marked, and one of Bach's contemporaries, Johann Adolph Scheibe, wrote in 1739 that free (that is, not chorale-related) preluding "generally takes place with the full organ" [166, p. 157]. Niedt and Adlung back up this statement.

Some of the earliest central German preludes, including youthful works of J. S.

Bach and Walther and compositions by Brunckhorst (who, working in Celle, was in the northernmost corner of the region), are rooted in the earlier *stylus fantasticus*. They are best played with the more-restrained older style of principal-plenum. In later works, especially those written in the second quarter of the century, the denser and more robust plenum of Adlung—tierces, 16's, and all—should not be ruled out, especially in preludes of a more open and chordal texture. However, more restraint may be needed in a fugue of significant contrapuntal complexity, and a plenum minus the mixtures may even be indicated in some of these.

The changing of manuals becomes a hard-to-avoid question in some of the ritornello-like preludes of Bach's middle period, where significant alternations of character and texture occur. The Prelude in C minor (BWV 546) is a good case in point; at the very least, two contrasting plena, while not actually called for in any known manuscript source, are not inappropriate in such pieces. Students would do well to study the structure of a particular piece before applying any specific approach.

Indeed, as many sources indicate, each division (including the Pedal) was regarded as having its own plenum, and it is quite probable that *pro organo pleno* assumes the full combination to be drawn on all manuals, uncoupled (although Adlung and Agricola note that coupling is sometimes an option). Since each had its own dynamic level, transference from, say, the Hauptwerk plenum to the Oberwerk plenum, when suggested by the character of the composition, does not violate the "organo pleno" direction. This may also be applicable to Bach's Passacaglia (BWV 582), a very sectional piece which is sometimes subjected to a lot of registrational silliness. Although no autograph exists of this work, an early copy is marked *con Pedal pro Organo pleno*; and this finds some confirmation in a statement by Mattheson that ciaconas (like passacaglias) should be improvised "with the full organ" [167, p. 197]. But plenum-to-plenum manual changes are not necessarily ruled out in such a context.

The well-known "St. Anne" Prelude in E-flat major (BWV 552), with its "concerto grosso" opening and echo effects, is another piece which seems to ask for manual changes. Indeed, it is one of the few that might even ask for a three-manual organ, although in the published version (one of the few such works to be published in his lifetime), Bach actually calls for manual changes only in his "forte" and "piano" markings of the echo sections. He specifies manual changes in only one other piece of this type, the "Dorian" Toccata in D minor (BWV 538), where again a kind of echo effect is written.

It has been argued that because Bach did designate certain pieces to be played on two manuals (mostly chorale-preludes, with the above-noted exceptions), and because there are no voice-crossings or telltale beaming changes in the preludes and fugues not so marked, these latter were meant to be played on the plenum of a single manual throughout [166, p. 161]. It can also be argued that since the only places actually marked in these two pieces are echo sections (which the composer perhaps did not want the player to miss—similar indications occur in works of Bruhns and others), players were expected to rely on their good taste and common sense in making manual changes (from major pleno to secondary pleno) in some of the sectional or ritornello-like preludes. Bach's G minor Fantasia (BWV 572), to cite but one (admittedly untypical) example, appears to have structural foundation for some judicious manual changes.

Even assuming that every prelude was meant to be played on the same registration throughout, there is still controversy as to whether all prelude-and-fugue pieces should be played on full plenum. The answer may lie in the nature of the piece and—as the old writers keep admonishing us—on the taste of the player. There is more than one kind of prelude and fugue, and, as we have seen, more than one kind of plenum, but no rule that says that all such pieces must be played on the same kind of plenum, nor indeed any that says that a fugue cannot be played on a different sort of plenum than the prelude. For that matter, the presence of a climactic "tailpiece" in some works, such as Bach's fugues in C minor (BWV 549) and A minor (BWV 543), is probably justification for reserving some of the loudest or most brilliant plenum stops for addition at the end, especially if this section is preceded by a pause or a cadence.

There is enough evidence now for some sort of plenum combination in preludes and fugues that some of the distortions of the not-too-distant past can no longer be countenanced—cute little gapped combinations to open Bach's G minor Fantasia (BWV 572), beginning a fugue on an 8' flute and changing stops every dozen measures, etc. But players must still use their brains, taste, and knowledge of the instruments, and not submit unquestioningly to whatever the current dogmas may be when it comes to registering individual pieces.

Another recurring controversy is whether the instruments of Gottfried Silbermann and his school are in fact the best vehicles for all of the music of J. S. Bach (and, by extension, certain of his contemporaries). Bach certainly knew these instruments in his later life, and his son Wilhelm Friedemann played one in Dresden, for which his father is said to have written the Prelude and Fugue in G major (BWV 541), one of the "organo pleno" pieces. But one must remember that Bach also played many organs by other builders, and he recommended or otherwise approved the instruments of several who worked in a somewhat different (and, for the region, more typical) style than did Silbermann. Even Silbermann's own pupils, such as Hildebrandt, tended toward a more eclectic style. To the frustration of those who would like their information neatly packaged and delivered, Bach seems to have played no favorites, and thus knowledge of Silbermann organs and registrations must always be tempered by knowledge of what Silbermann's more avant-garde contemporaries, such as Trost and Wagner, did and said.

Although born in the foothills of the Saxon Erzgebirge, Silbermann received his training from his elder brother Andreas in Strassburg in Alsace; and his instruments, while adhering to most of the basic practices of central German organ building, had an unmistakable stamp of their own. His extensive use of tin, French-style double-block manual reeds, and light suspended actions and, perhaps most significantly, his tonal conservatism, all set him apart from such colleagues as Trebs, Trost, Scheibe, Schröter, Wagner, and Fincke.

Despite the length of his organ-building career—over 40 years—Silbermann's organs changed little. All his smaller organs, especially the many two-manual instruments, had similar stoplists (as well as similar case designs); and his last three-manual organ, begun in 1750 for the great Catholic Hofkirche in Dresden, is remarkably like his first, begun in 1710 for Freiberg Cathedral. While people like Trost were multiplying 8' and 4' stops and experimenting with new voices, such as strings and harmonic flutes, the 47-stop Dresden organ had but a single Gamba, in the Hauptwerk. The only Unda Maris Silbermann is ever known to have made is in the Oberwerk. And even it may have been an addition by Hildebrandt, who completed the instrument after his master's death.

Silbermann is of interest not because of his style, or even because of the splendid and often movingly beautiful sound of his instruments, which were so well designed and built that an extraordinary number survive intact. He is of particular interest because in two instances he wrote out some registrations for his organs. In 1741 he completed a fairly typical two-manual organ for the church in Grosshart-mannsdorf, and the following year he finished a similar instrument in Fraureuth. For both of them he left similar sets of registrations, most of them solo combinations and accompaniments, presumably for chorale-prelude use. The registrations for the Grosshartmannsdorf organ are as follows:

1. "Pure" plenum:
   Hauptwerk: Principal 8', Rohrflöte 8', Octave 4', Quinta 2 2/3', Octave 2', Mixtur IV
   Oberwerk: Gedackt 8', Rohrflöte 4', Octave 2', Quinta 1 1/3', Cymbel II, Sifflöte 1'
   Pedal: Subbass 16' [probably with coupler]
2. Flute registration:
   Hauptwerk: Rohrflöte 8', Spitzflöte 4'
   Oberwerk: Gedackt 8', Rohrflöte 4'
3. Sifflöte registration:
   Oberwerk: Gedackt 8', Rohrflöte 4', Sifflöte 1'
4. *Lieblich* [elegant] flute registration:
   Hauptwerk: Quintadena 8', with Spitzflöte 4' or Rohrflöte 8', or Hauptwerk: Principal 8' and Spitzflöte 4'
   Oberwerk: Gedackt 8', Rohrflöte 4', Gemshorn 2'
5. Cornet registration:
   Hauptwerk: Principal 8', Rohrflöte 8', Octave 4', Cornet III, to be used as a solo with:
6. Lute registration:
   Oberwerk: Gedackt 8', Rohrflöte 4' or Gemshorn 2' as an accompaniment
7. Oberwerk Cornet registration:
   Oberwerk: Gedackt 8', Nassat 2 2/3', Tertia 1 3/5' as solo
8. Nassat registration:
   Oberwerk: Gedackt 8', Rohrflöte 4', Nassat 2 2/3' as solo
   Hauptwerk: Rohrflöte 8', Spitzflöte 4' as accompaniment
9. Tertien registration:
   Oberwerk: Gedackt 8', Rohrflöte 4', Nassat 2 2/3', Octave 2', Tertia 1 3/5' as a "Canto solo"

10. *Stahlspiel* registration:
  Oberwerk: Gedackt 8', Nassat 2 2/3',Tertia 1 3/5', Quinta 1 1/3' as solo
  Hauptwerk: Rohrflöte 8' and Spitzflöte 4' as accompaniment [52, p. 144]

Stahlspiel is another name for metal bar chimes or Glockenspiel, and such percussion instruments were known in Germany and the Low Countries from the seventeenth century. Silbermann's *Stahlspiel* would appear to be a novelty registration; the off-unison mutations and gapped makeup do indeed produce a bright metallic effect. The other registrations offer no real surprises, although No. 7 runs contrary to Adlung's Cornet in that the 4' flute is missing. The *Nassat* is the classic French *Jeu de nasard* and the *Tertien* a separated Cornet combination, or what Bach called Sesquialter at Muhlhausen.

The Fraureuth registrations are almost identical to the Grosshartmannsdorf ones, except that the Pedal receives greater mention. Usually the 16' Subbass is used with the solo combinations, the Posaunenbass 16' and manual-to-pedal coupler with the louder combinations. It would appear that the coupler is not indicated for the softer ones, and, as extant examples prove, a Silbermann 16' Subbass has enough octave in it to manage very nicely by itself. Only in the Fraureuth directions is the Tremulant mentioned, with the instruction that it may be used when the Principal 8', Rohrflöte 8', and Quintadena 8' are played alone [52, p. 145]. Silbermann's Tremulants were usually of the internal, *tremblant doux* type rather than the more common German external type, sometimes called *Bocktremulant* (Billy goat tremulant!) and used more commonly in the North. The internal tremulant, widely used by the French, is more suave and expressive, and it varies in intensity with the number of stops drawn or notes played.

Silbermann's registrations were probably drawn up to aid the organists of the churches in registering chorale-preludes. While certain ones are similar to some suggested by Kauffman, the particular colors recommended by Silbermann are in general more conservative and have an unmistakable hint of France about them (*Cornet,Jeu de nasard,Jeu de tierce, Flûtes*, etc.). His mostly principal (andTierce-less) "pure plenum," while very akin to a *Plein jeu*, is a far cry from the hodgepodge of full organ combinations proposed by Adlung or his fellow theorist to the north, Mattheson—although this may be the very reason that Silbermann used the term "pure."

Certainly Silbermann's combinations are applicable on an organ of the Silbermann stripe, but they are somewhat less applicable to an organ such as Trost's Altenburg or Waltershausen instruments than are some of Kauffman's. Yet even Kauffman does not tell us too much about the use of the newer string stops, save that it is all right to mix them with flutes and reeds (as in his No. 34, *Komm heiliger Geist*, where Vox humana 8', Salicional 8', and Spillflöte 4' are called for), while the organ builder Wagner suggests the combination of strings with principals and flutes [181, p. 163], and Boxburg considers strings useful for the *continuo* [223]. Certainly by the 1730s and 1740s older dogmas regarding the mixing of wide and narrow stops, using only one stop per pitch, and even those concerning tierces in the ensemble and gapped combinations, were being seriously eroded. Very possibly J. S. Bach was in the forefront of the eroders; although we have very little first-hand knowledge of the exact registrations he used in playing trios or chorale-preludes, his contemporaries seem to agree that they were sometimes surprising and adventurous.

Where does this all leave us with regard to the interpretation of the music—that of Bach and of the other central Germans? Because of the changes in organ design and shifts in opinion concerning older registration conventions during the period under consideration, which were in many ways more radical that what was occurring in other areas, it probably behooves us to study with some care the chronological aspect. A piece written in 1710 might require adherence to the older ideals and a curb on registrations of the more adventurous sort; a piece written in 1745, even by the same composer, might call for a quite different approach, and a more creative use of the available resources. It would certainly seem that in some of the later music a more "orchestral" approach should be considered for pieces of a certain type—trio sonatas, transcriptions, and some chorale-preludes, for instance—if kept within the restraints of mid-eighteenth-century organ design and instrumental color.

In terms of modern organs, it may also be that central German music will be at least as accessible on a late-twentieth-century eclectic instrument (or even one of the better "American classic" instruments) as it is on an organ based on the Renaissance or seventeenth-century northern style. With the exception of some Silbermann-style instruments, few new organs have been inspired by the more robust and forward-looking central German organ of the mid-eighteenth century.

Perhaps not too surprisingly, some of this music can also sound well on some of the larger American organs of the third quarter of the nineteenth century, since there was a very real German influence in American organ factories of the 1860s and 1870s. Sadly, most of the "neo-Baroque" instruments of the 1950s and 1960s lack the "gravity" and many of the rich and colorful 16' and 8' stops that Bach, Walther, Kauffman, Adlung, and Agricola deemed important. Certainly the registration of central German music of the eighteenth century should be approached and studied with an informed but open mind. With the fall of the "iron curtain" the historic organs of central Germany have become more accessible, and in the light of what is being learned about them, performers should feel free to scrutinize critically some of the concepts editorially promulgated in older editions (and in performance on older phonograph records), as well as some of the dogmas in vogue in more recent times.

South Germany, Austria, and Eastern Europe

Composers

Johann Baptist Beyer (c1678–1733)
Daniel Croner (Coronensis) (1656–1740)
Bohuslav Matej Czernohorsky (1684–1742)
Johann Ernst Eberlin (1702–1762)
Johann Friedrich Fasch (1688–1722)
Johann Kaspar Ferdinand Fischer (1665/70–1746)
Johann Philipp Förtsch (1652–1732)
Karlmann Kolb (1703–1765)
August Gottlieb (Theophile) Muffat (1690–1770)
Georg Muffat (1653–1704)
Franz Xaver Anton Murschhauser (1663–1738)
Johann Xavier Nauss (c1690–1761)
Johann Jakob de Neufville (1684–1712)
Wilhelm Pachelbel (1686–1746)
Jan Podbielski (fl. 1679–1731)
Georg Reutter (1656–1738)
Ferdinand Tobias Richter (1649–1711)
Conrad Michael Schneider (1673–1752)
Johann Speth (1664–1719)
Franz Matthias Techelmann (1648/9–1714)
Jan Zach (1699–1773)

Representative Organs

TÝN CHURCH, PRAGUE, CZECHOSLOVAKIA
J. H. Mundt, 1671–73 [181, p. 72]

Hauptwerk
Bourdon 16'

Rückpositiv
Coppel major 8' (wood)

Prinzipal 8'
Flöte 8' (open wood)
Salizional 8'
Coppel major 8'
Quintadena 8'
Oktave 4'
Coppel minor 4'
Quinte major 2 2/3'
Superoktave 2'
Quinte minor 1 1/3'
Sedecima 1' (22nd)
Mixtur VI (2')
Zimbel IV (1')

Prinzipal 4'
Coppel minor 4'
Oktave 2'
Quinte 1 1/3'
Superoktave 1'
Rauschquint II (1 1/3')
Mixtur III (1')

Pedal
Subbass I 16' (open wood)
Subbass II 16' (stopped)
Oktave 8' (wood)
Quinte 5 1/3' (orig. 2 2/3')
Superoktave 4'
Mixtur IV

Accessory Stops
2 Zimbelsterns
Hauptwerk-Rückpositiv Shove coupler

CHURCH OF ST. IGNATIUS, MAINZ
Johann Friedrich Macrander, 1699 [181, p. 73]

Manual
Coppel/Bordun 8'
Prinzipal 4'
Flöte 4'
Quinte 2 2/3'
Dublet 2'
Cornett IV (4')
Sesquialter II
Mixtur III
Zimbel (I?) 1'

Pedal
Subbass 16'

CATHEDRAL, SALZBURG, AUSTRIA
Johann Christoph Egedacher, 1703–6 [168, p. 127]

Hauptwerk
Prinzipal 8'
Holzprinzipal 8'
Coppel 8'
Quintadena 8'
Oktave 4'
Nachthorn 4'
Flöte 4'
Quinte 2 2/3'
Oktav 2'
Horn-Sesquialtera IV (Cornet)
Mixtur VI (2 2/3')
Zimbel IV (1')

Oberwerk
Prinzipal 8'
Flöte 4'
Flute dous 4' (wood)
Piffaro 4' (undulating)
Flageolet 2'
Schwegel 2'
Corni II (2')
Trompa 8'
Fagott 8'
Posaun 8'
Scharf or Scarpa 4' (regal?)
Schalmey 4'

Positiv
Viola 8'

Pedal
Infrabass 32'

Salicional 8'
Oktav 4'
Rohrflöte 4'
Quint 2 2/3'
Waldflöte 2'
Rauschwerk XII
Harfe 16' (regal)

Bordun 16'
Subbass 16' & 8'
Prinzipal 8'
Oktav 4'
Suboktav 4' (wood)
Rauschwerk X (8')
Mixtur VIII (2 2/3')
Bombarde 16'
Sordun II (8', reed)

Accessory Stops
Vogelgesang (bird)
Heerpauken (drums)

CHURCH OF ST. STEPHAN, MAINZ
Johann Hofmann, 1715 [168, p. 81]

Manual I (Hauptwerk)
Prinzipal 8'
Bordun 8'
Flöte im Discant 8' (treble)
Oktav 4'
Flöte im Bass 4' (bass)
Oktav 2'
Quint 1 1/3'
Sesquialter II (2 2/3')
Mixtur IV (1')

Manual II (Oberwerk?)
Gedackt 8'
Quintade 8'
Gamba 8'
Salizional 8'
Prinzipal 4'
Spitzflöte 4'
Quinte 2 2/3'
Oktav 2'
Krummhorn 8'

Pedal
Violon 16'
Prinzipal 8'
Oktav 4'
Mixtur (2')
Posaune 8'

CHURCH OF ST. BARTHOLOMEW, SLOVENSKA BISTRICA, SLOVENIA
Andreas Schwarz of Graz, 1724 [17, p. 30]

Hauptwerk
Principal 8'
Bordon 8'
Salicional 8'
Octav 4'
Rohrflöte 4'
Fugara 4'
Quint 2 2/3'
Superoctav 2'
Doublete 1'

Rückpositiv
Quintadena 8'
Praestant 4'
Flöte 4'
Traverso 4'
Picolo 2'
Quint 1 1/3'

Pedal
Principalbass 16'
Octavbass 8'
Flötenbass 8'
Quintabass 5 1/3'
Octav 4'

BENEDICTINE ABBEY, KLADRAU, BOHEMIA
Leopold Burckhardt, 1726 [168, p. 129]

Hauptwerk
Copula-Bass 16'
Prinzipal 8'
Oktav 4'
Quinte 2 2/3'
Superoktav 2'
Quint minor 1 1/3'
Mixtur V

Pedal
Prinzipal 16'
Subbass 16'
Oktav 8'
Quinte 5 1/3'
Superoktav 4'
Mixtur IV (2')

Oberwerk
Copula major 8'
Gamba 8'
Salicional 8'
Quintade 8'
Flöte 8'
Prinzipal 4'
Fugara 4'
Copula minor 4'
Oktav 2'
Quint 1 1/3'
Mixtur III (1')

ABBEY CHURCH, OCHSENHAUSEN, SILESIA
Josef Gabler, 1728–34, with additions by Gabler, 1751–52 [81, p. 153]

Hauptwerk
Bourdon 16'
Principal 8'
Koppel 8' (stopped)
Flauto 8' (conical)
Hohlflöte 8' (open wood)
Quintade 8' (treble)
Violoncell 8'
Salicional 8'
Viola 8' (wood)
Gamba 8'
Quinte 5 1/3'
Octave 4'
Flauto Traverso 4'
Rohrflöte 4'
Fugara 4'
Piffaro II 4' (undulating)
Superoctave 2'
Kornett III–V
Sesquialtera III–IV
Mixture IV
Trompete 8'

Pedal
Prestant 16'
Subbass 16' (open wood)
Violon II 16' & 8' (wood & metal)
Octave 8'
Quinte 5 1/3'

Rückpositiv
Koppelflöte 8' (wood)
Quintade 8'
Unda maris 8' (bass 8ve 4')
Principal 4'
Flûte douce 4' (wood)
Flageolet 2' (conical)
Kornett III–IV
Mixture III
Vox humana 8'
Schalmei 4'

Echowerk
Principal 8' (treble)
Quintade 8'
Rohrflöte 8'
Dolcian 8' (string)
Octave 4'
Flauto 4'
Violoncell 4'
Doublette 2'
Zimbel III
Hautbois 8'

Mixture III
Posaune 16' (wood)
Trompete 8' (wood)

Accessory Stops
Tremulant (Rückpositiv)
Cuckoo
Couplers: Hauptwerk-Pedal, Rückpositiv-Hauptwerk, Echowerk-Hauptwerk

[The Ochsenhausen Manuscript of music at Yale University indicates that the organ had additionally a Glockenspiel and a "Cimbel Glöcklein," a Drum, a "Nachtigal and Stern" (bird and Cymbelstern drawn from the same knob?) and not one but two Tremulants—"Allegro" and "Adagio" (presumably *fort* and *doux*). It also had a punning Ochsenhausen "toy" stop perched over the Positiv—a little house with an ox that moved in and out. Keeping the ox company was the four-pipe Cuckoo stop [261, p. 60].]

PARISH CHURCH, FÜRSTENFELD, BAVARIA
Johann Fux, 1736–41 [168, p. 130]

Hauptwerk	**Oberwerk**
Gamba 16'	Gedackt 8'
Prinzipal 8'	Flöte 8'
Hohlflöte 8'	Salizional 8'
Gedackt 8'	Gamba 8'
Quintade 8'	Prinzipal 4'
Oktav 4'	Flageolett 2'
Flöte 4'	Quinte II (1 1/3' and 4/5')
Quinte 2 2/3'	Scharf IV (1/2')
Terz II (2' and 1 3/5')	
Oktav 2'	**Pedal**
Mixtur V (1 1/3')	Untersatz 32'
	Prinzipal 16'
	Subbass 16'
	Oktave 8'
	Quinte 5 1/3'
	Superoktave 4'
	Kornett VI (4')
	Posaune 16'

Accessory Stops
2 Pauken (drums)

[Presumably this organ also had couplers and a Tremulant.]

MONASTERY CHURCH, MURI, SWITZERLAND
Epistle organ, Joseph and Victor F. Bossard, 1743–44 [119, p. 35]

Manual	**Pedal**
Principale 8'	Subbass 16' (wood)
Coppel 8'	Octavbass 8' (stopped wood)
Gamba 8'	Fagottbass 8'
Octava 4'	
Flute dous 4'	

Nazard 2 2/3'
Superoctava 2'
Terz 1 3/5'
Corno V (treble, from c1)
Sesquialtera II
Mixtur III (2')
Trompe 8'
Cleron 4'

Registration

The organ of northern and central Germany was a Protestant organ; among its most important functions were the accompaniment of congregational singing and the playing of chorale-preludes. The organ of southern Germany (Bavaria, Silesia, and Swabia), Austria, Switzerland, and the adjacent eastern regions (Bohemia, Romania, Moravia, and Slovenia) was a Catholic organ, and as such its major function was the accompaniment and embellishment of the mass.

As in the previous period, Italy exerted a strong influence on the musicians, but there was some influence from the immediate north as well. Johann Pachelbel worked in southern Germany and Vienna as well as in central Germany. While the elder Krieger studied in Venice and worked in Bayreuth, he spent most of his life in Halle and Weissenfels; the younger Krieger followed somewhat in his steps, ending up in the border region of Zittau in Lusatia. Depending on where they may have been living at the time, these composers produced Lutheran chorale-preludes as well as music for the Catholic liturgy (e.g., Johann Pachelbel's delightful miniature "Magnificat" fugues); but they are generally classed with the central German group.

Of those who spent all of their musical lives in the South, many were organists of the cathedrals or major churches of important cities such as Ulm (Schneider), Augsburg (Nauss), Salzburg (Eberlin), and Prague (Czernohorsky), or in large court chapels such as those in Passau (G. Muffat), Vienna (A. G. Muffat), and Baden (J. K. F. Fischer). Such positions called for the composition of more than just chant-based music, so the output of this school also includes preludes and fugues, variation sets, and smaller works in Italianate idioms such as the toccata, pastorale, aria, and ciacona.

The appearance in this period of substantial fugues, or preludes and fugues, marks a significant change from the previous period, especially since many, such as those by Eberlin, contain obbligato pedal parts. Stylistically these works owe much to central German influence, just as the toccatas of both Johann and Wilhelm Pachelbel (even though sometimes containing typical Italian pedal-points) are largely northern in their style. The toccatas of the elder Muffat, published in his *Apparatus musico-organisticus* of 1690, are an interesting blend of German and Italian styles. Leaning somewhat more on the latter than the former, they are an important link with the earlier Froberger tradition; unlike the freer toccatas of the younger Muffat, they make only limited use of the Pedal.

Many of the published works of the southern school were either didactic or were intended for liturgical use. Often they were given fanciful titles, such as Nauss's *Der spielende Muse,* a collection of preludes and versets based on the church tones, intended for students. In the same vein but of greater importance were Fischer's *Ariadne Musica Neo-Organoedum* (1702; reissued in 1715), a set of twenty Preludes and Fugues in as many keys (anticipating J. S. Bach's *Wohltemperierte Klavier*), and his *Blumenstrauss* (published posthumously), based on the eight church tones. The works in this last publication are in the form of a prelude with several short fugues, concluding with a brief finale, and were probably meant to be performed *alternatim* fashion between the verses of the Magnificat.

With the exception of works by composers having significant central German connections (J. Pachelbel, the Kriegers), one finds few chorale-based works in the southern literature. In *Ariadne,* Fischer includes five ricercars based on melodies used in the Catholic church, such as *Ave Maria klare* and *Komm heiliger Geist,* and Murschhauser contributes a charming set of variations (interwoven with "cuckoo" effects) on the Christmas carol *Lasst uns das Kindelein wiegen.*

The organs of the region continue in the tradition of the previous period, but as the area prospered, organs of more substantial size began appearing in cathedrals, abbey churches, and court chapels. On the whole, the southern instruments may be said to have a generic link with those of the central German region. Manual reeds are sparse, and some fairly sizable organs have no reeds at all. The Pedal divisions are limited to the most necessary stops and, as in the central area, often contain the only reed stop in the organ. Rückpositivs were still being built, but organs are also found in which the secondary manual is an Oberwerk.

What one does observe is a proliferation of unison voices exceeding even that in the central region; indeed, it would appear that this characteristic, along with a multiplying of string-toned stops, had its origin in this area, particularly in the eastern part. The concentration of 8' flutes and strings is often confined to one manual, usually the Oberwerk but occasionally the Hauptwerk. Changes in the type of music played (or, more likely, improvised) during the mass may have had something to do with the growing taste for these imitative voices.

Registrations do not appear in the music of this period, but, as in Italy, some directions from other sources survive. In 1707 the builder Theodor Agadoni left some registrations for the organ he had built in 1701 in the Cathedral of Olmütz, some of which specify the type of music to which they apply:

For lively syncopated arpeggios: Quintadena 8' alone
For slow broken chords: Viola di Gamba 8' alone
For arpeggio figures in slow tempo: Waldflöte 8' and Gamba 8'
For "Viennese" harmonies in slow tempo: Bifra 8' [an undulating stop]
For *lieblich* sound in slow music: Flöte 8' in the Positiv
For Praeludia of strong, sharp character: Various Principal chorus combinations (plena) [193, p. 51].

In the same year that Agadoni left his instructions, Johann Baptist Samber, organist of Salzburg Cathedral, published his *Continuatio ad manuductionem organicam,* a treatise intended for his fellow Catholic organists. He too cites combinations associated with various types of music:

Elevations: Holzflöte or Octave alone

Versets: Copula (8'), Quinte (2 2/3'), and Decima (1 3/5'), or Sesquialtera; or Viola and Zimbel.

Galante music: Copula [8' flute] alone

Running passages: Copula, Quinte, Decima, and Duodecima (1')

Concertos: Principal 8' alone or with the Zimbel

Toccatas: Wood Copula (8'), Octave (4'), and Zimbel

Fantasias: Spitzflöte alone, or metal Gedackt with Viola and Copula, or Flöte with Zimbel

Preludes: Copula and Flöte (4'), or Copula, Flöte, and Superoctave (2')

Fugues: Copula and Duodecima; or Copula and Mixtur; or Principal, Octave, Quinte, and Superoctave; or Copula, Quinte, and Superoctave; or Copula, Superoctave, and Zimbel; or Copula, Flöte, and Duodecima; or Flöte, Quinte, and Superoctave [54II, p. 1032].

Plainly, we at last have an organist with no reservations about gapped combinations. The number of very different "Fugue" combinations may be explained by the great variety of fugue styles represented by the southern school—from the little manual fugues of Fischer to the full-scale Preludes and Fugues of Eberlin. Regarding string stops, Samber singles out the Viola for praise. It can be used with the Copula (stopped flute), but it is also very elegant when used alone; the same holds true for the Principal 8'. Samber's plenum is the standard Principal-plenum, without wide-scaled stops or reeds—indeed, Samber says very little about reeds— and is used with the full Pedal, including the 5 1/3' Quinte. Concerning the accessory stops, he notes that there should be both a weak and a strong Tremulant, and that the drums may be used with the strong reeds.

In 1734 the Swabian builder Gabler completed a large organ for the Abbey Church of Ochsenhausen, and a year later an anonymous organist penned a description of the way the new organ should be used. It is an interesting document, in that it describes registrations by means of little console diagrams and illustrates their use by giving short musical examples. What is curious is that only one of them appears to have any direct liturgical connection. The rest are little secular pieces with titles like Postilion, Echo, Siciliana, Courante, Sarabande, Allemande, Gavotte, Marche, and Polonaise, along with a few Fugas and Fantasias—which, however, may have been intended for use as versets or in other liturgical contexts. Most are of only two-part texture, and none have any indication for the use of pedals [261, p. 55].

The stops that may be used alone are the Principal, Octav, Flute dous (with Tremulant), Spitzflöte, Copula, Nachthorn, Bourdon, and Schwebel-pfeifen (the last apparently an undulating stop). The Glockenspiel (a percussion stop) may also be used alone, or with the Principal and Superoctave, accompanied by string and reed combinations, or by the Quintadena and Vox humana. The relevant illustrative piece makes much use of repeated staccato notes.

Strings and flutes drawn together are featured in several of the combinations, usually with Adagio or Andante musical examples. Reeds, when specified, are almost always accompanied by flues, frequently the Quintadena and sometimes the

Rohrflöte. Sometimes more than one reed stop is called for, as in a combination of Quintadena, Rohrflöte, Vox humana 8', and Schalmey 4'; the accompaniment for such combinations is usually flutes at 8' and 4', sometimes with the 2' added.

The Principal with Tremulant is called for more than once, but the Tremulant is also used with flutes. The Traverse Flute 8' is used as a solo with the Octave 4', against the 8' Principal or Rohrflöte. Most of the combinations are based on the 8' pitch, but in one instance the Flageolet 2' is used alone against 4' flutes on other manuals; the two illustrative pieces are an Allegro and one entitled *Carnary* (Canaries), both of which are heavily ornamented. While the organ had a Cornet and a Sesquialtera, neither is mentioned, nor are any Plenum combinations or other uses of the mixtures given.

In many ways the Ochsenhausen registrations contrast sharply with those of Samber in ways that cannot be satisfactorily explained by the less than thirty years that separate them. Samber is obviously more concerned with liturgical music, while the Ochsenhausen emphasis seems more secular. One wonders whether either one truly represents common practice, or whether both should be taken with a grain of salt. Less-than-common repertoire is involved in each (although Samber does mention elevations and versets), and one must question how much the Ochsenhausen music has to do with a monastic organist playing for the mass. Toward the end of this period, though, one begins to find in all areas occasional outbursts from a cleric or a music critic against the use of dances, operatic airs, and other secularisms in the church service. The rather spare unison-based combinations of Agadoni were probably still more the norm in common liturgical practice.

While the literature of this period contains some works of substance, much is of the *Gebrauchsmusik* type, designed for use in the Catholic liturgy. One finds little evidence of the type of secular music described in the Ochsenhausen manuscript, which may have been largely improvised. The liturgical music is generally of an uncomplicated nature, and thus does not make unusual demands on most modern organs, even fairly small ones. Georg Muffat's music, like Froberger's, could benefit from straightforward Italianate Principal and Flute registrations, with changes between sections, and only asks for some lightness and good articulation. Some of Fischer's music, while often more transparent, will sound well with some of the later flute and string combinations, provided that the flutes are not too opaque and the strings are not too raspy or slow-speaking. Some of the ricercars seem to require little more than just a light Principal, alone or backed up with a light Gedackt.

For some of the more ambitious southern preludes, fugues, and Toccatas, an 8' plenum through the mixture (without reeds) is suggested. The Czechoslovakian and Polish works in this genre tend to be generally straightforward and sober, and should be registered accordingly. None of the known registration directions indicate the use of manual 16' stops, even though many of the southern organs had them—quite a contrast to the fairly extensive use of the 16' pitch in central Germany.

Both Agadoni and Samber key some of their registrations to particular types of music, and a little experimentation with some of these formulas will yield interesting and colorful results on an organ having the necessary resources. Some of Murschhauser's music, particularly the light-textured variations, may be a suitable vehicle for some of the more quirky and adventurous combinations suggested by Samber and the Ochsenhausen writer, but for the liturgical music more restraint is probably in order.

Significant changes in musical styles do not happen overnight, but it is not uncommon for them to blossom after a period of political unrest. The Seven Years' War, which pitted France, Austria, Russia, Saxony, and Sweden under Maria Theresa against Prussia, Hanover, and England under Frederick the Great, lasted from 1756 to 1763. At its conclusion Prussia emerged as the leading continental power, and England (with Hanoverian King George III on the throne) as a leading colonial power. The ensuing period was not entirely peaceful; the American Revolution against England followed on the heels of the French and Indian wars in the New World, and there were the beginnings of unrest in France. All told, it is perhaps fortunate that both Frederick of Prussia and the various British Georges were patrons of music.

The seeds of the Classical period, which is generally regarded as extending from the end of the Seven Years' War into the early years of the nineteenth century, were sown in the late Baroque, with its increasing interest in expression and the "galant" style. Thus the stage was set for Mozart, Haydn, C. P. E. Bach, and Beethoven. They all had had connections with the Church in their early years, but they also prepared the way into the secular musical world that was to be increasingly cultivated by their successors. The late eighteenth century also saw the rapid emergence of the newly invented pianoforte as the keyboard instrument of choice and the growth of the small court orchestra toward the full-blown symphony orchestra of the nineteenth century. Along with these developments came a new audience in the form of the prosperous middle class, which since the middle of the eighteenth century had been acquiring a taste for symphonies, operas, and oratorios.

For the organ, it was in many ways a period of temporary eclipse, a somewhat static hiatus between the glories of the Baroque and the emergence of the Romantic organ in the mid-nineteenth century. The organ and its music were beginning to retreat more behind the timeless doors of the Church, becoming in the process more conservative, less mainstream, and, above all, less noticeable to the musical world at large. Even there it often took a back seat to an instrumental ensemble, not only in larger urban establishments but also in the smaller court chapels and even in the humble churches of the Moravian sect.

No extraordinary changes or developments in the tonal or mechanical design of the organ occurred in this period, and for the first time in history none of the major composers were primarily organists. Indeed, any up-and-coming composer who wished to be recognized found it much more prudent to find employment in the court rather than in the Church, even though many began their youthful careers as church organists. And if they wished to perform on or compose for a keyboard instrument, they quickly discovered that the piano had a larger and better-paying audience than the organ.

And yet, curiously, the organ continued to exert its old fascination for some. Although Mozart did not write any major works for it, he was one of those fascinated by the organ. Even as a young virtuoso on tour he delighted in climbing up on the organ bench and improvising whenever he came across a church with an interesting instrument. Beethoven, on the other hand, seemed to have a very clear view of where his future lay, and he abandoned the organ as soon as he could, his only organ works being a few youthful (and rather dull) student pieces. It was the expressive fortepiano, not the block-dynamic organ (with its still primitive expressive division), that inspired the Classical imagination as it was groping toward the Romantic ideal.

As if to recapture and preserve past glories, the theorists and historians of the last decades of the eighteenth century wrote down and codified organ-building and registration practices of an already receding era. We owe to the French monk Dom Bédos de Celles much of what we know about the construction theories of the French organ of the "golden age," although only a few more decades were left to it when Bédos published his monumental work in 1766–78. Around the same time Jan Hess of Gouda compiled his valuable record of the stoplists of notable older Dutch organs, published in 1774. In England during the 1790s several organists were codifying the registration practices of the eighteenth century. During the same period the German theorists Petri, Türk, and Knecht published the first of a long line of conservative tutors for church organists, which extended into both the nineteenth century and the New World. Backward-looking though many of these writings were, they provide a valuable summation of the standard practices of the immediate past as well as some intimations of what was to come.

The Music

In the period following the deaths of Bach and Handel, one looks in vain for major organ works from the most notable composers. The closest one comes are the Organ Concertos of C. P. E. Bach and Haydn and the "Epistle Sonatas" of Mozart. All these quite delightful pieces were intended for church use, underscoring, in a way, the importance of the instrumental ensemble in church music as well as the increasingly subservient role of the organ. Those of Bach and Haydn are early works, written in the period 1755–60, stylistically linking the fading Baroque ideal to the emerging Classical idiom. Mozart's concerted works are later and more fully Classical in style, although it is significant that only in the later ones is the organ given anything like a fully developed obbligato part; in the earlier ones it functions largely as a *continuo* instrument.

Haydn composed a few short and rather inconsequential organ pieces for church use, again in his younger years; and the musicologist Robin Langley has gone to some pains to establish a tenuous connection between certain of Mozart's short keyboard works and the organ. C. P. E. Bach did write some significant works for organ solo, but, except for a few early fugues, the most substantial of these compositions were composed in that increasingly popular all-purpose musical form, the sonata.

It is ironic that most of the rest of the so-called organ music written by the better-known masters was secular music commissioned for the self-playing "clock organs" (*Flötenuhr*) or barrel organs, which were the current technological status symbols of the wealthy artistocracy. Of these, only Mozart's, which have been successfully transcribed for performance on the organ, have any real substance. Those by C. P. E. Bach, Haydn, and Beethoven (with the exception of *Wellington's Victory*, a potboiler composed for a large barrel organ called the Panharmonicon but now usually played by orchestras) are at best delightful miniatures.

Beyond this august circle, the best and most authentic organ compositions are the work of the *Kleinmeisters*, and they are not confined to any particular country. In France, they included Corrette and Balbastre, the latter known chiefly for his lively *Noëls*; in Spain the most familiar name is that of Antonio Soler, who is best known for his organ duets. Galuppi and Martini are probably the most notable of the Italians; and in England, Stanley, Green, and Boyce dominate the early part of the period, while Charles and Samuel Wesley stand at the end of it. In Protestant Germany the best-known organ composers were largely members of the Bach circle—Johann Sebastian's sons and students—and much literature of enduring value emanated from this source. From Catholic Austria, we have some worthwhile if retrospective works, including organ duets, by Beethoven's early mentor, Albrechtsberger.

Stylistically the organ music written in all quarters during this period demonstrates the movement away from the Baroque, although in a conservative and often reluctant way. Fugal writing was almost the only holdover, and sonatas, trios, sicilianos, and other instrumentally derived forms gained in popularity. The free forms (voluntaries, fantasias, toccatas, etc.) lent themselves well to the new "galant" style and were often well laced with Classical inventions of a not particularly organistic sort, such as Alberti basses, arpeggios, syncopations, and broken chords. As we have seen, some of these musical devices made their first appearances in southern Europe toward the end of the Baroque period. One of the most intriguing tendencies in the organ music of this period was the lessening importance of the Pedal, even in Germany. Almost the only forms in which composers seem to have felt bound to give a nod to the receding Baroque aesthetic were the chorale-prelude, the voluntary, and variations such as the French noëls.

The Organs

Remnants of the Baroque organ culture continued to influence organ design until the early nineteenth century, although they were somewhat diminished in focus. In France the Revolution put an abrupt end to the "French Classic" tradition, perhaps preparing the way for that country to spearhead the Romantic movement later on. In Spain and Italy the general orientation of organ design remained firmly attached to the Renaissance ideal, although the music written for the organ was becoming thoroughly Classical in style. In Protestant Germany and Holland, organ design seemed locked into the basic Baroque matrix, whether inherited from Schnitger, Müller, or Silbermann; yet the steady incursion of strings, overblowing flutes, and imitative reeds not only suited very nicely the requirements of late eighteenth-century composers but set the stage for the innovations of the Romantic period.

The end of the Baroque and the beginning of the Classical period saw some very large and pretentious organs being built for wealthy monastery churches, particularly in southern Germany and Austria, but the occupation by the French following the Revolution led to the secularization of the monasteries (as well as many churches) in France, Austria, and eastern Europe, and this in turn led to further stagnation in these countries. Although few organs were actually destroyed, many were allowed to go to ruin, and any new organs that were built tended to be small and functional.

Organs of significant size continued to be built in England, Holland, parts of Germany, Italy, and Spain, and throughout the period a number of English organs (plus a few German and French ones) were exported to North America. Central America by this time already had a well-established school of native organ builders, particularly in Mexico, and a few builders were beginning to emerge in the British and German colonies on the northeast coast of North America.

Tonal and mechanical design was throughout the entire period still based on tried and true classical principles, although registration aids of all kinds appear with increasing frequency during the late eighteenth century, perhaps pointing toward a growing tendency to change registrations within a composition. About the only new tonal idea to stand the test of time was the free reed, which was first developed in practical form in the last years of the eighteenth century. It had occasional (but geographically widespread) use in organs between 1800 and 1900, but its most enduring application occurred in an entirely new instrument, the harmonium, or reed organ, which was to achieve enormous popularity in both Europe and America during the nineteenth century.

The only real iconoclast to emerge in the Classical period was the eccentric Abbé Georg Joseph Vogler—court musician, composer, popular recitalist, and teacher of Weber and Meyerbeer. Intrigued with the theory of difference tones and the compactness of free reeds, he designed a traveling orchestrion and noisily propounded his "Simplification System" to all who would listen. Fortunately few did, and as a result history was spared the loss of the organ's 32' stops, beating reeds, and mixtures [cf. 156].

Composers

John Alcock, Sr. (1715–1806)
John Alcock, Jr. (1740–1791)
Jonathan Battishill (1738–1801)
John Christmas Beckwith (1750–1794)
John Bennett (1735?–1784)
Jonas Blewitt (1757–1805)
Robert Broderip (c1758–1808)
Charles Burney (1726–1814)
Matthew Camidge (1758–1844)
Benjamin Carr (1769–1831)
Benjamin Cooke (1734–1793)
William Crotch (1775–1847)
Thomas Sanders Dupuis (1733–1796)
William Flackton (1709–1798)
Starling Goodwin (d. 1774)
George Guest (1771–1831)
Matthias Hawdon (d. 1787)
Philip Hayes (1738–1797)
Henry Heron (d. 1795)
James Hook (1746–1827)
Jacob Kirkman (d. 1812)
Francis Linley (1771–1800)
Samuel Long (d. 1764)
John Marsh (1752–1828)
William Russell (1777–1813)
William Selby (1739–1798)
Samuel P. Taylor (1779–1875)
Raynor Taylor (1747–1825)
Thomas Thorley (fl. 1775–1820)

Charles Wesley (1757–1834)
Samuel Wesley (1766–1837)
John Worgan (1724–1790)

Representative Organs

ST. MARY'S CHURCH, ROTHERHITHE, LONDON
John Byfield, 1764 [113, p. 8]

Great
Open Diapason 8'
Stop Diapason 8'
Principal 4'
Nason 4' (chimney flute)
Twelfth 2 2/3'
Fifteenth 2'
Cornet V (treble, mounted)
Sesquialtera IV
Trumpet 8'
Clarion 4'

Choir
Stop Diapason 8'
Principal 4'
Flute 4'
Fifteenth 2'
Vox Humana 8'

Swell (short compass)
Open Diapason 8'
Stop Diapason 8'
Principal 4'
Cornet III
Trumpet 8'
Hautboy 8'

ST. PETER'S CHURCH, DROGHEDA, IRELAND
John Snetzler, 1770 [70]

Great
Open Diapason 8'
Stopt Diapason 8'
Principal 4'
Twelfth 2 2/3'
Fifteenth 2'
Cornet
Sesquialtera

Choir
Stopt Diapason 8'
Principal 4'
Flute 4'

Echo (short compass)
Open Diapason 8'
Principal 4'
Hautboy 8'

[N.B. This organ had only two keyboards; the Echo was a short-compass enclosed division, played from the Choir manual.]

ST. JAMES'S CHURCH, BATH
Richard Seede, 1782 [122, p. 127]

Great
Open Diapason 8'
Stopped Diapason 8'
Principal 4'
Twelfth 2 2/3'
Fifteenth 2'
Cornet IV (treble)
Sesquialtera IV
Trumpet 8'

Swell (short compass)
Open Diapason 8'
Stopped Diapason 8'
Principal 4'
Cornet III
Trumpet 8'

[N. B. A four-stop Choir division and an octave of pulldown pedals were added to this organ around the turn of the century.]

CATHEDRAL, SALISBURY
Samuel Green, 1792 [98, p. 15]

Great
Open Diapason I 8'
Open Diapason II 8'
Stopped Diapason 8'
Principal 4'
Twelfth 2 2/3'
Fifteenth 2'
Cornet IV (treble)
Sesquialtera III
Fourniture II
Trumpet 8' (divided)

Choir
Stopped Diapason 8'
Dulciana 8' (tenor C)
Principal 4'
Flute 4'
Fifteenth 2'
Bassoon 8'

Swell
Open Diapason 8'
Stopped Diapason 8'
Dulciana 8'
Principal 4'
Cornet III
Trumpet 8'
Hautboy 8'

OPERA HOUSE, COVENT GARDEN, LONDON
Samuel Green, 1794 [122, p. 160]

Great
Open Diapason I 8'
Open Diapason II 8'
Stopped Diapason 8'
Principal 4'
Twelfth 2 2/3'
Fifteenth 2'
Sesquialtera III
Trumpet 8'

Swell (short compass)
Open Diapason 8'
Stopped Diapason 8'
Dulciana 8'
Principal 4'
Cornet III
Trumpet 8'
Hautboy 8'

CHRIST LUTHERAN CHURCH, NEW YORK
John Geib, 1798–99 [116, p. 187]

Great
Open Diapason 8'
Stop Diapason 8'
Principal 4'
Twelfth 2 2/3'
Fifteenth 2'
Tierce 2 3/5'
Cornet III (treble)
Sesquialtera III (bass)
Trumpet 8'

Accessory Stops
Tremulant (Swell)

Swell (short compass)
Open Diapason or Dulciana 8'
Stop Diapason 8'
Principal 4'
Hautbois 8'

ST. PAUL'S CHAPEL, NEW YORK
George Pike England, 1802 [116, p. 188]

Great
Open Diapason 8'
Stop Diapason 8'
Principal 4'
Twelfth 2 2/3'
Fifteenth 2'
Tierce 1 3/5'
Cornet V (mounted)
Sesquialtera III
Trumpet 8'

Choir
Stop Diapason 8'
Dulceana 8'
Principal 4'
Flute 4'
Vox Humana 8'

Swell (short compass)
Open Diapason 8'
Stop Diapason 8'
Principal 4'
Hautboy 8'
Trumpet 8'

NEW THEATRE ROYAL, COVENT GARDEN, LONDON
Hugh Russell, 1809 [122, p. 161]

Manual
Open Diapason 8'
Stopped Diapason 8'
Principal 4'
Flute 4'
Twelfth 2 2/3'
Fifteenth 2'
Sesquialtera III

PARISH CHURCH, THAXTED, ESSEX
Henry Cephas Lincoln, 1821 [174, p. 8]

Great
Open Diapason Front 8'
Open Diapason II 8' (Tenor C)
Stopped Diapason 8'
Principal 4'
Twelfth 2 2/3'
Fifteenth 2'
Sesquialtera IV (bass)
Cornet IV (treble from c)
Mixture II
Trumpet 8'

Pedal
"Pedals" (8' wood pipes)

Swell (from Tenor E)
Open Diapason 8'
Stopped Diapason 8'
Principal 4'
Cremona 8'
Hautboy 8'
Trumpet 8'

Choir
Stopped Diapason 8'
Dulciana 8'
Principal 4'
Flute 4'
Fifteenth 2'
Bassoon 8'

Accessory Stops
Couplers: Swell–Great, Great–Pedal, Choir–Pedal

OLD SOUTH CHURCH, BOSTON
Thomas Elliot, 1822 [120, p. 424]

Great
Open Diapason I 8'
Open Diapason II 8'
Stopped Diapason 8'
Principal 4'
Twelfth 2 2/3'
Fifteenth 2'
Sesquialtera III
Mixture II
Trumpet 8'
Clarion 4'

Pedal
Coupled to Great

Choir
Stopped Diapason 8'
Dulciana 8'
Principal 4'
Flute 4'
Fifteenth 2'
Cremona 8'

Swell (short compass)
Open Diapason 8'
Stopped Diapason 8'
Principal 4'
Trumpet 8'
Hautboy 8'

ST. MARY'S CHURCH, PRESTWICH, LANCASHIRE
Renn & Boston, 1825 [149, p. 72]

Great
Double Stop [Diapason] 16'
Open Diapason I 8'
Open Diapason II 8'
Stop Diapason 8'
Principal 4'
Flute 4'
Twelfth 2 2/3'
Fifteenth 2'
Sesquialtera (bass)
Cornet (treble)
Trumpet 8'

Swell (from Tenor C)
Open Diapason 8'
Stop Diapason 8' [with bass octave]
Dulciana 8'
Principal 4'
Cornet
Hautboy 8'

Pedal
"Pedal Pipes" 16'

Accessory Stops
Couplers: Great-Pedal, Swell-Great
2 shifting pedals affecting (1) 4' Flute and (2) upperwork and Trumpet

CENTRE CONGREGATIONAL CHURCH, HARTFORD, CONN.
Thomas Appleton, 1835 [120, p. 429]

Great
Open Diapason I 8'
Open Diapason II 8'
Stopt Diapason I 8'
Stopt Diapason II 8'
Principal 4'
Twelfth 2 2/3'
Fifteenth 2'
Tierce 1 3/5'
Cornet V (treble)
Sesquialtera III (bass)

Choir
Open Diapason 8'
Stopt Diapason 8'
Dulciana 8'
Principal 4'
Flute 4'
Cremona 8'
Bassoon 8'

Swell (short compass)
Open Diapason 8'
Stopt Diapason 8'

Mixture III   Dulciana 8'
Trumpet 8'   Principal 4'
Clarion 4'   Cornet III

Pedal   Hautboy 8'
Sub Bass 16'

Accessory Stops
Tremulant (Swell)
Couplers: Great-Pedal, Choir-Pedal, Swell Great, Choir-Great

Registration

By the middle decades of the eighteenth century, the British organ had become locked into a pattern as standard and predictable as that of the French or the Italian organ. The stoplists above were not chosen for their conformity to this pattern; indeed, it is virtually impossible to find an English or Anglo-American stoplist prior to the 1840s that does not conform to it. The basic ingredients do not always turn up in quite the same arrangement in every organ, but they know their place and rarely vary from it. Experimentation with novel stops ceased quite early in the eighteenth century, almost as if the organists and builders had tacitly agreed among themselves as to what was musically necessary and what was not.

This does not mean that no changes occurred, but rather that they came about slowly, often by means of evolution or substitution. Thistlethwaite credits the popularity of the orchestral clarinet (used extensively by Mozart, Spohr, and Weber, composers who were popular in England) for the reappearance around 1800 of the cylindrical Cremona—its name a corruption of the Restoration-period Cromorne [174, p. 90]. By the early nineteenth century this stop had usurped the place of the Vox Humana and Bassoon on the secondary manuals, and Joshua Done observed that combined with the Stopped Diapason it made "an excellent imitation of the Clarionet"[38, p. 16]. The appearance of the first truly new stop since Snetzler's Dulciana—the foundational 8' Clarabella or Claribel Flute (an open wood flute), introduced by J. C. Bishop—did not occur until near the end of the period, around 1819, but it quickly became popular as a solo stop (usually displacing the older Cornet) and was widely imitated [318, p. 16]. As such it was a somewhat belated addition to the British tonal palette, for strong solo 8' flutes had been in use in some areas of the Continent for almost a century.

Yet despite these minor changes, certain physical features remained the same. The Cornet was always a treble-compass stop, the Tremulant only affected the Swell, and although the Great and the Choir (except in the smallest organs) extended down to GGG below modern CC (occasionally even to FFF), the Swell (or Echo) was always of short compass, usually beginning at "fiddle G" (G below middle C) and only occasionally lower. Rarely was there any Pedal until around the turn of the century, and even then it was usually only a pulldown Pedal with no independent pipes, even in large organs; so-called German (C-compass) pedals were unknown before the 1820s.

These details are important to remember when registering the music according to the composer's directions. If, for instance, a section of a voluntary is marked simply "Swell," but the left-hand compass descends below "fiddle G," it should be understood that only the right hand plays on the Swell; the left hand plays on the Choir or on the soft stops of the Great. And, although on organs of modern compass the Pedal is sometimes needed to sound occasional manual notes written below low C, the player should beware of corrupt editions with editorially added independent Pedal parts, which invariably destroy the balance and concept of the music.

The standard organ layout was a small-to-moderately sized three manual, with full compass Great and Choir, short compass Swell, and usually no Pedal. The Great/Choir two-manual organ of the Restoration period had, by mid-century, given way to a Great/Swell two-manual. By the beginning of the nineteenth century an unenclosed "choir bass" of one or two stops was sometimes added to the Swell in two-manual organs, so that this manual could take over some of the duties assigned to the Choir in three-manual organs. A one-manual organ of this period, unless it was a small chamber organ, was simply a Great, minus the other divisions. Very occasionally, toward the end of the period, a few of its softer stops were enclosed, and sometimes in chamber organs one finds all the pipes in a primitive swell enclosure.

The standard British style crossed the ocean to the eastern United States with imported organs from the London workshops of Green, Snetzler, Bridge, Elliot, England, Avery, and others. Builders such as Geib, Hall, and Erben in New York, and Goodrich, Appleton, and Hook in Boston, built organs in virtually the same style, and with the same standard stoplists, almost up to the middle of the nineteenth century. From the period immediately preceding the War of Independence through the early 1800s, several British organist-composers emigrated to the eastern United States, including Selby, Linley, Hayter, Carr, Reinagle, R. Taylor, and S. P. Taylor. These musicians and their students doubtless helped to perpetuate the "standard" English organ tonal design in this area.

The British organ music of the late eighteenth and early nineteenth cenuries, while making its bow to the continental influences of Italian keyboard players and German symphonists, was almost as conservative as the organ designs. The multi-sectional type of voluntary pioneered by Stanley was taken up with gusto by Heron, Hook, Russell, and Charles Wesley, but many others continued to write in the older two-sectional style, usually a prelude and a fugue, or a Cornet, Flute, or Trumpet movement preceded by a Diapason or Full Organ movement.

With the notable exception of the eccentric Samuel Wesley—one of the first English organists to "discover" J. S. Bach—there were few forays into other forms, although toward the end of the period one finds an occasional short air or march, and two composers of the Anglo-American group (Carr and R. Taylor) have left us attractive hymn-tune variations. Organ concertos continued to be written by Arne, Camidge, Russell, Hook, and the Wesleys. In general they tended to be more adventurous than the voluntaries written by the same composers, doubtless because they were secular works and more in the instrumental mainstream.

Transcriptions from instrumental music were a part of the repertoire of the late Baroque and Classical periods, and indeed earlier, as the Handelian borrowings in

Reading's 1737 manuscript attest. Italian music was very popular, and movements from Corelli, Scarlatti, etc., turn up in published sources and in manuscript collections compiled by organists. Instrumentally inspired overtures, sicilianos, pastorales, gavottes, and marches infiltrated and sometimes replaced the traditional voluntary.

Camidge's Six Concertos "for the Organ or Grand Piano Forte," published around the turn of the century, are a case in point; the title page states that the composer "has Endeavored to imitate the particular Style of Music . . . of HANDEL & CORELLI." It is interesting that Camidge calls his pieces "Concertos," since, despite their Italianate hints, they are in fact little different from the expanded multi-partite voluntaries of some of his contemporaries. Some of the segments are straightforward slow movements, full organ movements, and fugues—but there are also marches, minuets, and gavottes. Camidge's registration directions in these pieces are somewhat of a departure from the norm; with the exception of the usual "Diapasons," they do not refer to specific stops, but to manuals and dynamic levels—"Full Organ," "Soft Organ," "Soli," "Tutti," etc. Camidge gives the piano as an alternative instrument to the organ for the performance of these pieces (perhaps to increase sales?) yet he also indicates occasional use of the pedals, mostly for sustained notes, as did his contemporaries Wesley and Russell.

In England, perhaps more than in any other area save possibly Italy and Iberia, the Classical period was a conservative outgrowth of the Baroque period in the world of the organ, which was, with the interesting exception of the popular public "music rooms," increasingly becoming the world of the Church. Thus one has the anachronism of anthems and voluntaries being composed in archaic styles for the Church, while out in the secular world French and Italian operas vied with the symphonies of Haydn and the expatriate J. C. Bach for the ears of concertgoers.

This conservatism is mirrored dramatically in the several registration treatises and directions which appeared during the last decade of the eighteenth century. Of particular importance are those written by three relatively minor figures who incorporated their observations on registration into the prefaces to sets of voluntaries: John Marsh, whose *Eighteen Voluntaries for the Organ* was published in 1791; Jonas Blewitt, with *A Complete Treatise on the Organ to which is added a Set of Explanatory Voluntaries,* published around 1795; and Francis Linley, whose *A Practical Introduction to the Organ* appeared at about the same time. Their rules are applicable to the music of much of the eighteenth century, and since a few of their comments pointed to more current trends, they are likewise applicable to music from the early years of the nineteenth century. Because these authors generally corroborate each other, their comments on the stops and their uses are conflated in the following summary.

Diapasons, Open and Stopped 8'

They are always to be used together, and "no other stops used without them" [Marsh].

"The Diapasons are the grand foundation of the instrument, and consequently must never be omitted; as without them, no other stop (excepting the flute) can have a proper effect" [Linley].

"No stop whatever should be used without these stops, except the Flute" [Blewitt].

The Open Diapason may be used alone for "slow fugues and imitations," but, "when the Open Diapason is enlivened by the Stop Diapason, Airs of a more sprightly nature may with propriety be used" [Blewitt].

"The Treble part of the [Open] Diapason, if the pipes be brilliantly voiced, greatly resembles the tone of a German Flute; and when accompanied upon the Swell in semi-quavers, imitating the Tenor Fiddle, it is productive of a very agreeable melody" [Blewitt]. Note here the typical Classical assumption of the organ's imitative role, as well as a new role for the Diapason.

"The Stop Diapason likewise has a happy effect as a relief to a Trumpet piece" [i.e., as an "echo"; Blewitt].

"The Stop Diapason, and the Principal, on the Choir Organ, have a happy effect in an Andante movement. The Stop Diapason and the Flute are to accompany a Solo Voice" [Blewitt]. The latter practice can be traced back at least as far as Handel.

Dulciana 8'

The Dulciana "has a peculiar sweetness of tone, and may be used quite alone" [Marsh].

The "Dulceano" resembles "a delicate open Diapason, which, when the Flute is added to it, resembles the Cymbal [*sic*]. If the Dulceano be in the Choir . . . or the Great organ, the Flute may be blended with it" [Blewitt].

The Dulciana "is, in fact, an Open Diapason, but voiced much softer and sweeter, the pipes being on a smaller scale" [Linley].

In the Choir, the Stopped Diapason and Dulciana may be used together, and Principals 4' and 2' may be added [Marsh].

Principal 4'

The Principal "renders the Diapasons more brilliant," and with the Dulciana "makes an accompaniment for antiphonal singers" [Marsh]—a rather interesting comment.

"The Principal . . . should never be used singly, in manner of a Flute, because it doth not answer quick to the finger; but, when blended with the Stop Diapason, in an airy style, it is shown to the greatest advantage . . . this is the best mixture of stops in the organ" [Blewitt]. But note in this regard the single exception of the solo use of the Principal, cited in the previous section, found in a 1780 edition of Handel's Voluntaries.

Flute 4'

The Flute is "frequently used alone (as an imitation of the common flute or flageolet) but is more properly joined in the [Stopt] Diapason (or the Dulciana at pleasure), which two stops are the proper accompaniment in Solo or Verse parts in Anthems" [Marsh].

"The Flute, or Flageolet ... requires airy music.... It likewise has a pleasing effect when accompanied with the Swell; and is a relief to the Diapason in a movement designed to imitate the Horns" [Blewitt].

In the Choir, the Flute "can be used like the Principal [i.e., with the 8' stops] or alone" [Marsh].

It must be remembered that the stop called "Flute" on an English organ of this period is always of 4' pitch, and was often used as a solo stop to imitate (in "airy music") the orchestral flute or flageolet.

Upperwork

The Twelfth is never drawn without the Diapasons, Principal, and Fifteenth; the Twelfth and Fifteenth "are never drawn without each other, or alone." However, the Diapasons, Principal, Twelfth and Fifteenth together "form a proper mixture [plenum] to accompany the Choral Parts of the Service in Cathedrals ... and to accompany a small congregation in the psalms in Parish Churches" [Marsh].

"Neither the Twelfth, nor Fifteenth, is used singly, being only calculated for full pieces; or for a mixture, such [as] with the Diapasons, the Principal, the Twelfth and Fifteenth" [Blewitt].

The independent Tierce and Larigot are described only as "stops used by the ancient builders," although they "now form a part of the Sesquialtera" [Blewitt]. Marsh regarded them as something builders put in "merely to make a show of stops to draw, at small expense."

These writers notwithstanding, Tierces did in fact continue frequently to appear as independent stops well into the nineteenth century, and were regarded as part of the chorus, subject to the same rules as the Twelfth and Fifteenth. The Tierce, or Seventeenth, was also (as Blewitt implies) a standard component of the Sesquialtera—which was a chorus mixture—until past the middle of the nineteenth century in both England and America, no doubt because meantone-based tuning systems were retained in these areas.

Cornet

The Cornet "must never be used in the full organ. It is only proper to be used in conjunction with the Diapasons, in giving out psalm tunes, voluntaries, Symphonies of anthems, etc." [Linley].

The Cornet, "being a half stop, it ought never to be used in the Full Organ, but only with the Diapasons, in Voluntaries, giving out Psalm Tunes, Symphonies of Anthems, etc." [Marsh].

"The Cornet stop requires light airy music, and is generally accompanied by a moving bass." "Never . . . use the Cornet Stop in a Full-Organ Piece on any occasion whatever" [Blewitt]. All the writers are quite emphatic on this score!

"Never use the Cornet in the Swell, except it be full Swell, or as an Echo to that in the Great Organ" [Blewitt].

Mixtures

The Sesquialtera should never be used without the Diapason, Principal, Twelfth, and Fifteenth "for Full Organ"; the Mixture or Furniture is "shriller [more high-pitched] than the Sesquialtera, and should not be used without it [Marsh]. In other words, the full organ is to be built up in the traditional way, from bottom to top.

"The Sesquialtera is wholly adapted to the Full Organ, although it has sometimes been made use of as a single stop, and as such written for by Authors. I may remark, that where there is no Cornet, the Sesquialtera is a tolerable substitute" [Blewitt]. "Tolerable" is probably the operative word here, for the Sesquialtera was a principal-scaled stop, and thus not as full-sounding as the wide-scaled Cornet.

Full Organ

Marsh specifies five different kinds of full organ: 1. Great up to Sesquialtera; 2. The same, with the Furniture added; 3. The same, with Trumpet instead of Furniture; 4. The same, with both Trumpet and Furniture; and 5. The foregoing, with the Clarion 4' added.

"After a Trumpet Piece, to conclude with the same subject on a Full Organ, has a very grand effect" [Blewitt].

For the full organ, "I know of no pieces more proper than a Largo, a Fugue, or a slow Adagio" [Blewitt].

Full Swell consists of all stops "through the Principal," with the reeds [Marsh].

Reed Stops

The Trumpet "renders the chorus more full and brilliant"; the Clarion "strengthens the chorus comparatively, as the Principal does the Diapasons" [Linley].

The Trumpet may be used instead of the Mixture; the Clarion is used "only in addition to" the Trumpet. "When the Trumpet is used imitative of the real Trumpet, it is then only joined with the Diapasons" [Marsh]. In other words, the 8' foundations are needed to give body to the Trumpet in solo use.

The Trumpet stop should be used for imitative music that is "martial and grand," and should be accompanied by the Choir Diapasons. "The Bass of the Trumpet . . . is very coarse, unless when used in the Full Organ" [Blewitt].

"The Clarion is never used but in a full piece" [Blewitt].

The Choir Bassoon, Cremona, and Vox Humana are "seldom used but as fancy [i.e., solo] stops in voluntaries" [Linley].

The Choir Bassoon, Vox Humana, and Cremona should be drawn with the 8' stops (Stopt Diapason and Dulciana) "when used as a fancy stop in voluntaries" [Marsh].

"The Cremona, Vox Humane, and Bassoon [are] . . . generally used in an adagio or grave movement. . . . Such passages as are written for the Violoncello are best calculated for these Stops" [Blewitt].

The Swell Hautboy and Trumpet "may be used singly or both together, but always with the Diapasons" [Marsh].

"If the Hautboy Stop in the Swell be used, [the organist] must only use the Stop Diapason with it," accompanied "only with the Stop Diapason in the Choir organ" [Blewitt].

During the ensuing decades, these registration directions of the 1790s were extensively copied, with little variation, by a number of authors on both sides of the Atlantic. Samuel P. Taylor, a pupil of Russell, emigrated to New York in 1806. Shortly afterward he published his *Practical School for the Organ*, in which the description of the stops and their uses was plagiarized almost word for word from Marsh. Articles on organ stops and their uses appeared in various American periodicals during the 1820s and 30s, and seem to be based largely on the same source; the material in "The Organ, and a Description of its Use," which appeared in the May 6, 1820 issue of *The Euterpeiad*, a Boston publication, is quoted verbatim from Marsh, probably via Taylor [cf. 277].

As late as 1830 the New York organ builder Henry Erben was distilling the same dogmas in a preface written for *Harmonia Sacra,* a collection of hymns and anthems: The Diapasons (open and stopped) are the "foundation, upon which all other stops are built" and other stops should never be used without them; the Open Diapason should be used with the Trumpet in solos, and the Stopped Diapason with the Cremona or Oboe; the chorus should be built up from the bottom to the top, the reeds being added last. Other "pleasing" combinations cited include Open Diapason 8', Dulciana 8', Principal 4', and Flute 4' on the Great, and Dulciana 8', Flute 4', and Hautboy 8' on the Swell.

Although significant changes in English organ design and usage began to occur in the 1830s, Busby's *Dictionary of Music*, published in 1827, makes a few references to the use of stops that are quite in harmony with the older tradition. The Diapasons are always to be used with solo reeds, and it is desirable to use the Trumpet in Full Organ [149, p. 42]. That a distinction between the two types of Full Organ was still observed, however, is shown in some books of mass accompaniments from the 1820s found in Lulworth Castle, which specify both "Full to Fifteenth" and "Full with trumpet" [287, p. 30].

Change came even slower in the United States. "On the Use of the Stops of the Organ," which appeared in the February 25, 1845 issue of *The American Journal of Music*, still hewed remarkably closely to the dictates of a half-century previous with regard to the uses of the Diapasons, the reed stops, and the 4' Flute, adding only some cautions on the judicious use of the swellbox [278].

Comments made by various authors regarding the overuse of "fancy stops" and "light, airy music"—and probably, by implication, transcriptions—suggest a growing conservatism in church circles at the turn of the century, even as the practices of the previous half-century were being carved in stone by various authors. In the preface to his *Ten Church Pieces*, published in 1798, the cleric-composer Rev. William Jones of Nayland makes these observations:

> I use the organ chiefly in the Diapasons, the Swell, and the chorus, as best accommodated to the Music of the Church. A stop approaching to vocality, such as the Bassoon, Cremona, or Vox-humana, has a very agreeable effect, and may well be admitted when used with discretion; but I must confess myself much less affected by the noise and levity of the Cornet and Trumpet than I used to be. [306]

What bothered Jones was probably not the stops themselves, but the increasingly brilliant and showy voluntaries being written for them in this period. But there is ample evidence that the Cornet was still commonly used to "give out" the psalm tunes for congregational singing in this period.

The dicta of Marsh and his imitators were concerned with the church organ and its use in playing voluntaries and accompanying the voice. But another type of organ was very much in vogue in this period. Chamber organs had been around since the days of the Tudors, but it was during the second half of the eighteenth century and the early decades of the nineteenth that domestic keyboard music flourished. Not only among the aristocracy but also in the homes of the merchant class, the chamber organ vied with the harpsichord and spinet (and, later, the fortepiano) for pride of place. Some professional musicians were known to have owned chamber organs or claviorgana, and many homes had several keyboard instruments of various types.

Chamber organs could also be found in increasing numbers in theatres, "music rooms," assembly rooms, "pleasure gardens," spas, and even taverns. They were frequently used as an ensemble or accompanimental instrument, but there is evidence that solo voluntaries were played on them as well, and church organists often did double duty in such places.

There is nothing to suggest that registrations such as those from Byfield and Gray, cited in chapter 9, did not continue to be applicable to small organs for some time. Their recommendations were reiterated in 1779 by John Arnold, who described in verse his manner of registering his "fine organ" of ten stops:

> On Diapasons, grave Adagios,
> And on the Cornet, brisk Allegros.
> With beats and shakes and other Graces,
> And on the Trumpet play Vivaces; [*sic!*]
> According as my pieces suit,
> Forte full Organ, Piano Flute.
> And as I chuse my stops to alter,

In playing full I take Sesqualter;
In order, for to do it well,
I likewise take the Principal,
Great Twelfth, Fifteenth, Cremona brave,
For, in all, ten stops I have.

[10, p. 420]

The references to the types of music requiring certain registrations are interesting, although there are no surprises. No gapped combinations appear, but the 4' Flute may be used for quiet passages, and there is the possible implication that Arnold added the mixture to his Full Organ last, after the reed.

Registrations, often detailed, appeared in virtually all published music from the middle of the eighteenth century until well into the nineteenth. Samuel Wesley, in his *Twelve Short Pieces*, includes a thirteenth, a "Full Voluntary" of the prelude-and-fugue type. The Prelude is registered for Full Organ with Trumpet, and the Fugue for Full Organ without Trumpet; this practice was probably fairly common with this type of voluntary, unless other directions are given. In the familiar miniature usually called "Air" and paired with a Gavotte, Wesley also shows how solo stops such as the Cremona and the Flute can be charmingly contrasted.

One of the first pieces with detailed registration found in America is a long and showy sectional voluntary written early in the nineteenth century by Benjamin Carr for the dedication of an organ built by another expatriate Englishman for a Philadephia church. It includes segments for such standard formulae as Diapasons, Full Organ, and flute and reed solos. The only apparent variant from the standard practice is a tenor-register solo for "Violoncello," but it is unknown whether the organ actually had a stop of this name, or whether this is an example of the use of the Open Diapason "imitating the tenor fiddle," as had been suggested by Blewitt.

"Diapasons," "Swell," and "Full Organ" are still the most common registrations for the introductory section of a voluntary, but "Diapasons with Principal"—Open and Stopped 8', with the 4' Principal—sometimes also appears, and Russell experimented with different types of introductions and combinations such as the Stopt Diapason and Principal on the Choir. Russell may also be credited with developing the Cornet (and Hautboy) voluntary into a more melodic type of piece, often replacing the old "echo" device with a more sophisticated dialogue. He also occasionally used unorthodox registrations, such as combining the Swell Diapasons with the reeds in a Pastorale—very similar to Italian usage, in fact—and tended to use reeds and flutes in a more imitative way [290, p. 54].

Along with Russell, James Hook, organist of Vauxhall Gardens, may have been one of the last to write Cornet voluntaries. But he also foreshadowed some of the trends that would develop more fully later on in his use of Swell Oboe solos, manual changes, and unusual registrations such as are found in his Voluntary in D, which calls for "Oboe or Cremona" in the right hand and "Basson or Vox Humana" in the left hand, in a movement reminiscent of some French trios. T. S. Dupuis even calls for the Bassoon to be played an octave lower in a right-hand solo, placing it largely in the tenor register, where indeed this stop may have sounded best.

Another experimenter was Henry Heron. In his *Voluntary 1* a double Trumpet figure is echoed an octave lower on "Horns" (presumably Diapasons) and a solo is given to "Flute or Diapason." In *Voluntary 8* something even more unusual occurs: The Full Organ (Great) enters into a dialogue with a lively duo played with the right hand on the "Eccho" (probably full Swell) and the left on the Choir Flute and Fifteenth. As the Flute in this period is always a 4' stop, the two lines are on the same pitch level, and they cross and recross in effective interplay. Likewise somewhat unorthodox is a registration calling for 8', 4', and 2 2/3' (no 2') in a c1793 voluntary by Mathias Hawdon. Such usages were still very much the exception, however, and the vast majority of registrations found in English music until well into the nineteenth century are still cast in the time-honored Marsh-Blewitt-Linley mold.

Most of the cautions applying to the performance of earlier English music on modern organs still apply to the music of this period. The color of the "Diapasons" was still as suave and generally understated as in the previous period, even though a second, louder Open Diapason was often found in the Great of larger turn-of-the-century organs (the softer Diapason becoming "Diapason II"). While a literal interpretation of 8' Principal and 8' Stopped Flute may work on some organs, an excessively powerful or sizzly principal or a loud hooty flute can totally destroy the desired effect. Sixteen-foot stops were still extremely scarce until well into the nineteenth century, and thus have no place in the full organ, where the goal is still balance and brightness rather than volume. Nor are high-pressure solo Trumpets (or Tubas) appropriate for Trumpet voluntaries; the choice of stops on many organs must be carefully made, and sometimes principals or reeds on a secondary manual will be preferable to those on the Great.

Players having access to an unaltered American organ of the mid-nineteenth century or earlier will have a distinct advantage, for the quality of the individual stops in such organs is very close to what Marsh et al. had in mind, and most of the old combinations will work nicely. Although Cornets and/or independent Tierces are not common save in the earliest nineteenth-century instruments, it is possible to use the Sesquialtera chorus mixture (which will contain a tierce) with 8' and 4' flutes, a substitution which is indeed condoned by some English writers. The available flutes will generally include an authentic Stopped Diapason (in the Swell if not in the Great) and usually a sweet-toned 4' flute suitable for solos. And the reed stops on these organs (and even some later ones) will be found to be ideal, since until around 1870 most of the East Coast builders were still basing their reed stops on early nineteenth-century English models rather than on the more contemporary (and more Romantic) continental ones, particularly for smaller instruments.

Composers

Claude-Bénigne Balbastre (1727–1799)
Jacques-Marie Beauvarlet-Charpentier (1766–1834)
Jean-Jacques Beauvarlet-Charpentier (1734–1794)
Alexandre Pierre François Boëly (1785–1858)
Michel Corrette (1709–1795)
Armand-Louis Couperin (1727–1789)
Dufour (d. 1786)
Pierre Février (1715–c1780)
Matthias van den Gheyn (1721–1785)
Guillaume Lasceux (1740–1831)
Jean-Nicolas Marrigues (1757–1834)
Louis-Nicolas Séjan (1786–1849)
Nicolas Séjan (1745–1819)
Jean-François Taperay (1738–1819)

Representative Organs

CHURCH OF ST. NICOLAS-DES-CHAMPS, PARIS
François-Henri Cliquot, 1772–77 [65, p. 19]

Grand Orgue	**Positif**
Montre 16'	Montre 8'
Bourdon 16'	Bourdon 8'
Montre 8'	Flûte 8' (treble)
Dessus de Flûte 8' (treble)	Prestant 4'
Bourdon 8'	Nasard 2 2/3'
Prestant 4'	Quarte 2'
Double Tierce 3 1/5'	Tierce 1 3/5'

Nasard 2 2/3'
Doublette 2'
Quarte 2'
Tierce 1 3/5'
Grand Cornet V (treble)
Fourniture IV
Cymbale V
Trompette I 8'
Trompette II 8'
Voix Humaine 8'
Clairon 4'

Echo (short compass)
Bourdon 8'
Flûte 4'
Trompette 8'

Pedalier
Flûte 16' (stopped)
Flûte 8' (principal)
Flûte 4'
Bombarde 16'
Trompette 8'
Clairon 4'

Accessory Stops
Not listed, but presumably included one or two Tremulants.

PROTESTANT CHURCH, GRIES, BAS-RHIN
Jean-Andreas Silbermann, 1781 [86, p. 36]

Manual
Bourdon 8'
Prestant 4'
Flûte 4'
Nasard 2 2/3'
Doublette 2'
Tierce 1 3/5'
Sifflet 1'
Cornet IV
Fourniture III
Cymbale II

Pédale
Soubass 16'
Bourdon 8'
Flûte 4'

ABBEY CHURCH, SOUVIGNY
François-Henri Cliquot, 1782 [86, p. 74]

Grand Orgue
Montre 8'
Bourdon 8'
Prestant 4'
Nasard 2 2/3'
Doublette 2'
Quarte de Nasard 2'

Positif
Bourdon 8'
Flûte 8' (treble)
Prestant 4'
Nasard 2 2/3'
Doublette 2'
Tierce 1 3/5'

Cornet V (treble)
Fourniture III
Cymbale II
Cromorne 8'
Dessus de Hautbois 8' (treble)
Basse de Basson 8' (bass)
Voix Humaine 8'
Clairon 4'

Récit (short compass)
Flûte 4'
Cornet
Hautbois 8'

Bombarde
Bombarde 16'
Trompette 8'

Tierce 1 3/5'
Cornet V (treble)
Plein Jeu VI
Trompette 8'
Voix humaine 8'
Clairon 4'

Pédale
Flûte 8'
Flûte 4'
Trompette 8'
Clairon 4'

Accessory Stops
Coupler: Grand Orgue–Positif
2 Tremblants (Doux and Fort)

Plein Jeu V
Trompette 8'
Cromorne 8'

Récit (short compass)
Bourdon 8'
Cornet IV
Hautbois 8'

PARISH CHURCH, ST. GUILHEM-LE-DESERT, HÉRAULT
Jean-Pierre Cavaillé, 1788 [86, p. 62]

Grand Orgue
Montre 8'
Bourdon 8'
Flûte 8'–4'
Prestant 4'
Nasard 2 2/3'
Doublette 2'
Quarte 2'
Tierce 1 3/5'
Cornet V (treble)
Fourniture
Cymbale
Trompette 8'
Cromorne 8'
Voix Humaine 8'
Clairon 4'

Positif
Bourdon 8'
Montre 4'
Nasard 2 2/3'
Doublette 2'
Tierce 1 3/5'
Larigot 1 1/3'
Plein Jeu
Trompette 8'
Cromorne 8'

Récit (short compass)
Cornet V

Pédale
Flûte 8'
Trompette 8'

Accessory Stops
Coupler: Grand Orgue–Positif (shove coupler)
Tremblant doux

PARISH CHURCH, WESTREM, EAST FLANDERS
Van Peteghem, 1790 [107, II, p. 144]

Manual
Montre 8'
Bourdon 8'
Prestant 4'
Fluit 4'
Nazard 2 2/3'
Doublette 2'
Cornet V (treble)

Fourniture III
Trompet 8' (divided?)

CHURCH OF THE ESCARINES, NICE
Grinda Fréres, 1791 [stoplist from extant organ]

Manual
Montre 8'
Bourdon 8'
Dessus de flûte 8' (treble)
Prestant 4'
Nasard 2 2/3'
Doublette 2'
Tierce 1 3/5'
Cornet (treble)
Plein Jeu VI
Trompette 8'
Voix humaine 8'
Clairon 4'

Pédale
Pédale de 8'

Accessory Stops
Rossignol (bird)

ST. PETER'S CATHEDRAL, POITIERS
François-Henri Cliquot, 1791 [315, p. 99]

Grand Orgue
Montre 16'
Bourdon 16'
Montre 8'
Bourdon 8'
Flûte 8'
Prestant 4'
Grande Tierce 3 1/5'
Nazard 2 2/3'
Doublette 2'
Quarte 2'
Tierce 1 3/5'
Grand Cornet V (treble)
Fourniture V
Cymbale IV
Bombarde 8'–16'★
Trompette 8'
Cromorne 8'
Voix Humaine 8'
Clairon I 4'
Clairon II 4'

Pédale
Flûte 16' (stopped)
Flûte 8' (open)
Flûte 4' (open)

Positif
Montre 8'
Bourdon 8'
Flûte 8' (treble)
Prestant 4'
Nazard 2 2/3'
Doublette 2'
Tierce 1 3/5'
Grand Cornet V (treble)
Plein Jeu VII
Trompette 8'
Cromorne 8'
Clairon 4'

Récit (short compass)
Flûte 8'
Grand Cornet V★★
Trompette 8'
Hautbois 8'

Echo (short compass)
Bourdon 8'
Flûte 4'
Trompette 8'

Bombarde 16'†
Trompette 8'†
Clairon 4'†

Accessory Stops
Coupler: Grand Orgue–Positif (shove coupler)
Tremblant doux, Tremblant fort

*Added by Dallery early in the nineteenth century; originally Trompette 8'
**Originally called Cornet de Récit; from Tenor G
†Stop goes down to AAA

PARISH CHURCH, MOLLAU, HAUT-RHIN
Jos. Callinet, 1833 [103, p. 23]

Grand Orgue
Bourdon 16'
Montre 8'
Bourdon 8'
Gambe 8'
Prestant 4'
Flûte 4'
Nazard 2 2/3'
Doublette 2'
Sifflet 1'
Cornet V
Fourniture V
Trompette 8'

Positif
Bourdon 8'
Salicional 8'
Flûte traversière 8'–4'
Montre 4'
Nazard 2 2/3'
Doublette 2'
Cromorne 8'
Basson-Hautbois 8'

Pédale
Bourdon 16'
Flûte 8'
Flûte 4' Clairon 4'
Trompette 8'
Clairon 4'

Accessory Stops
Coupler: Grand Orgue–Positif
Tremblant

Registration

The history of the French organ in this period can be said to have two parts, riven by the Revolution. The true French Classic period came to an abrupt end as the weak and bankrupt monarchy was toppled in Paris at the very time that Cliquot was completing his last great masterpiece in Poitiers to the southwest. Full-scale warfare broke out in 1792, as France invaded Austria and other nearby countries, and did not subside for a decade. In the meantime, the revolutionary government had suppressed the worship of the Catholic Church and secularized the churches as "Temples of Reason"; some organs were destroyed, and many others suffered from neglect, but, as normalcy began to return, some were used for secular recitals.

The early years of the nineteenth century were chaotic from a cultural and religious standpoint, particularly in Paris. The areas least affected were probably Alsace-Lorraine and the Southeast, where the French organ tradition survived after a fashion in the work of Riepp, Cavaillé, and inheritors of the Silbermann tradition, such as Callinet. In the area of present-day Belgium, little change occurred, and several organ-building families continued to make organs of a very conservative style until well into the nineteenth century.

In Paris, members of the Dallery family occupied themselves during the first two decades of the nineteenth century by repairing and re-installing damaged or dismantled organs in Paris. In the process, perhaps unwittingly, they also started another revolution by suppressing or replacing some of the upperwork and mutations in many of the organs they repaired. In 1808 Pierre-François Dallery replaced a Bourdon with a Flûte Ouverte in St. Nicolas-des-Champs, and in 1813 he replaced mixtures and a Larigot with reeds in St. Gervais [211, p. 63]. Despite such changes, the Dallerys must be given credit for having preserved a number of the surviving works of the Cliquots and other older builders, works which might otherwise have perished.

French historians seem to regard the period immediately before and after the Revolution as one of decadence, at least as far as organ music is concerned. Like the English, they deplored the "bizarre themes" and "theatre music" (not to mention operatic overtures) that invaded the organ loft in the second half of the eighteenth century [230, p. 129]. Improvisation was practiced in France, as everywhere, and it found popular approval in "thunderstorm" *Te Deums*, which were related in spirit to the battle pieces of Spain and the descriptive genre that was to flourish in the nineteenth century. Ostensibly depicting such ecclesiastically acceptable themes as the Last Judgment or the battle between good and evil, they were tolerated by the clergy and loved by the people.

It is certainly true that some of the *Noëls* and other pieces by Balbastre, Corrette, and their contemporaries seem insubstantial and even frivolous compared to the masterworks of François Couperin and Nicolas deGrigny. The music for the mass was in unquestionable decline, yet Corrette's Mass on the 8th Tone is thoroughly worthy of the earlier tradition; and the elder Beauvarlet-Charpentier and others could still write creditable fugues in the new *Fugue de mouvement* style. From a vantage point two centuries removed it is quite possible to find much of charm, and even an occasional bit of substance, in the music of this period.

Lasceux, along with the Séjans, father and son, helped to bridge the gap between Balbastre and Boëly. Lasceux was one of the few Parisian organists to keep his post through the troubled revolutionary years. He was organist of the church of St. Etienne du Mont from 1774 to 1819, and during that time he published a number of organ works. He also wrote an "Essai Théoretique et Pratique sur l'Art de l'Orgue" (1809; never published), which contains registration directions very much in the Classical mold. The younger Séjan, organist of the Chapel Royal, lost his post during the Revolution, but in 1807 he became organist of the Invalides in Paris; he too was a prolific writer. Both paved the way for Boëly, a somewhat eccentric and solitary figure reminiscent of Samuel Wesley, who nonetheless influenced the younger generation. Boëly also shared Wesley's delight in the rediscovery of J. S. Bach, and while Boëly's later works are decidedly Romantic, his earlier compositions reflect a Bachian austerity too pronounced to be accidental.

All the composers of this period continued to write *alternatim* liturgical music (versets) and *Noëls* in the time-honored formats, but Balbastre also wrote a stirring version of *La Marseillaise*, which he is said to have played in a Paris church during the Revolution; and Corrette wrote a bombastic "thunder" piece, with directions to place a board on the pedal keys and stamp on it wherever thunder is indicated. Some of the post-Revolutionary organists carried things to much greater excess by routinely playing marches, dances, and opera music during the mass. But in general the composers under discussion here tended to look backward toward the late Baroque period for their inspiration. While some of his contemporaries were playing their secular ditties, the younger Séjan wrote a sober Prelude and Fugue on a Kyrie by the seventeenth-century composer duMont, whose choral settings were still being used in alternation to the organ settings in the liturgy well into the nineteenth century.

Perhaps because of this conservatism, as well as the inescapable presence of the surviving seventeenth- and eighteenth-century organs, registration practices changed little until the third decade of the nineteenth century. This is not to say that there had been no change at all since the end of the seventeenth century, for, just as slow changes were occurring in the still very standard stoplists (the introduction of the solo 8' Flûte toward the end of the eighteenth century, for example, as well as the more frequent occurrence of 16' Pedal stops, notably the Bombarde) so too were registration habits slowly altering. Yet in 1772, Armand-Louis Couperin was recorded as having improvised a *Te Deum* in which he alternated tutti sections on the *Grand Jeu* with sections in which the Hautbois was accompanied by the *Jeu de Nazard* [230, p. 131]. Probably the Hautbois was played by the left hand, in which case the *Jeu de Nazard* in the right hand would correspond to the accompaniment for reed bass solos specified by Raison, Boyvin, and others a century earlier.

Dom Bédos de Celles, who codified the practices of French classic organ building only a few decades before its eclipse, also gives some valuable glimpses into changing registrational practices in the last quarter of the eighteenth century. Fenner Douglass [212, p. 105] has pointed out certain of these changes by comparing Dom Bédos's recommendations with those of Lebègue, which were written a century before. The following is a summary of Douglass's findings:

For *fugues graves* use the Trompette and Clairon, with the Bourdon 8' and Prestant 4' [Lebègue]. For *fugues graves* use the Prestant and all the Trompettes and Clairons on the Grand Orgue, as well as the Trompette, Cromorne, and Clairon on the Positif [Dom Bédos].

The strong Tremulant (*Tremblant fort*) may be used with the *Grand Jeu* (an opinion also held by Raison, Chaumont, and G. Corrette) [Lebègue]. While many organists still use the strong Tremulant with the *Grand Jue*, this is never done by "the ablest and most tasteful players" because it bothers the speech of the pipes [Dom Bédos].

The accompaniment to a Tierce or Cromorne *en Taille* should be played on Montre or Bourdon 16', Petit Bourdon 8', and Prestant 4' [Lebègue]. If the 8' Principal and 8' Bourdon are too weak for an accompaniment, add the Flute or Prestant 4', but not the 16' stops (except on the Pedal) [Dom Bédos].

A *Basse de Trompette* can be played on a Trompette with 8' flues, or on the Positif Cromorne with the Montre, Nazard, and Tierce [Lebègue]. Although some use the Nazard with the Cromorne, and while this may be all right if the Cromorne is not full enough, a really good Cromorne should never be combined with a Nazard [Dom Bédos].

Duos should be played boldly and lightly; on large organs with the treble on the Positif *Jeu de Tierce* and the bass on the Grosse Tierce with the Bourdon 16' [Lebègue]. For duos, use for the bass the foundation stops on the Grande Orgue, even the 32' if there is one, along with all Nazards, Tierces, and the Quarte or Doublette (*Grand jeu de Tierce*), but play at a moderately slow tempo, since "to play rapidly in the bass will have no effect" [Dom Bédos].

Much of what Dom Bédos says about registration corroborates the older sources, but the differences noted show a tendency to thicker registrations (as well as larger instruments, and stronger-sounding reeds) in the late eighteenth century. His registrations tend to be similar to but often thicker than those of the earlier writers. Dom Bédos seems to be cautioning his readers that some older usages (such as using the strong Tremulant with the *Grand jeu*), still practiced by some organists, will no longer have the desired musical effect and can in fact spoil the music.

Another facet of late eighteenth-century registration is the greater variety recommended by Bédos. Where earlier writers were content to cite only one or two possibilities for duos and trios, he offers no fewer than nine possible duo registrations and ten for trios; and his other registrations tend to be a bit thicker than the older ones. In other respects, however, Bédos is quite consistent with the usages of the preceding period, and his writings illustrate how little the general registrational conventions had changed by the end of the era.

Duos and trios occur in the music of this late period not only in liturgical contexts but also in many of the *Noël* variations, free compositions, and sectional pieces such as Boëly's *Easter Offertory*. In view of the popularity of these pieces, Bédos's combinations are of interest:

Duos

1. Treble: Positif *Jeu de Tierce* (Montre and Bourdon 8', Prestant 4', Nasard, Quarte or Doublette, Tierce). Bass: Grand Orgue *Grand jeu de Tierce* (all foundations, even 32' if available, with 4', 2', and all fifth and third mutations).
2. Treble: Récit Cornet. Bass: Positif Prestant 4' and Cromorne 8'.
3. Treble: Grand Orgue Grand Cornet alone, or *Petit jeu de Tierce* (Montre and Bourdon 8', Prestant 4', Nasard, Quarte, Tierce). Bass: Positif Prestant and Cromorne.
4. Treble: Récit Cornet. Bass: Positif Trompette.
5. Treble: Récit Trompette. Bass: Positif *Jeu de Tierce* (as in No. 1).
6. Treble: Positif Cromorne and Prestant. Bass: Grand Orgue *Grand jeu de Tierce* (as in No. 1).
7. Both parts on Grand Orgue with Trompettes, Clairons, and Prestant 4'.
8. Treble: Positif Montre and Bourdon 8', Flute 4', and Nasard; or Cromorne and Prestant. Bass: Grand Orgue Montre and Bourdon 16', Clairon 4'.
9. Treble: Récit Cornet. Bass: Grand Orgue foundations, Positif. Cromorne and Prestant coupled.

Trios with Two Trebles

1. Treble I: Récit Cornet. Treble II: Positif Cromorne and Prestant. Bass: Pedal foundations with *Jeu de Tierce* if available.

2. Treble I: Positif *Jeu de Tierce* without Larigot. Treble II: Récit Trompette or Grand Orgue Trompette with Prestant. Bass: Pedal Flûtes (at all available pitches) or *Jeu de Tierce*.

3. Treble I: Récit Cornet. Treble II: *Jeu de Tierce*. Bass: Pedal same as No. 2.

4. Treble I: Grand Orgue and Positif coupled, all 8' stops. Treble II: Récit Trompette or Cornet. Bass: Pedal same as No. 2.

5. Treble I: Grand Orgue 8' stops. Treble II: Positif Cromorne and Prestant. Bass: Pedal same as No. 2.

6. Treble I: Grand Orgue Montre and Bourdon 8', Nasard 2 2/3', Flute 4' if available. Treble II: Positif Cromorne and Prestant. Bass: Pedal same as No. 2.

7. Treble I: Récit or Grand Orgue Trompette. Treble II: Positif Montre and Bourdon 8', Flute 4', Nasard. Bass: Pedal same as No. 2.

8. Treble I: Positif *Jeu de Tierce*. Treble II: Grand Orgue all 8' stops. Bass: Pedal same as No. 2.

9. Treble I: Récit Cornet; or two 8's; or two 8's with Flute 4' and Nasard. Treble II: Positif Voix Humaine, Bourdon 8', Flute or Prestant 4'. Bass: Pedal Flûtes with Tremblant Doux.

10. Both Trebles on Grand Orgue and Positif coupled, with all 8' stops. Bass: Pedal Flûtes.

Bédos notes that in combinations 6, 7, and 8 the two trebles can be reversed [232, p. 169].

It is interesting that Bédos mentions only one type of piece not dealt with by the earlier writers. The *fugue de mouvement* was a lighter and livelier piece than the older *fugue grave*, and examples are found among the works of Séjan, Marrigues, Lasceux, Beauvarlet-Charpentier, and Boëly. Bédos suggests either the *Grand Jeu*, or the *Jeu de Tierce* on the Positif coupled to the *Grand jeu de Tierce* on the Grand Orgue—a significant departure from the standard combinations for the *fugue grave*, which almost always consisted of flues and reeds at 8' and 4'. Indeed, the turn–of–the–century *fugue de mouvement* has much in common with the standard short fugue of England and the southern Germanic countries in both structure and registration; it subtly marks the inroads of outside influences on French organ music.

The interest in imitating other instruments on the organ, so universal in the Classical period, is also reflected in Bédos's registrations, although in a curiously antique way. The imitative registrations, presumably all intended for solo use, include the following:

German (traverse) flute: All the 8' stops on the Grand Orgue and Positif, coupled, but no 4' Prestant or Flûte, and no 16' stops.

Recorder: Prestants and flutes 4' on the Grand Orgue and Positif, coupled.

Fife: Play the melody on the Grand Orgue, with 4' Petit Bourdon and Quarte and Doublette 2'; on the Positif draw both the 8' stops with the Larigot, and "beat on the Positif keyboard to imitate the tambourine." (This sort of thing is called for in *Tambourin* sections of *Noëls* as early as Dandrieu, who, however, writes out the left-hand part in repeated chords.)

Flageolet (Piccolo): Quarte and Doublette 2' on the Grand Orgue, accompanied by the two 8' stops on the Positif.

Musette (Bagpipe): If there is a Musette stop, use it with the 8' Bourdon; if not, use the Cromorne. Accompany it on the two 8' stops (Montre and Bourdon). "One usually puts pieces of lead on the tonic and dominant [keys] in the lower register" (to give the effect of a drone; this too is found in written-out form in some of the *Noëls*).

Little Birds: *Petit Nasards* on the Grand Orgue and Positif, coupled. "One can imitate the twittering of little birds by playing staccatos, roulades, or trills." (This would seem to be strictly for improvisatory purposes.)

Bédos makes only slight reference to the accompanimental use of the organ. While he does not specifically say so, he is probably referring not to the large organ in the west-end gallery of the church but to the smaller choir organ in the chancel. For accompanying a large choir he recommends the *Plein Jeu* with 8' and 4' Pedal reeds. With a smaller group, singing several to a part, only three or four 8' stops are needed; for "mediocre" voices, just the two 8' stops on the Positif, and if the voices are "feeble," just a light Bourdon.

Only one registration table has come down to us from the post-Revolutionary, pre-Romantic period—a list of twenty combinations found in Lasceux's "Essai." It is an interesting collage of older and newer usages [235, p. 255]:

1. *Fonds d'Orgue*: On the Grand Orgue the Bourdon 16', Montre 8', Bourdon 8', Prestant 4', and all other flutes.

2. Four-part Plainchant: All the above stops with the 2' Doublette and mixtures [i.e., an ordinary *Plein Jeu*] on either the Grand Orgue or the Positif. The chant is played on the Pedal 16', 8', and 4' reeds.

3. Three-part Plainchant, melody on manual: Trompettes, Clairon, and Prestant on Grand Orgue, accompanied by flutes and principals 8', 4', and 2' with mixtures on Positif.

4. *Grand Choeur* Plainchant: Reeds, Prestants, and Cornets on both manuals, coupled, with reeds at 16', 8', and 4' in Pedal.

5. Cornet duo: Cornet on Récit; reeds 8' and 4' plus Prestant on Positif.

6. Voix Humaine and Hautbois duo or dialogue: Bourdon and Hautbois on Positif; Bourdon 16', Montre and Petit Bourdon 8', Prestant 4', and Voix Humaine on Grand Orgue.

7. Grosse Tierce trio: Prestant and Cromorne on Positif (right hand); principals and flutes 16', 8', and 4' with Nazards and Tierces on Grand Orgue (left hand).

8. Trio for Pedals, or for three manuals: Right hand on Récit Cornet, left hand on Grand Orgue Bourdon 8', Prestant 4', and Cromorne, and third part on Pedals with 8' and 4' stops (and 16' if available). Ritornellos can be played on the Positif Montre and Bourdon 8'.

9. Quartet: Same combinations as No. 8.

10. Cromorne with foundations: Positif Bourdon, all flutes, Prestant, and Cromorne; Grand Orgue Bourdons at 16' and 8', all flutes, and Prestant, both manuals coupled, with 16', 8', and 4' in Pedal.

11. Voix Humaine: Grand Orgue Bourdons 16', 8', and 4', Montre 8', Prestant 4', and Voix Humaine; Positif Bourdon, Prestant, flutes, and Nazard, coupled to Grand Orgue; Pedal 16', 8', and 4' stops.

12. Solo Hautbois: Bourdon and Hautbois on Positif, accompanied on Grand Orgue by Montre and Flûtes 8' with 4' Bourdon, and 16', 8', and 4' in the Pedal.

13. Solo Cromorne: Same as No. 12, but with the Cromorne substituted for the Hautbois.

14. Solo Trompette on Positif: Same as No. 12, but with Trompette and Prestant instead of Hautbois.

15. Flute pieces: There are many possibilities for using the Flûtes and Bourdons, for example, Bourdon and Flûtes on Positif and Grand Orgue, also on other manuals if they have a Flûte. Positif and Grand Orgue may be coupled, and Flûtes in the Pedal may be used.

16. Cromorne in the Tenor: Same as No. 13.

17. Military band: Positif Bourdon, Flûtes, Prestant, Cromornes and Hautbois; Grand Orgue Bourdons 16' and 8', Prestant 4', Flûtes and Clarion 4', coupled to Positif Pedal Flûtes, "and to imitate the Trombone, one adds the Trompette to the Pedal." For Echo effects, the Bourdon and Trompette on the fourth manual.

18. Hautbois concerto: If the Hautbois is on the third manual (Récit), one draws the Hautbois and Bourdon on this manual, and accompanies with the Bourdon and Flûtes on the Positif. If the Hautbois is on the Positif, it can be accompanied by the Bourdon and Flûte on the fourth (i.e., the softest) manual. Since a concerto consists of solos contrasted with tutti passages, the latter should be played on the Grand Orgue with Prestant, Grand Cornet, Trompette, and Clairon, with Flûtes on the Pedal.

19. Flute concerto: Same as No. 18, but with the Positif Bourdon and Flûtes for a solo.

20. Symphony Concertante for two instruments: Hautbois or Cornet on the Récit; Trompette, Cromorne, and Prestant on the Positif, with the tutti on the Grand Orgue, as in No. 18.

The last three examples confirm the growing post-Revolutionary trend toward transcriptions (or transcription-like organ pieces or improvisations) and various types of concertos (for organ solo or with orchestra). Beauvarlet-Charpentier wrote an offertoire in "symphony concertante" style. As in England, concertos for organ and chamber orchestra were written for secular use (notably the Parisian *Concerts spirituels*) in the second half of the eighteenth century by Corrette, Balbastre, and Taperay.

While Lasceux's work includes some short fanfares and marches, it is largely in the older forms, as is that of the younger Boëly. Although the latter's *Offertoire pour le Jour de Paques* (Easter Offertory) is a late work (1858, the year of the composer's death; and Franck was already active), it is old-fashioned in style, reminiscent of a turn-of-the-century sectional *Noël* with an added overture. The registrations are largely those found in Lasceux, but with explicit instructions for stop changes within the piece—a significant departure from the older practice of setting everything up at the beginning and using only manual changes to obtain registrational variety.

Much of the music written in the pre-Revolutionary (late eighteenth-century) period can, and indeed should, be registered in the classical manner. Certain modifications are dictated by the increasing size of the instruments and the general thickening of some ensemble registrations suggested by Bédos. Many modern "French classic" organs are more closely linked to the late eighteenth-century aesthetic of Bédos than that of the earlier period, and are thus ideal for this music, as are certain French-biased eclectic instruments.

The same also largely applies to the music of composers active both before and after the Revolution. They were all older men, and none had any really first-hand connection with the new style of organs that began to appear in the 1840s; Boëly, for instance, played older instruments at the churches of St. Gervais (the "Couperin" church) and St. Germain l'Auxerrois in Paris, and his music is designed for these classical instruments. It is thus the aesthetic of Cliquot and Dom Bédos, rather than that of Cavaillé-Coll, that must be kept in mind when registering the music of the late eighteenth and early nineteenth centuries on a modern organ that might offer opportunities for both styles.

20

Italy

Composers

Gian Domenico Cattenacci (c1735–c1800)
Giovan Battista Cervellini (1735–1801)
Luigi Cherubini (1760–1842)
Baldassare Galuppi (1706–1785)
Carlo Gervasoni (1762–1819)
Giuseppe Gherardeschi (1759–1815)
Andrea Lucchesi (1741–1801)
Giambattista Martini (1706–1784)
Carlo Monza (c1735–1801)
Giovan Battista Oradini (fl. 1770–83)
Giuseppe Paolucci (1726–1776)
Giovanni Battista Pescetti (1704–1766)
Gaetano Piazza (fl. late eighteenth century)
Ferdinando Provesi (1770–1833)
Antonio Salieri (1750–1825)
Giuseppe Sarti (1724–1802)
Gaetano Valeri (1760–1822)
Giovanni Battista Viotti (1753–1824)

Representative Organs

ACCADEMIA DI MUSICA ITALIANA, PISTOIA
Domenico Gentili, 1762 [stoplist taken from extant organ]

Manuale
Principale 8' (stopped bass)
Voce umana 8' (from middle c♯)
Ottava 4' (2' below tenor G)

Pedale (8 notes)
Coupled to manual

Duodecima 2 2/3' (1 1/3' in bass)
Decimaquinta 2' (1' in bass)
Decimanona 1 1/3' (2/3' in bass)

CATHEDRAL, TRIESTE
Francesco Dacci, 1780 [108, p. 406]

Grand'Organo
Principale 8' (divided)
Voce umana 8' (treble)
Ottava 4'
Flauto in ottava 4' (divided)
Flauto in duodecima 2 2/3'
Decimaquinta 2'
Cornetta 1 3/5'
Decimanona 1 1/3'
Vigesimaseconda 1'
Vigesimasesta 2/3'
Vigesimanona 1/2'
Trigesimaterza 1/3'
Trigesimasesta 1/4'
Tromboncini 8' (divided)

Organo di Riposta (positiv)
Principale 8' (divided)
Voce umana 8' (treble)
Ottava 4' (divided)
Flauto in ottava 4' (divided)
Violetta 8' (bass)
Decimaquinta 2'
Cornetta 1 3/5' (treble)
Decimanona 1 1/3'
Vigesimaseconda 1'
Vigesimasesta 2/3'
Vigesimanona 1/2'
Tromboncini 8' (divided)

Pedale
Contrabassi 16'
Contrabassi in ottava 8'
Quinta 5 1/3'
Tromboni 8'

Accessory Stops
Tamburo (drum)

CHURCH OF S. MICHELE, TREPPIO
Pietro Agati, 1794 [23, p. 15]

Manuale
Principale I 8'
Principale II 8' (from middle d)
Voce umana 8' (from middle c)
Flauto in selva 8' (stopped)
Ottava 4' (doubled from middle d)
Flauto in ottava 4'
Violoncello bassi 4' (half stop, bass)
Duodecima 2 2/3'
Decimaquinta 2'
Decimanona 1 1/3'
Vigesimasesta e nona 2/3' and 1/2'
Cornetto IV (4'–2 2/3'–2'–1 3/5')
Mosetto soprani (reed half stop, treble)
Trombe 8' (divided)

Accessory Stops
Tamburo (drum, 2 pipes)
Usignoli (bird, 4 pipes)

Pedale
Contrabassi tappati 16' (stopped)

CHURCH OF THE CARMINE, LUGO DI ROMAGNA
Gaetano Callido, 1797 [106, p. 17]

Manuale
Principale 16' (12') (divided)
Ottava 8'
Voce umana 8' (treble?)
Violoncello 8' (divided)
Quintadecima 4'
Flauto in ottava 4' (divided)
Viola 4' (divided)
Flauto in duodecima 2 2/3'
Decimanona 2 2/3'
Vigesimaseconda 2'
Vigesimasesta 1 1/3'
Vigesimanona 1'
Trigesimaterza 2/3'
Trigesimasesta 1/2'
Cornetta soprani (mixture, treble)
Tromboncini 8' (divided)

Accessory Stops
Manual to Pedal coupler
Terza mano
Tremolo
Tamburo (drum)
Combinazione "alla lombarda" (adjustable combination)

Pedale
Contrabassi e Ottave 16' and 8'
Tromboni 8'

PARISH CHURCH, VIVERONE
Fratelli Serassi, 1818 [108, p. 410]

Manuale
Principale I 8' (divided)
Principale II 8' (divided)
Voce umana 8' (treble)
Flauto traversiere 8' (treble)
Ottava 4' (divided)
Flauto in ottava 4' (divided)
Viola 4' (bass)
Duodecima 2 2/3'
Decimaquinta 2'
Ottavino 2'
Decimanona 1 1/3'
Vigesimaseconda 1'
Flagioletto 1'
Vigesimasesta e nona (2/3' and 1/2')
Trigesimaterza e sesta (1/3' and 1/4')
Cornetto I (4' and 2 2/3', treble)
Cornetto II (2 2/3'–2'–1 3/5', treble)
Corni dolci 16' (reed, treble)

Pedale
Contrabassi con ottava 16' and 8'
Tromboni 8'

Accessory Stops
Campanini (bells, played from Manual)
Timballi in 12 toni (drums, played from Pedal)

CHURCH OF S. LEONARDI, S. ZENO
Michaele Angelo Paoli, 1819 [260]

Manual
Principale 8'
Voce umana 8' (from middle f)
Ottava 4' (from middle c)
Flauto in ottava 4' (from middle f)
Decimaquinta 2' (from middle c)
Decimanona 1 1/3' (from middle c)
Vigesimaseconda 1' (from middle c)
Cornetto dolce 2 2/3' (from middle f)
Cornettino 1 3/5' (from middle f)

CHURCH OF ANGELO RAFFAELE, VENICE
Antonio and Agostino Callido, 1821 [208, p. 29]

Organo Grosso
Principale 8' (divided)
Ottava 4'
Flauto in ottava 4' (divided)
Viola 4' (divided)
Flauto in duodecima 2 2/3'
Quintadecima 2'
Decimanona 1 1/3'
Vigesimaseconda 1'
Vigesimasesta 2/3'
Vigesimanona 1/2'
Trigesimaterza 1/3'
Trigesimasesta 1/2'
Cornetta
Tromboncino 8' (divided)
Corni 4' (?)

Organo Eco (enclosed)
Principale 8' (divided)
Flutta reale 8'
Violoncello 8' (divided)
Ottava 4'
Quintadecima 2'
Ottavino 2'
Decimanona 1 1/3'
Vigesimaseconda 1'
Tromboncino 8' (divided)

Pedale
Contrabassi 16'
Ottava 8'
Ottava di ottava 4'
Trombone 16'

Accessory Stops
Manual Coupler
Terza Mano (octave coupler, Manual II)
Full Swell (foot lever)
Swell Pedal
Banda militare (percussions)

PRIORY OF S. MARTINO, FOGNANO, MONTALE
Giosué Agati, 1831 [147, p. 54]

Manuale
Principale 8' (divided)

Pedale
Coupled to manual

Voce Angelica 8' (treble)
Ottava 4' (divided)
Flauto in ottava 4'
Decimaquinta 2'
Ottavino 2' (treble)
Decimanona 1 1/3'
Ventiduesima 1'
Cornetto II (treble)
Trombe 8' (divided)

Accessory Stops
Tirapieno (full organ)
Timpano (drum)
Usignoli (bird)

Registration

As in other countries, the interest of composers and performers in Italy toward the end of the eighteenth century was shifting away from the organ and church music, and toward the concert stage and the opera house. Opera was undergoing a vigorous revival, and, near the end of the Classical period, it was attracting the leading composers: Rossini wrote *The Barber of Seville* in 1816, Bellini composed *Norma* in 1831, and Donizetti created *Lucrezia Borgia* in 1833.

Of these well-known masters, only Rossini is known to have left a few small organ works. Cherubini, who is also better known as an opera composer, also left a few organ works, including a substantial duet for two organs. But for significant organ output, we must look to lesser-known late eighteenth-century keyboardists and church musicians: the Venetians Galuppi (immortalized by Robert Browning) and Pescetti (both of whom also wrote operas), Padre Martini of Bologna, and the prolific Gherardeschi, organist of the Cathedral in Pistoia.

Music for the liturgy was still being written. Although slow, introspective pieces still accompanied the elevation, the broad and flowing toccata style of Frescobaldi had virtually vanished. Lively Post Communios and loud Offertorios were prominent, along with light versetti. Pastorales, pivas, rondos, and sonatas were increasingly taking their place in the repertoire, some of the last being quite long and showy. Novelties such as organ duets began to appear, and in general the stage was being set for the popular style of the ensuing period. As in France, the epithet of decadence has been attached to the organ music of Italy in this period. While some of it is indeed little more than good fun, one also finds works of surprising elegance and beauty.

In organ building, the area of greatest activity in this period lay between Rome and the northern border. Many influences were coming over that border, but the core of the distinctive Italian organ remained curiously intact. The average instrument was still a one-manual organ with a rudimentary Pedal, but now, in all but the smallest organs, the Pedal usually had some stops of its own, sometimes including reed stops, which were becoming more and more common during this period. Most of them were still of the old short-length Tromboncino type, but full-length Trombes (Trumpets) and imitative Oboes, English Horns, and French Horns (*Corni di caccia*) began to appear in larger organs from the late eighteenth century onward. In instruments of more than one manual, enclosed divisions (Organo Eco or Organo Espressivo) appear with increasing frequency after the turn of the century, as do divided stops.

The principal-toned Ripieno, with its many fractional-length upperwork ranks, remained the core of the instrument, but flute-toned stops, no longer limited to the old 4' and 2 2/3' pitches, began to appear increasingly at 8' pitch, sometimes as an imitative Flauto traversiere. String-toned stops also made their debut in this period, usually as an 8' Violoncello or a 4' Viola—the latter, of medium scale and often quite scratchy in tone, was almost always a bass half-stop. Tierce-containing Cornettos, which only occasionally occurred in earlier organs (usually those built or influenced by the Flemings), became more and more a standard feature, as indeed they were everywhere in this period.

The Serassi family of builders, who were active in the Lombardy and Piedmont areas to the north, were in the forefront in introducing some of these innovations in the late eighteenth century; but other northern and central builders were not slow to follow, and it is clear that the new stops found favor with the organist-composers. One thing that remained constant was the unforced, vocal quality of the 8' Principale.

While the one-manual organ remained the norm, two-manual organs were occasionally built, and, more rarely, three-manual instruments. Serassi built one in 1782 for the church of S. Alessandro in Bergamo; among other things, it contained one of the earliest known Italian Pedal mixtures, a Ripieno of five ranks. A 16' organ, it had a full 16' Ripieno on Manuals I and III, and an 8' Ripieno on Manual II, the Organo Eco (enclosed division, possibly inexpressive). But it also contained a variety of reeds, strings, and a Cornetto on each manual [108, p. 409]. A slightly later three-manual Serassi, built in 1796 for the church of San Liborio, Colorno, has strings, open and chimneyed flutes, an English Horn, and a French Horn [105, p. 11].

Another extraordinary three-manual organ, extant but unplayable and in critical need of restoration, is in the church of S. Pier Maggiore in Pistoia. It was built by Benedetto Tronci c1815. The Grand'Organo has a full 16' Ripieno, but it also contains 8' flutes, reeds at 16' and 8', and a Campanella (bells). The Piccol'Organo is actually an Organo Eco (Swell) containing several flutes and flute mutations. Of particular interest is the Organo di Concerto division, which contains flutes and flute mutations, a low-pitched Cornet curiously called Cornetto Chinese, and some reeds divided in the Spanish fashion (8' and 4' in bass, 16' in treble) [147, p. 155]. If this organ is ever restored, it will provide players and scholars with an important window on the more adventurous Italian literature of the Classical period.

The use of the Renaissance "toy" stops was dying out in most of the rest of Europe. The Hispanic countries clung to their bird stops and the Germanic countries still produced an occasional Cymbalstern, but only in Italy does one still find the full complement in use. Birds, drums, and drones continued to be standard equipment well into the nineteenth century, along with Campanellas (saucer bells), crickets, and the uniquely Italian *banda militare*, a percussion effect that could include everything from a bass drum and cymbals to the Turkish "jingling Johnny," also called *Capello Cinese* (Chinese hat). Curiously, the ubiquitous Tremulant was usually absent, perhaps because, as in the preceding period, the undulating Voce Umana made it unneccessary.

Composers of this period were more inclined to put registrations in their music than were those of earlier times, but we also have several registration lists from organ builders, as well as a late eighteenth-century list found by Umberto Pineschi with a number of musical manuscripts from the same period in the public library of Montecatini Termi, near Pistoia. It gives six registrations, intended for an organ of eight stops, and indicates the type of music in which they are to be used:

1. For pieces in the Legato or Fugato style, or Allegro as in an introduction: Principale with all other stops save the Flauto

2. For *Cantabile largo* pieces with detached chords in the bass: Principale 8' and Flauto 4'

3. For florid Andantino pieces with detached chords in the bass, or for singing: Principale 8', Ottava 4', Duodecimo 2'

4. For florid Allegro pieces in eighth notes, with a "singing" bass, like a Cornetto: Principale, Flauto, 1 1/3', 1', 2/3'

5. For Andantinos or arpeggiated Allegros, with Pedals ad lib, or a Cantabile Allegro with a detached bass: Flauto 4' alone

6. For an Andante (or *Cantabile serio*), with answering bass: Principale 8', Ottava 4', Flauto 4', Duodecima 2' [284, II]

This source also gives some hints for the use of the Pedal. According to the taste of the player, the Pedal may be used at the beginning of a piece, and it should definitely be used at cadences. In the middle sections it is better left out. The player should avoid playing the lower keys with the left hand when using the pedals, and it is helpful to sustain the Pedal note at a cadence to help the choir get its pitch—presumably during performance within the liturgy.

Another set of registrations for a small organ was recently found during the restoration of an organ built in 1819 by Michaele Angelo Paoli of Prato for the church of S. Leonardi in the town of S. Zeno. It is written on the stopjamb and appears to be contemporary with the instrument:

1. The Ripieno is composed of the Principale, Ottava, Decimaquinta, Decimanona, and Vigesimaseconda.

2. For "sinfonias" one should add the Cornettino and Cornetto dolce.

3. The Cornetto [registration] is composed of the Principale, Ottava, and both the Cornetti [i.e., the 2 2/3' and 1 3/5'].

4. The Cornetto dolce [registration] is composed of the Principale, Flauto, and Cornetto dolce.

5. The Cornettino [registration] is composed of the Flauto and Cornettino.

6. The Voce umana goes with the Principale [260].

Nos. 1. and 6. are very standard, going back to the time of the Antegnatis, but the others underscore the increasing importance of the flute-toned mutations, which is also reflected in the registrations for the larger organs. In the S. Zeno organ, all stops except the Principale are treble half-stops, so it follows that Nos. 2–5 are essentially solo combinations, giving the effect of a two-manual organ if the left hand remains below middle C. No. 5, based on the 4' pitch, is probably intended for light music played in the treble register, as sometimes occurs in sections of pastorales.

Registration lists for two large organs by Callido—an instrument of 1799 in the Church of S. Martino Vescovo, Venice [88], and one built a few years later for the Cathedral of Feltre [35, p. 114]—point to new trends in composing and improvising. There was still the classic simple Ripieno (*ripieno semplice*) consisting of the 8' Principali and full chorus of upperwork (with the Contrabassi in the Pedal), but Callido also records other, newer types of Ripieno. They included the *ripieno misto* (mixed Ripieno), in which the Flauto 2 2/3' and Cornetto are added to the simple Ripieno, the *ripieno orchestra*, in which the reed stop is added, and a Ripieno "in the march with drums manner," which combined the mixed and orchestral versions, adding the drum stop.

Similarly, while the time-honored registration of Principale and Voce umana still applied to the sombre Adagio music that accompanied the Elevation in the mass, Callido cites some variants in which the bass half of the Violoncello or Tromboncino is added, perhaps to give a more orchestral effect. This is one of the earliest references to the usage of divided stops, which were appearing with ever greater frequency. These bass stops could also be added to vary the *Cantabile* registration of Principale, Voce umana, and Flauto in ottava, and the *Andante* registration of Principale and Flauto in ottava. For use on the secondary manual (Organo Piccolo) an unusual *Adagio* registration calls for the bass half of the Principale and the treble half of the Tromboncino.

For livelier pieces, registrations for *Spiritoso* and *Allegro* are given. For the former, a gapped combination of Principale 8' and Flauto 2 2/3' is suggested, to which the Ottava and Cornetto may be added if desired; the *Granito spiritoso* combination adds to these the Tromboncino. A similar combination on the Organo Piccolo is suggested for *Allegro*. These combinations accord with the gapped registrations coming into use for quick and light music in England and Germany in this period. Instrumentally imitative combinations are also much in evidence, including:

Oboe or Fagotto: Principale, Flauto 2 2/3', Tromboncini
Flauto dolce (recorder): Flauto 4', also recommended for duets
Traverse flute: Ottava 4', Flauto in ottava 4'
Organ and flute: Principale with Flauto 2 2/3' treble
Harp: Ottava 4' with Tromboncino 8'

It must be remembered that the Tromboncino was still a short-length reed of rather thin nasal tone. It was often located in the organ façade and was of the same general type as the German Harfenregal of the Renaissance. Perhaps the most unusual combination given by Callido consists of Principale, Voce umana, Vigesimanona 1 1/3', and Pedal Contrabassi; it was intended for playing elevations (probably improvised) "in imitation of bells" and resembles "bell" registrations found in other countries.

Callido's San Martino registration list gives several combinations utilizing divided stops on the secondary manual:

Principale 8' treble, Ottava 4' bass
Principale treble, Ottava bass, both halves of the Tromboncini 8'
Principale treble and Tromboncini bass
Principale treble, Tromboncini bass, both halves of Ottava 4'
Principale and Flauto 4' treble, Tromboncini bass, both halves of Ottava
Principale and Flauto 4' in treble, both halves of Ottava and Tromboncini, and Cornetto [88]

With the exception of some of the imitative registrations, the Principale remains the basis of all combinations, although most of the "coloring" in these particular registrations is done with flutes and reeds, rather than with the higher-pitched principal mutations, as previously. The 2 2/3' flute occasionally appears in gapped combinations, and a few combinations are based not on the 8' Principal but on the 4' flute or principal. There is a resemblance between some of these practices and some of the new registrations appearing in France in this period.

In 1808, a few years after Callido's publications, Giuseppe Serassi completed a substantial organ for the church of SS. Crocifisso dell'Annunziata in Como. It was similar in content to Callido's large instruments, having a Grand'Organo with a full Principal Ripieno, an enclosed division, and several imitative stops—by Serassi's own count, 55 Ripieno registers and 31 "instrumental" registers. His description of the organ makes specific mention of its use in imitating military bands, noting that it is provided with all the necessary stops, and explaining that they may also be combined to give the effect of individual instruments. Serassi points out that his instrument can express all musical sentiments from grave and tender to powerful and ferocious, the latter effects being especially suitable for the "storm" and "battle" pieces becoming popular with improvisors [162].

In his registration list, Serassi deals with each division of the organ separately. For the Grand Organo:

Ripieno: Includes all principal-toned chorus stops except the 32' Principale, with the Pedal Contrabassi and Ripieno. The Voce umana, flutes, and orchestral stops are not to be used in the Ripieno.

The Voce umana may be used with the Principali and Contrabassi.
The Cornetti may be used with the Principale treble.
The Fagotto may be used with the Principale bass, or with the Ottava.
The Trombe may be used with the Principale treble.
The Corno Inglese may be used with the Principale 32' [sic].
The Violone bass may be used alone, or with Principale bass.
The Viola may be used alone, or with Ottava bass or Violone.
The Viola may be used with the Quintadecima, and accompanied by the Flauto on the other manual, played with the right hand.
The Flauto traverso may be used alone.
The Flauto in ottava may be used alone, or with the Ottava.

Special instructions are given for making orchestral effects and imitating various instruments. Serassi cites the following as stops of the *banda*: In the Grand Organo, the Violone, Viola, Fagotto, Voce puerile, Trombe, Corno inglese, Bombarde, and Trombone; in the Organo Eco, the Serpentone, Violoncello, and Cornamusa; in the Pedal, the Trombe, along with the bells and the drums. Some additional instruments can be imitated as follows:

Clarinet: Principale treble, Flauto traverso, Trombe
Oboe: Trombe and Ottava treble, or Cornamusa, Principale and Ottava
Harp: Serpentone, Cornamusa, Ottava, and Flauto treble
Guitar: Ottava treble, Trombe, Cornetto, Quintadecima, Decimanona, and the four highest Ripieno stops
Mandolin: Cornetto, Decimanona, Vigesimaseconda, Violino, Sesquialtera
Psaltery: Cornetto, Trombe, Voce puerile, Duodecima, Quintadecima, and the four highest Ripieno stops
Lute: Serpentone, Violoncello, Voce puerile, Flauto in ottava, Violino, Duodecima, Vigesimaseconda

The several combinations imitating plucked stringed instruments will appear curious to the modern organist; for these effects Serassi instructs the player to strike the keys in a pizzicato manner and to use string-toned stops for accompaniment. In all probability such effects were used largely by improvisors. It is interesting that despite the proliferation of imitative stops in large organs of this period, it was still thought necessary to provide combinations for sounds that could not be imitated by individual organ stops.

The increasing role of the flute stops is underscored by the number of flute combinations suggested by Serassi: the 8' Flute can be used with the Principale 16' treble, the *Corni e Fluttoni* (French horns and 4' flutes), the *Campanini* (bells), and the Trombe. The Principale, versatile as always, may be used with Fagotti, Voce puerile, Corni, Fluttoni, Corno inglese, Trombe, Bombarde, or Tromboni; with Fagotti, Trombe de caccia, Corni, and Trombe; with Decimanona, Vigesimaseconda, Fluttoni, Flauto in ottava, Ottava, Cornetti, Duodecima, and Corno Inglese—"and many other variations are possible" [162, pp. 15–24]. As in France, the combinations are becoming thicker and more complex, while retaining ties to the older traditions.

A special registration is cited for the increasingly popular pastorale, or piva: Tromboni, Fagotti, Voce puerile, Trombe, Principale, Ottava Cornetto, and Cornetto III on the main manual; Serpentone, Principale treble, Cornetto, and Cornamusa on the Organo Eco; Trombe and Timballi (drums) on the Pedal. While reeds figure heavily in some of these combinations, it must always be borne in mind that even in the early nineteenth century Italian reeds, with the possible exception of the Trombe, were still on the light side and speaking on fairly low wind pressure. Even so, such complex combinations give to the pastorale a much more robust quality than one is used to hearing, since many present-day players tend to confine their registration of these pieces to single flutes and light reeds. The more authentic type of registration is not difficult to obtain on most modern organs if an Oboe or Clarinet on a secondary manual is combined with principals at 8' and 4' and a mutation or two.

The usages cited in these late eighteenth- and early nineteenth-century sources are borne out by registration directions found in much of the music of the period.

Indeed, registrations sometimes even appear in the titles of pieces, as in Galuppi's *Sonata con ripieni e flauti*. This straightforward dialogue between full organ and flutes can easily be played on a single-manual organ by drawing or retiring the Tiratutti in the rests between the *Forte* and *Piano* sections (although it can also, of course, be played on two manuals). Valeri gives a registration of Principale and Flauti for his Sonata in G major, and his Sonata in B-flat major requires the Tromboncini.

The use of divided stops is called for in Gherardeschi's *Cantabile per il Traverso solo con Clarone nei bassi*—an early example of the use of one of the "new" stops, the imitative 8' Flauto traverso. In the same composer's twelve *Versetti concertati*, each has its registration clearly spelled out, including places where the Timpani and Usignoli are to be used—something that was usually left up to the player by earlier composers. Many of these registrations are virtually the same as some of those called for by Callido. Gherardeschi's *Banda militare* Sonata has similar explicit directions, starting with a registration of reeds, flutes at 8', 4', and 2', with drums (played staccato) and birds. In this piece the use of the Pedal and the drums is again carefully marked, although they are used largely for emphasis.

A new term comes into use toward the end of this period—*organo aperto* (literally, "open organ"), meaning full organ, and interchangeable with *pieno* and *tutti*, which are also sometimes used. It means more than just the Principal Ripieno; from the context in which it appears it almost certainly includes reeds—in other words, the Italian version of the "reed plenum." Gherardeschi in fact specifically asks in one piece for the full Ripieno with Trombe and Cornetti for his *organo aperto*; he also calls for *organo aperto* at the opening and closing of a Pastorale, in which sections for Principal 8' and Flute 4' alternate with light treble passages for 4' flute alone.

Yet some old usages are unchanged. The classic Ripieno, the backbone of the Italian organ, remained intact almost to the end of the nineteenth century, despite more modern and Romantic additions; and it was certainly still used in the old Renaissance manner during the Classical period. Gervasoni, in his *La scuola della musica* of 1800, points out that reeds are still not used alone, but "are always to be accompanied by the Principali, since, by themselves, they are usually too weak or too harsh" [283, p. xxx]. This corresponds to the English admonitions to always use the Diapasons with the reeds, and the French combinations of reeds and Bourdons— a virtually universal practice since the seventeenth century in all countries.

Registration changes within a piece become more frequent in this period and require the use of the Tiratutti mechanism and the divided stops to achieve solo and echo effects. Although an increasing number of larger instruments were being built, the great majority of Italian organs still had but one keyboard, and virtually all music from this period was written with this in mind. On modern organs, two manuals can of course be used, and combination pedals or pistons may be employed in place of the Tiratutti.

In choosing stops for this music, the present-day organist should keep in mind the harmonic complexity of the combinations cited as well as the general understated richness of the Italian organ sound. Solo 8' flutes (Melodias, Harmonic Flutes) and light imitative reeds such as the Oboe, English Horn, and Clarinet are suitable where such colors are called for in music of this period, especially in the quieter portions of pastorales, the brighter portions of which require a cheerful and balanced chorus sound based on 8' pitch that avoids top- or bottom-heaviness.

Overly smooth, foundational reeds should be avoided, however, as well as excessively smooth, loud, or edgy 8' Principals. Players should not be misled by the light and fluty "Italian Principals" found in some organs, for the true Principale 8' of Italy remained a rich, suave, and harmonically complex *mezzo-forte* sound until well into the nineteenth century.

21

Spain, Portugal, and Latin America

Composers

Rafael Anglés (1731–1816)
Pedro José Blanco (c1750–1811)
Joao de Sousa Carvalho (1745–1798)
Narciso Casanovas (1747–1799)
José Ferrer (c1745–1815)
José Larrañaga (d. 1806)
José Lidon (1752–1827)
Juan Andrés de Lonbide (fl. 1765–75)
Félix Máximo Lopez (1742–1821)
Joaquin Martinez de Oxinaga (fl. 1765–75)
Juan Moreno y Polo (d. 1776)
Felipe Rodriguez (1759–1814)
Juan de Sessé y Balaguer (1736–1801)
Antonio Soler (1729–1783)
Manuel Sostoa (1749–after 1802)
Anselm Viola (1739–1798)

Representative Organs

PARISH CHURCH, ATÁUN, SPAIN
Lorenzo de Arrazola, 1761 [313]

Manual
Violón 16' (treble)
Flautado 8'
Flautado-Violón 8'
Octava 4'
Docena clara 2 2/3'

Docena nasarda 2 2/3'
Quincena nasarda 2'
Decinovena clara 1 1/3'
Decinovena nasarda 1 1/3'
Compuesto de lleno IV (mixture)
Címbala III
Sobrecímbala III
Corneta VII (treble)
Corneto en eco V (treble, enclosed)
Clarin en eco 8' (treble, enclosed)

Accessory Stops
Tambor (small drum)
Timbal (kettledrum)
Pájaros (birds)
Cascabeles (sleighbells)
Campanillas (small bells)
Echo pedal: affects Violón, Corneto en eco, Clarin en eco

CATHEDRAL, SEGOVIA
Pedro de Echevarría, 1770 [317, p. 44]

Organo Principal
Flautado 16'
Flautado 8'
Violón 8'
Octava 4'
Quinzena 2'
Repiano IV (1', mixture)
Nasardos IV (bass)
Flauta II (treble)
Corneta VI (treble)
Trompeta real 8' (interior)
Trompeta magna 8' (treble, ext.)
Clarin de Campagna 8'(?) (exterior)
Clarin 8' (or 4'?) (exterior)
Orlos 8' (reed, exterior)

Organo de Expressión (enclosed)
Violón 8'
Flautado 8' (treble)
Tapadillo 4' (stopped flute)
Quinzena 2'
Desinovena 1 1/3'
Lleno (mixture)
Corneta V (treble)
Clarin de ecos 8'
Voz humana 8' (reed)
Obue 8' (treble)
Bajoncillo 4' (bass)

Organo Segundo (Cadireta)
Flautado 8'
Octava 4'
Docena 2 2/3'
Quinzena 2'
Lleno (mixture)
Zimbala (mixture)
Trompeta real 8' (interior)
Trompeta magna 8' (exterior)
Trompeta de batalla (exterior)
Dulzaina 8' (reed, exterior)
Violeta 4'(?) (reed, interior)

Pedal
Contras 16'

Accessory Stops
Drums at D and A

ROYAL PALACE, MADRID
Jorge Bernat-Veri, 1778 [313, p. 155]

Organo Grande
Flautado 16'
Violón 16'
Flautado 8'
Violón 8'
Flauta dulce II 8' (treble)
Octava 4'
Tapadillo 4'
Corneto VI (treble)
Corneta tolosana III (treble)
Nasardos III (bass)
Lleno IV–V
Docequinzenovena III
Trompeta magna 16' (treble)
Orlos 16' (bass)
Trompeta real 8'
Clarin 8' (treble)
Orlos 8'
Clarin bajo 8' (bass)
Clarin 8' (treble)
Fagote 8'
Obue 8' (treble)
Viejas 8' (vox humana?)
Chirimía 4'
Claron 2' (treble)
Violeta 2' (bass)

Organo Segundo
Flautado 8'
Violón 8'
Flauta Traversa II 8' (treble)
Tapadillo 4' (stopped flute)
Corneta V (treble)
Nasardos III (bass)
Lleno VI
Zimbala IV
Trompeta magna 16' (bass)
Trompeta real 8'
Clarin 8' (treble)
Bajoncillo 4' (bass)
Chirimía alta 4' (treble)

Cadireta (enclosed, interior)
Violón 8'
Tapadillo 4'
Octava corneta 4' (treble)
Quinzena 2'
Corneta III (treble)
Nasardos III (bass)
Lleno III
Teorba 16' (regal, treble)
Trompeta 8'
Voz humana a la francese 8'

Pedal
Open wood basses 16' and 8' (single stop)

Accessory Stops
Not cited, but probably included the usual birds, bells, etc.

PARISH CHURCH, ESTRELA, PORTUGAL
A. X. Machado de Cerveira, 1791 [254, p. 114]

Manual
Flautado 8' (bass)
Flautado 8' (treble, façade)
Flautado 4' (bass, façade)
Flautado tapado 4' (stopped flute)
Piffano II 4' (treble)
Quinzena 2'
Compostas II–III (bass)
Vintedozena III (treble)
Clarao IV (bass)

Corneta III (treble)
Voz humana 8'
Dulcaina 8' (bass, 1/4-length reed, exterior)
Clarim 8' (treble, full-length reed, exterior)

FRANCISCAN MONASTERY, SAN MARTIN TEXMELUCÁN, PUEBLA, MEXICO
Unknown Mexican builder, 1794 [222, p. 60]

Bass	**Treble**
Flautado mayor 8'	Flautado de 26 16'
Nazardo violón 8' (stopped)	Flautado mayor 8'
Octava brillante 4'	Violón 8'
Octava parda 4' (flute)	Octava mayor 4'
Quinta 2 2/3'	Octava parda 4'
Quincena 2'	Quinta 2 2/3'
Diez y setena 1 3/5'	Quincena 2'
Diez y novena 1 1/3'	Lleno III
Lleno III	Corneta clara
Trompetas 8' (half-length)	Trompetas 16' (half-length)
Trompetas 4' (half-length)	Trompetas 8' (half-length)

Accessory Stops
Sirena (large open pipes at ends of case)
Tambores and Cimbales (bass drum and cymbal, struck together)
Pajaros agua (bird)

CATHEDRAL, CADIZ
Antonio Otin Calvete, 1808 [11, p. 58]

Organo Mayor	**Cadireta**
Flautado 8'	Flautado de violón 8'
Ottava general 4'	Tapadillo 4' (stopped flute)
Quincena 2'	Quincena 2'
Lleno III	Lleno II
Zimbala III	Zimbala II
Corneta IV–V	Corneta III
Trompeta real 8' (interior)	
Bajoncillo 8' (exterior)	
Clarin claro 8' (exterior, treble)	
Clarin en quincene 1' (exterior, bass)	
Viejos 8' (regal, interior)	

[All stops on both manuals are divided; apparently there was no Pedal.]

PARISH CHURCH, OEIRAS, PORTUGAL
A. J. Fontanez, 1829 [181, p. 262]

Manual	**Pedal**
Principal 8'	Pulldown coupler only
Bordao 8' (stopped flute)	
Principal 4'	

Flauta 2 2/3' and 4' (bass)
Flauta 2' and 4' (treble)
Octava 2' and 2 2/3' (bass)
Octava 2' and 2 2/3' (treble)
Quinta 1 1/3' and 2' (bass)
Principal 1' and 2' (bass)
Mistura IV
Cheio III (mixture)
Trompeta batalha 4' (exterior, bass)
Trompeta batalha 8' (exterior, treble)

[N.B. All stops are divided at middle c/c♯; the stops of two pitches "break back," as in Italian organs.]

Registration

Like the organs of Italy, the Iberian and Ibero-American organs were slowly evolving from their Renaissance roots, without actually breaking away from those roots. Small and medium-sized organs continued to have but one manual, although by this time it was not uncommon to find everything divided (usually between middle C and C♯), with many stops found only in either the bass (often higher-pitched) or the treble (often lower-pitched, including the 16'). This characteristic became particularly idiomatic in Central American organs, which by the end of the eighteenth century were evolving along slightly different lines from the organs of the mother countries, tending to be more conservative after the turn of the century. Toward the end of the eighteenth century larger organs of as many as three manuals appeared occasionally in Spain and Portugal; like the larger Italian organs, they sometimes included an expressive division.

Pedals, if they existed at all, continued to be very rudimentary; most had only eight notes (short compass), and even the large organ in the Royal Palace of Madrid had only twelve pedal keys. The keys themselves were often nothing more than short stubs of wood, or wooden "mushrooms," projecting from a box on the floor. As in other countries, 8' solo flute stops, some overblowing, began to appear in organs of this period. String stops were still a rarity, and certain names on a stoplist can be confusing—the so-called Violón is actually a stopped flute, and the Violeta is a short-length reed stop. Reeds, both full- and fractional-length, continued to be a prominent feature, and, as in England and France, Oboe stops began to appear.

Again, as in Italy, the old Renaissance "toy" stops, especially drums and birds, continued to be a necessary element, even in small organs. Bird stops (*Pajaro, Pajarito*) were common everywhere, and were of the classic type made by immersing the tops of three or four small pipes in a cup filled with water. The large organ built by Julien de la Ordén in 1783 for Malaga Cathedral had drums in D and A, and—somewhat less usual—"suave" and "fierce" tremulants, corresponding to the weak and strong tremulants of France.

As in other areas, more registration aids began to appear in the late eighteenth century. The 1789 organ in Jaén Cathedral had four foot and knee levers affecting the Flautado 8', Llenos, Nasardos, Flutes, Cornets, and six reed stops in both treble and bass. Knee-lever mechanisms are peculiar to Iberian organs. They served the same function as hand- or foot-operated tutti and combination mechanisms in other countries, making it possible for the player to change registrations or achieve echo effects more quickly and easily.

After the turn of the century more foreign influences began to be felt. Some Italian organs were exported to Spain and to Latin America, and examples still exist in Uruguay and Argentina. In the north of the Iberian peninsula, particularly in Catalonia, expatriate Frenchmen such as the Cavaillés came to work after the Revolution of 1789, and during the nineteenth century some Germans and Swiss emigrated to the area.

As in Italy, a lighter and more secular style of organ composition and improvisation became predominant as the period progressed, although it was still integrated into ecclesiastical usage and compatible with the resources of the instruments. Only two Iberian keyboard composers achieved any real prominence in the late eighteenth century, and both were influenced by Italy: the Portuguese Sousa Carvalho studied there, and Antonio Soler, by far the best-known Spaniard, was a pupil of Domenico Scarlatti.

Unlike their counterparts in most other countries, the Iberian composers left little in the way of registrational directions in their music. Many seem to have intended their free compositions (toccatas, tientos, xácaras, sonatas, variations, etc.) for more than one type of keyboard instrument. Lidon, for example, subtitled his Sonata on the First Tone *para clave or para órgano con trompeta real* (for harpsichord or for an organ with an interior trumpet stop), and this lively but thinly textured piece seems well adapted for playing on the prompt and brilliant Spanish Trompetas. Padre Soler, despite his extensive compositional output, left few clues to registration. One is in his third concerto for two organs, where the *Minué* movement contains a light middle section marked *Flautin*, which probably denotes a 4' flute stop. In Iberian organs, as in Italian ones, the most common flute was at 4' pitch (the so-called Flautado 8', it must be remembered, is actually a Principal), and indeed this light *Minué* is not unlike some of the movements in Italian pastorales which call for the use of the 4' flute. This is thus a valuable clue to both the use of the 4' flute in Iberia and to the contrasting nature of sections within certain compositions.

Lonbide, a composer in Bilbao, wrote a treatise for organists, but, alas, it says virtually nothing about registration. However, as in Italy, some organ builders left registration lists. One of these, probably by Echevarría, pertains to the large organ in Segovia Cathedral, built in 1770. It may have been written to assist the Cathedral organists, who were used to an older single-manual organ, in finding their way around on the new three-manual instrument. That may also have been the intent of another list, written by the builder of the large 1789 three-manual organ in the Cathedral of Jaén.

The registration suggestions given for the Segovia organ imply that the organists would know all the standard older registration conventions. Those cited by Echevarría seem largely concerned with the new things that one could do with a three-manual instrument in which all stops were divided. His suggestions are quoted here verbatim:

1. With Nasardos [flutes with 2 2/3'] drawn in both hands [on two manuals] one can play in four parts, providing that the music has a few rests [to change manuals or hand position?].

2. Corneta in the right hand and Nasardos in the left is a good registration, but the right hand should have running figures [*glosadas*]. The Trompeta Magna can also be added.

3. Corneta in the right hand with the Trompeta Real and the Chirimía [Schalmey] in the left hand.

4. The Corneta [right hand] with the Clarin [4'?] in the left hand.

5. The Orlos must not be played in chords; the Dulzayna the same; and these two [short-length reed] stops do not mix well with the full-length reeds (*lenguetaria*).

6. Orlos and Dulzayna in the left hand have a good effect with the echoes; the Orlos with the Corneta Clara [Manual II] and the Dulzayna with the echo Corneta [Manual III].

7. In Manual I Trompeta de Batalla, in Manual II Clarin for the left hand, Flauta for the right hand, in Manual III Clarin de Ecos [right hand] with Flautados in the left hand: this makes very agreeable music, imitating the orchestra of trumpets, horns, and flute or flutes.

8. In Manual I the full chorus (*lleno*); in II the full-length reeds (*lenguetaria*); in III the flue or reed chorus: this has a good effect.

9. In Manual I the flue chorus right hand; in the left hand the reed chorus. In Manual II the full flue chorus (*ripieno*) for the right hand, the full-length reeds for the left hand; in Manual III Trompeta for the left hand, flue chorus for the right hand. If you play each half-manual individually, there seem to be many organs.

10. The same combination one sometimes plays thus: reeds in Manual I right hand, flue chorus in the left hand, etc.

11. Flue chorus in the right hand and Orlo in the left hand is a good registration.

12. The full-length reeds in Manual II and the echo stops in Manual III have a good effect.

13. Flautados and Flute [8'] in the left hand with the Trompeta de Batalla on Manual I in the right hand and Echo Clarin on Manual III has a good effect when playing trumpet calls.

14. On Manual I the Trompeta de Batalla in the left hand with the Violeta make a good accompaniment for the Cornets [Manual II] [317, p. 45].

Most of these directions have to do with special effects, some of them intentionally imitative, and there are no real hints concerning the musical (or liturgical) usage. No. 9, in particular, consciously exploits the variety obtainable from three divided manuals. If registered as suggested, they give the effect of six divisions, especially if the organist was a clever improvisor, as some undoubtedly were. Indeed, such an effect could only be produced on a modern American three-manual organ by the frequent use of combination pistons. One might ask why it was still thought necessary to divide manuals when the trend was away from single-manual instruments. These registrations suggest that organists regarded the divided manual as a registration aid to obtain the maximum variety and contrast (as well as orchestral effects) without having to change stops.

Mechanical registration aids occur with greater frequency in this period, however, and since Pedals were still rudimentary (and only used in the old ways for pedal-points and cadential emphasis), the organist's knees and feet were put to use in the operation of these mechanisms, which were simply extra sliders in the manner of English "shifting movements." The purpose of the four knee and foot levers in the Jaén Cathedral organ is explained in a document left by the builder, which also gives some insights into registration practice [209, p. 79].

The left foot lever operated the two halves of the Flautado II on the main manual, and the right foot lever operated the Flauta Alemana and Traversera (chimney and traverse flutes 8' and 4'); the right knee lever operated the Trompeta de Batalla and Clarin on the main manual, and the left knee lever the reeds on the back façade of the double-fronted organ. This system was complicated, perhaps, but it is full of possibilities since the stops affected could be added to or subtracted from whatever combination of stops was already drawn. And surely the effect of adding the horizontal reeds in sequence during the course of a piece (perhaps a "battle" piece) must have been dramatic. As the writer notes that this could be done without removing the hands from the keys, the effect was thus similar to the adding of reeds by means of a ventil pedal in later French Romantic organs. The two knee levers, by being moved together to the right or left, also made it easy to alternate the front and back reeds during the course of a piece, making a kind of antiphonal effect possible (as well as providing a certain amount of abdominal excercise for the organist!).

In 1790, de Madrid, the builder of the Jaén organ, published a treatise entitled *Cartas instructivas sobre los órganos.* He gives some basic registration rules which confirm that, new tricks and gadgets notwithstanding, many of the older registration conventions still applied to normal usage. De Madrid cites the following, summarized by G. A. C. de Graaf:

1. Principals and Stopped Flutes 8' and 4' may each be used alone, or together in six possible combinations.

2. Cornets and Open Flutes [8'] should never be used in the Plenum, or combined with reeds.

3. However, the 8' and 4' Stopped Flutes can be part of the plenum.

4. To play a *partido de mano izquierda* (left-hand solo piece): Clarin 2' [left hand] with Trompeta Magna 8' [right hand], or Clarin 2' with Principal 8', or Clarin 2' with a flute combination.

5. The Flauta Traversera is always a [treble] solo stop, accompanied by a Stopped Flute in the left hand.

6. Stops of the Echo division should never be combined with those of other manuals [209, p. 84].

Note that the overblowing Traverse Flute, which appeared in all countries after the the middle of the eighteenth century, is, as elsewhere, strictly a solo stop and should not be used in combination with other stops.

Little mention is made in any of these sources of the accessory stops, but we can safely assume that they were, as in other countries, meant to be used at the organist's discretion to heighten the dramatic effect of various types of music, and no doubt they were indispensable in "battle" music. Julian de la Ordén, in his contract for the large Malaga organ, gives some hints concerning the use of the two tremulants, perhaps because they were less common than other accessory stops:

> one *suave* [weak], which when used with the Flautados [Principals 8'] is very agreeable and majestic; the other *feroce* [strong], whose movement has a major effect on the Voz humana, Traverse flute, Bajón, Cornetas, Flautados, and other registers according to common practice and the good taste of the organist. [181, p. 297]

The Iberian organ may be said to have reached the apex of its idiomatic development in the Classical period. The larger Spanish organs are indeed unique with regard to both tonal appointments and mechanical design. The multiplication of reed stops (interior and exterior), the exploitation of the possibilities of divided manuals, the development of registration aids, and the increasing size of instruments in major locations—this all put a wealth of color and variety at the disposal of organists, which they undoubtedly put to good use in the colorful (if often insubstantial) music of the period.

To achieve some of the same effects on modern organs is not always easy. At least two manuals are necessary to obtain the effect of the *medio registro* (divided-manual) pieces, and bright reeds (preferably at more than one pitch) as well as rich foundations and colorful mutations are necessary for all but the simplest pieces. If such resources are not available (and used liberally) much of the essential élan of these pieces will be lost. While some of the better new eclectic instruments will indeed do justice to this music, few fully Iberian-inspired organs have yet been built in North America. Yet in Mexico, there is a vast number of authentic instruments dating from the late seventeenth to the mid-nineteenth century. Happily, more and more of these once-neglected instruments are being restored, played, and even recorded; and several recent organized tours have introduced North Americans to this treasury of historic organs that one does not have to cross an ocean to see and play. Iberian music of the late Baroque takes on much charm when played on these bright, often brash-sounding instruments, and it is this light and cheerful character that one should try to emulate on a modern organ.

As in the previous period, there are registrations which call for an 8' (or 4', or even 2') basis for the left hand and a 16' (or 8') basis for the right hand. This rarely occurs in other literature, but the player should always keep this possibility in mind when playing Baroque or Classical Iberian music. One should try different pitch levels to judge the effect in an actual piece of music before settling on a registration having the same pitch level in treble and bass.

Although there are still some corrupt editions with added editorial pedal parts (often awkward), the pedals should in fact still be used very sparingly (cadentially, or in pedal-points), as in English, French, and Italian organ music of the same period. Or, since Iberian organ manuals still sometimes employed the "short octave" in the bass, the pedals may be used to play an occasional bass note that is out of reach on modern manuals. But in any case, the pitch line of the pedals should correspond to that of the manual.

Composers

Johann Friedrich Agricola (1720–1774)
Carl Philipp Emanuel Bach (1714–1788)
Johann Christian Bach (1735–1782)
Johann Christoph Friedrich Bach (1732–1795)
Wilhelm Friedemann Bach (1710–1784)
Johan Daniel Berlin (1714–1787)
Johan Henrik Berlin (1741–1807)
Johann Friedrich Doles (1715–1797)
Michael Gotthardt Fischer (1773–1829)
Johann Wilhelm Hertel (1727–1789)
Gottfried Homilius (1714–1785)
Johann Peter Kellner (1705–1772)
Johann Philipp Kirnberger (1721–1783)
Johann Christian Kittel (1732–1809)
Johann Ludwig Krebs (1713–1780)
Johann Christoph Kuhnau (1735–1805)
Friedrich Wilhelm Marpurg (1718–1795)
Johann Christoph Oley (c1738–1789)
Philippus Pool (b. 1734)
Johann Ernst Rembt (1749–1810)
Christian Friedrich Rüppe (1753–1826)
Johann Adolf Scheibe (1708–1776)
Johann Schneider (1702–1788)
Georg Michael Telemann (1748–1831)
Johann Gottfried Vierling (1750–1813)

Representative Organs

CHURCH OF ST. MAXIMILIAN, DÜSSELDORF
Christian Ludwig König, 1755 [81, p. 154]

Hauptwerk
Bourdon 16' (metal, divided)
Prestant 8'
Rohrgedackt 8'
Viola da Gamba 8'
Quintgedackt 5 1/3'
Octave 4'
Superoctave 2'
Sesquialtera II (2 2/3'–1 3/5')
Cornett III
Mixtur IV
Trompete 8' (divided)

Echowerk
Grobgedackt 8'
Kleingedackt 4'
Principal 2'
Carillon II
Zimbel II
Vox humana 8'
Trompete 8' (treble)
Vox angelica 1' (bass)

Positiv
Bourdon 8'
Flauto traverso 8' (treble)
Principal 4'
Flûte douce 4'
Salicional 4'
Quinte 2 2/3'
Superoctave 2'
Quintflöte 1 1/3'
Zimbel III
Vox humana 8'
Hautbois 8' (treble)
Klarine 4' (bass)

Pedal (20 notes)
Subbass 16' (metal, stopped)
Prestant 8'
Rohrflöte 8'
Viola da Gamba 8'
Mixtur
Posaune 16'
Trompete 8'
Klarine 4'

Accessory Stops
Tremulants to Positiv and Echowerk

CHURCH OF ST. MICHAEL, HAMBURG
J. G. Hildebrandt, 1762–67 [181, p. 125]

Hauptwerk
Prinzipal 16'
Quintadena 16'
Oktave 8' (2rks in treble)
Gedackt 8'
Gemshorn 8'
Viola da Gamba 8'
Quinte 5 1/3'
Oktave 4'
Gemshorn 4'
Nasat 2 2/3'
Oktave 2'
Sesquialtera II
Cornet V
Mixtur VIII (2')
Scharf V (1 1/3')
Trompete 16'
Trompete 8'

Oberwerk
Bourdon 16'
Prinzipal 8' (2rks in treble)
Spitzflöte 8'
Quintatön 8'
Unda maris 8' (treble)
Oktave 4'
Spitzflöte 4'
Quinte 2 2/3'
Oktave 2'
Rauschpfeife II
Echo Cornet V
Zimbel V (1 1/3')
Trompete 8' (2rks in treble)
Vox humana 8'

Brustwerk (Unterwerk)
Rohrflöte 16'
Prinzipal 8' (2rks in treble)

Pedal
Prinzipal 32'
Subbass 32' (wood, stopped)
Prinzipal 16'
Subbass 16' (wood, stopped)
Rohrquinte 10 2/3'
Oktave 8'
Quinte 5 1/3'
Oktave 4'
Mixtur X (2')
Posaune 32'
Posaune 16'
Fagott 16'
Trompete 8'
Trompete 4'

Flauto traverso 8'
Gedackt 8'
Rohrflöte 8'
Oktave 4'
Rohrflöte 4'
Nasat 2 2/3'
Oktave 2'
Tierce 1 3/5'
Quinte 1 1/3'
Sifflöte 1'
Rauschpfeife II–III
Zimbel V
Chalumeau 8'

Accessory Stops
Tremulant to HW
Schwebung (gentle tremulant) to Oberwerk
Zimbelstern
Coupler Hauptwerk-Pedal

[Three stops of the Oberwerk (presumably including the Echo Cornet) were said to have been enclosed in a simple swellbox.]

CHURCH OF ST. MARY, GRÜNENDEICH/STADE
Dietrich Christoph Gloger, 1766 [62, p. 92]

Hauptwerk
Quintadena 16'
Prinzipal 8'
Octav 4'
Quinte 2 2/3'
Octav 2'
Gemshorn 2'
Mixtur III–IV
Dulcian 16'
Trompete 8'
Cornett 2'

Brustwerk
Gedact 8'
Flöte 4'
Nasat 2 2/3'
Octav 2'
Sesquialter II
Scharf III
Krummhorn 8'

Pedal
Coupled to Hauptwerk

Accessory Stops
Tremulant
Cimbelstern
Sperrventil

PARISH CHURCH, LOHMEN, SAXONY
Johann Christian Kayser, 1789 [stoplist from extant organ]

Hauptwerk
Bordun 16' (wood)
Principal 8'
Gedackt 8'
Octava 4'
Gedackt 4'

Oberwerk
Rohrflöte 8'
Principal 4'
Rohrflöte 4'
Octava 2'
Quinta 1 1/3'

Quinta 2 2/3'
Octava 2'
Cornet III
Mixtur III

Sifflöt 1'

Pedal
Subbass 16'
Octavbass 8'
Posaunenbass 16'

Accessory Stops
Tremulant
Hauptwerk-Oberwerk Coupler (shove coupler)
Bass ventile (for Pedal stops)

ZION LUTHERAN CHURCH, PHILADELPHIA
David Tannenberg, 1790 [8, p. 101]

Hauptwerk
Quintaden 16'
Principal 8'
Gambe 8'
Gemshorn 8'
Gedackt 8'
Octave 4'
Flöte 4'
Quinte 2 2/3'
Octave 2'
Mixture IV–VI

Pedal
Principal Bass 16'
Subbass 16'
Octav Bass 8'
Quinta 5 1/3'
Octave 4'

Oberwerk
Princip[al] dulce 8'
Quintadena 8'
Flöte amab[ile] 8'
Gedackt 8'
Nachthorn 4'
Salicet 4'
Fistelquint 2 2/3'
Hohlflöte 2'
Cimbel III

Echowerk (short compass)
Rohrflöte 8'
Flöte traver[so] 8'
Echo Bass 8' (lowest 20 notes)
Fistula oct[av] 4' (chimney flute)
Nachthorn 4'
Dulcian 8'
Hautbois 8'

Accessory Stops
Tremolo
Cimbel Stern
Bells (to be added later?)
Sperrventil
Two couplers

[N.B. Tannenberg was a Saxon immigrant who apprenticed with J. G. Klemm of Dresden, a fellow immigrant. This instrument was his largest.]

PARISH CHURCH, ROTHENKIRCHEN/AUERBACH
J. G. & C. Trampeli, 1798–1800 [83, p. 64]

Hauptwerk
Bourdon 16'
Principal 8'
Viola di Gamba 8'
Stark Gedackt 8'

Oberwerk
Lieblich Gedackt 8'
Quintadena 8'
Principal Diskant 8' (treble)
Principal 4'

Octave 4'
Flaut douce 4'
Quinte 2 2/3'
Octave 2'
Flageolett 1'
Cornetti III (treble)
Mixtur IV

Flauto amabile 4'
Octave 2'
Quinte 1 1/3'
Siffloete 1'
Mixtur III
Vox humana 8'

Pedal
Subbass 16'
Violonbass 16'
Octavenbass 8'
Posaunenbass 16'

Accessory Stops
Tremulant to Oberwerk
Manual and Pedal couplers

REFORMED CHURCH, OLDEHOLTPADE, FRIESLAND
H. A. Meijer, 1800 [61, p. 6]

Lower Manual
Bourdon 16' (treble)
Prestant 8' (treble)
Holpijp 8'
Prestant 4'
Quint 2 2/3'
Octaaf 2'
Terts 1 3/5'
Dulciaan 8' (short–length reed)

Upper Manual
Viola di Gamba 8' (treble)
Gemshoorn 8' (treble)
Roerfluit 8'
Octaaf 4'
Fluit 4'
Woudfluit 2'

Pedal
Coupled to main manual

Accessory Stops
Ventil
Manual coupler (shove coupler)

[N.B. This is a large chamber organ, probably originally designed for residential use.]

PARISH CHURCH, EKEBYBORNA, SWEDEN
Pehr Schiörlin, 1806 [47, p. 40]

Manual
Principal 16' (treble)
Gedackt 8'
Offenflöjt 8' (open flute, treble)
Piffaro 8' (2rks, treble)
Gamba 4' (bass)
Salicional 4' (bass)
Principal 4' (divided)
Gedacktflöjt 4'
Waldflöjt 2'
Scharf II
Trumpet 8' (divided)

Pedal
Coupled to manual

ST. MICHAEL'S & ZION CHURCH, PHILADELPHIA
Andrew Krauss, 1815 [22, p. 142]

Manual
Principal 8'
Quint Dehn 8' (Quintadena)
Grob Gedackt 8' (wood)
Floet 8' (wood; open?)
Viola di Gamba 8'
Principal 4'
Klein Gedackt 4' (wood)
Gems Horn 4'
Quinta 3'
Sub Octav [*sic*] 2'
Mixtur III

Pedal
Subbass 16' (wood)
Octav Bass 8' (wood)

Accessory Stops
Coppel (Manual to Pedal coupler)

PARISH CHURCH, DORNBERG, THURINGIA
Ernst Gerhard, 1821 [stoplist from extant organ]

Hauptwerk
Bourdon 16'
Principal 8'
Gemshorn 8'
Gedeckt 8'
Hohlflöte 8'
Viol da Gamba 8'
Octava 4'
Flute douce 4'
Kleingedackt 4'
Quinta 2 2/3'
Superoctav 2'
Cornet III (treble)
Terzian II
Mixtur IV

Oberwerk
Principal 8' (treble)
Lieblich Gedackt 8'
Flauto amabile 8'
Flauto traverso 8' (treble)
Principal 4'
Spitzflöte 4'
Salicet 4'
Nasat 2 2/3'
Waldflöte 2'
Mixtur III

Pedal (all stops of wood)
Principalbass 16'
Violone 16'
Subbass 16'
Octavbass 8'
Posaune 16'

Accessory Stops
Glockenakkord (bells)
2 Cimbelsterns
Coupler Hauptwerk-Pedal

MENNONITE CHURCH, LEER, OSTFRIESLAND
Wilhelm Eilert Schmid, 1825 [76, p. 159]

Manual
Prinzipal 8'
Gedackt 8'
Traversflöte 8' (wood, treble?)
Gamba 8' (stopped bass)

Oktave 4'
Rohrflöte 4'
Fugara 4'
Waldflöte 2'
Mixtur III
Trompete 8' (divided)

Accessory Stops
Tremulant

PARISH CHURCH, FARMSUM, HOLLAND
Nicolaas Anthonie Lohman, 1828 [stoplist from extant organ]

Hoofdwerk	**Rugpositief**
Bourdon 16'	Fluit 16' (treble)
Praestant 8'	Holpijp 8'
Quintadena 8'	Fluit travers 8' (treble)
Viola di Gamba 8'	Fluit 4' (stopped)
Octaaf 4'	Woudfluit 2'
Roerfluit 4'	Flageolet 1'
Quint 2 2/3'	Dulciaan 8' (reed, divided)
Octaaf 2'	**Pedaal**
Cornet III (treble)	Originally coupled; 8 independent stops
Mixtuur III–IV	added 1869
Trompet 8' (divided)	
Vox Humana 8'	

Accessory Stops
Tremulant
Manual coupler (divided bass/treble)
Sperrventile

Registration

Although the stylistic line of demarcation between the organs of central Germany and the Baltic Sea area was fairly sharp during the high Baroque period, it became increasingly blurred in the years following the deaths of Schnitger and Silbermann. Organists tended to be more mobile in the area: C. P. E. Bach went from Leipzig to Hamburg, Pool and Ruppe from central Germany to Holland, Scheibe from Leipzig to Copenhagen, and the younger Telemann from Holstein to Riga. Marpurg spent much of his youth in Paris and returned to Hamburg in his early thirties. Although some builders in northern Holland and Ostfriesland clung to a style of organ building that had changed little since the end of the seventeenth century, the central German style was spreading northwest toward the mouth of the Rhine. The purchase by St. Michael's Church in Hamburg of an organ by a leading central German builder (the son of Zacharias Hildebrand of Saxony) signaled the end of the old "Hamburg tradition."

More and more the organs of Protestant Germany were falling into the progressive pattern that had originated in central Germany in the previous period.

Rückpositivs, along with Brustwerks of the old over-the-keydesk type, had virtually disappeared everywhere save in the extreme north; and Pedal pipes were increasingly relegated to the back of the organ. Enclosed divisions—Echowerks—were making a tentative appearance in the Rhenish region. Eight-foot stops continued to multiply; the Gamba and the solo Flauto Traverso were found on all but the smallest organs, even in conservative Holland.

Musically, there was some significant overlapping from the previous period. And it is impossible to ignore the sizable number of composers in the list heading this chapter who can be readily identified with the "Bach circle." These musicians occupy a unique historical niche. Many of them wrote convincingly in the older forms, but at the same time they often engaged in bold adventures into the "galant" and Italianate idioms. More than one writer has commented on the ability of some of these composers to feel comfortable in both the Baroque and the Classical idioms. Thus Krebs and C. P. E. Bach could write quite conservative fugues and chorale-preludes but also venture into Classical sonatas, trios, and Italianate fantasias.

In Central Germany, particularly, many organists—including Krebs in Altenburg and W. F. Bach in Dresden—played substantial organs that had been built during the previous period. Thus many of the conclusions concerning the registration of those organs are still valid for this period, especially as they apply to the chorale-based compositions written for the church service.

There was an increase in stylistic cross-fertilization during this period as well. Not only were builders like Riepp introducing German ideas into French organs, but organists like Marpurg were bringing French ideas to Germany. As early as 1749, Marpurg, ostensibly a Protestant (and the composer of many Protestant chorale-preludes), wrote some articles for his periodical, *Der kritische Musicus an der Spree*, which were directed toward the education of Catholic organists. A so-called typical organ, which he describes, looks more like a French organ with German nomenclature; his Brustwerk, for example, is really a two-stop (Trumpet and Cornet) *Récit*. Perhaps the most German element was a six-stop Pedal of flues and reeds at 16', 8', and 4'.

It is doubtful if such an organ ever actually existed in Germany, but it would appear that a hybrid of this stripe was Marpurg's personal preference. For this "typical" organ, Marpurg proposed some registrations for French-style dialogues (a *Plein jeu* type of chorus on both manuals, coupled, with reeds in the Pedal) and fugues (principals and reeds at 8' and 4', but with the Terz and Nazard added to the Positive). Registrations for duos, trios, and solo pieces are likewise adapted from standard French formulas, although, interestingly, there is no tierce in his *tierce en taille*, but rather the Spitzflöte 1', which recalls a similar variant in one of the earlier Gottfried Silbermann registrations [332, pp. 44–61]. Indeed, Silbermann, with his Alsatian training, may have at least opened the door to French-influenced registrations. His introduction of wide-scaled solo Cornets proved to be lasting, for such stops appear frequently in the otherwise typical central German organs of followers such as Wagner and Hildebrandt.

The strong influence of ensemble music creeps in everywhere in this period, as indeed it always has to some extent; but it is aided and abetted by the up-to-date imitative stops now found in virtually all the organs. J. U. Sponsel, writing in 1771, mentions the "new stops" (Gamba, Salicional, Fugara, Piffaro, Vox angelica, Vox humana—most of which had actually been around since the beginning of the eighteenth century) and implies that nothing can imitate instruments (flute, trumpet, gamba, etc.) better than the organ [165, p. 11].

The Flauto Traverso was usually found at 8' rather than 16' pitch, but an excellent early example of this stop—a wooden, overblowing "harmonic" rank—is in fact found at 16' pitch in the Trost organ Krebs played at Altenburg, and it will be recalled that Agricola mentioned the effectiveness of this stop with the 8' Gamba. Krebs may have had something like this registration in mind for his *Fantasia à giusto italiano*, with its quarter-note chords in the right hand. The 16' and 8' Violones found in so many central German organs would be the obvious choice for the cello-like quarter-note Pedal part that complements the right-hand chords, and for the rather "instrumental" left-hand solo one of the combinations of reeds and flues might be suitable.

Organ composers of this period were no more likely to provide registrations for their music than their predecessors. The general philosophy seems to be summed up by two of the theorists who wrote instruction books for church organists in this period. J. S. Petri (1782) stated that "Rules for the use of various stops are really superfluous, since each organist should know his instrument and trust his ear" [54II, p. 1009]. Even though German organs were becoming somewhat more uniform, D. G. Türk could still say in 1787 that

> every organ has its unique disposition; therefore I will not presume to dictate what stops should be used in this or that situation. The safest rule is this: that the organist understands his instrument, and learns from experience which stops sound best together; then, whatever the stoplist of a particular organ, he can put each stop to its best use. [54II, p. 1008]

Good advice in any context!

Nonetheless, both Petri and Türk did make some general (and very similar) suggestions, which can be summarized as follows:

The Pedal 32' Untersatz should not be used without the 16' and 8' stops [Petri]. Stops of 32' or 16' pitch should be balanced with stops of higher pitches [Türk]. The 8' Principal and other elegant (*lieblich*) stops are suitable for Preludes [Petri].

The Gamba and Quintatön 8' together work well in slow pieces, but are not good for fast passages [Petri].

For pieces of a soft or sad character, use Flutes and Gedeckts at 8' with the Tremulant; Quintatön and Gamba may be added [Türk].

For mourning or funeral chorales, flutes are best; for praise chorales play as strongly as you wish; for prayer chorales, play medium loud, not strong or screamy, but not as mild as for funeral music [Petri].

The Nassat, Cornet, and Sesquialtera should be drawn with the Principal 8'; otherwise they scream or sound nasal. Use this for a right-hand melody in half notes. The Tremulant may be used if it is a mild one (*Schwebung*) [Petri].

Mixtures and mutations should not be used without sufficient 8' foundation [Türk].

Start with a foundation of two or three 8' stops, to which may be added the 16', 4', 2 2/3', 2' and Mixture [Türk].

Softer reeds are good for chorale melodies; stronger ones bring out a *cantus firmus* with more power [Petri].

Flutes without the Principal, combined with 2 2/3', 2', and 1' stops, "sound like a nightingale," and should be accompanied by an 8' Flute [Petri].

The Glockenspiel [bells] is sometimes better than high-pitched stops [Türk].

Go easy on the full organ; have pity on the poor organ blower [Petri]!

The comment on the off-unison mutations and mixtures (Nassat, Cornet, Sesquialtera) is interesting. It represents a slight shift from earlier practice in that Petri seems to regard the strong unison Principal necessary to take some of the edge off these stops. Increasing emphasis on a strong unison is also found in Türk's recommendation of building the chorus not on a single 8' stop, but on two or three; indeed, in most of the German organs of this period, even some fairly small ones, the main division usually had at least three 8' stops—a Principal, a Flute, and a Gamba. Also interesting is the comment concerning the Glockenspiel; one suspects that the "high-pitched stops" referred to were probably the Zimbel or the 1' flute, which had earlier been used to impart a tinkling or bell-like quality to combinations.

Some further registration suggestions are contained in a manuscript dated 1798, discovered by Hans Löffler in Eisenach, Thuringia. The author of this treatise, like Türk and Petri, favors using several 8' stops together and regards Gedeckt, Fugara, Quintadena, and Hohlflöte as a particularly attractive combination. While there were still some reservations about the use of multiple 8's during the previous period, it was recommended by some, and doubtless practiced by many organists; by the second half of the eighteenth century it seems to have become standard usage. No doubt improvements in the wind supply, advocated by Bach, Mattheson, and others in the previous period, encouraged such registrations. This should not be construed to mean that the wind characteristic of late eighteenth-century organs was becoming significantly less flexible, but rather that it was becoming more plentiful and thus better able to supply an increased demand with less danger of sagging or drawing.

For trios, which were becoming very popular in the late eighteenth century, the Eisenach writer regards Quintadena 16' and Hohlflöte 4', or Flute 8' and Reed 4', as particularly useful. For solos he suggests some gapped combinations: Gedeckt 8', Sesquialtera, and Octave 1', or, for fast melodies, Bourdon 16' and Sifflöte 1'. Another favored solo combination has a distinctly French character: Gedeckt 16', Bourdon 8', Octave 4', Nassat 2 2/3', Octave 2', and Terz 1 3/5', accompanied by the Principal 8' with two 8' flutes [264, p. 140]. Krebs's trios for two manuals and Pedal would be a very suitable vehicle for experimenting with such combinations.

One wonders if this writer may have been influenced by Marpurg, who two decades earlier had also recommended the 16' and 1' combination for rapid passages in solos or trios, as well as another gapped combination, Quintatön 16' and Flute 4'. But in general Marpurg recommends that the difference in pitch between two stops should not exceed the octave, that a 2' should not be added to an 8' without an intermediary 4' stop, and that high-pitched unison stops (2' or 1') always be used with Quints and Tierces. So gapped combinations, while occasionally used in some of the light-textured forms such as trios, are still to be regarded as novelties—the exception rather than the rule.

Although the turn-of-the-century period produced a number of other organ tutors, few seem to have had much to say about registration. Kittel's *Die angehende praktische Organist* of 1808 includes many chorale-preludes, but none with any registration suggestions other than obvious generalities (e.g., prayerful music should be played on soft stops). At the end are several preludes in various styles, almost all marked *Pro organo Pleno*, which, if nothing else, suggests that full organ was a common registration for such pieces.

While the conservative organ-building style of the North Sea area suggests correspondingly conservative registrations, the practices in the Dutch cities appear to have been similar to those prevalent in Germany. In 1791 C. F. Ruppe, a German who had spent most of his musical career in Leyden, published a collection of eighteen organ pieces in which he gave two sets of registrations for each piece—one for church organs, and one for chamber organs, attesting to the popularity of organs as domestic instruments in Holland during this period.

Ruppe's registrations included Full Organ combinations, usually Principals 16' through Mixture, with the 8' Flute (and occasionally the 4' Flute), although sometimes the Mixture was omitted or a reed was added. This was in line with German practice. J. H. Knecht, in his *Völlstandigen Orgeschule* (1795), praises the mixing of principal, flute, and reed colors, even in full organ, which includes the Principal 16' [79, p. 187]. It would seem that Adlung's rather revolutionary concept of plenum had by this time become the norm. J. C. Kuhnau, writing a few years earlier, in 1786, recommended a "Trumpet registration" consisting of Bordun 16', Principal 8', Rohrflöte 4', and Trompete 8', but noted that only 8' flues should be used with the softer reed stops [54II, p. 1011].

Aside from the plenum registrations, most of Ruppe's combinations consisted of Principals and Flutes at 8' and 4' pitches, often with three or four 8' stops. A *Dolce* registration included Prestants, Flutes, and the Quintadena at 8', with a 4' Flute for the church organ; for the chamber organ, only the 8' stops. *Mezzo Forte* combinations again included several 8' and 4' Principals, Flutes, and Quintadenas, usually with the addition of a 2' stop or one of the softer reeds, such as the Vox Humana. The only gapped combination adds the 2' Octave to the 8' Principal and 8' Flute; stops are rarely used alone, the only example being a *Pianissimo* registration of Holpyp 8'. From Ruppe's examples it would seem that the central German predilection for massed unison sound had spread to at least the urban areas of Holland by the end of the eighteenth century [307II, p. 278].

Perhaps nowhere more than in Protestant Europe does one find organ design, musical style, and registration practice looking both forward and backward during this period—forward in the area of secular and instrumentally influenced music, and backward with regard to free compositions and to music for the church service. Depending on the music, then, it is not uncommon to find compositional and registrational practices of the Baroque era occurring side-by-side with others that might be termed pre-Romantic. Perhaps this was why Germanic writers seem so reluctant to set down any hard-and-fast rules for registration, repeatedly admonishing organists to rely instead on their own common sense and taste.

It is only in recent times that the music of this region from the post-Bach years has attracted serious attention. The works of W. F. Bach, C. P. E. Bach, Krebs, and such lesser-known writers as Kellner, Kittel, Doles, and Oley are appearing in new scholarly editions and on recitals. As can be seen from some of the registrations cited above, this music is less demanding of the resources of modern organs than that of earlier periods. Although larger organs of the period still possessed mutations and cornets, colorful manual reeds had all but disappeared. Organists were relying increasingly on unison combinations and the newer imitative stops, such as broad strings (Gambas) and overblowing flutes, which are available on a wide variety of present-day organs.

Despite the greater emphasis on "gravity" and massed 8' tone, extremes such as overpowering diapasons, acidy strings, and woolly flutes should still be avoided in favor of more moderate (but definitely not top-heavy) sounds. This music sounds well on many well-designed eclectic modern organs, as well as on some nineteenth-century American instruments, including mid-century examples built by immigrant German builders.

Composers

Johann Georg Albrechtsberger (1736–1809)
Ludwig van Beethoven (1770–1827)
František Xavery Brixi (1732–1771)
Franz Danzi (1763–1826)
Joseph Grätz (1760–1826)
Franz Joseph Haydn (1732–1809)
Johann Michael Haydn (1737–1806)
Johann Nepomuk Hummel (1778–1837)
Johann Gottlieb Janitsch (1708–1763)
Justin Heinrich Knecht (1752–1817)
Karel Blazej Kopriva (1756–1785)
Jan Krital Kuchar (1756–1829)
Jiřík Ignác Linka (1725–1791)
Leopold Mozart (1719–1787)
Wolfgang Amadeus Mozart (1756–1791)
Ferenc Miklós Novotny (1742–1773)
Georg von Pasterwitz (1730–1803)
Peter Sebastian Prixner (1744–1799)
Anton Reicha (Rejcha) (1770–1836)
Ferenc Pál Rigler (c1748–c1775)
Heinrich Schmoll (d. 1792)
Franz Xavier Schnizer (1740–1785)
Josef Ferdinand Norbert Seger (Seeger) (1716–1782)
Johann Caspar Simon (1701–1776)
Georg Andreas Sorge (1703–1778)
Maximilian Stadler (1748–1833)
Jan Krtitl Vanhal (Wanhal) (1739–1813)
Georg Joseph Vogler (1749–1814)
Antal Zimmermann (c1741–1781)

Representative Organs

PRAEMONSTRATIAN ABBEY, TEPL, AUSTRIA
Anton Gertner, 1763 [131, p. 52]

Hauptwerk
Grosscopula 16'
Principal 8'
Copula 8'
Flauta 8'
Gamba 8'
Quintade 8'
Octav 4'
Flauta 4'
Gemshorn 4'
Quint 2 2/3'
Superoctav 2'
Terz 1 3/5'
Quint minor 1 1/3'
Mixture IV–V (1 1/3')
Cembalo IV (1', Cimbel)

Rückpositiv
Gedackt 8'
Flauta 8'
Spitzflöte 4'
Principal 2'
Octav 1'

Oberwerk
Copula maior 8'
Copula minor 8' (4'?)
Salicional 8'
Principal 4'
Fugara 4'
Octav 2'
Flageolet 2'
Quint 1 1/3'
Mixtur

Pedal
Subbass 16'
Subbass ged[ackt] 16'
Octav 8'
Quint 5 1/3'
Superoctav 4'

BENEDICTINE ABBEY, AMORBACH
Heinrich Stumm, 1774–82 [181, p. 83]

Hauptwerk
Prinzipal 16'
Bourdon 16'
Oktave 8'
Quintatön 8'
Gedackt 8' (wood)
Viola da Gamba 8'
Superoktave 4'
Kleingedackt 4'
Quinte 2 2/3'
Superoktave 2'
Mixture VI (2')
Zimbel III (1')
Cornet V (mounted, treble)
Trompete 8' (divided)
Vox angelica 2' (bass)

Echo
Holpfeife 8'

Positiv (Oberwerk)
Prinzipal 8'
Gedackt 8' (wood)
Flauto traverso 8' (treble, wood)
Salizional 8'
Oktave 4'
Rohrflöte 4'
Quinte 2 2/3'
Superoktave 2'
Tierce 1 3/5'
Mixtur IV (1')
Krummhorn 8'
Vox humana 8' (with its own tremulant)

Pedal
Offener Bass 13' [sic] (open wood)
Subbass 16' (stopped wood)
Violon 16' (open wood)
Oktave 8'

Flöte 4'
Oktave 2'
Gemshorn 2'
Quinte 1 1/3'
Flageolet 1'
Vox humana 8'
Krummhorn 8' (bass)
Hautboy 8' (treble)

Superoktave 4'
Mixtur VI (2')
Posaune 16'
Fagott 16'
Klarinett 4' (Clarion)
Cornet 2' (reed)

Accessory Stops
Tremulant (Echo)
Glockenspiel (Echo; steel bars)
Coupler: Hauptwerk-Pedal

PARISH CHURCH, PRUSKÉ, CZECHOSLOVAKIA
Ondrej Pazicky, 1777 [79, p. 181]

Hauptwerk
Principal 8'
Fl[auta] maior 8'
Quintadena 8'
Salicional 8'
Octava 4'
Spitzflauta 4'
Quinta 2 2/3'
Superoctava 2'
Mixtura IV

Tischpositiv ("dynamically weaker")
Copula 8'
Principal 4'
Fl[auta] minor 4'
Octava 2'
Superoctava 1'

Pedal
Portunalbass 16'
Subbass 16'
Octavbass 8'
Principalbass 8'

Accessory Stops
Campani (Glockenspiel)
Manual Coupler

CHURCH OF ST. MARTIN, EISENSTADT, AUSTRIA
Johann Gottfried Malleck, 1778 [197, p. 33]

Hauptwerk
Prinzipal 8'
Gedeckt 8' (wood)
Quintadena 8'
Oktave 4'
Flöte 4' (wood)
Gambe 4'
Quinte 2 2/3'
Oktave 2'
Mixtur III–IV (1 1/3')

Rückpositiv
Koppel 8'
Principal 4'
Koppel 4'
Oktave 2'
Mixtur II (1')

Pedal
Subbass 16'
Oktave 8'
Bourdonbass 8'
Oktave 4'
Pausaune 16'

Accessory Stops
Couplers: Rückpositiv-Hauptwerk, Hauptwerk-Pedal

CASTLE CHURCH, KARLSRUHE, SWABIA
Johann Matthäus Schmahl, 1797 [298, p. 341]

Hauptwerk
Bourdon 16'
Principal 8'
Viola da Gamba 8'
Grobgedeckt 8' (wood)
Quintatön 8'
Praestant 4'
Gemshorn Quint 2 2/3'
Superoctav 2'
Cornet V (treble)
Mixtur Crescendo [sic]
Trompetten 8' (divided)

Positiv
Stillgedeckt 8'
Flautraversiere 8' (metal)
Principal 4'
Waldflöte 4' (wood)
Rohrflöte 4'
Octav 2'
Mixtur III
Crumhorn 8'
Vox humana 8'

Pedal
Subbass 16' (open)
Octavbass 8'
Posaunenbass 16' (metal)
Trompeten Bass 8' (metal)
Clarion Bass 4'

Accessory Stops
Tremulant

[A note in the contract states that the Traverse Flute is of metal because it will sound more like an actual overblowing flute.]

CHURCH OF THE HOLY TRINITY, HROVACA, SLOVENIA
Anton Scholz, 1782 [17, p. 76]

Manual
Principal 8'
Portun 8' (Bourdon)
Copula [maior] 8'
Octav 4'
Copula [minor] 4'
Fugara 4'
Quint 2 2/3'
Superoctav 2'
Mixtur (1 1/3')

Pedal
Subbass 16'
Principalbass 8'
Octavbass 4'

TOWN CHURCH, DARMSTADT
J. Oberndorfer, 1805 [102, p. 33]

Unterwerk (Hauptwerk)
Prinzipal 16'
Prinzipal 8'
Flöte 8'
Gedackt 8'
Oktave 4'
Gedackt 4'
Nassat 4' (?)
Quinte 2 2/3'

Oberwerk
Quintatön 8'
Viola da Gamba 8'
Prinzipal 4'
Flöte 4' (8' pitch?)
Salizional 4'
Oktave 2'
Vox humana 8'

Flöte 2'
Mixtur
Zimbel
Trompete 8'

Pedal
Subbass 16'
Oktavbass 8'
Prinzipal 4'
Oktav 2'
Posaune 16'
Trompete 8'

MOTHER OF GOD CHAPEL, RITZINGERFELD, SWITZERLAND
Joseph Anton Carlen, 1813 [198, p. 88]

Manual
Principal 8'
Copell 8' (stopped flute)
Suavial 8' (flute, treble)
Octaf 4'
Flütten 4' (conical flute)
Tranzquint 2 2/3' (conical)
Superoctaf 2'
Quint 1 1/3' (breaking back)
Mixtur III (1 3/5'–1 1/3'–1', breaking at c's and g's)

Pedal
Paas 16' and 8' (Bourdon and Spitzflöte)

CHURCH OF THE BIRTH OF THE VIRGIN MARY, CERKNICA, SLOVENIA
Johann Gottfried Kunat, c1820 [17, p. 98]

Hauptwerk
Principal 8'
Portun 8' (Bourdon)
Gamba 8'
Salicional 8' (bass)
Vox humana 8' (flue, treble)
Octav 4'
Fugara 4'
Superoctav 2'
Quint 1 1/3'
Mixtur II (2 2/3'–2')

Tischpositiv
Copula 8' (stopped, metal)
Principal 4'
Flauto minor 4' (Fugara)
Octav 2'

Pedal
Contra Bass 16'
Principal Bass 8'
Quint Bass 5 1/3'
Octav Bass 4'

CISTERCIAN ABBEY, OSSEGG, BOHEMIA
Franz Feller, 1838 [131, p. 56]

Hauptwerk
Bordunat 16' (stopped flute)
Quintade 16'
Principal 8'
Spitzflote 8'
Flöte 8' (open flute?)
Gemshorn 8'
Salicional 8'
Quinta 5 1/3'
Octav 4'
Basetta 4' (wide-scaled flute)

Rückpositiv
Principal 8'
Bordunat 8'
Flöte 8'
Copula maior 8' (flute)
Octav 4'
Flöte minor 4'
Fugara 4'
Quint 2 2/3'
Superoctav 2'
Mixture III (1')

Superbasetta 2'
Rauschpfeif IV (2')
Mixtur V (2')

Pedal
Untersatz gedeckt 32'
Principal 16'
Violon 16'
Quinta 10 2/3'
Principal 8'
Octav 8'
Quint/Superoctav 5 1/3' and 4'
Superoctav 4'
Schalmei 4'

Registration

In the South, as well as in the central and northern regions, one sees a greater uniformity of tonal design in this period; indeed, the differences between the organs of the Germanic and Slavic countries in this region had become almost negligible by the beginning of the nineteenth century. The so-called *Werk-prinzip* had been virtually abandoned everywhere, although the Rückpositiv was still employed as the second manual division in some parts of the South, and in the Slavic countries one sometimes finds the Rückpositiv combined with a detached keydesk facing the altar (Tischpositiv).

Detached keydesks that permitted the organist to face the altar (and also to have better visibility of singers and instrumentalists in an often deep gallery), seem to have developed in the Catholic South and Southeast early in the eighteenth century and spread west to France in the nineteenth century. The Protestant countries, on the other hand, generally continued to employ the attached (and usually recessed) keydesk in organs of medium and small size until near the end of the nineteenth century.

As in central Germany (and, to an increasing extent, the northern areas), the number and variety of reed stops decreased. Many organs had only Pedal reeds, if any, and only the largest instruments were likely to have more than one reed stop to a manual division. The number of 8' and 4' flue stops continued to increase, although not entirely at the expense of mutations, and string-toned stops (Gamba, Salicional, Fugara) were found even in small instruments. There is a more than a hint of French influence in the work of the southern builder Riepp, and one cannot discount a certain amount of subtle Italian influence. Organs from Italian workshops are indeed found in some numbers in the parts of Austria, Switzerland, and Slovenia bordering northern Italy, and organ builders occasionally crossed the border in both directions. This Italian influence is found not so much in the stoplists, which still adhere fairly closely to the Germanic format, but in the gentler, suaver voicing of the southern organs and often in the simpler case designs.

From the Catholic South in this period came perhaps the first self-styled "organ expert," Abbé G. J. Vogler. The activities of this facile and charismatic (if eccentric) musician centered largely around Vienna, Mannheim, and Darmstadt, although he also spent a few years in the Swedish court. His iconoclastic and pre-Romantic approach to music spared neither traditional harmony and composition, performance, nor organ design.

As a composer Vogler was undistinguished, and as a performer he leaned heavily on the improvisation of thunderstorms and other crowd-pleasers such as "The Fall of the Walls of Jericho." But his radical ideas of "simplifying" the organ by doing away with the lowest- and highest-pitched stops (32' stops and mixtures) and replacing beating reeds with free reeds, did briefly find a few supporters around the turn of the century. It is probable that Vogler was at least partly responsible for the appearance of Quint stops at 10 2/3' pitch in the Pedal (which with the 16' synthesized a 32' sound) in the early nineteenth century, as well as the popularity of free reeds around the middle of the century, but historically his influence on organ building in general must be regarded as minimal.

The above list of composers includes a number of "greats," but not many of them left anything of substance for the organ. Beethoven studied the organ in his youth, but his few organ compositions are rather ordinary student pieces that would probably have been forgotten if they did not bear the name of a master. With the Haydns we fare a little better, but only because both Joseph and Michael were associated with Catholic court chapels. From Michael we have a set of short but well-crafted versets in the eight church tones, intended for *alternatim* use in the mass; from Joseph some pleasing little preludes, also clearly for church use.

Joseph Haydn's most enduring contributions to the organ literature are unquestionably his delightful concertos for organ and chamber orchestra. Court chapels, cathedrals, and large urban churches of the Catholic south in this period usually maintained an instrumental ensemble as well as a choir and an organist. Haydn worked in such a situation during his long tenure as Kapellmeister to Prince Esterházy, and the concertos were written in this context.

Mozart follows the same pattern. He wrote little if anything for organ solo (the Fantasy and Fugue in C and a few shorter keyboard pieces are believed by some to be organ works). His most important compositions for the organ are the seventeen "Epistle" Sonatas for organ and string orchestra, to be played between the Epistle and the Gospel during the high mass at Salzburg Cathedral. They date from 1772–80, while Mozart was in the service of the Archbishop of Salzburg, and were written for the Cathedral's Egedacher organ, whose stoplist is cited in chapter 17.

Because it involves compositions by all three of the classical "greats"—Haydn, Mozart, and Beethoven—one other curious source of organ music from this period should be mentioned. Mechanically played organs and organ-playing clocks, combining the two most "high tech" mechanical arts of the pre-industrial era, had been known for centuries throughout Europe. One of the oldest self-playing organs, a sixteenth-century tower *Hornwerk*, known as the "Salzburg Stier," is still in existence in Austria. It is played by a pinned barrel, and during the eighteenth century music was written for it by both Haydns, both Mozarts, and J. E. Eberlin [24, p. 61].

During the Classical period smaller indoor barrel organs became popular, and the more elaborate examples were exhibited in museums and concert halls. During the last half of the eighteenth century domestic clocks containing a small organ of flute pipes became one of the status symbols of the wealthy. They were known throughout Europe, from England to Italy, but were especially popular in Austria and its surrounding area, from southern Germany to Prague. Composers both distinguished and obscure were commissioned to write music for these mechanical organs, and it is ironic—in view of his oft-quoted comment about the organ being the "King of Instruments"—that the most inspired of Mozart's organ compositions, the 1790 Fantasia in F Minor (K594), was originally written for a large barrel organ called an Orchestrion, which contained flutes and strings and at least one reed stop, mostly at 8' pitch.

Mozart's pieces have been transcribed for a normal organ and are most effective in this form. Beethoven too was commissioned to write a piece for a large orchestrion, called the Panharmonicon, the work of his ingenious friend J. N. Maelzel, better known as the inventor of the metronome. Beethoven's orchestrion piece was *Wellington's Victory, or the Battle of Vittora*; it was later rewritten for orchestra, but was apparently never transcribed for organ. The orchestrion, as its name implies, was a barrel organ designed as a mechanical imitation of an orchestra; in addition to playing pieces specifically written for it, it played transcriptions of orchestral and operatic favorites. Thus its tonal resources tended toward 8' imitative tone—reeds, flutes, and strings—rather than true organ tone. When registering orchestrion music transcribed for organ, bear in mind that in the orchestrion, reeds rather than mixtures provided the brilliance.

Outnumbering the orchestrions were the flute-clocks, for which Handel and others had written in the Baroque period. Although Mozart claimed not to care for them—"lots of little pipes which sound too high and childish" [118, p. 224], he did write for these smaller mechanical instruments, as his works numbered K594, K608, and K616 attest. Beethoven too wrote some pleasing pieces for the flute-clock, as did Salieri, C. P. E. Bach, Cherubini, the pianist Anton Eberl, and others, but the largest number by far (32) came from the pen of Joseph Haydn. They were written between 1772 and 1793 for mechanisms built by the Esterházy clockmaker, P. P. Niemecz, and they are as charming as they are brief.

The compass of the organ movements in flute-clocks was small, usually beginning around middle C or the F or G below it. The pipes were lightly voiced stopped or open flutes of unison pitches, although one description of the flute-clock Mozart wrote for states that it included a "Bassoon"—most probably a short-length reed stop [243, p. 12]. It is thus appropriate when registering these little pieces to limit the stops used to mild but bright 8' and 4' flutes (with the possible addition of a mild reed in the case of the Mozart works) and let the variety of styles and tempi in the pieces themselves provide the contrasts and interest.

The best-known composers of the Viennese school left little for the organ, but there were others, not so well known, who produced quality work. Among them was Michael Haydn's pupil and Beethoven's teacher, Albrechtsberger, organist of the Cathedral in Vienna, who wrote prolifically in the free forms—preludes, fugues, sonatas, and trios. Some of the most interesting and substantial organ music of the period comes not from Vienna but from Czechoslovakia, where the school founded by Czernohorsky produced the organ composers Seger, Brixi, Kuchar, Reicha, and

Vanhal, whose well-crafted works are deserving of more attention than they are usually afforded.

Like their Germanic Protestant counterparts, these Catholic composers rarely put registrations in their music, but a few registration lists do survive. One, apparently written in the late eighteenth century, pertains to a one-manual thirteen-stop organ of the Stumm type with a divided Trumpet in a church near Cologne, and suggests the following:

To accompany chorales or the choir: Prestant and Bourdon 8', Octave 4', Superoctave 2', or Nasard 2 2/3'

For a solo voice: Prestant, Bourdon, Octave, Flute 4', Nasard, Tierce, Larigot, and Trompete [essentially a French *Grand Jeu*]

For Preludes: Full organ with Mixture and Trumpet

For a strong bass: Bourdon, Octave, Nasard, Trompete bass

For a strong treble: Bourdon, Octave, Nasard, Cornet, Trompete treble

To imitate the orchestral flute: Prestant and Bourdon

Use the Sesquialtera with Prestant, Bourdon, Octave (plus optional 2').

Use the Cornet with Prestant, Bourdon, Octave, and Flute 4' "for rapidly running [*laufende*] interludes."

Use the Vox humana with Bourdon and Flute 4'; optional Nasard and Tremulant. [Hummel calls for Vox humana and 8' Flute in one of his pieces, an Andante.]

To imitate the Glockenspiel: Bourdon 8' and Superoctave 2'

For Clarinet or Horn effects: Trompete, Bourdon, Prestant, Octave, and Nasard

For a variation: Bourdon, Prestant, and Flute

To imitate fifes: Octave 4' and Flute 4' [181, p. 84]

This list gives insight into the way one organist coped with the limitations of a small instrument in obtaining desired effects. Carrying some of these ideas further with a larger organ in mind are the "recipes" given by Karl J. Riepp for his French-influenced organ at the Benedictine Abbey of Ottobeuren in Swabia, completed in 1766. He calls for such standard French combinations as the *Grand jeu, Plein jeu,* and *Jeu de Tierce.* For solos he suggests such combinations as Gamba with Principals 8' and 4' accompanied by the two 8' flutes in the Echo, and Vox Humana with Copel (flute) 8' and Octave 4' [328, p. 573]. The culinary simile also applies to Riepp's suggestions for "seasonings": Quintatön (sauerkraut), Superoctave (salt), Larigot (cream), Salicional (loaf sugar), Pedal (Burgundy wine), and Echo (coffee) [181, p. 83]. However, both the Cologne and Riepp directions pertain more to the western part of the region than to the eastern, where, as in the previous period, there was less use of off-unison colors.

In 1765 P. Rathard Meyer, music director of the Parish Church in Diessen/Ammersee, made a lengthy list of registrations for the new König organ there, which was arranged around a west gallery window, as many southern German organs were in this period. His several *Cantabile* registrations are various combinations of 8' and 4' principals, flutes, and strings on both manuals; and one consisting of four 8' stops (two flutes, Quintade, and Gamba) reflects the trend toward unison sounds in the North. The Pedal 16' alone (occasionally with an 8') is used with most of these combinations. Many of the solo combinations are also mixtures of 8' and 4' flue stops, although a couple of solo combinations call for 4' and 2' pitches only, and one consists of Principal 8', Octave and Flute 4', and Zimbel.

The Meyer list is one of the very few to cite Pedal solo registrations; the three listed are Principal 8' alone; Subbass 16', Octave 8', and Fagott 16'; and Pedal Plenum. Gapped combinations, found under the heading of *Allegretto*, confirm sources from other regions suggesting that such registrations are permissible for light-textured and fast-moving music in this period [132, pp. 21–23].

Although Abbé Vogler, in his *Orgelschule* of 1797, gives some suggestions for registration, they probably did not all reflect common usage and should be taken with a grain of salt. Some do seem fairly in line with other sources: Quintatön 8' and Rohrflöte 4', Gamba 8' and Superoctave 4', Gamba and Traverse Flute 8'. But he also recommends many gapped combinations (Quintatön 8' and Gemshorn 2', Gedackt 8' and Waldflute 2', and even Rohrflute 4' and Flageolet 1'), which were probably used for more esoteric effects, as was his "Dutch carillon" registration, which colored 16' or 8' stops with either the Quint 2 2/3' and the Terz 4/5' or the Gemshorn 4' and the Terz 3 1/5' [156, p. 35]. Such combinations should be employed with great caution, and only in novelty pieces or improvisations.

The Czech composers were as reticent as the Germans and Austrians with regard to putting registrations in their music, but the similarity of the organs, as well as the literature and the usage, suggest that registration practices were similar. One source from the very end of the period, a textbook for organists published in 1834 by the Prague organ builder Josef Gartner, tends to confirm this. Most of his stop combinations (aside from full organ) ring a great many changes on the various 8' and 4' flue stops; they largely ignore the higher-pitched stops with which the average Czech organ was still quite well endowed and may have been intended primarily for liturgical music. Gartner makes one small addition to our knowledge of what organists were doing when he condones the coupling of manuals to achieve a desired color [79, p. 179]. In general, the few registration indications we have from this period tend to echo those of the previous period, with their emphasis on combinations of unison pitches.

What was said concerning the adaptation of north and central German music to modern organs applies here also—perhaps even more so. The preludes, fugues, sonatas, and other free compositions of the southeastern school are quite straight-forward, and generally do not require overly colorful registrations that are hard to achieve on the average small or medium-sized organ. Occasionally one encounters an example where the overblowing flute (Traverse Flute, Harmonic Flute) seems called for, as in the Italianate pastorale section of Kuchar's Fantasia in G minor. Most modern organs have such a stop, and those that do not often have a Melodia or a Clarabella, which will serve almost as well.

In the concerted music of Mozart, Haydn, Albrechtsberger, and others, even the obbligato parts are not complex; and in many (including some of Mozart's "Epistle" Sonatas), the organ part is hardly more than a *continuo* part. The seemingly stock 8' and 4' flue combinations were probably expected to be used in much of this music, with perhaps a 2' added if more clarity was needed in an obbligato section. In this regard, note that, in general, neither off-unison mutations nor reeds sound good in light ensemble music; they seem to clash with the harmonics of the strings and woodwinds, especially when the organ is used with the small chamber ensembles for which the concerted music of the Baroque and Classical periods was written. As far back as Handel there is evidence for the use of only unison pitches in concertos. Considering the increasing emphasis put on unison combinations at the end of the eighteenth century, there is no reason to suppose that anything spicier (or more imitative) than basic flute and principal tone was employed in the works of the Classical period written for organ with other instruments.

APPENDIX I

Restored Historic Organs in North America

These authentic period instruments, from various countries, date from the seventeenth century to early in the ninetenth. Most of them are small, and as far as can be determined, all of them are well restored, relatively unaltered, and in playable condition.

A = American G = German
D = Dutch I = Italian
E = English P = Portuguese
F = French Sw = Swiss

Location	Builder and Date	Type	Size
CALIFORNIA			
Berkeley, University of California	Unknown, 1789	I	1-7
	Unknown, 18th century	G	1-4
	Unknown, 1783	D	1-7
CONNECTICUT			
Middle Haddam, Second Congregational Church	Thomas Appleton, 1827	A	2-15
Milton, Episcopal Church	Thomas Hall, 1823	A	1-7
New Haven, Belle Skinner Collection (Yale)	John Snetzler, 1742	E	1-5
DISTRICT OF COLUMBIA			
Washington, Smithsonian Institution	Jacob Hilbus, c1812	A	1-9
	Eben Goodrich, c1815	A	1-4
	John Snetzler, 1761	E	1-5
FLORIDA			
Tallahassee, University of Florida	Hill & Davison, 1837	E	1-5
ILLINOIS			
Elgin, Church of Brethren Board	J. C. Harttman, 1698	G	1-3
MASSACHUSETTS			
Boston, Museum of Fine Arts	John Avery, 1792	E	1-3
	Unknown, c1700	G	1-4
	Simon Bauer, 1692	G	Regal
Cambridge, Christ Episcopal Church	William Gray, 1805	E	1-7
Phillipston, Congregational Church	Goodrich & Appleton, 1812	A	1-4
Salem, Essex Institute	George Hook, 1827	A	1-6
South Dennis, Congregational Church	John Snetzler, 1762	E	1-9
Sturbridge, Old Sturbridge Village	Eben Goodrich, c1815	A	1-5
MICHIGAN			
Ann Arbor, University of Michigan	Unknown, 18th century	I	1-3

Location	Builder and Date	Type	Size
MINNESOTA			
St. Paul, House of Hope Church	H. A. Meijer, 1785	D	2–10
	Ducroquet, 1852	F	1–7
NEW HAMPSHIRE			
Portsmouth,	Unknown, c1700	E	1–4
St. John's Episcopal Church			
Seabrook, Historical Society	R. P. Morss, 1838	A	1–6
Winchester, Public Library	Henry Pratt, 1799	A	1–4
	Henry Pratt, c1815	A	1–4
NEW YORK			
Geneva, Trinity Episcopal Church	Wm. Redstone, c1811	A	1–5
New York, Metropolitan Museum	Thomas Appleton, 1830	A	2–13
	R. M. Ferris, c1850	A	1–3
	William Crowell, 1852	A	1–4
	Unknown, c1700	G	1–3
	George Voll, 1575	G	Regal
New York, St. David's School	Unknown, c1670	E	1–4
NORTH CAROLINA			
Concord, Mill Hill	J. Stirewalt, 1821	G/A	1–3
Winston-Salem, Old Salem, Inc.	David Tannenberg, 1789	G/A	1–5
PENNSYLVANIA			
Camp Hill, Peace Church	Conrad Doll, 1807	G/A	1–6
Lititz, Moravian Church Hall	David Tannenberg, 1787	G/A	1–9
Lititz, Single Brothers' House	David Tannenberg, 1793	G/A	1–4
Nazareth, Whitefield House	David Tannenberg, 1776	G/A	1–4
Northumberland, Priestley Chapel	John Wind, 1815	G/A	1–2
Pittsburgh, Old St. Luke's Church	Unknown, c1823	E	1–5
Reading, Historical Society	J. Dieffenbach, c1800	G/A	1–3
York, Historical Society	David Tannenberg, 1804	G/A	1–11
SOUTH DAKOTA			
Vermillion, Shrine to Music	Josef Looser, 1786	Sw	1–6
	Jacob Hanss(?), c1620	G	1–6
	Chr. Dieffenbach, 1808	G/A	1–6
TEXAS			
Dallas, Meadows Museum (SMU)	Pascoal Caetano, 1762	P	1–7
VIRGINIA			
Madison, Hebron Lutheran Church	David Tannenberg, 1800	G/A	1–7
Williamsburg, Wren Chapel	J. Snetzler(?), c1760	E	1–8

APPENDIX II

Modern Historically Based Organs in North America

These instruments are direct copies of historic organs or are strongly based on the tonal work of a particular school. Some have other authentic period features, such as short-octave keyboards; most have flexible winding, and virtually all are tuned in non-equal temperament. A few have modern console features and case designs, but all have mechanical key and stop action. Every attempt has been made to make this list as complete as possible regarding instruments in public places; organs in private ownership are not listed.

A = American	MR = Medio Registro (divided keyboard)
CG = Central German	LO = Long Octave (English GG)
D = Dutch	SO = Short (bass) Octave
E = English	SS = Subsemitones (split keys)
F = French	
G = German	
I = Italian	
NG = North German	
P = Portuguese	
S = Spanish	
Sw = Swiss	

Location	Builder	Style/Period	Size
ARIZONA			
Tempe, Arizona State University	Paul Fritts	NG/17th c.	2-26
BRITISH COLUMBIA			
Vancouver, St. Andrew's Church	Goetze & Gwynn	E/18th c. SO	1-10
CALIFORNIA			
Berkeley, University of California	Greg Harrold	S/17th c. SO,MR	1-17
	Greg Harrold	NG/17th c	2-20
Berkeley, St. John's Presbyterian Ch.	John Brombaugh	NG/17th c.	2-22
Chico, California State University	Munetaka Yokota	CG/18th c.	2-37
Fremont, Mission San José	Manuel Rosales	S/18th c. MR	1-16
San Diego, All Souls Church	Fritts-Richards	D,G/17th c.	3-34
Stanford, Stanford University	C. B. Fisk	F,G/17th c.	4-53
	Paul Fritts	NG/17th c. MR	1-8
Yuba City, First Lutheran Church	Munetaka Yokota	CG/18th c.	2-17
CONNECTICUT			
New Haven, Yale School of Music	C. B. Fisk	E/18th c. MR,LO	1-7
Stamford, St. John's Lutheran Church	Richards, Fowkes	CG/18th	2-20
Storrs, St. Mark's Chapel	John Brombaugh	NG/17th c.	2-22
DISTRICT OF COLUMBIA			
Washington, Georgetown University	Gene Bedient	CG/18th c.	2-19
FLORIDA			
Tallahassee, First Presbyterian Church	Taylor & Boody	NG/17th c.	2-25

Location	Builder	Style/Period	Size
GEORGIA			
Atlanta, Glenn Memorial Methodist Church	Taylor & Boody	E/18th c.	2-9
Decatur, Agnes Scott College	John Brombaugh	G/17th c. MR	1-6
ILLINOIS			
Elmhurst, Elmhurst College	John Brombaugh	G/17th c. MR	1-6
Rock Island, Augustana College	Gene Bedient	G/17th c. MR,SO	1-11
INDIANA			
Bloomington, Indiana University	Lynn Dobson	I/18th c.	2-23
Evansville, Aldersgate Methodist Church	Daniel Jaeckel	CG/18th c.	2-17
Indianapolis, Christ Church Cathedral	Taylor & Boody	NG/17th c.	3-37
IOWA			
Ames, Iowa State University	John Brombaugh	NG/17th c.	3-34
Iowa City, University of Iowa	Taylor & Boody	NG/17th c.	2-17
MARYLAND			
Baltimore, Mt. Calvary Episcopal Church	C. B. Fisk	D/17-18th c.	2-36
MASSACHUSETTS			
Boston, New England Conservatory	C. B. Fisk	E/18th c. MR,LO	1-7
	Fritz Noack	NG/17th c. SO	1-5
Boston, Christ Church (Old North)	A. D. Moore	E,A 18-19th c.	2-29
Roxbury, St. Margaret's Convent	A. D. Moore	G/17th c.	2-11
So. Hadley, Mt. Holyoke College Chapel	C. B. Fisk	I,G/17th c.	2-27
Sudbury, Episcopal Church	William Drake	E/18th c.	2-12
Wellesley, Wellesley College Chapel	C. B. Fisk	NG/17th c. SO,SS	3-30
Wellesley Hills, Congregational Church	Fritz Noack	G/17th c. MR	1-10
Westfield, First Congregational Church	C. B. Fisk	CG/18th c.	2-18
Worcester, Holy Cross College Chapel	Taylor & Boody	NG/17th c.	4-45
MICHIGAN			
Ann Arbor, University of Michigan	C. B. Fisk	CG/18th c.	2-27
Grand Rapids, St. Mark's Church	Gene Bedient	F/18th c.	3-40
NEW JERSEY			
Red Bank, United Methodist Church	Oberbergen	G/18th c. SO	1-4
NEW YORK			
Flushing, Queens College	Gene Bedient	G/17th c.	3-34
Rochester, Eastman School of Music	Goetze & Gwynn	E/18th c.	1-6

Location	Builder	Style/Period	Size
Stony Brook, State University of New York	Bozeman-Gibson	CG/18th c.	2-22
NORTH CAROLINA			
Durham, Duke University Chapel	D. A. Flentrop	D,F/18th c.	4-66
OHIO			
Cincinnati, North Presbyterian Church	Taylor & Boody	NG/17-18th c.	2-21
Cleveland Heights, St. Paul's Church	Gerhard Hradetzky	I/17-18th c.	2-22
Oberlin, Oberlin Conservatory	Fritz Noack	NG/17th c. SO	1-5
	D. A. Flentrop	D/18th c.	3-46
Oberlin, Oberlin College, Fairchild Chapel	John Brombaugh	NG/17th c. SO,SS	2-15
Toledo, Ashland Ave. Baptist Church	John Brombaugh	D/17th c.	2-19
University Heights, Carroll University	Patrick Collon	S/18th c. MR,SO	2-25
ONTARIO			
Sarnia, St. Giles Presbyterian Church	Halbert Gober	G/18th c.	2-20
Toronto, University of Toronto	Hellmuth Wolff	NG/17-18th c.	3-30
OREGON			
Eugene, Central Lutheran Church	John Brombaugh	NG/17-18th c.	3-38
PENNSYLVANIA			
York Springs, Trinity Lutheran Church	Taylor & Boody	NG/17th c.	2-12
QUEBEC			
Montreal, Grand Seminaire	Guilbault-Thérien	F/18th c.	4-39
Montreal, Sacré-Coeur Chapel	Guilbault-Thérien	F/18th c.	2-25
Montreal, McGill University	Hellmuth Wolff	F/18th c.	3-37
Montreal, Chiesa Madonna della difesa	Karl Wilhelm	I/ 18th c.	2-10
TENNESSEE			
Collegedale, Southern College	John Brombaugh	NG/16-17th c.SO	2-14
TEXAS			
Houston, Christ the King Lutheran Church	Fritz Noack	CG/18th c.	2-30
VERMONT			
Burlington, University of Vermont	C. B. Fisk	F/18th c.	2-28
VIRGINIA			
Charlottesville, Westminster Church	Taylor & Boody	NG/17-18th c.	2-18

Location	Builder	Style/Period	Size
Richmond, Bethlehem Lutheran Church	Taylor & Boody	NG/17–18th c.	2-24
Yorktown, Grace Church	J. W. Walker	E/18th c.	2-6
WASHINGTON			
Ellensburg, Grace Episcopal Church	John Brombaugh	D/17th c. MR	1-11
Tacoma, Christ Episcopal Church	John Brombaugh	NG/17th c.	2-22
Tacoma, University of Puget Sound	Paul Fritts	G/17–18th c.	2-33
Seattle, St. Alphonsus Church	Paul Fritts	D/17th c.	2-33
WISCONSIN			
Reedsburg, St. John Lutheran Church	Fritz Noack	NG/18th c.	2-15
Wausau, Salem Lutheran Church	Daniel Jaeckel	NG/17th c.	3-38

BIBLIOGRAPHY

Books, Pamphlets, and Dissertations

1. Adlung, Jakob. *Musica Mechanica Organoedi.* Berlin, 1768.
2. Amezua y Noriega, R. G. *Perspectivas para la Historia del órgano Español.* Madrid, 1970.
3. Anderson, Poul-Gerhard. *Organ Building and Design* (trans. Joanne Curnutt). New York: Oxford University Press, 1969.
4. Angel de la Lama, Jesus. *El órgano en Valladolid.* Valladolid, 1982.
5. Antegnati, Costanzo. *L'arte organica.* Brescia: Tebaldino, 1608. (Ms. translation by Luigi Tagliavini.)
6. Anthony, James R. *French Baroque Music from Beaujoyeulx to Rameau.* New York: W. W. Norton, 1981.
7. Apel, Willi. *The History of Keyboard Music to 1700.* Bloomington: Indiana University Press, 1972.
8. Armstrong, William H. *Organs for America.* Philadelphia: University of Pennsylvania Press, 1967.
9. Arnold, Corliss R. *Organ Literature: A Comprehensive Survey.* Metuchen: Scarecrow Press, 1973; rev. eds., 1987, 1995.
10. Arnold, John. *The Complete Psalmodist.* Fendon, 1779.
11. Ausseil, Louis. *L'Orgue espagnol du XVIe au XIXe siècle.* Paris: L'Orgue, 1980.
12. Baffert, Jean-Marc. *Les Orgues de Lyon du XVIe au XVIIIe siècle.* Paris: L'Orgue, 1974.
13. Banchieri, Adriano. *Organo suonarino.* Venice: Alessandro Vincenti, 1638.
14. ———. *Conclusions for Playing the Organ* (trans. Lee Garrett). Colorado Springs, 1982.
15. Bédos de Celles, Dom F. *L'Art de Facteur d'Orgues,* 2 vols. Paris, 1766–78.
16. Bijtelaar, B. *De Orgels van de Oude Kerk in Amsterdam.* Amsterdam: Stichting Orgelcentrum, 1975.
17. Bizjak, Milko, and Edo Skulj. *Pipe Organs in Slovenia.* Ljubljana, 1985.
18. Blanchard, Homer D. *The Bach Organ Book.* Delaware, OH: Praestant Press, 1985.
19. Blewett, P. R. W. *The Duddyngton Manuscripts at All-Hallows-by-the-Tower, London.* London, 1977.
20. Blewitt, Jonas. *A Complete Treatise on the Organ, to which is added a Set of Explanatory Volunteries.* London: Longman & Broderip, 1795(?).
21. Bornemann, Walther. *Kleine Geschichte der Lüdingworther Orgel.* Lüdingworth, 1961.
22. Brunner, Raymond J. *That Ingenious Business.* Birdsboro: Pennsylvania German Society, 1990.
23. Bruschi, Mario, and P. P. Donati. *L'organo della chiesa di Treppio.* Pistoia, 1981.
24. Buchner, Alexander. *Mechanical Musical Instruments.* London: Batchworth Press, n.d.
25. Busch, Hermann J., ed. *Orgeln in Paris.* 2d ed. Kassel: Merseberger, 1979.
26. Caldwell, John. *English Keyboard Music before the Nineteenth Century.* Oxford: Basil Blackwell, 1973.
27. Cantagrel, Gilles, and Harry Halbreich. *Le Livre d'or de l'orgue Français.* Paris: Calliope-Marvel, 1976.
28. Cellier, Alexandre and Henri Bachelin. *L'orgue—Ses éléments—Son histoire—Son esthétique.* Paris: Delagrave, 1933.
29. Chase, Gilbert. *The Music of Spain.* 2d ed. New York: Dover, 1959.
30. Clutton, Cecil, and Austin Niland. *The British Organ.* London: B.T. Batsford, 1963; rev. ed., Eyre Methuen, 1982.
31. Cocheril, Michel. *Les orgues de Bretagne.* Rennes: Ouest France, 1981.

32. Colchester, L. S. *A Short History of the Organs*. Wells: Wells Cathedral, 1953.

33. Dähnert, Ulrich. *Die Orgeln Gottfried Silbermanns in Mitteldeutschland*. Amsterdam: Frits Knuf, 1971.

34. ———. *Der Orgel- und Instrumentbauer Zacharias Hildebrandt*. Leipzig, 1962.

35. Dalla Libera, Sandro. *L'organo*. Milan: Ricordi, 1956.

36. David, Hans T., and Arthur Mendel. *The Bach Reader*. New York: Norton, 1966.

37. Donati, Pier Paolo et al., eds. *Arte nell'Aretino*. Firenze: Editrice Edam, 1980.

38. Done, Joshua. *A Complete Treatise on the Organ*. London: Balls & Son, 1837.

39. Douglass, Fenner. *The Language of the Classical French Organ*. New Haven: Yale University Press, 1969.

40. Dufourcq, Norbert. *Documents inédits relatifs à l'orgue français*. 2 vols. Paris: Picard, 1934/5.

41. ———. *La Musique d'Orgue Française de Jehan Titelouze à Jehan Alain*. Paris: Librairie Floury, 1949.

42. ———. *Le livre de l'orgue français: Tome IV, La musique*. Paris: Picard, 1972.

43. Edskes, H.A., et al., eds. *Arp Schnitger en zijn werk in het Groningerland*. Groningen: Stichting Groningen Orgelland, 1969.

44. Edskes, H.A. *De nagelaten geschriften van de orgelmaker Arp Schnitger*. Sneek: Boeijenga, 1968.

45. *Einweihung der rekonstruierten Orgel in der Kapelle der Weissenfelser Schlosses Neu-Augustusburg*. Weissenfels, 1985.

46. Elvin, Laurence. *Bishop & Son, Organ Builders*. Swanpool: Elvin, 1984.

47. Erici, Einar. *Inventarium över bevarde äldre kyrkorglar i Sverige*. Stockholm: Kyrkomusikernas Riksförbund, 1965.

48. Fellerer, Karl Gustav. *Studien zur Orgelmusik*. Kassel: Bärenreiter, 1932.

49. Fesperman, John. *A Snetzler Chamber Organ of 1761*. Washington, DC: Smithsonian Institution Press, 1970.

50. ———. *Organs in Mexico*. Raleigh: Sunbury Press, 1980.

51. Fessy, A[lexandre]. *Manuel d'Orgue à l'Usage des Eglises Catholiques*. Paris: Troupenax & Cie., 1845.

52. Flade, Ernst. *Gottfried Silbermann*. Leipzig: Breitkopf & Härtel, 1953.

53. Flentrop, Dirk A., and John Fesperman. *The Organs of Mexico City Cathedral*. Washington, DC: Smithsonian Institution Press, 1986.

54. Frotscher, Gotthold. *Geschichte des Orgelspiels und der Orgelkomposition*. 2 vols. Berlin: Merseberger, 1959.

55. Freeman, Andrew, and John Rowntree. *Father Smith*. Oxford: Praestant Press, 1977.

56. Friedrich, Felix, ed. *Geschichte und Rekonstruktion der Trost-Orgel in der Konzerthalle Schlosskirche Altenburg*. Altenburg, 1987.

57. Galpin, Francis W. *Old English Instruments of Music*. London: Methuen, 1932.

58. Gates, Eugene M. "Towards an Authentic Interpretation of Mendelssohn's Organ Works." Master's thesis, McMaster University, 1985.

59. Geer, E. Harold. *Organ Registration in Theory and Practice*. Glen Rock: J. Fischer, 1957.

60. Germani, Fernando. *Metodo per Organo*, Part IV. Rome: Edizioni de Santis, 1953.

61. Gierveld, Arend Jan. *Die Niederländsche Hausorgel in Frühern Jahrhunderten*. Buren: Frits Knuf, 1981.

62. Golon, Peter. *Historische Orgeln im Landkreis Stade*. Stade: Verlag Schaumberg, 1983.

63. Hardouin, Pierre. *Le Grand Orgue de Notre-Dame de Paris*. Kassel: Bärenreiter, 1973.

64. ———. *Le Grand Orgue de Saint-Gervais a Paris*. Paris: Librairie Floury, 1949.

65. ———. *Le Grand Orgue de Saint Nicolas des Champs*. Paris: J. P. Mure, 1977.

66. Harmon, Thomas. *The Registration of J. S. Bach's Organ Works*. Ph. D. diss., Washington University, 1971; reprint Buren: Frits Knuf, 1978.

67. Haupt, Hartmut. *Orgeln in Bezirk Suhl*. Meiningen: Staatliche Museen, 1985.

68. ———. *Die Orgel der Kapelle im Schloss Wilhelmsburg*. Schmalkalden, n.d.
69. Hawkins, John. *A General History of the Science and Practice of Music*. 2 vols. London: Novello, 1875.
70. Henly, Randal L. *The Snetzler Organ, St. Peter's Church, Drogheda*. Drogheda, c1965.
71. Hess, Joachim. *Luister van het Orgel* (1772). Utrecht: J. A. H. Wagenaar, 1945.
72. Hopkins, Edward J., and E. F. Rimbault. *The Organ, Its History and Construction*. London: Robert Cocks & Co., 1855.
73. Jongepier, Jan. *Frieslands Orgelpracht*. Sneek: Boeijenga, 1970.
74. Kastner, M. S. (trans. B. Brauchli). *The Interpretation of 16th- and 17th-Century Iberian Keyboard Music*. Stuyvesant, NY: Pendragon Press, 1987.
75. Kauffmann, George Friedrich. *Harmonische Seelenlust*. Leipzig, 1733.
76. Kaufmann, Walter G. *Die Orgeln Ostfrieslands*. Aurich: Verlag Ostfriesische Landschaft, 1968.
77. ———. *Die Orgeln des alten Herzogtums Oldenburg*. Oldenburg, 1962.
78. Keller, Hermann. *Der Orgelwerke Bachs*. Leipzig: Peters, n.d.
79. Klinda, Ferdinand. *Orgelregistrierung, Klanggestaltung der Orgelmusik*. Leipzig: VEB Breitkopf & Härtel, 1987.
80. Klotz, Hans. *Pro Organo Pleno: Norm und Vielfalt der Registriervorschrift Joh. Seb. Bachs*. Wiesbaden: Breitkopf & Härtel, 1978.
81. ———. *The Organ Handbook* (trans. G. Krapf). St. Louis: Concordia, 1969.
82. Kosnik, James W. "The Toccatas of J. J. Froberger." D.M.A. diss., University of Rochester, 1979.
83. Krummacher, Christoph, ed. *Wege zur Orgel*. Kassel: Merseburger, 1988.
84. Langley, Robin, ed. *Music in Restoration England*. Oxford; Oxford University Press, 1981.
85. Lasceux, Guillaume. "Essai théorique et pratique sur l'art de l'orgue." Ms., 1809.
86. Lindow, Ch.-W. *Historic Organs in France*. Delaware, OH: Praestant Press, 1980.
87. Linley, F. *A Practical Introduction to the Organ*. London: A. Hamilton, 179?
88. *L'organo Doppio della chiesa San Martino Vescovo in Venezia*. Venice: Australian Committee for Venice, 1984.
89. Lukas, Viktor. *A Guide to Organ Music*. Portland: Amadeus Press, 1989.
90. Lunelli, Renato. *Studi i documenta de storia organaria Veneta*. Firenze, 1973.
91. ———. *Der Orgelbau in Italien in seinem Meisterwerken*. Mainz, 1956.
92. Lüttmann, Reinhard. *Das Orgelregister und sein instrumentales Vorbild in Frankreich und Spanien vor 1800*. Kassel: Bärenreiter, 1979.
93. Mace, Thomas. *Musick's Monument*. Cambridge, 1676.
94. Marpurg, F.W. *Historisch-Kritisch Beyträge zur Aufnahme der Musik*, Vol. III. Berlin, 1754–78.
95. Marsh, John. *Eighteen Voluntaries for the Organ*. London: Preston & Son, 1791. Preface.
96. Mattheson, Johann. *Das Neu-Eröffnete Orchestre*. Hamburg, 1713.
97. Matthews, Betty. *The Organs and Organists of Exeter Cathedral*. Exeter, n.d.
98. ———. *The Organs and Organists of Salisbury Cathedral*. Salisbury, 1972.
99. ———. *The Organs and Organists of Winchester Cathedral*. Winchester, 1975.
100. Mayes, Stanley. *An Organ for the Sultan*. London: Putnam, 1956.
101. Merian, Wilhelm. *Der Tanz in den Deutschen Tablaturbüchern*. Hildesheim: Georg Olms, 1968.
102. Metzler, Wolfgang. *Romantischer Orgelbau in Deutschland*. Ludwigsburg: E. F. Walcker, 1962.
103. Meyer-Siat, P. *L'Orgue Joseph Callinet de Mollau*. Strasbourg, 1963.
104. Miné, M. *Nouveau Manuel Complet de l'Organiste*, Part III. Paris: Librairie Roret, n.d.
105. Mischiati, Oscar. *L'organo Serassi della Chiesa di San Liborio*. Parma, 1985.
106. ———. *L'Organo della Chiesa del Carmine di Lugo di Romagna*. Bologna: Editrice Citron, 1968.

107. Moortgat, Gaby. *Oude Orgels in Vlaanderen.* Antwerp: Belgisch Radio en Televisie, 1964 (Vol. I) and 1965 (Vol. II).

108. Moretti, Corrado. *L'organo italiano.* 2d ed. Milan: Eco, 1973.

109. Müller, Werner. *Auf den Spuren von Gottfried Silbermann.* Berlin: Evangelische Verlaganstalt, 1969.

110. Münger, Fritz. *Schweizer Orgeln von der Gotik bis zur Gegenwart.* Bern: Verlag Krompholz, 1961.

111. Nassarre, Pablo. *Escuela Mùsica.* Zaragoza, 1723/4.

112. Nicholson, Henry D. *The Organ Manual.* Boston: Ditson, 1866.

113. Niland, Austin. *The Organ at St. Mary's, Rotherhithe.* Oxford, 1983.

114. Norman, John. *The Organs of Britain.* London: David & Charles, 1984.

115. Ochse, Orpha. *The History of the Organ in the United States.* Bloomington: Indiana University Press, 1975.

116. Ogasapian, John. *Organ Building in New York City: 1700–1900.* Braintree: Organ Literature Foundation, 1977.

117. ———. *Henry Erben: Portrait of a 19th-Century American Organ Builder.* Braintree: Organ Literature Foundation, 1980.

118. Ord-Hume, A. W. J. G. *Barrel Organ.* New York: A. S. Barnes, 1978.

119. *Die Orgel in der Klosterkirche Muri.* Lauffen/Neckar: ISO Information, 1975.

120. Owen, Barbara. *The Organ in New England.* Raleigh: Sunbury Press, 1979.

121. Pape, Uwe. *Die Orgeln der Stadt Wolfenbüttel.* Berlin: Verlag Pape, 1973.

122. Pearce, Charles W. *Notes on English Organs.* London: Vincent, 1911.

123. ———. *The Evolution of the Pedal Organ.* London: Musical Opinion, 1927.

124. Pfatteicher, Carl. *John Redford, Organist and Almoner of St. Paul's Cathedral.* Kassel: Bärenreiter, 1934.

125. Pfeiffer-Durkop, Hilde, et al. *Klingendes Ostfalen.* Cuxhaven: Verlag Oliva, 1967.

126. Pirro, André. *Johann Sebastian Bach, the Organist* (trans. W. Goodrich). New York: G. Schirmer, 1902.

127. Pitsch, G. *Geschichte der Musik in Worms bis zur Mitte des 16. Jahrhunderts,* Vol. III. Worms, 1556.

128. Praetorius, Michael. *Syntagma Musicum* (trans. H. Blumenfeld). New York: Da Capo Press, 1980.

129. *Psalmodia Evangelica.* New York: Elam Bliss, 1830.

130. Purey Cust, A. P. *Organs and Organists of York Minster.* York, 1899.

131. Quoika, Rudolf. *Die Altösterreichische Orgel.* Kassel: Bärenreiter, 1953.

132. ———. *Die König-Orgel in Diessen am Ammersee.* Diessen am Ammersee: Cäcilienverein, 1960.

133. ———. *Vom Blockwerk zur Registerorgel.* Kassel: Bärenreiter, 1966.

134. Radeker, Johannes. *Korte Beschreyving van het Orgel in de Groote of St. Bavoos-Kerk te Haarlem.* Reprint, ed. H. S. J. Zandt. Amsterdam: Fritz Knuf, 1974.

135. Raugel, Félix. *Les Grandes Orgues des églises de Paris et du Département de la Seine.* Paris: Fischbacher, 1927.

136. ———. *Les Orgues de l'abbaye de Saint-Mihiel.* Paris: L'echo Musical, 1919.

137. Rehm, Gottfried. *Die Orgeln des Kreises Fulda.* Berlin: Pape Verlag, 1978.

138. Reinburg, Peggy Kelley. *Arp Schnitger, Organ Builder.* Bloomington: Indiana University Press, 1982.

139. Reuter, Rudolf. *Organos Españoles.* Madrid: Valera, 1963.

140. ———. *Orgeln in Westfalen.* Kassel: Bärenreiter, 1965.

141. Riemenschneider, Albert. *The Use of the Flutes in the Works of J. S. Bach.* Washington: Library of Congress, 1950.

142. Riley, Vicki Ann Hale. "Innovation and Conservatism in the Organ Hymns of Jehan Titelouze." D.M.A. diss., Stanford University, 1987.

143. Rinck, J. C. H. *Practical School for the Organ*. New York: William Hall & Son, 1850.

144. Routh, Francis. *Early English Organ Music from the Middle Ages to 1837*. London: Barrie & Jenkins, 1973.

145. Rubardt, Paul. *Die Silbermannorgeln in Rötha*. Leipzig: Breitkopf & Härtel, 1953.

146. Russell, Gillian Ward. "William Russell and the Foundling Hospital 1801–1813." M. Phil. thesis, Colchester Institute School of Music, 1988.

147. Sadko, Keith. *Gli Organi Storici della Provincia di Pistoia*. Pisa: Pacini Editore, 1988.

148. Salmen, Walter, ed. *Orgel und Orgelspiel im 16 Jahrhundert*. Innsbruck: Helbling, 1978.

149. Sayer, Michael. *Samuel Renn, English Organ Builder*. London: Hillimore, 1974.

150. Saurez Molino, Maria Teresa de Jesus. "La Caja de Organo en Nueva España Durante el Barroco." Thesis, Universidad Iberoamerica, 1981.

151. Scheibert, Beverly. *Jean-Henry D'Anglebert and the 17th-Century Clavecin School*. Bloomington: Indiana University Press, 1986.

152. Schlick, Arnolt. *Spiegel der Orgelmacher und Organisten*. Mainz, 1511. Ms. trans. Elizabeth Berry Barber.

153. Scholes, Percy. *The Puritans and Music in England and New England*. New York: Russell & Russell, 1962.

154. Scholten, Y., ed. *Nederlandse Orgelpracht*. Haarlem: Tjeenk Willink & Zoon, 1961.

155. Schott, Howard. *Catalogue of Musical Instruments*, Vol. I. London: Victoria & Albert Museum, 1985.

156. Schweiger, Hertha. *Abbé G. J. Vogler's Orgellehre*. Vienna: Joh. Kmoch, 1938.

157. Seggermann, Günter. *Klingendes Friesland. Orgeln zwischen Weser und Ems*. Cuxhaven: Verlag Oliva, 1959.

158. ———. *Klingendes Schätze. Orgel-Land zwischen Elbe und Weser*. Cuxhaven: Verlag Oliva, 1961.

159. ———, and Wolfgang Weidenbach. *Denkmalorgeln zwischen Weser und Ems*. Kassel: Merseburger, 1980.

160. Seidel, J. J. *The Organ and its Construction*. London: Ewer & Co., 1855.

161. Seijbel, Maarten. *Orgels in Overijssel*. Sneek: Boeijenga, 1965.

162. Serassi, Giuseppe. *Descrizione de Osservazioni pel nuovo Organo nella Chiesa posto del SS Crocifisso dell'Annunziata di Como*. Como: Presso Ostinelli, 1808.

163. Shannon, John R. *Organ Literature of the Seventeenth Century*. Raleigh: Sunbury Press, 1978

164. Snyder, Kerala. *Dieterich Buxtehude, Organist in Lübeck*. New York: Schirmer Books, 1987.

165. Sponsel, Johann Ulrich. *Orgelhistorie*. Nuremberg, 1771.

166. Stauffer, George B. *The Organ Preludes of Johann Sebastian Bach*. Ann Arbor: UMI Research Press, 1980.

167. Stauffer, George, and Ernest May, eds. *J. S. Bach as Organist*. Bloomington: Indiana University Press, 1986.

168. Supper, Walter, ed. *Der Barock, seine Orgeln und seine Musik in Oberschwaben*. Berlin: Merseburger, 1951.

169. Sumner, William L. *The Organ: Its Evolution, Principles of Construction, and Use*. 4th ed. London: MacDonald & Jane's, 1973.

170. ———. *Bach's Organ-Registration*. London: Hinrichsen Edition, 1961.

171. Terry, Charles Sanford. *Bach: A Biography*. London: Oxford University Press, 1949.

172. Thistlethwaite, Nicholas J. *Organs at Eton*. Eton, 1987.

173. ———. *A History of the Birmingham Town Hall Organ*. Birmingham: City Council, 1984.

174. ———. *The Making of the Victorian Organ*. Cambridge: Cambridge University Press, 1990.

175. Vallotton, Pierre. *Orgues en Normandie*. Saint-Dié: Organa Europae, 1985.

176. Vente, Maarten A. *Die Brabanter Orgel.* Amsterdam: H. J. Paris, 1958.
177. ———. *Proeve van een repertorium van de archivalia betrekking hebbende op het Nederlandse Orgel en zijn makers tot omstreeks 1630.* Bruxelles: Palais des Académies, 1956.
178. *Voces del Arte: Inventario de órganos tubulares.* Mexico City: SEDUE, 1989.
179. Werckmeister, Andreas. *Erweiterte und verbessert Orgelprobe* (trans. G. Krapf). Raleigh: Sunbury Press, 1976.
180. Wickens, David C. *The Instruments of Samuel Green.* London: Macmillan, 1987.
181. Williams, Peter. *The European Organ, 1450–1850.* Nashua: Organ Literature Foudation, 1967.
182. ———. *A New History of the Organ.* Bloomington: Indiana University Press, 1980.
183. ———, and Barbara Owen. *The Organ.* London: Macmillan, 1988.
184. Wilson, Michael. *The English Chamber Organ.* Oxford: Cassirer, 1968.
185. Winter, Helmut, ed. *Orgel-Studien I. Die Huss-Orgel in Stade.* Hamburg: Verlag Wagner, 1979.
186. ———. *Orgel-Studien II. Die Schnitger-Orgel in Cappel.* Hamburg: Verlag Wagner, 1977.
187. Wisgerhof, Bert. *Orgeln in den Niederlanden.* Berlin: Merseburger, 1981.
188. Wölfel, Dietrich, ed. *Die Kleine Orgel in St. Jakobi zu Lübeck.* Lübeck, 1978.

Articles in Periodicals, Anthologies, and Encyclopedias

189. Albrecht, Christoph. "Current Problems in the Interpretation of Bach's Organ Works." *The Diapason,* Vol. 80, No. 1 (January 1990).
190. Anglès, Hyginii. Preface to Johannes Cabanilles, *Opera omnia.* Barcelona: Biblioteca de Cataluña, 1927.
191. Bicknell, Stephen. "English Organ-Building 1642–1685." *BIOS Journal,* No. 5 (1981).
192. Baldello, F. "Organos y organeros en Barcelona, siglos XIII–XIX." *Anuario Musical,* Vol. I (1946).
193. Bastiaens, Luk. "Registriekunst in Zuidduitse bronnen (1500–1800). *Orgelkunst* (March 1985, March 1986, September 1986, June 1988).
194. Blindow, Martin. "Die Trier Orgelakten." *Musik und Kirche,* Vol. 31, No. 3 (May/June 1961).
195. Bolt, Klaas. "The Character and Function of the Dutch Organ in the Seventeenth and Eighteenth Centuries," in Fenner Douglas, Owen Jander, and Barbara Owen, eds., *Charles Brenton Fisk, Organ Builder.* Vol. I. Easthampton: The Westfield Center, 1986.
196. Bozeman, George. "The Bach/Silbermann organ at SUNY-Stonybrook." *Journal of Church Music* (April 1985).
197. ———. "The Haydn Organs of Eisenstadt." *Art of the Organ,* Vol. 1, No. 1 (March 1971) and Vol. 1, No. 2 (June 1971).
198. Bruhin, Rudolf. "Historische Kapellenorgeln im Oberwallis," in *Visitatio Organorum I.* Buren: Frits Knuf, 1980.
199. Bruinsma, Henry A. "The Organ Controversy in the Netherlands Reformation to 1640." *Journal of the American Musicological Society,* Vol. VII, No. 3 (1954).
200. Butler, H. Joseph. "The Teachings of André Raison." *The American Organist,* Vol. 24, No. 3 (March 1990).
201. Campbell, S., and W. S. Sumner. "The Organs and Organists of St. George's Chapel, Windsor Castle." *The Organ,* Vol. XLV, No. 180 (April 1966).
202. Cocheril, Michel. "The Dallams in Brittany." *BIOS Journal,* Vol. VI (1982).
203. Corry, Mary Jane. "Spanish Baroque: The Organ and its Music." *Music,* Vol. III, No. 4 (April 1969).
204. Cox, Geoffrey. "John Blow and the Earliest English Cornet Voluntaries." *BIOS Journal,* Vol. VII (1983).

205. Culley, Thomas. "Organo fiamminghi a S. Apollinare a Roma." *L'Organo*, Vol. V, No. 1 (1967).
206. Dähnert, Ulrich. "Johann Sebastian Bach's Ideal Organ." *Organ Yearbook*, Vol. I (1970).
207. ———. "Organs Played and Tested by Bach," in G. Stauffer and E. May, eds., *J. S. Bach as Organist*. Bloomington: Indiana University Press, 1986.
208. dalla Libera, Sandro. "Organs in Venice." *Organ Yearbook*, Vol. IV (1973).
209. de Graaf, G. A. C. "A Spanish Registration List of 1789." *Organ Yearbook*, Vol. VII (1976).
210. ———. "The Gothic Organ in the Chapel of St. Bartholomew in Salamanca." *ISO-Information*, No. 22 (August 1982).
211. Delosme, René. "L'orgue français de transition, première moitié du XIXe siècle." *La Revue Musicale*, No. 295–96 (1977).
212. Douglass, Fenner. "Should Dom Bédos play Lebègue?" *Organ Yearbook*, Vol. IV (1973).
213. ———, and M. A. Vente. "French Organ Registration in the Early XVIth Century." *Musical Quarterly*, Vol. X (1965).
214. Drewes, Michael. "Further Notes on Mexican Organs of the 18th and 19th Centuries." *Organ Yearbook*, Vol. XIV (1983).
215. Dufourcq, Norbert. "Recent Researches into French Organ-building from the 15th to the 17th Century." *Galpin Society Journal*, Vol. X (May 1957).
216. ———. "L'Orgue Silbermann de Marmoutier en Alsace." *L'Orgue*, No. 77 (October–December 1955).
217. ———. Preface to *Premier livre d'orgue de Gilles Jullien*. Paris: Heugel, 1952.
218. Edmonds, B. B. "The Chaire Organ, An Episode." *BIOS Journal*, Vol. IV (1980).
219. Ellison, Ross Wesley. "Baroque Organ Registration." (Trans. of Chapter 8 of Adlung's *Musica Mechanica Organoedi*). *Music*, Vol. 8, No. 1 (January 1974).
220. Faulkner, Quentin. "Jacob Adlung's *Musica mechanica organoedi* and the 'Bach Organ.'" *Early Keyboard Studies Newsletter*, Vol. V, No. 2 (May 1990).
221. ———. "Information on Organ Registration from a Student of J. S. Bach." *Early Keyboard Studies Newsletter*, Vol. VII, No. 1 (January 1993).
222. Fesperman, John, and D. W. Hinshaw. "New Light on America's Oldest Instruments: Mexico." *Organ Yearbook*, Vol. III (1972).
223. Flade, Ernst. "The Organ Builder Gottfried Silbermann (I)." *Organ Institute Quarterly*, Vol. 3, No. 3 (Summer 1953).
224. Fock, Gustav. "Hamburgs Anteil am Orgelbau im Niederdeutschen Kulturgebiet." *Zeitschrift des Vereins für Hamburgische Geschichte* (1939).
225. Freeman, Andrew. "John Snetzler and his Organs." *The Organ*, Vol. XIV, No. 53 (July 1934).
226. ———. "The Organs of the Abbey Church at Westminster." *The Organ*, Vol. II, No. 7 (January 1923).
227. ———. "The Organs of Canterbury Cathedral." *The Organ*, Vol. III, No. 9 (July 1923).
228. ———. "The Organs of Worcester Cathedral." *The Organ*, Vol. V, No. 18 (October 1925).
229. Frotscher, Gotthold. "Zur Registrierkunst des 18. Jahrhunderts," in W. Gurlitt, ed., *Bericht über die Freiburger Tagung für Deutsche Orgelkunst, 1926*. Kassel: Bärenreiter, 1973.
230. Fuller, David. "Zenith and Nadir: The Organ versus its Music in Late 18th Century France," in D. Mackey, ed., *L'Orgue à notre époque*. Montreal: McGill University, 1981.
231. Gallat-Morin, Elizabeth. "Un manuscrit inédit de musique d'orgue à Montréal au 18e siècle," in D. Mackey, ed. *L'Orgue à notre époque*. Montreal: McGill University, 1981.
232. Gay, Claude. "Notes pour servirà la Registration de la Musique d'Orgue Française des XVII et XVIII siècles." *L'Organo*, Vol. II (1961).
233. Garcia Chico, Esteban. "Documentos para el Estudio del Arte en Castilla." *Anuario Musical*, Vol. VIII (1953).
234. Gleim, Helmut. "Die Reichel-Orgel auf der Ostempore der Markt-Kirche in Halle (Saale)." *Organ Yearbook*, Vol. VI (1975).

235. Golos, Jerzy. "Note di storia organaria Polacca." *L'Organo*, Vol. V, No. 1 (1967).

236. Gravet, Nicole. "L'Orgue et l'Art de la Registration en France." *L'Orgue*, Vol. 100 (October/December 1961).

237. Gudger, William. "Registration in the Handel Organ Concertos." *The American Organist*, Vol. 19, No. 2 (February 1985).

238. ———. "Registration in the 18th Century British Organ Voluntary." *The Diapason*, Vol. 19, No. 2 (1986).

239. Hardouin, Pierre. "Jeux d'orgues au XVIe siècle." *Revue de Musicologie*, Vol. LII, No. 2 (1966).

240. ———. "Naissance et élaboration de l'orgue français classique d'aprés sa composition." *La Revue Musicale*, Nos. 295–96 (1977).

241. Harmon, Thomas. "Gottfried Silbermann: The French Connection in German Baroque Organ Building," in D. Mackey, ed., *L'Orgue à notre époque*. Montreal: McGill University, 1981.

242. Harris, C. David. "Viennese Keyboard Music at Mid-Baroque." *The Diapason*, Vol. 60, No. 6 (May 1969).

243. Haselboeck, Hans. "New Information About Mozart's Clockwork Pieces." *The Diapason*, Vol. 68, No. 12 (November 1977).

244. Haupt, Hartmut. "Bach Organs in Thuringia," in Stauffer and May, eds., *J. S. Bach as Organist*. Bloomington: Indiana University Press, 1986.

245. Higginbottom, Edward. "Jehan Titelouze, c1563–1633." *The Musical Times*, Vol. CXXIV, No. 1687 (September 1983).

246. Holland, Jon. "Performance Practice and Correa de Arauxo's *Facultad Organica*, Part 2." *The Diapason*, Vol. 78, No. 6 (June 1987).

247. Hooper, J. Graham. "The Organs and Organists of St. James's, Bristol." *The Organ*, Vol. XXVIII, No. 110 (October 1948).

248. Horning, Joseph. "The Italian Organ." *The American Organist*, Vol. 25, No. 2 (February 1991).

249. Howell, Almonte. "Organos, Organeros and Organistas of Spain during the Scarlatti Years." *The American Organist*, Vol. 19, No. 10 (October 1985).

250. Jakob, Friedrich. "Der Hausorgelbau im Toggenburg." *Musik und Gottesdienst*, Vol. 6 (1967).

251. Johnstone, H. Diack. "The RCO Manuscript Re-examined." *The Musical Times*, Vol. CXXVI, No. 1706 (April 1985).

252. Kastner, Santiago. "Ursprung und Sinn des Medio registro." *Anuario Musical*, Vol. XIX (1966).

253. ———. Preface to Cabezon's *Tientos und Fugen*. Mainz: Schott, 1958.

254. Kearns, Michael. "The Instruments of the Late 18th Century Portuguese Organ Builder Antonio Xavier Machado e Cerviera," in D. Mackey, ed., *L'Orgue à notre époque*. Montreal: McGill University, 1981.

255. Kent, Christopher. "A Revolution in Registration—Marsh to Mendelssohn: A View of English Music 1788–1847." *BIOS Journal*, Vol. XIII (1989).

256. Kjersgaard, Mads. "Orglets ABC (XIII) Orgelpositivet." *Orglet*, No. 27 (December 1984).

257. Klinda, Ferdinand. "Gedanken zur Bach-Registrierung," in C. Wolff, ed., *Orgel, Orgelmusik und Orgelspiel*. Kassel: Bärenreiter, 1985.

258. Klotz, Hans. "Die nordfranzösische Registrierkunst im letzten Drittel des 17. Jahrhunderts und die Orgeldisposition Gottfried Silbermanns von 1710 für die Leipziger Pauliner-kirche," in A. Dunning, ed., *Visitatio Organorum* (Vol. 2). Buren: Frits Knuf, 1980.

259. Kramer, Gale, trans. "The Prefaces to the Organ Works of Jehan Titelouze." *Organ Yearbook*, Vol. IX (1978).

260. Kremer, Rudolph. "A Workshop dedicated to Italian Organ Restoration." *The Diapason*, No. 850 (September 1980).

261. Krigbaum, Charles. "A Description of the Ochsenhausen Manuscript (1735)," in W. Dehnhard & G. Ritter, eds., *Bachstunden: Festschrift für Helmut Walcha*. Frankfurt/Main: Evangelischer Pressverband, 1979.

262. Leaver, Robin A. "Psalm Singing and Organ Regulations in a London Church c1700." *The Hymn*, Vol. 35, No. 1 (January 1984).

263. Liberman, Marc L. "A Scientist's Account of the French Organ in 1704." *The Diapason*, Vol. 72, No. 2 (February 1982).

264. Löffler, Hans. "Ein unbekanntes Thüringer Orgelmanuscript von 1798." *Musik und Kirche*, Vol. III (1931).

265. ———. "J. H. Trost und die Altenburger Schlossorgel." *Musik und Kirche*, Vol. IV (1932).

266. L[udham], W[illiam]. "A Short Account of the Several Sorts of Organs used for Church Service." *Gentleman's Magazine*, Vol. XLII (December 1772).

267. Luy, André. "L'orgue en France (entre 1630 et la Révolution) et sa registration," in C. Wolff, ed., *Orgel, Orgelmusik, und Orgelspiel*. Kassel: Bärenreiter, 1985.

268. Marcase, Donald E. "Adriano Banchieri's *L'Organo Suonarino*," Part III. *The Diapason*, Vol. 64, No. 11 (October 1973).

269. Marigold, W. G. "Some Organs and Organ Builders of Franconia." *The Organ*, Vol. XLVII, No. 188 (April 1968).

270. Matthews, Betty. "Christian Smith and the Organ of St. Mary Magadalen, Bermondsey." *BIOS Journal*, Vol XI (1987).

271. May, Stephen M. "St.-Michel Reconsidered." *The Diapason*, Vol. 74, No. 1 (January 1983).

272. Mischiati, Oscar. "La terza nel ripieno italiano." *L'Organo*. Vol. VI, No. 1 (1968).

273. ———. "Profilo storico e lineamenti del restauro," in *Il restauro degli organi di S. Petronio*. Bologna, 1982.

274. Musch, Hans. "Eine Spiel- und Registriermöglichkeit für das Mitteldeutsche Orgeltrio des 18 Jahrhunderts." *Ars Organi*, Vol. 29, No. 3 (September 1981).

275. Noisette de Crauzat, Claude. "L'Orgue Romantique." *La Revue Musicale*, Nos. 295–96 (1977).

276. Oldham, Guy. "Louis Couperin: A New Source of French Keyboard Music of the Mid 17th Century." *Recherches*, Vol. I (1960).

277. "On the Use of the Stops of the Organ." *The Euterpeiad*, Vol. I, No. 8 (May 20, 1820).

278. "On the Use of the Stops of the Organ." *American Journal of Music*, February 25, 1845.

279. Owen, Barbara. "The Henrician Heyday of the Regal." *Continuo*, Vol. 7, No. 10 (September 1984).

280. ———. "Dr. Edward Hodges of Bristol and New York." *BIOS Journal*, Vol. 13 (1990).

281. ———. "The One-Manual Anglo-Breton Organ of the Seventeenth Century and its Musical Implications," in Fenner Douglas, Owen Jander, and Barbara Owen, eds., *Charles Brenton Fisk, Organ Builder*, Vol. I. Easthampton: The Westfield Center, 1986.

282. ———. "Two Richard Bridge Organs in New England." *The Organ*, Vol. 68, No. 267 (July 1989).

283. Pineschi, Umberto. "L'uso dei registri dell'organo pistoiese nei secoli XVIII e XIX." *L'Organo*, Vol. XII (1974).

284. ———. Prefaces to *Musiche Pistoiesi per organo*. 2 vols. Brescia: Paideia, 1978, 1990.

285. ———. "Restoration of Historical Organs in Pistoia, Italy, and Its Area." *The Diapason* (May 1975).

286. Plumley, Nicholas. "The Harris/Byfield Connection; Some Recent Findings." *BIOS Journal*, Vol. III (1979).

287. Rowntree, John. "Lulworth Castle Chapel—The Early Music of the Chapel." *BIOS Journal*, No. 11 (1987).

288. Renshaw, Martin. "An Early 17th Century British Organ." *BIOS Journal*, No. 4 (1980).

289. ———. "Anatomy of an Organ, Part 2." *The Organ*, Vol. XLVIII, No. 190 (October 1968).

290. Russell, Gillian Ward. "The Organ Music of William Russell." *BIOS Journal*, No. 13 (1989).

291. Sawyer, Philip. "A Neglected Late 18th Century Organ Treatise." *BIOS Journal*, Vol. X (1986).

292. Schrammek, Winfried. "Fragen des Orgelgebrauchs in Bachs Aufführungen der Matthaus-Passion." *Bach-Jahrbuch*, 1975.

293. Selfridge-Field, Eleanor. "Gabrieli and the Organ." *Organ Yearbook*, Vol. VIII (1977).

294. Shay, Edmund. "French Baroque Organ Registrations." *The Diapason*, Vol. 60, No. 12 (November 1969).

295. Shewring, Walter. "Organs in Italy: Brescia and Verona." *The Organ*, Vol. XXXV, No. 140 (April 1956).

296. ———. "Organs in Italy: Venice, Treviso, Trent." *The Organ*, Vol. XXXVI, No. 141 (July 1956).

297. Soehnlein, Edward J. "Diruta and his Contemporaries: Tradition and Innovation in the Art of Registration c1610." *Organ Yearbook*, Vol. X (1979).

298. Sulzmann, Bernd. "Mitteilungen über das Wirken schwäbischer Orgelmacher in badischen Landen vom 16. bis 19 Jahrhundert," in *Mundus Organorum*. Berlin: Merseburger, 1978.

299. Sumner, William L. "The Organ of Bach," in Max Henrichsen, ed., *Eighth Music Book*. London: Hinrichsen, 1956.

300. Tagliavini, Luigi Ferdinando. "Remarks on the Compositions for Organ of Domenico Scarlatti." *The American Organist*, Vol. 19, No. 10 (October 1985).

301. ———. "The Old Italian Organ and its Music." *The Diapason*, Vol. 59, No. 3 (February 1966).

302. ———. "Il ripieno." *L'Organo*, Vol. 1, No. 2 (1960).

303. ———. "Registrazioni organistiche nei Magnificat de Vespri Monteverdiani." *Revista Italiana de Musicologia*, Vol. II, No. 2 (1967).

304. ———. Preface to D. Zipoli, *Orgel- und Cembalowerke*. Heidelberg, 1957.

305. Tattershall, Susan. "A Chronicle of the Restoration of a Mexican Colonial Organ," in Fenner Douglas, Owen Jander, and Barbara Owen, eds., *Charles Brenton Fisk, Organ Builder*, Vol. I. Easthampton: Westfield Center, 1986.

306. "The Tune 'St. Stephen's.'" *The Musical Times*, May 1, 1903.

307. van Dijk, Peter. "Registratiekunst in Duitse bronnen." *Het Orgel*, Vol. 73, No. 10 (October 1977), Vol. 74, No. 9 (September 1978); Vol. 75, No. 3 (March 1979); Vol. 75, No. 4 (April 1979).

308. ———. "Registratiekunst in 18e eeuwse Nederlandse bronnen." *Het Orgel*.

309. Vendome, Richard. "Spanish Netherlands Keyboard Music, 1596–1633." *BIOS Journal*, Vol. VII (1983).

310. Vennum, Thomas Jr. "The Registration of Frescobaldi's Organ Music." *Organ Institute Quarterly*, Vol. II, No 1 (1964); Vol. II, No. 2 (1964).

311. Vente, M. A. "L'influence des Flamands sur les Français en matière de construction d'Orgues (II)." *L'Orgue*, Vol. 49 (October/December 1948).

312. ———, and D. A. Flentrop. "The Renaissance Organ of Evora Cathedral." *The Organ Yearbook*, Vol. I (1970).

313. ———, and W. Kok. "Organs in Spain and Portugal." *The Organ*, Vol. XXXV, No. 138 (October 1955); No. 139 (January 1956); Vol. XXXVI, No. 143 (January 1957); No. 144 (April 1957), Vol. XXXVII, No. 145 (July 1957).

314. Viderø, Finn. "Some Reflections on the Registration Practice in the Time of Bach." *Art of the Organ*, Vol. 2, No. 2 (June 1972).

315. Villard, Jean-Albert. "Facteurs du Roy: Robert, Louis-Alexandre et François Cliquot." *La Revue Musicale*, Nos. 295–96 (1977).

316. Vogel, Harald. "North German Organ Building of the Late 17th Century: Registration and Tuning," in Stauffer and May, eds., *J. S. Bach as Organist*. Bloomington: Indiana University Press, 1986.

317. Walter, Rudolf. "A Spanish Registration List of c1770." *Organ Yearbook*, Vol. IV (1973).

318. Wickens, David C. "The Introduction of New Organ Stops in English Organ-Building in the 18th and 19th Centuries." *BIOS Journal*, Vol. 13 (1989).

319. Williams, Peter. "The Registration of Schnitger's Organs." *The Organ*, Vol. XLVII No. 188 (April 1968).

320. ———. "Diapason." *Musical Times*, Vol. CVI (June 1965).

321. ———. "Handel und die Englische Orgelmusik." *Handel-Jahrbuch*, Vol. 12 (1966).

322. ———. "Some Tercentenary Questions for the Performer." *The American Organist*, Vol. 19, No. 1 (January 1985).

323. Wyly, James. "Historical Notes on Spanish Façade Trumpets." *Organ Yearbook*, Vol. VIII (1977).

324. ———. "La Registrazione della musica organistica de Francisco Correa de Arauxo." *L'Organo*, Vol. VIII, No. 1 (1970).

325. ———. "Registration of the Organ Works of Francisco Correa de Arauxo." *Art of the Organ*, Vol. 1 No. 4 (December 1971).

326. ———. "Seventeenth Century Spanish Trumpets by the Echevarrias." *Art of the Organ*, Vol. II, No. 4 (December 1972).

327. Young, Percy. "'A Sweet Pretty Instrument': Sir Samuel Hellier's Obsession." *BIOS Journal*, Vol. 12 (1988).

Addenda

328. Baggs, Robin. "Organs in Swabia." *Musical Times*, Vol. 116, No. 1588 (June 1975).

329. Boeringer, James. *Organa Brittanica*, Vol. 3. Lewisburg: Bucknell University Presses, 1989.

330. Busch, Hermann J. "Unbekannte Registrierungsanweisungen aus dem Umkreis Johann Sebastian Bach." *Ars Organi*, Vol. 33 (June 1985).

331. Christiansen, Clay. "Toward More Innovative, Creative, and Less Rigid Registration of J. S. Bach's Organ Works." *The Diapason*, Vol. 86, No. 3 (March 1995).

332. Crowell, Gregory F. "Friedrich Wilhelm Marpurg and French Registration Practices in Central Germany in the Middle of the 18th Century." D.M.A. dissertation, University of Cincinnati, 1993.

333. Dalton, James. "Studies in Registration—1: 17th and 18th Century English Music." *Organists' Review*, Vol. LXI, No. 243 (Autumn 1975).

334. ———. "Studies in Registration—2: 17th Century German Music." *Organists' Review*, Vol. LX, No. 240 (Summer 1976).

335. Davidsson, Hans. *Mathias Weckmann: The Interpretation of his Organ Works*. 3 vols. Stockholm: Gehrmans, 1992.

336. Foccroulle, Bernard. "Le 'Liber Fratrum Cruciforum' (1617). Contiendrait-il les premiers Récits de Cornet et Basses de Trompette?" *Organ Yearbook*, Vol. XVII (1986).

337. Friedrich, Felix. "Beobachten zu den Glockenspielen in Thüringer Orgeln." *Ars Organi*, Vol. 41, No. 1 (March 1993).

338. Hardouin, Pierre. "Les variations d'equilibres dans l'orgue français classique," in D. Mackey, ed. *L'Orgue à notre époque*. Montreal: McGill University, 1981.

339. Kloppers, Jacobus. "A Criterion for Manual Changes in the Organ Works of J. S. Bach." *Organ Yearbook*, Vol. VII (1976).

340. Panetta, Vincent. "An Early Handbook for Organ Inspection." *Organ Yearbook*, Vol. XXI (1990).

341. Peeters, Flor, and M. A. Vente. *The Organ and its Music in the Netherlands 1500–1800.* Antwerp: Mercatorfonds, 1971.

342. Praetorius, Michael, and Esaias Compenius. *Orgeln Verdingnis* (ed. Friedrich Blume). Wolfenbüttel: Kallmeyer Verlag, 1936.

343. Ritchie, George. "Störmthal: Organo pleno, the Terz, and Bach Fugues." *Early Keyboard Studies Newsletter,* No. 5 (July 1991).

Some Primary Sources Cited in the Bibliography

English: 10, 20, 38, 72, 87, 95, 262, 277, 327
French: 15, 40, 85, 259
German: 1, 75, 94, 96, 128, 152, 165, 179, 194, 264, 342
Italian: 5, 13, 14, 162, 284, 297
Spanish: 111, 209, 317

In addition, the prefaces to good modern editions (or facsimiles) of the works of the French composers Nivers, Lebègue, Gigault, Raison, Boyvin, Jullien, Chaumont, and Corrette include the composers' original registration tables; some of these are also reproduced in #39. Good modern editions of eighteenth-century English voluntaries include the composers' original registrations in the score; the Oxford University Press facsimile edition of Stanley's Voluntaries (3 volumes, 1957) is especially useful in this regard. Original registration indications in music written before the middle of the seventeenth century, as well as in German, Dutch, Italian, and Iberian music of any period, are rare, save in the case of Kauffmann's *Harmonisches Seelenlust,* and the specific examples cited in the text. Detailed registrations in modern editions of music in these categories may be assumed to be editorial unless specifically noted otherwise.

For Further Background Study

See 3, 7, 9, 26, 30, 39, 54, 81, 89, 115, 144, 163, 167, 169, 181, 182, 183, 341.

Also recommended are articles on the organ, organ music, and organ builders in *The New Grove Dictionary of Music* and *The New Grove Dictionary of Musical Instruments.*

INDEX

Barbara Owen is active as a lecturer, teacher, recitalist, and organ consultant. She is Music Director of the First Religious Society, Newburyport, Massachusetts, Librarian of the Organ Library at Boston University, and author of *The Organ in New England, E. Power Biggs: Concert Organist,* and articles in *The New Grove Dictionary of Music and Musicians* and many organ journals.